# Benchmark Papers in Behavior Series

**Editors: Martin W. Schein — West Virginia University
Carol Sue Carter-Porges — University of Illinois at
Urbana-Champaign**

# FOUNDATIONS OF COMPARATIVE PSYCHOLOGY

Edited by

## DONALD A. DEWSBURY
**University of Florida**

A Hutchinson Ross Benchmark® Book

 **VAN NOSTRAND REINHOLD COMPANY**

m

Published by Van Nostrand Reinhold Company Inc.
135 West 50th Street
New York, New York 10020

Van Nostrand Reinhold Company Limited
Molly Millars Lane
Wokingham, Berkshire RG11 2PY, England

Van Nostrand Reinhold
480 Latrobe Street
Melbourne, Victoria 3000, Australia

Macmillan of Canada
Division of Gage Publishing Limited
164 Commander Boulevard
Agincourt, Ontario MIS 3C7, Canada

15   14   13   12   11   10   9   8   7   6   5   4   3   2   1

**Library of Congress Cataloging in Publication Data**
Main entry under title:
Foundations of comparative psychology.
   (Benchmark papers in behavior; v. 17)
   "A Hutchinson Ross Benchmark book."
   Includes indexes.
   1. Animal behavior—Addresses, essays, lectures.
2. Psychology, Comparative—Addresses, essays, lectures.
I. Dewsbury, Donald A., 1939-      II. Series: Benchmark
papers in behavior; 17.
QL751.6.F68   1984       591.51       84-10372
ISBN 0-442-21753-6

4/4/85

# CONTENTS

# Contents

# SERIES EDITORS' FOREWORD

In response to the steadily increasing and overwhelming volume of information in all areas of behavior, the Benchmark Papers in Behavior series was launched some years ago as an open-ended set of single topic volumes designed to be some things to some people. Each volume contained a collection of what an expert considered to be *the* classic research papers on a given topic. Each volume served several purposes. To teachers, a Benchmark volume served as a supplement to other and perhaps more current written materials assigned to students; it permitted an in-depth consideration of a particular topic while at the same time confronting students (often for the first time) with original research papers of outstanding quality. To researchers, a Benchmark volume saved countless hours of digging through the various journals to find *the* basic articles in a specific area of itnerest; often the journals were not easily available. To students, a Benchmark volume pro- vided a readily accessible set of original papers on a topic, a set that formed the core of the more extensive bibliography that they were likely to compile; it also permitted them to see first hand what an "expert" thought was important in the topic area and to react accordingly. Finally, to librarians, a Benchmark volume represented a collection of important papers from many diverse sources, thus making readily available materials that might other- wise not be economically possible to obtain or physically possible to keep in stock.

The present volume is somewhat different from earlier volumes in the series, although it follows the same (and seemingly successful) format. The topic area is significantly broader than in previous volumes—it encompasses the whole field of comparative psychology. The volume is also different in that it is designed to serve dual purposes: it can stand alone, as do other Benchmark volumes, or it can serve as a companion volume to Dr. Dewsbury's excellent monograph *Comparative Psychology in the Twentieth Century* (Hutchinson Ross, 1983). Our concept is that while the monograph will be revised in future years to incorporate new ideas and developments, it will simply be added to as current and future papers also become "classics."

We are especially pleased that Dr. Dewsbury agreed to edit this volume.

MARTIN W. SCHEIN
CAROL SUE CARTER-PORGES

# PREFACE

The image of comparative psychology presented by many authors is that of a few ill-trained psychologists studying learning in a few domestic species in an effort to make generalizations about human behavior. The image is one in which a few creative scientists are said to have espoused a broadly based, biologically oriented approach to animal behavior within psychology at the beginning of the century only to have the tradition die out around 1920. Although this image was drummed into me in paper after paper, I continued to encounter research that ran counter to it. The work of Robert Yerkes, Karl Lashley, Calvin Stone, T. C. Schneirla, Frank Beach, Harry Harlow, C. R. Carpenter, Henry Nissen, Daniel Lehrman, Eckhard Hess, and many others simply did not fit this picture. This discrepancy bothered me for many years.

In the past few years, several events occurred at about the same time that resulted in increasing my displeasure with the discrepancy between the picture presented by most authors and the reality I saw. This stimulated me to try to do something about it. Comparative psychologists became somewhat sensitized as the first real efforts toward organization were initiated by the formation of the National Committee on the Status of Comparative Psychology, led initially by Ethel Tobach, and the publication of the *Comparative Psychology Newsletter,* edited by Jack Demarest. Secondly, I became involved in the efforts within the American Psychological Association to restore the *Journal of Comparative Psychology* as a separate journal within APA. Finally, the publication of W. H. Thorpe's *The Origins and Rise of Ethology* may have been the proverbial straw that broke the camel's back. I have great respect and deep affection for the ethologists and for all that they represent. However, comparative psychology has much of which to be proud as well. This tradition was portrayed neither by Thorpe nor by many other authors.

The result was a period of intense library research, mounting photocopy bills, and finally the production of a book, — *Comparative Psychology in the Twentieth Century.* In that book I portray my view of the image and history of comparative psychology in this century in an effort to present between a single set of covers a comprehensive picture of some of the positive accomplishments of comparative psychology.

The book was published by Hutchinson Ross, which is noted for its Benchmark series (one volume of which I had previously edited). During discussions regarding the publication of the book, the possibility of a Benchmark volume produced in association with the other book arose. In *Comparative Psychology in the Twentieth Century,* I tried to interpret, summarize, and integrate the thought and efforts of a great many comparative psychologists. In a Benchmark book I could assemble examples of worthwhile and influential writings from comparative psychologists and bring to the reader in a convenient form the original words of the authors. The two volumes thus complement each other,—one providing an attempt at synthesis and the present volume making available classic works in the original authors' own words. I have tried to prepare this book to stand on its own. However, I believe that it will have greater impact when used in conjunction with *Comparative Psychology in the Twentieth Century.*

I have endeavored to select a group of papers that illustrate the tremendous and exciting diversity that characterizes comparative psychology. Far from a small band of rat runners of limited vision, comparative psychologists throughout the century have turned their attention toward a vast array of diverse behavior in a considerable variety of species. There is no way to do justice to this diversity in a mere 300 pages of reprinted material. However, I hope that I have selected papers that convey the flavor and excitement that has that has been and is comparative psychology in the twentieth century.

The editors at Van Nostrand Reinhold (formerly Hutchinson Ross) have been most encouraging, efficient, and helpful during the production of both books. As always, I thank my family, Joyce, Bryan, and Laura, for bearing with me during production of the book. Portions of the manuscript were expertly typed by Susan M. Fuentes.

DONALD A. DEWSBURY

# CONTENTS BY AUTHOR

# FOUNDATIONS OF
# COMPARATIVE
# PSYCHOLOGY

# INTRODUCTION

This volume and the accompanying volume, *Comparative Psychology in the Twentieth Century* (Dewsbury, 1984), represent an effort to correct what I perceive as a broadly held misperception of comparative psychology, its nature and its history. In the accompanying book, I have developed an integrated picture of comparative psychology. For this book, I have selected original works that will help solidify my point. On the assumption that many readers have not read the accompanying volume, I shall reiterate some of its major points, for these points provide the basis for the selection of papers in the present volume.

The first issue relates to the image of comparative psychology, which is generally unfavorable. I have proposed ten myths about the field that I believe are widely accepted by many writers. In an effort to be positive, I will now list them as positive statements and note that most authors who have written about the field have regarded most or all as false statements.

1. The rationale for comparative psychology does not come exclusively or primarily from a human orientation or from an effort to make direct generalizations about human behavior.

2. Psychologists often have a sense of appreciation for animals and for their place in nature.

3. Comparative psychologists have often addressed problems of the evolution of behavior.

4. Comparative psychologists, although working primarily in laboratory settings, have conducted a significant number of important investigations of animal behavior under natural conditions.

5. Comparative psychologists have studied a broad range of species.

6. Comparative psychologists have studied both domesticated and nondomesticated species.

7. Comparative psychologists have sometimes compared closely related species as well as those more distantly related.

8. Comparative psychologists have often been interested in the

1

animals under study and have been close to them, and have not been merely preoccupied with instrumentation.

9. Comparative psychologists have often been attentive to the importance of careful descriptions of naturally occurring behavior in addition to being concerned about the need for experimentation.

10. Comparative psychologists have studied a wide variety of behavioral patterns, many of which are of considerable ecological significance.

A second issue relates to the history of comparative psychology. The view often promulgated is that there were a few comparative psychologists early in the century whose work might be described by these ten statements, but that during the period from roughly 1920 through 1960 this tradition died in psychology and was replaced by an extremely environmentalistic approach exclusively directed toward the study of learning in rats. I believe that this view comes in part from various content analyses of papers published in the *Journal of Animal Behavior*, the *Journal of Comparative Psychology*, and the *Journal of Comparative and Physiological Psychology* (e.g., Papers 3 and 4 of this volume). I have argued that these analyses have hidden biases that lead one to overestimate the diversity of approach of some early comparative psychologists and to underestimate the contributions of those that came later, thus producing this distorted view of history. It was with amusement that, after selecting the twenty-six papers for the present volume, I discovered that I had quite unintentionally included none from the three journals whose contents have been used to portray the history of the field.

The third issue relates to the definition of comparative psychology. I believe that most scientists are reasonably intelligent and that the criticism leveled against comparative psychology did not arise in a vacuum as the product of the imaginations of lesser beings. Rather, I believe that much of the discrepancy between my view of comparative psychology and the views of others stems from differences in what we define as subject matter encompassed by the field. I cannot do justice to all alternative definitions of comparative psychology here (see Dewsbury, 1984). I use the term "animal psychology" to include all studies by psychologists working with nonhuman animals. Within animal psychology, I view comparative psychology as a broadly based, biologically oriented approach to the study of animal behavior. It is associated with the work of such individuals as C. Lloyd Morgan, E. L. Thorndike, J. Mark Baldwin, T. Wesley Mills, John B. Watson, Linus Kline, W. S. Small, Margaret Floy Washburn, Robert M. Yerkes, Karl Lashley, Carl J. Warden, T. C. Schneirla, Frank A. Beach, C. Ray Carpenter, Henry Nissen, Zing Yang Kuo, Winthrop N. Kellogg, Harry F.

Harlow, Daniel S. Lehrman, and many others. With this definition I exclude much of animal psychology, especially most process-oriented studies of learning and most physiological analyses. Comparative psychologists have generally studied some unusual species, some naturally occurring behavioral pattern, or both. I do not wish to criticize the remainder of animal psychology. Rather, I believe that the goals and traditions within these fields differ from those of comparative psychology and that a failure to differentiate them from comparative psychology can lead to considerable confusion. I cannot give a fully adequate, simple definition of just what distinguishes comparative psychology from the rest of animal psychology. Perhaps the ten statements listed above and the papers reprinted in this volume will convey the approach I am trying to portray. My tripartite division of animal psychology is very close to the present three-journal program of the American Psychological Association, which publishes the *Journal of Comparative Psychology, Behavioral Neuroscience,* and the *Journal of Experimental Psychology (Animal Behavior Processes)*.

The book is organized into nine sections, each designed to present one aspect of the complex field that is comparative psychology. The first group of papers is a collection of general treatments of comparative psychology and illustrates how perceptions of the field changed through the first half of the century. The papers in Part II illustrate the role of comparative psychologists in field studies. The continuing interest of comparative psychologists in the study of social behavior is presented in Part III. Far from being extreme environmentalists, comparative psychologists have played a leading role in the development of behavior genetics; this is presented in Part IV. In developing an area of behavior genetics, comparative psychologists have not lost sight of the importance of environmental influences or of the complex interactions between genotype and environment; this is presented in Part V. Approaches to the study of instinct are discussed in Part VI. The problem of instinct may be the central issue in the field throughout its history. The topic of Part VII is the comparative analysis of learning, a topic so focal that some authors treat it as synonymous with the field of comparative psychology. In Part VIII will be found papers representative of the long-standing interest of comparative psychologists in sensory-perceptual function. The final section, Part IX, concerns evolution, the topic that led to the development of comparative psychology and which has provided its backbone throughout its history.

I hope that by bringing these many faces of comparative psychology into focus I can transmit the level of understanding and appreciation for nature and animals that I believe these comparative psychologists developed. My hope is that, each in its own way, the present volume and the accompanying book lead to a greater appreciation and understanding of the richness to be found in comparative psychology.

## REFERENCE

Dewsbury, D. A., 1984, *Comparative Psychology in the Twentieth Century*, Hutchinson Ross, Stroudsburg, Pa.

Part I

# GENERAL TREATMENTS OF COMPARATIVE PSYCHOLOGY

# Editor's Comments
# on Papers 1 Through 4

My theme is that throughout the twentieth century comparative psychology has had a continuous history as a broadly based, biologically oriented approach to behavior. However, individual comparative psychologists have not always perceived the field in that manner. The papers in this section illustrate the ways in which various comparative psychologists have viewed the discipline at particular points in its history.

Although Linus Kline's career in comparative psychology was limited to a few years at the end of the nineteenth century while he was a graduate student at Clark University, his work illustrates some of the best characteristics of the field. Many of these characteristics can be seen in his construction of a laboratory course (Paper 1). Kline's course would utilize a wide variety of species, both invertebrate and vertebrate, and start with a consideration of the naturally occurring behavior of each species as expressed outside of captivity. Kline's students would be exposed to a diverse array of behavioral patterns and topics, such as instinctive behavior, sensory function, and learning. He even discusses research on sticklebacks, animals that would later become beloved subjects of European ethologists.

Probably no individual exerted a more sustained and lasting influence on comparative psychology than Robert M. Yerkes. A decade after Kline's paper, Yerkes reviewed recent progress in the field (Paper 2). The sense of excitement should be readily apparent. Yerkes's view was that more progress had been made in the two years preceding his review than in any previous comparable period. Yerkes discusses the work of such authors as Sherrington, Watson, Porter, Cole, and Berry. He looks forward to the application of the comparative method in abnormal psychology.

Comparative psychology changed over the next few decades, influenced by changes in personnel, difficult economic conditions, two world wars, and many other factors. Perceptions of comparative psychology changed as well. In his 1946 assessment of the status of comparative psychology, Schneirla (Paper 3) was far less sanguine than Yerkes had been. Schneirla questioned whether we even have a "comparative psychology" and postulated a trend away from a broadly biological approach to the study of behavior.

In his often-cited paper "The Snark was a Boojum" (Paper 4), Frank Beach carried the analysis even further. Beach's paper features a cartoon caricaturing the progress of experimental psychology and also features graphs portraying the results of content analyses of articles in major journals of the field. Beach concludes that comparative psychology became dominated by the study of learning in rats and proposes that the field would profit by a return to a broader perspective.

The trend toward criticism of comparative psychology has continued ever since. Hodos and Campbell (1969) wrote a paper with the subtitle, "Why There Is No Theory in Comparative Psychology." Robert Lockard (1971) followed with his "Reflections of the Fall of Comparative Psychology." Robert Boice (1971) countered that "comparative psychology has never had the elevation from which to fall" (p. 858).

I believe that self-criticism has had beneficial effects within comparative psychology, although it has damaged the perception of comparative psychology within the broad field of psychology. However, I believe that the historical picture painted in these papers is misleading (Dewsbury, 1984). The journal content analyses contain hidden biases. The picture portrayed by Schneirla and Beach impresses me as generally accurate for animal psychology. However, within animal psychology, the comparative study of behavior continued on an even and orderly progression throughout the century. Its apparent demise is an illusion created by the contrast effect of viewing it next to the dramatic growth of more behavioristic studies of learning. Like its European counterpart, ethology, comparative psychology was practiced by relatively few prominent scientists (e.g., Watson, Yerkes, Lashley, Beach, Schneirla, Stone, Harlow) throughout much of the century and has shown substantial growth only in recent years. This century of continuous progress has generated an active and exciting discipline in the 1980s.

7

## REFERENCES

Boice, R., 1971, On the Fall of Comparative Psychology, *Am. Psychol.* **26:**858–859.

Dewsbury, D. A., 1984, *Comparative Psychology in the Twentieth Century,* Hutchinson Ross, Stroudsburg, Pa.

Hodos, W., and C. B. G. Campbell, 1969, *Scala naturae:* Why There Is No Theory in Comparative Psychology, *Psychol. Rev.* **76:**337–350.

Lockard, R. B., 1971, Reflections on the Fall of Comparative Psychology: Is There a Message for Us All? *Am. Psychol.* **26:**168–179.

# 1

Reprinted from *Am. J. Psychol.* **10**:399–430 (1899)

## SUGGESTIONS TOWARD A LABORATORY COURSE IN COMPARATIVE PSYCHOLOGY.

By LINUS W. KLINE, Ph. D.

"In no case may we interpret an action as the outcome of the exercise of a higher psychical faculty, if it can be interpreted as the outcome of the exercise of one which stands lower in the psychological scale."—*C. Lloyd Morgan.*

"But why should we bind ourselves by a hard and fast rule. . . ? Is it not the truth at which we wish to get? For myself, I am becoming more and more skeptical as to the validity of simple explanations for the manifestation of animal life whether physical or psychical."—*Wesley Mills.*

The following experiments in comparative psychology were devised to fill a small part of the work offered at Clark University in the Psychological Practicum.[1]

I have been guided by two principles in selecting animals for experimentation: (1) general distribution of the species; (2) an animal little influenced by captivity and permitting a variety of experiments of a psychological value.

The animals thus selected are regarded as typal, *e. g.*, earth worms of vermes, slugs of mollusca. A careful study of the instincts, dominant traits and habits of an animal as expressed in its free life—in brief its natural history should precede as far as possible any experimental study. Procedure in the latter case, *i. e.*, by the experimental method, must of necessity be largely controlled by the knowledge gained through the former, *i. e.*, by the natural method. In setting any task for an animal to learn and perform, two questions should be asked: (1) Does it appeal to some strong instinct? (2) Is it adapted to the animal's range of customary activities?

The adage, "Make haste slowly," is highly applicable to the present field of scientific work, not only in working with the animals, the manual execution, but especially in the matter of drawing inferences and interpreting the facts.

The work as a whole, on account of its newness, must be regarded as tentative. And notwithstanding the fact that the problems and experiments here outlined have been largely

---

[1] Experiments on Arthropoda (daphnia, crayfish, bees, ants, and wasps), Amphibia (frog, newt), Reptilia (lizard, turtle), and Canidae (dog) are omitted from this paper for the reason that many of them are yet untested or are in the process of making.

selected from the works of the foremost scientists in their respective fields, and further that I have retested their "workableness" in many cases from the standpoint of psychology, they still belong to the suggestive stage and must remain such until they are extensively tested—not merely discussed—by student and teacher in a number of laboratories.

The literature given here, although by no means exhaustive, contains in every case matter pertinent to the subject. The aim is to acquaint the learner with a few of the best works in the field, leaving the minor ones to his own industry.

The hope that the present outline will awaken a wider interest and enlist a larger co-operation in testing the value of the methods here set forth is my only justification for presenting this paper.

The nature of this work has necessarily put me under obligations to many persons.

For the greater part of the material itself I am indebted to those from whose works I have drawn and to whom I make acknowledgments in the references accompanying the experiments. For the original plan of the work, and for seeing that ample laboratory material was provided me, together with much assistance in the arrangement of the subject matter of this paper, I make grateful acknowledgments to Dr. Edmund C. Sanford.

I am thankful to President Hall for the loan of books from his library, and for the inspiration received from his hearty approval of the work itself.

To Dr. C. B. Davenport, of Harvard University, I feel greatly indebted, not only for the several experiments selected from his published works, and citations to literature, but also for personal suggestions and his keen interest in the purposes of the work.

## AMOEBA.

The chief psychological interest in Amoeba is the variety of activities that it is able to perform with an apparently undifferentiated structure. It feeds, it gets rid of waste material, it reacts to stimuli, it moves from place to place, and it reproduces by division.

The student should observe carefully to what stimuli it appears responsive, and especially any cases of apparent selective activity in the taking of food, and in the latter case should consider whether or not the act in question requires a psychical explanation.

Probably[1] the simplest and surest method of securing Amoeba

---

[1] Behla, Robert: Die Amöben, inbesondere von Parasitären und culturellen Standpunkt. Berlin, 1898.
This excellent little monograph, besides containing a bibliography

is from green grasses taken from streams and ponds. Put a small handful of such green material in a large evaporating dish, and barely cover it with tap water. Amoeba may be found at once. I get better results by waiting three or four weeks, replacing in the meantime the evaporated water.

Such material answers every purpose for observing the life processes of the Amoeba. By permitting the glass slide to dry up by evaporation Amoeba's reaction to desiccation may be observed.

It is convenient[1] to rest the four corners of the cover slip on small bits of glass of uniform thickness cemented together, or better still on four wax feet which admit, by pressure, of regulating the space between cover slip and slide—say $1\frac{1}{2}$ mm. apart.

## VORTICELLA.

The qualities of this infusoria that lead to its selection for study here are: first the easy observation of the same individual for a considerable period of time, due to its permanent attachment; second, the variety and clear cut character of its activities and the fact that they are performed in a comparatively short cycle; and third, the fundamental and suggestive character of these activities, viz.: contraction of stalk, movements of cilia, food-taking, reproduction, etc.

Place in a medium size glass jar a bunch of grass blades gathered from a running stream, or pond; cover with water. Vorticella may be found in abundance on the decaying grass within a week or ten days. They will "hold their own" in the

---

and descriptive account of Amoeba in the interests of medicine, treats historically of the many attempts to obtain a pure culture of Amoeba. No one method is as yet satisfactory. Dr. Behla, himself, recommends the following: 25 grs. of flaxseed stalks, placed in a liter of water 48 hours. Filter, and to the filtrate add a 1% solution of agar and sodium carbonate until the solution becomes alkaline. *Amoeba Spinosa* develops in large quantities. Ogata, according to Behla, put into a large evaporating dish, partly filled with water, green grass taken from an open canal. It proved to contain Amoeba and Infusoria. He put a few drops of this water into a test tube, which was filled with the following nourishing solution kept in a sterilized vessel: a filtered solution of 50cc of tap water containing 2.5% grape sugar. To separate the infusoria from the bacteria he dipped into the the test tube capillary tubes 10-20 cm. long and 0.4-0.6 mm. in diameter filling them with the culture medium. Sealed the ends in a flame. The entire length of the tube was examined under a microscope and the region exceptionally plentiful in Amoeba, and freed from other forms, was marked and broken off.

[1] Those who may desire to study Amoeba's reactions to a single stimulus. *e. g.*, light, temperature or chemical, should consult Verworn's Psycho-Physiologische Protisten-Studien, Jena, 1889; J. Loeb's Der Heliotropismus der Thiere, pp. 118, Würzburg, 1890; and Davenport's Experimental Morphology, Vol. I, pp. 155–218.

aquarium for several weeks, after which they succumb to other forms.

Their form [1] and structure [2] are described in manuals of zoölogy.

Select one in a quiescent state, and by using magnification from 375 to 425 diameters, draw the following structures : calyx (the bell shaped body), the peristomal lip or lid to the calyx ; the stalk, and ribbon like contractile tissue (draw these contracted and extended), the contractile vesicle and band like nucleus.

*Activities.* I. Vegetative. Do you discover any rhythm in the contraction of the vesicle? Does the stalk contract when the calyx and cilia [3] come in contact with any rigid, resisting, unmanageable object, or is it indifferent to some, while it avoids others ;—*i. e.*, does it seem to distinguish between harmful and harmless objects?

Put Vorticella in a continuous current of distilled water brought from a reservoir by means of a glass syphon, drawn to a capillary point, placed at one side of the cover-slip and a filter-paper drip applied to the other side. Is there any uniformity in Vorticella's reactions to the current? [4] Put yeast [5] grains into the reservoir—note behavior toward them—try very fine pulverized chalk, salts of barium, pepsin. Do you find any uniformity in Vorticella's reaction toward these substances. Are the cilia selective in the matter of food getting, [6] or do they admit all sorts of material indifferently at one time and reject all food material whatever, at other times, owing, perhaps, in the latter case to satisfied hunger?

II. Reproductive. Reproduction in *Vorticella* may take place by fission or by gemmation. The former process may frequently be seen, the latter less frequently.

The first signs of multiplication by fission may be seen in the calyx taking on a roundish form, the longitudinal axis shortening. Follow and note all the changes from this stage on till complete division takes place. Note preparations made by the daughter Vorticella previous to its leaving the mother stalk. Do you observe anything that indicates a difference in the sensitivity on different parts of the calyx?

---

[1] Kent, Saville: Manual of Infusoria, p. 675.
[2] Nicholson, H. A.: A Manual of Zoölogy. p. 100.
[3] Hodge and Aikens: *Am. Jour. of Psychology*, Vol. VI, No. 4.
[4] Kline, L. W.: *Am. Jour. of Psychology*, 1899, Vol. X, No. 2, p. 260.
[5] Commercial yeast may be used—should be dissolved in sterilized water.
[6] Weir, James: The Dawn of Reason, N. Y., 1899, p. 8.

## PARAMECIA.

This hardy, prolific, and swiftly moving infusoria readily responds to a wide range of primitive stimuli, such as gravity, light, contact, temperature and chemical substances. Observations of the responses of such a one celled organism to this varid group of stimuli must be both interesting and instructive to the psychologists.

Paramecia occur in abundance in stagnant water containing decaying vegetable matter.[1] Two or three weeks before they are needed, put hay or grass in a jar of water, and keep in a warm room. In such a jar they may be kept for indefinite periods in immense numbers. To prevent the paramecia on the slide from moving too rapidly, it is advisable to put them in a 2.5% solution of gelatine in water. Study first with the low power, then with the high.

The following structures should be made out : the position and shape of the buccal cavity, nucleus, contracting vacuoles, non-contracting vacuoles, cilia, and trichocysts.

*Movements of Cilia.*[2] Remove a large number of Paramecia from the culture medium by means of a pipette on to a glass slide. Cover the preparation with a cover glass supported by glass rollers of capillary fineness and of *uniform thickness.* Thrust under the cover slip a couple of pieces of fine capillary glass tubing.[3] After the Paramecia begin to collect along these glass tubes as well as the glass rollers, run carmine water under the cover glass ; select a quiet individual and observe how the carmine grains pass by it. Indicate by arrows placed outside the periphery of your drawing the direction of movement of the carmine. What do you infer concerning the movement of the cilia ? Do the grains whirl as much about a moving individual as about a quiet one ? Can you explain?[4]

*Geotaxis.* The effect that gravity[5] has in determining the verticality of the body and thereby determining the direction

---

[1] Kent, Saville : A Manual of the Infusoria. Vol. II, pp. 483-488. Pl. 26, Figs. 28-30.

[2] Jennings, H. S. : Reactions of Ciliate Infusoria. Jour. Phys., 1897, Vol. XXI, p. 303.

[3] Ludloff in studying the motions of the cilia in electrotaxis confined the animals in a thick gelatine solution. Jennings considered their motion in such a medium as abnormal and recommends water containing carmine grains.

[4] Taken from Davenport's outline of requirements in zoölogy for use in preparing students for Harvard University.

[5] Verworn, Max : Ueber die Fühigkeit der Zelle, activ ihr specifisches Gewicht zu verändern. Pflüger's Archiv, Vol. LIII, 1892, pp. 140-155. See also by the same author : Psycho-Physiologische Protisten-Studien, pp. 121-122.

of locomotion is termed geotaxis.[1]   Creatures whose axial orientation and consequent locomotion are perceptibly influenced by this force are geotactic.[2]

(a).   Fill half full with the culture medium of Paramecia a glass tube 1 ½ cm. in diameter and 60 cm. in length.   Keep the tube vertical and in uniform temperature and light—not direct sunlight.   After a few hours the organisms will be found at and near the surface of the water.

(b).   Fill the remaining half of the tube with hydrant water, and, keeping it vertical as before, note the results.   Twelve or fifteen hours later they may be found 3 to 6 cm. from the surface of the water (see chemotaxis).   Turn the tube bottom side up and observe the time for complete migration to the upper[3] end.[4]

A rough and ready demonstration of this geotactic response may be found by filling a test tube nearly full of the culture medium.   To prevent the free end becoming richer in oxygen, seal with an impermeable plug of wax or a rubber stopper. Do not expose the tube to direct sunlight.   For the theoretical interpretations of the geotactic responses the student is referred to the works of Verworn, p. 141 ; Jensen, pp. 462-476 ; Davenport, pp. 122-124.   (See literature given below.)

*Chemotaxis.*   (a).   Remove a large number of Paramecia from their culture medium by means of a pipette on to a glass slide.   Drop into their midst a small bit of decaying vegetable or animal material.   Cover the preparation with a cover glass supported by capillary glass rollers of uniform thickness.   Note the behavior of Paramecia toward the decaying material.

(b).   Introduce under the cover glass, by means of a pipette drawn to capillary fineness, rancid oils, *e. g.*, olive oil, cod-liver oil.   Use also a drop of water from putrefying meat, beef ex-

---

[1] Jensen, Paul:   Ueber den Geotropismus niederer Organismen. Pflüger's Archiv, 1892, Vol. LIII, pp. 428-480.

[2] Davenport. C. B. :   Experimental Morphology   Vol. I, pp. 112-125.

[3] Advantage may be taken of the negative geotactic activity of Paramecia for securing large numbers in a small quantity of water. It also serves as a means for washing out the water in which they were bred.

[4] Miss Platt (The Amer. Nat., Vol. XXXIII, No. 385, Jan., 1899,) and Dr. Jennings (Amer. Jour. of Phys., Vol. II, 1899,) report that paramecia in this country are not so markedly geotactic as those used by European investigators.   During the fall and early winter of '98 I brought large numbers into small volumes of water by taking advantage of the geotactic responses which they then so readily displayed. In April, '99, I had an occasion to repeat the process.   My efforts failed.   The paramecia remained scattered throughout the length of the tubes for several days.   Both spring and fall cultures were of the same species and reared in similar mediums.

tract, etc. It is best to use a fresh lot of Paramecia for each new substance.

(c). The following salts, acids, and alkalies were used by Dr. Jennings.[1]

| Substance. | Wk. Sol. | Stg. Sol. | Substance. | Wk. Sol. | Stg. Sol. |
|---|---|---|---|---|---|
| Copper Sulphate | + ([2]) | — | Sodium chloride | — | — |
| Sulphuric acid | + | — | Sodium carbonate | — | — |
| Hydrochloric acid | + | — | Sodium bicarbonate | — | — |
| Acetic acid | + | — | Potassium hydroxide | — | — |
| Nitric acid | + | — | Sodium hydroxide | — | — |
| Tannic acid | + | — | Potassium bromate | — | — |
| Mercuric chloride | + | — | | | |

[2] + = positive and — = negative chemotaxis.

Solutions of $H_2 SO_4$ of the following strengths give positive chemotactic reactions: $\frac{1}{1000}$ %, $\frac{1}{2000}$ %, $\frac{1}{4000}$ %, $\frac{1}{8000}$ %, $\frac{1}{16000}$ %.

(d). Repeat experiment (b) under geotaxis and note that after they have gathered at the surface they recede or fall from 3 to 6 cm. from the surface. Can you explain?

(e). Repeat (a) using a bit of filter paper or a small piece of linen fibre. After they have collected in large numbers about these objects, withdraw by means of a capillary pipette a drop of water from within the area to which the Paramecia are confined. Inject this drop beneath the cover glass of a second preparation in which Paramecia are uniformly distributed. The behavior of Paramecia to this new fluid should be very carefully observed. Their behavior under conditions in experiments (d) and (e) is now believed to be due to the presence of $CO_2$ excreted in the respiratory process of the organisms. Jennings has shown that they are attracted by weak concentrations of $CO_2$ and repelled by strong.[2] This fact greatly complicates and oftentimes vitiates experiments in chemotaxis with these animals.

*Thigmotaxis.* The stimulus offered by mere contact with a solid body is termed thigmotaxis. Animals that have a tendency to cling to, or to move along solid bodies are thigmotactic. Bits of sponge, linen, cotton, or cloth fibre, filter paper or bits of glass may be employed to demonstrate thigmotactic activities of Paramecia. These substances should be sterilized before using. The first gathering of Paramecia about such inert, insoluble bodies is thigmotaxis, but experiments (d) and (e)

[1] Jennings, H. S.: *Loc. cit.*, pp. 258-322.
[2] For a very satisfactory exposition of this subject, together with tests for detecting the presence of $CO_2$, see the paper by Dr. Jennings already referred to. The same author has given an entirely new and far more satisfactory explanation of positive chemotaxis in a more recent study of Paramecia. See Am. Jour. Phys., Vol. II, May, 1899.

under chemotaxis suggest that a continuation of the gathering in one place is due to the presence of $CO_2$ excreted. Dr. Jennings[1] concludes that "the reactions which play the chief part in the normal life of Paramecia are *negative geotaxis, positive thigmotaxis,* and *positive chemotaxis toward carbon dioxide.*" This is very likely true and at first it might appear superfluous— at least for psychology—to investigate their reactions to any other kind of stimulation. Temperature, however, stands in such vital relations with life in general, necessitating through its frequent and wide variations, ever new adjustments, that it seems advisable to give a method of testing the reaction of Paramecia to temperature.

*Thermotaxis.* Mendelssohn[2] has demonstrated that Paramecia are negatively thermotactic to temperatures above and below 24°-28° C, and are positively thermotatic to temperatures within and including these limits,[3] *i. e.,* 24°-28° C is their optimum.[4]

An apparatus yielding results quite satisfactory for demonstrational purposes may be constructed on the following plan: (1). A wooden frame—consisting of two uprights 16 inches long and 6 inches apart joined at the top by a cross beam and firmly joined to a wooden foot about 1 foot square; (2) a glass tube 6 inches long and ⅞ inches in diameter with a ⅜ inch hole at its middle point. Close the ends of the tube with cork stoppers containing a ⅜ inch hole bored near the periphery. Insert the stoppers in the tube so that their holes will be as near the bottom of the tube as possible; (3) affix, transversely, on the inside of each upright, ten inches above the foot, a ¼ inch lead pipe one end of which carries a coil of two turns, of diameter barely sufficient to admit the glass tube.

The glass tube may also carry near its middle portion a movable pipe of one coil. Differences of temperature may now

---

[1] Jennings, H. S.: *Loc. cit.,* p. 321.

[2] Mendelssohn, M.: Archiv f. d. ges. Physiologie, Vol. LX, pp. 1-27.

[3] His apparatus was simple and excellent. It consisted of a brass plate 20 cm. x 6 cm. and 4 mm. thick, supported in a horizontal plane. To its under surface was attached, transversely, tubes through which hot or cold water was run at pleasure from a reservoir elevated above the plane of the brass plate. In the middle of the plate a space 10 cm. x 2 cm. and 2 mm. was cut out and into which a glass or ebonite trough was fitted. Small thermometers with bulbs at right angles to their stems were placed in the plane of the trough and served to measure the temperature at any point. Desired differences of temperature between any two points along the trough were secured by means of water of different temperatures running through the transverse tubes.

[4] Thermotactic axis-orientation is a reaction to the stimulus created by the difference of temperature between the anterior and posterior ends of an organism. See discussions by Davenport and Mendelssohn.

be secured according to Mendelssohn's method (see note p. 406), or, if connection with hydrant faucets is possible, interpose be-tween the faucets and the lead pipes two metal worms. By applying heat to one, and packing ice around the other, continuous streams of hot and cold water may be secured.

The following rough method readily shows the thermotaxis of Paramecia: Build a trough of wax on a glass slide 6½ x 1¼ inches. Fill the wax trough with "Paramecia water." Place the slide on two flat glass dishes juxtaposed. In one keep hot water, in the other ice. Let the hot water and ice barely touch the under surface of the glass slide. The movements of Paramecia may be followed with a hand lens.

(a). By means of geotaxis secure a large number of Paramecia in a small quantity of water. Pour into the glass tube "Paramecia water" until it barely covers the thermometer bulbs. Too much water will start up currents which impair the results. Find what temperatures attract and what repel Paramecia.

(b). Supposing that Paramecia migrate from a temperature $10°$ C to a temperature $18°$ C, and from temperature $32°$ C to temperature $26°$ C, make the further experimentation that is necessary to find their optimum.

(c). *Acclimatization.* Mendelssohn[1] found that, if Paramecia be kept in a temperature from $36°$-$38°$ C from 4-6 hours, and then placed in a rectangular vessel whose end temperatures are $24°$-$36°$ C respectively, they will occupy a position corresponding to $30°$-$32°$ C. If, however, they are kept in a temperature $18°$ C and then placed in the vessel whose end temperatures are suddenly raised, they reach their optimum at $24°$ C.[2] Repeat this experiment. What inferences may be drawn from the facts of acclimatization?

## HYDRA. (*Hydroidae.*)

These fresh water polypys belong to the primitive forms of double walled animals (coelenterata.) They (coelenterata) present to us for the first time organs and tissues composed of cells, and the *co-ordination* of different parts in the performance of certain activities, *e. g.*, simultaneous closing in of tentacles on some object of prey.

Fresh water hydra may be obtained by gathering from fresh pools Lemna, sticks, and grass and putting them into an aquarium. Hydras, which are attached to these objects, will then

---

[1] Mendelssohn, M.: *Loc. cit.*, pp. 19-20.
[2] Davenport, C. B.: *Loc. cit.*, 1899, pp. 27-32. See also Loew, O.: Ueber den verschiedenen Resistenz grad im Protoplasma. Archiv f. d. ges. Physiologie, 1885, Vol. XXXV, pp. 509-516.

usually migrate within a few days to the light side of the vessel. Hydras can be kept readily throughout the winter in a large glass jar containing Lemna, chara, water cress, and Entomostraca for food.[1]

*Touch.* Place a Hydra in a watch-glass full of water. Touch the tentacle with a needle. What movements?

*Selecting Food (Taste).* (a). Drop cautiously and at intervals of a few minutes upon the surface of the water over the tentacles of the Hydra a drop of water, of sugar solution, of acid. What differences in the movements?

(b). Bring a Daphnia (previously stranded) on the end of a needle to the tentacles of the Hydra. Note the result. With another Hydra, use a bit of plant tissue.

*Reaction to Light (Photopathy).*[2] Place in a small glass jar full of water containing Lemna and Entomostraca two or three large, budding Hydras. Cover the jar with a box, placing the slit next to the window. Means of aeration should be supplied the glass jar. Note at short intervals for two weeks the position and number of Hydras in the jar.[3]

"Place a Hydra in a watch-glass with a little water, and by means of a needle and a penknife cut it into two or three pieces. Let the pieces expand and draw them. By means of a clean pipette place the pieces in a small Stender dish, in clean water. Draw the pieces again after 24 hours, and after a longer period if necessary."

## EARTH WORMS. (*Lumbricus Agricola.*)

Worms changed the course of animal evolution from a radial to a bilateral form and established permanently the very fundamental principle of metamerism. Those that have migrated from water to land have, by reason of their crawling habits, greatly accentuated all those differences, begun in the sea, between ventral and dorsal parts, between anterior and posterior ends. These structural and physiological differentiations have an interest for the psychologist in that they express a correlation between the degree of sensitiveness and the relative use of the parts of an organism.

---

[1] For anatomical descriptions of Hydra see Manuals of Zoölogy.

[2] "The wandering of organisms into a more or less intensely illuminated region, the direction of locomotion being determined by a difference in intensity of illumination of the two poles of the organism, is photopathy." Davenport: Experimental Morphology. Part I, p. 180. See also Vitus Graber: Grundlinien zur Erforschung des Helligkeits und Farbensinnes der Thiere. pp. 318, Leipzig, 1884.

[3] Wilson, Edmund B.: The American Naturalist, Vol. XXV, pp. 413-425, 1891. This paper of Prof. Wilson's contains also an account of Hydras reactions to colored light.

The nature[1] of the soil, as to its compactness, moisture, fertility, that is most favorable to the presence of earth worms; the shape and contents of their burrows; the relation of the amount of their castings to the changes of the weather—all must be studied out of doors in their natural habitat.

*Sense Organs.* Miss Langdon's[2] anatomical studies have demonstrated very thoroughly, "that the sense organs are distributed over the entire surface of the body, but are most numerous and largest at each end."[3] It has also been found that the anterior and posterior portions of the body react to weaker solutions of strychnine and saccharine than do the middle portions.

*Reactions to Chemicals.* Apply very gently to different portions of the surface a few drops of strychnine varying in strength from 1: 10000 to 1: 100000; also solutions of different strengths, of saccharine and creosote.

*Touch.* Their sensitiveness to touch or a jar may be seen by tapping gently a vessel containing them. Blow the breath gently against the head end,—what effect?

*Sight.* Earth worms may be kept for an indefinite time in earthen jars containing rich soil. (a). Keep the entrance of their burrows illuminated all night, compare in the morning by weight the amount of castings with those of the previous morning. (b). Compare also the amount of food eaten with that of the previous night. (c). During the day expose (taking care to avoid jarring the vessel) the top of the vessel suddenly to the light—note how quickly the worms disappear beneath the surface when the light flashes on them. (d). Cover a pane of glass with moist filter paper, place a worm upon it and set the glass near a window—record the reactions of the worm. (e). Allow direct sunlight to fall upon the head end of the worm, the tail end, the middle. Make note of the reactions.

*Food.* Give at night three pieces each of the following vegetables—celery, potato, cabbage, apple and onion—all cut wedge shaped. Arrange the pieces of each vegetable, thus cut, in the form of a star, with their bases toward a common center. Note in the morning what pieces have been most eaten and the relative position of the pieces that have been

---

[1] Darwin, Charles: The Formation of Vegetable Mould through the Action of worms, with observations on their habits. D. Appleton & Co., New York, 1885, pp. 326. This book should be read by every student of nature, not merely for the subject matter *per se*, but more particularly for the method and spirit that is so admirably brought to bear on a group of commonplace facts.

[2] Langdon, Fanny E.: Am. Jour. of Morphology, 1895, Vol. VI, p. 218.

[3] Lenhossek, Michael V.: Ursprung, Verlauf und Endigung der sensibeln Nervenfasern bei Lumbricus. Arch. f. Micros. Anat., 1892, XXXIX, pp. 106-136.

disturbed.  This should be repeated often enough to establish with certainty the presence or absence of a preference for certain foods.

*Taste.*  Dip a piece of cabbage or celery into a strong solution of quinine and place it near a fresh piece of the same food, of same size and shape—notice whether the piece dipped in quinine is disturbed during the night.[1]

*Smell.*[2]  (a).  Bring near to the head end of the worm in succession bits of sponges or filter paper saturated with water, with sugar solution, with onion juice, with acetic acid, and with beef extract.  Does the worm react?  (b).  Bury in a hole about the size of a hen's egg a piece of onion.  Pack the earth firmly, bury a second piece near by in a similar way, but do not pack the earth.[3]  Notice which is first disturbed.

*Boring* (a).  Place three or four worms in a pot of loose earth and note the time in which they disappear.  (b).  Press and pack the earth and repeat the experiment.  (c).  Try different kinds of soils—note where the worms go down.  Do they swallow the earth while boring?  Methods and rate of boring may be conveniently observed in tall narrow glass jars.[4]

*Methods of Burying.*  (a).  Place without order in a jar over night fifty dead pine needles.  In another jar the same number of green pine needles.  Note the next morning the arrangement of dead and green needles.  (b).  Make the same experiment during the day time—after covering the top of the jar with a black cloth.  (c).  Put dead pine needles in both jars ; keep one jar in a temperature of about 22°C over night, and the other out doors uncovered.  Compare the number of needles drawn in.

### SLUGS.  (*Limax Maximus.*)

This species of *gastropoda* may be found[5] during the warmer seasons in gardens, orchards, dairy houses and the like, and during the winter seasons in greenhouses.  They seek dark, shady, damp places.

---

[1] Graber, Vitus: *Loc. cit.*, pp. 290-295.

[2] After Darwin's, probably no other work on the senses of earth worms is more helpful and suggestive than that of Nagel's.  Bibliotheca Zoölogica, Sept. 18, 1894, pp. 146-150.

[3] This experiment was used by Darwin to test the worms sense of smell.  The food placed in the loose earth was usually found first.  Might not this be partly due to the fact that the loose earth offered easier penetration to the worm?

[4] For the power of worms to regenerate lost parts see T. H. Morgan's paper in Anat. Anz. Bd. 25.  No. 21, s. 407, 1899.

[5] I keep them alive all winter in a wooden box partly filled with rotten wood and rich soil taken from their natural habitat.  They eat vegetables, fruits and meat.

Sense Organs:[1] Eyes, auditory vesicles (otocysts), tactile and olfactory organs are present.

Senses. They react to odors,[2] sound, touch, light, heat and gravity.

*Sense of Smell.*[3] (a). Reactions to odors in the form of liquids may be secured by putting a band or stream of the solution on a pane of glass at right angles to the snail's line of motion. Do you find characteristic reactions toward different odors. Look for objectionable and unobjectionable odors ; (b) note in seconds, in each case, the interval elapsing before the first responses.

*Sight.* (a). Do they discern objects?[4] Weir[5] is inclined to think that they do. "The snail carries its eyes in telescopic watch-towers . . . and, as semi-prominent and commanding view points are assigned to its organs of sight, one would naturally expect to find a comparatively high degree of development in them." His experimental test runs thus: At the end of a ten foot pole suspend, by means of a string, a white or black ball. The ball is made to describe a pendulum-like movement to and fro in front of the snail on a level with the tips of its horns. I suggest that a pane of glass be interposed between the snail and the swinging ball, thus preventing the possibility of creating disturbing air currents. (b). Put a specimen on a pane of glass 8 x 10, and place the glass horizontally near a window and let the slug be parallel to the window. Do not let direct sunlight fall upon it.[6] Plot the position of the slug at intervals of ten seconds.[7]

*Taste.*[8] Nagel[9] believes that the lips and mouth parts of the slug are moderately susceptible to taste stimulus. By means of a pipette, place one at a time, and at right angles to the snail's line of motion, a band of distilled water, of a weak solution of sugar, of acetic acid, of quinine, of alcohol, of cheese-water, of meat juice, etc.,—make a record of its behavior on reaching the different bands of solution.

*Locomotion.* Place the slug on the glass and study its locomotion from the under side of the plate.

---

[1] Claus and Sedgwick : Text-book of Zoölogy. 1884, Vol. II, p. 34.

[2] Spengel, J. W.: Die Geruchsorgane und das Nervensystem der Molluskin. Zeit. f. wiss. Zoöl., Vol. XXXIV.

[3] Nagel, Wilibald A.: Bibliotheca Zoölogica, heft, 18, pp. 163–168, 1894.

[4] Lubbock, Sir John: Senses, Instincts, and Intelligence of Animals. p. 140.

[5] Weir, James: *Loc. cit.*, pp. 18-20.

[6] Hot water or a solution of ether and alcohol will cleanse the glass of the slime which should frequently be removed.

[7] Loeb, J.: Der Heliotropismus der Thiere. Würzburg, 1890, pp. 93-100.

[8] Lubbock, Sir John: *Loc. cit.*, p. 22.

[9] Nagel, W. A.: *Loc. cit.*, p. 164.

*Geotactic Sense.* A rough and ready demonstrational method is to place the slug on a pane of glass, parallel to one edge of the pane, hold the pane vertical and shield from lateral lights. Represent graphically the position of the slug at the beginning of the experiment, and at intervals of ten seconds, for about a minute.

The geotactic sense of the slug has been so well demonstrated by Davenport[1] that I can do no better than give his methods. A dark, wooden box of cubical form about 35 cm. in diameter, a dense, opaque, black cloth to cover the open side of the box which must be directed upwards, are required; a glass plate about 30 cm.[2] square carries the slug and is so placed in the dark box that one edge fits into one of the lower angles of the box while the opposite edge may be elevated to any degree ranging from 0° to 90°. Measure the angles off, upon one side of the box, and bore a hole at every fifth degree, so that the glass plate may rest on plugs inserted into the holes. The angular deviation of the axis of the body during a given time from the position in which it was first placed may be measured off by means of a protractor.

If the student desire to pursue the question of geotaxis further, he may investigate to answer the following questions, which may readily be determined by experimentation. (a). "What relation exists between a variation in the pressure of gravity and the precision of orientation?" (b). "What is the limiting pressure which will call forth the geotactic response?"[3]

The former is demonstrated by ascertaining the angular deviation of the slug from a vertical position upon the plate at various inclinations from 0° to 90°, and after the lapse of a constant time (45 seconds). The data gained in answer to the first problem furnishes an answer to the second.

Preliminary to (a): Ascertain whether the *quickness* of the response of the slug is modified by the strength of the action of gravity, *i. e.*, does the slug respond as quickly and effect as complete an orientation at say 15° as at 75°? For this purpose, place the slug on the glass so that its long axis is parallel to the lower edge of the plate. Set the glass successively at 60°, 45°, 30°, 20° and 15°, and make five tests at each angle upon one and the same slug. Two time intervals should be taken: (1) the time elapsing before the first response to gravity occurs, and (2) the interval required for

[1] Davenport, C. B. : Jour. Phys., Vol. XXII, pp. 99-110, 1897-98.
[2] I receive satisfactory results from a box 10 x 8 x 7 inches deep.
[3] In addition to these questions, Dr. Davenport asks a third: What determines the position of the head end? A solution of this question involves experimentation beyond what is contemplated in this course.

the organism to place its entire axis in a vertical position. To avoid exposing the slug to the action of light during the preliminary experiment, the completeness of orientation should be observed after different periods of time, *e. g.*, at the end of 30, 40, and 50 seconds. That period in which orientation is just effected should be the time selected for future experiments.

(a). Set the plate at the following angles: 90°, 60°, 45°, 30°, 20°, 10° and 0°. At each angle make six determinations on each one of five slugs. For each angle find the mean of the thirty determinations of the angular deviation of the slug from the vertical position, (b) note the extreme deviations from the vertical in the case of each slug.[1]

## FISH.

A study of fishes in the interests of comparative psychology is exceedingly desirable, for the reason that they stand at the bottom of the great back-boned series of animal life presenting in a simple and fundamental form all the essential structures characteristic of that group. To the fish we owe a debt for having encased the nervous system in a bony vertebral column, for developing an efficient neuro-motor mechanism operating about a stiff longitudinal axis, and for having "staked out" or laid down the ground plan of the nervous system on which the forces of evolution have erected the complex structures of higher forms.

The following are some of the fish suitable for such a study; pickerel[2] (*Esox Americana*), perch (*Perca Americana*), goldfish (*Cyprinus Auratus*), horned pout, common bull head (*Ameiurus nebulosus*) and shiners and spotted tail minnows (*Notropus hudsonius*) and stickle-back (*Eucalia inconstans*). Both pickerel and perch should be kept in large aquaria supplied with a continuous flow of water—a forced stream is preferable. Chara, water cress, or other water grasses should be supplied and, of course, permitted to *grow*. Shiners, earth worms, newts, young frogs serve as food. Gold fish do not require constant running water. It should be changed, however, every week or two. Supply the aquaria with sand and pebbles, and grasses —like water cress, cabomba, chara.

Food for gold fish may be had of the dealers.

*Food.* (a) Feed regularly—daily or every other day depend-

---

[1] See also Geotaxis by Davenport, Experimental Morphology, Part I, p. 119.

[2] The scientific names of North American fishes can be found in U. S. Com. of Fish and Fisheries, report of 1895, pp. 209-590. This work was prepared by President David Starr Jordan and Dr. B. W. Evermann.

ing on the species and somewhat on the season.  Note the
time required for the different species to recognize your approach
and presence.[1]  Do some never learn to recognize you?  (b).
Compare the manner in which, e. g., perch[2] and pickerel
seize their food (live minnows).  Can you account for the difference?  (c).  See if you can detect a carnivorous fish stalking
its prey.  (d).  Cut the rice wafer preparation for gold fish into
pieces about 1 cm. square.  Give the fish, along with the two
or three pieces of wafer, a piece of decided yellow paper cut
like the wafer in size and shape.  Note carefully the results.
Repeat the experiment often enough to justify a conclusion.
Next give them paper of a much lighter yellow and observe
their behavior toward it.  Is it touch or taste or both that ac-
quaints them with the paper?  Finally, give them cut pieces
of white filter paper, which very closely resembles the rice
wafer.  At each experiment do not give more than two or three
bits of rice wafer with the one piece of paper.  It would be of
great interest to find out if the gold fish would ever learn not
to strike at the white filter paper.  (e).  Feed[3] perch on shiners
for three months, then partition off a portion of their aquarium
with a pane of glass.  Every other day, at the feeding hour, put
shiners in the new division.  Note on each occasion the number of attempts made by the perch to catch the minnows.
Remove the minnows from the tank at the end of each observation.  Feed the perch earth worms on days not experimenting.
Should the perch finally become indifferent toward the minnows,
remove the glass partition.  Note the effect.  (f).  Some fish, like
pickerel, appear to have " table manners," others, like sticklebacks, snatch at times the food from each other's mouths as do
the hens.

   *Temperature.*[4]  The sensitiveness[5] of fish to temperature
varies greatly among different species.  (a).  If a minnow be
transferred from a temperature of about 20°C to 2°–4°C, and
allowed to remain ½ minute, it will soon appear as dead.  If,

---

   [1]McIntosh, W. C.: Note on the Memory of Fishes.  Journal of
Mental Science, Vol. XLIV, pp. 231–235, 1898.
   [2]Neither pickerel nor perch eat dead fish.
   [3]This experiment was suggested by the famous experiment of Möbius
on pike.  The story runs that pike, having lived for some time in a
tank separated by a glass plate from another in which small fish were
living finally desisted from trying to catch them, and on the glass plate
being removed made no attempt to molest the small fish.  See interpretation by Prof. Bateson.  Journal of Marine Biological Association,
pp. 243, 1890.
   [4]For an account of some experimentation and observation on the
Sense-Organs and Perceptions of Fishes, see W. Bateson in Journal of
Marine Biological Association, Vol. I, pp. 239–248.
   [5]Goode, G. Brown: U. S. Fish Com. Report, 1877, pp. 51–72.

after a minute, it be transferred successively through 10°C, 15° C, and back to 20°C, life returns;—transferring directly from 2° to 20°C often kills the fish.

(b)[1] The following apparatus may be used not only for testing their sensitiveness to temperature, but also for finding their optimum. (I suggest that the test be made with shiners, using

20 or 30 at a time). A zinc trough about 20 cm. deep, 16 cm. wide and 2.4 meters long supported by a wooden frame. [See cut.] Solder to the bottom of the trough 16 cm. from one end a tin box 12 cm. wide, 15 cm. long and 6 cm. deep. The box receives water through a hole cut in the zinc trough. Solder a stand-pipe to the zinc trough about the hole leading to the tin box. Apply heat to the tin box. The water in the trough should not exceed 2½ inches in depth. The end opposite the tin box should rest on iced sawdust. Ice may be applied to the sides of the trough, and also put in the water to secure desired differences of temperature. Lay lengthwise of the trough a strip of board containing ¼ inch holes about six inches apart. Thrust thermometers through the holes and into the water two inches below its surface.

*Sight.*[2] Observations[3] made on different species readily show that there are wide differences in their range of vision, *e. g.*, perch appear to recognize the human figure about 30 feet away, minnows 20 to 25 feet away and pickerel 10 to 15 feet.

With the room darkened and with a magic lantern mounted

---

[1] An apparatus of this sort gave satisfactory results in searching for the optimum temperature of tadpoles. See *Am. Jour. of Psychology*, 1898, Vol X, No. 1, pp. 8-10.

[2] Bateson, W.: *Loc. cit.*, pp. 242-248.

[3] One may connect with observations on the sight of fishes experiments and observations on their color changes. The horned pout is said to alter its color when transferred from a white to a dark dish. Abbott and others cite cases of color changes during emotional excitement. The different hues on my perch are more pronounced after an exciting chase for a minnow. It appears that changes in the intensity of light causes apparent changes in color.

on a rotating table placed about three feet from the aquarium,
throw a bright light on the aquarium in the region of the fish.
Should the fish finally move away or just out of the zone of
light, rotate the table until the light covers his entire body.
See if, by repeating this process, you can drive them back and
forth between the ends of the aquarium.   It would be interesting to see if they react toward colored light as toward white.
Bateson found no appreciable difference in the reaction toward
white and colored light among the species tested by him.[1]  Give
to a species of day feeders food at night,—note their behavior
by means of a dark lantern.

*Hearing*.   Ichthyologists[2] are generally agreed that fish do
not hear sounds transmitted by air waves.[3]  The ear apparatus
is usually interpreted as an organ for equilibration.   They do
respond to vibratile motions imparted to the water by solid
bodies.   Some fish are known to make noises, and even musical sounds which are heard by other fishes of their kind.
Would acuteness of hearing be of any advantage to the fish?

*Emotions*.   The works of Romanes, Brehm, Günther, Darwin, Abbott and others cite instances of the activities of fish
that are expressive of fear, pugnacity, social, sexual and
parental feelings, anger, jealousy, play and curiosity.   How
many of these emotions do you notice?[4]

## CHICKS.

"I have now described, perhaps in undue detail, a few of my observations as noted down at the time.  To some they may seem trivial,
and scarcely worth the making and the noting.  To us, as students
of comparative psychology, their interest lies in the light they throw
on the beginnings of psychical life and activity in the chick or
duck."—*Morgan*.

---

[1] Bateson, W.: *Loc. cit.*, pp. 251-252.

[2] Lee, F. S.: A Study of the Sense of Equilibrium in Fishes.  Jour.
of Physiology, Vol. XV, pp. 311-348.

[3] Kreidl, Alois: Ueber die Schallperception der Fische.  Archiv f.
d. ges. Physiology, 1895, Vol. LXI, pp. 450-464; also Ein weiterer
Versuch über das angebliche Hören eines Glockenzeichens durch die
Fische.  Archiv f. d. ges. Physiologie, 1896, Vol. LXIII, pp. 581-586.

[4] From my observations on shiners, I am persuaded that they, at
least, possess the capacity for feigning death.  Pickerel will not eat
dead fish—at any rate mine do not.  Sometimes they are not successful at the first two or three attempts in seizing a shiner.  These
unsuccessful attempts greatly excite the small fish, which dart
hither and thither pursued by the pickerel.  The chase may finally
be given up or the pickerel may seize one, after which all becomes
quiet.  It is at this period that the lucky shiner seeks a dark place
and lies flat on one side as when dead.  I have been deceived several
times myself when, on going to remove them from the tank, thinking
they were dead, they would dart with lightning speed to some new
quarter.

The fact that chicks can be reared under test conditions and by the care of foster-parents, makes it possible to see more clearly just what responses are due to inheritance, *e. g.*, pecking, cuddling, making their toilet ; and what are due to sense-experience, operating under the principles of association, *e. g.*, responses to agreeable and disagreeable foods.

*First Day. Senses*[1]. (a). While peeping in the shell,[2] whistle,[3] clap the hands near the egg, hold a tuning-fork near—is there a response to these sounds?

(b). After they have recovered from the " catastrophe of birth," repeat the sounds made in (a) and others that suggest themselves. Repeat this at ages 12, 24, 36, and 48[4] hours, respectively, and note the differences in responses both as to the increasing perfection of the sense of hearing and in the expression of the emotions.

(c). Has tapping on the floor near the food with a pencil any suggestive[5] value—through the auditory sense—to the chicks pecking?

2. Note behavior toward different odors, *e. g.*, spearmint, iodoform, cologne, cheese, asafœtida, etc. Odors may conveniently be presented on bits of cotton batting held by forceps.

3. At about the age of 12 hours test the field of vision by dropping bright bits of shell or meal before them. Move the food back and forth, up and down, before them. Do they peck at food beyond their reach?[6] Is it necessary to touch the eye to get a winking reflex?

4. Touch their feet with cold, medium, and quite warm wire—note the response in each case. Note fondness for sunshine.

*Instinctive Movements.*[7] (a). Note efforts to stand,[8] to walk[9] follow moving objects[10]—do they show preferences here? Note position of head and neck when sitting. Whenever possible early movements of other birds should be noted and

---

[1] Suggestions and directions for hatching chicks by means of an incubator may be had by writing to any reputable manufacturer of incubators.

[2] Morgan, C. Lloyd: Habit and Instinct, 1896, pp. 31-32.

[3] Hudson, W. H.: Naturalist in La Plata, 1892, pp. 99.

[4] Spalding, D. A.: Instinct. Macmillan's Magazine, Feb., 1873, Vol. XXVII.

[5] Darwin, Charles: Expression of the Emotions, 1872, p. 47.

[6] Preyer, W.: The Mind of the Child, p. 239. Translated by H. W. Brown, 1888.

[7] Preyer, W.: *Loc. cit.*

[8] Morgan, C. Lloyd: Habit and Instinct. Chapter 3.

[9] Mills, Wesley: The Nature and Development of Animal Intelligence.

[10] Groos, Karl: The Play of Animals. Chapter 3.

compared with those of chicks, *e. g.*, standing, walking, and swimming of the duck. (b). Make a list of all those activities that may be regarded as instinctive, *i. e.*, "congenitally perfect," as pecking, cuddling (do they show a preference here or do they cuddle indifferently under any object)? Do loud, sharp sounds shock or frighten them?

*Voice.* How many distinct sounds can be distinguished at this age?

*Second Day.* 1. Repeat experiments on the senses, adding to the list experiments on taste by giving them bits of lemon and orange[1] peelings, or a bit of blotting paper of pronounced color saturated with quinine. Note with special care the increased perfection of sight and hearing.

2. Note all activities of food getting, such as pecking, seizing, bill-movements, swallowing, etc. Offer them water (water should not be offered earlier than the second day), and observe just how they come to drink. Offer them an earth worm, beetle, or the like, and note the effects of competition. Imitative[2] acts are liable to occur at the end of the second and the beginning of the third day. For discovery[3] and accurate description they require careful observation.[4] What is the nature of the activities imitated, racial or acquired?

3. Observe the following: (a) certain activities fading out, (b) new ones appearing,[5] *e. g.*, preening feathers, flapping wings, wallowing, scratching—will they scratch on a bare surface, or do they require a bit of sand or grain to touch off the scratching apparatus? these may not occur until third and fourth days. (c) Are there any which they do from individual experience?

*Memory and Associations.*[6] To study the formation of associations in the chick the sense of taste may easily be employed. Offer them some bitter or disagreeable substance of a pronounced color as food. The number of experiences which the chick has with the disagreeable substance before it avoids or neglects it altogether is a rough measure of the time required for a permanent association to be formed between the color of the food and its disagreeable effects when taken into the mouth[7]

---

[1] Hunt, H. E.: *Am. Jour. of Psychology*, 1897, Vol. IX, pp. 125-127.
[2] Morgan, C. Lloyd: *Loc. cit.*, pp. 166-185.
[3] Romanes: Mental Evolution in Animals, pp. 222-223.
[4] For imitative movements in the child, see Preyer: The Senses and the Will. Tr. by H. W. Brown. pp. 282-292.
[5] James, W.: Psychology, Vol. II, pp. 394-402. See Transitoriness of Instincts.
[6] Thorndike, E. L.: Animal Intelligence. Supp. Psy. Rev., 1898, pp. 65-78.
[7] Morgan, C. Lloyd: Introduction to Comparative Psychology, 1894. Chapter 5, Association of Ideas in Animals.

An experiment of this sort may require several successive days of observation. The permanency of the association should be tested by offering the objectionable substance several days apart.[1]

*Third Day. Instinctive Activities.* Note the first appearance of attempts to scratch the head, to wallow, to play, and under what conditions these things occur.

*Emotions.* Joy, fear, anger may be expressed at this age.

*Solitude and Society.* The effect of solitude may be observed by isolating one chick completely from his kind—not even letting it hear the voices of other chicks. Feed it on a limited variety of diet. At the end of four or five[2] days, introduce it to a flock that have enjoyed society and a larger variety of experience. Observe its initiation into this larger world.

The above outline, covering the first three days of chick life, and indicating the kind of observations to be made for the advantage of psychology may be continued with profit twelve to fourteen days, the duration depending largely upon the problems set for the chicks to do.

## The White Rat.

"No ghost story or tale of horrid murder has been considered quite complete without its rat peering from some dark corner."—*Cram.*

To Mr. Willard S. Small I am greatly indebted for both the form and matter of this section. The outline here presented by Mr. Small for studying this rodent is based on his own very painstaking investigations, which have extended over nearly two years. With appropriate variations—dictated of course by the instincts, dominant traits, etc., of the rodent to be studied, the outline may serve for further investigations on other members of that family.

The white rat presents some modifications of the psychical character of his wild congeners,[3] but these are comparatively slight. The description given by Brehm[4] of the character of *mus decumanus* applies to the domesticated white rat with almost equal accuracy. The principal difference in psychic outfit is the inferiority of vision in the white rat. The eye is unpigmented and seems to be a much less important instrument than with the wild varieties.[5]

On account of their early maturity, healthiness (under nor-

[1] Kline, L. W.: *Am. Jour. of Psychology*, Vol. X, p. 273.
[2] *Ibid.*, pp. 271-272.
[3] Brehm: Thierleben (Saügethiere, Vol. II, p. 342 ff.). A characterization of the species *Muridae*.
[4] Brehm: *Loc. cit.*, p. 349.
[5] Rodwell, James: The Rat (London: Routledge and Sons) is a mine of anecdotal literature upon the rat,

mal conditions[1]), gentleness and cleanliness white rats are well adapted for experimental studies.

*1.   The Psychic Development of the Young Rat.*   The white rat, born blind and deaf, passes through two distinct phases of psychic development:[2] the period before, and the period after, sight and hearing begin to function.   The method in this section is to follow the development of the animal's psychical activities from birth until the age of five or six weeks.   The only factor appearing after this age is the sex instinct.   This appears about the ninth or tenth week.

SENSATION.[3]   *First day.*   1. *Smell.*   Test[4] with several substances, *e. g.*, fresh milk, cologne water, hydrochloric acid. Observe:   (a) the character of the reactions—how many kinds? (b) whether the reactions seem to indicate pleasure or displeasure in each case;   (c) can you distinguish between the act of sensing and the motor reaction?   (d) do you distinguish the vibratory movements of the nostrils so characteristic of the rodents?

2.   *Taste.*   Open the mouth and place upon the tongue: fresh milk, honey or sugar solution, aloes or quinine solution, or other substances.   Observe:   (a) the reactions;   (b) whether they seem to indicate discrimination of tastes.[5]

3.   *Tactile Sensibility.*   (a) Touch the skin lightly on various parts of the body;   (b) draw a bristle across the back, flank or side, and over the nose;   (c) pinch very lightly the tail, foot, and sides or flank;   (d) touch any part with a cold wire (32°), and then with a hot wire (not hot enough to burn);   (e) notice also the rats' extreme sensitiveness to changes of atmospheric

---

[1] The following conditions should be observed :   (1) the rats must be kept in a warm room—temperature not lower than 50° F.; (2) the floors of the cages should be covered one inch deep with clean sawdust; this should be changed at least once a week; (3) the cages should be so arranged as to protect the rats from strong light ; (4) a simple diet of dog biscuit and milk and occasional green stuff, *e. g.*, apples or lettuce, gives good results.   Fresh water each day.   Offensive odors are minimized by carefully observing (2) and (4).

An excellent observation cage may be made as follows: dimensions, length, 20 inches; height, 16 inches; width, 16 inches; floor, back, and top of wood; one end of wire mesh (¼ inch) for ventilation; front and other end of glass.   This insures observation of all activities, and is large enough for the introduction of necessary apparatus.

[2] Mills, Wesley:  Animal Intelligence, p. 167.

[3] In connection with the observations upon sensation, it will prove interesting and suggestive to note the conditions of the sense organs.

[4] Bits of paper held by forceps are convenient for this purpose.   The odorous substance should be held from 2 to 5 mm. from the nostrils. Other odors and irritating fluids should be used.   For similar tests upon other rodents, cf. Mills, W.: *Loc. cit.*, p. 234, 241.   Distinguish carefully between the effects of odors and irritating fluids.

[5] Mills, Wesley: *Loc. cit.*

temperature as indicated by rapid lowering of bodily temperature and retardation of heart-beat when brought from the nest into a cooler atmosphere; (f) observe also their apparent satisfaction when covered with the hand.

4. "*Sense of Support.*"[1] Place the young rat near the edge of the table, and note whether it crawls off or hesitates at the edge and shows uneasiness.[2]

5. *Sense of Position.*[3] Place the rat upon a pane of glass in horizontal position, with the sagittal axis of body parallel with two sides of the pane; then tip the pane—each end and side in turn—and note the angle required to elicit a response, *i. e.*, an effort to compensate the inclination of the pane.

*Second to fifteenth day.*[4] Follow the same line of observation, noting these more general points.[5]

1. *Smell.* (a). The tests may be made with the same substances, or variations may be introduced. In the former case, note the effect of growing familiarity upon the reactions; (b) note whether there is any diminution in the time required for sensing the stimulus; and (c) distinguish between sensing of stimulus and motor response.

2. *Taste.*[6] The experiments need not be repeated more than twice during the first week; after that, every second day.

3. *Instinctive Activities.*[7] *First day.* 1. When the young rats are held in the hand, observe their tendency to roll up into a ball. 2. Place them upon a smooth table and observe their efforts;[8] (a) to stand, (b) to crawl, (c) to hold up and move the head from side to side; (d) observe further whether they seek to get together; explain the reason of this movement and consider whether it has any significance for

[1] Mills, Wesley: Animal Intelligence, pp. 118, 150, 176, 225. Morgan, C. Lloyd: Habit and Instinct, p. 107.

[2] This experiment *may* be impracticable the first day on account of the limited locomotion of the rats.

[3] Sanford, E. C.: Experimental Psychology, p. 36. Lee, F. S.: Jour. of Physiology, Vols. XV and XVII.

[4] Weigh the rat and measure length of body and head from time to time.

[5] Mills, W.: *Loc. cit.* Prof. Mills's work should be familiar. The differences brought out in his studies, between young animals of different species, are most instructive. Preyer, W.: The Mind of the Child—the Senses and Will. (Tr. by H. W. Brown.) p. 257 ff.

[6] The experiments on taste and smell may be varied profitably by introducing the factors of hunger and satiety. Compare rats taken at random from the nest with some that have been segregated for two to four hours, according to age. (N. B. Keep them warm.)

[7] Morgan, C. Lloyd: Habit and Instincts. Ch. 5. For a discussion of "Instinct," cf. Ch. 1. Also Groos, Karl: The Play of Animals. Marshall, H. R.: Instinct and Reason (MacMillan, 1898). James, W.: Psychology, Vol. II, Ch. 24.

[8] For comparison with other rodents, cf. Mills, W.: *Loc. cit.*

the origin of the "social instinct." 3. Turn them over upon their backs; note their efforts to turn over upon their bellies; note also the variety of movements in these efforts and the lack of muscular co-ordination.

4. Try to observe the sucking activity from the first.[1] (a) Do the new-born rats find the mother's teats immediately by a "congenitally perfect instinct," or is there accident in the process? (b). Do they suck any other part of the mother than the teats? (c). Does the mother render assistance?

5. Test their clinging power—letting them cling, unsupported, to your finger.[2] The attempt should be made constantly to infer the sensational and affective states correlative with the instinctive activities.

6. *Vocal Expressions.* Note carefully the number of sounds you can distinguish clearly, and what affective states they severally indicate.[3]

The eyes and ears begin to function about the fifteenth day. Between the second and the fifteenth days, two facts of a general nature relating to motor activities should be noted : (a) the increasing vigor of movements, and (b) definiteness of muscular co-ordination. Note especially, the progressively effective use of the paws in sucking.

In respect to vocal activities, it should be noted whether they increase in variety, and whether they are indulged in more or less frequently.

New features in development may be looked for as follows :

*About the seventh day*, note that they begin to move about more freely, selecting their paths to some extent and avoiding obstacles.

*Tenth to thirteenth day.* 1. Look for the appearance of some very characteristic "rat" activities : (a) orientation, by rising slightly upon the hind legs and sniffing about, when they are moved into a new place ; (b) climbing up on the mother's back and up the side of the cage ; (c) scratching the body with the hind foot ;[4] (d) washing the face with the fore paws. 2. Observe about this time also that they may leave the nest and follow the mother in order to suck.[5]

---

[1] Mills, W.: *Loc. cit.*, p. 118 ff.   Morgan, C. L.: *Loc. cit.*, p. 113. Hudson, W. H.: The Naturalist in La Plata, p. 106.   Wallace, A. R.: Contributions to the Theory of Natural Selection, p. 206.   Preyer, W.: The Senses and Will, p. 257.

[2] Robinson, Dr. Louis:   Nineteenth Century, Nov., 1891.   (This instinct in the human child.)

[3] Contrast with rabbit, Mills, W.:   Animal Intelligence, p. 134.

[4] This is called by Romanes a pure reflex.   Cf. Romanes, G. J., Darwin and after Darwin, part 2, p. 80.

[5] I have seen one leave the nest and go directly to the mother, a foot away, eating her supper.   Whether this was by chance or by smell is an interesting question.

A test for instinctive fear may be made by rubbing a cat and then presenting the hand to the nostril of the rats.[1]

At the end of the first period, it will be well to "take account of stock," summarizing the psychical elements that have now appeared, noting their time of appearance—congenital or later—and their order of development.

## SECOND PERIOD.

The following suggestions for this period may serve for a general outline, to be varied or discontinued at discretion.

SENSATION. 1. *Smell.* Tests should be made now especially with food substances, *e. g.*, milk, cheese, honey, meat, etc. Tests may be made also with essential oils.[2]

2. *Test.* Discrimination of taste, by putting edible and non-edible substances into the mouths of the rats, *e. g.*, dog biscuit and sealing wax.

3. *Hearing.*[3] (a). Tests should be made for hearing just before the external meatus is completely open, by clapping the hands, clucking, hissing, whistling, etc. Be careful that a current of air is not thrown upon the rats with explosive noises. (b). Generally the sense of hearing becomes acute about the fifteenth day. (c). Try a number and variety of sounds, especially musical tones (a gamut of tuning forks is desirable). Also introduce variations in loudness.

In these experiments observe the small variety in the reactions at first. What is the inference?

(d). The test should be repeated daily for a few days noting the progress in discrimination of sounds and the emotional concomitants. (e). At the age of about three weeks, test for æsthetic sense in connection with sound.[4] An air played softly upon a violin or even sung softly will serve for test.

4. *Vision.*[5] Make tests as soon as the eyes begin to open. (a). Bring the rats into a strong light. (b). Strike the hand across the field of vision an inch or two in front of the eyes.

---

[1] Mills, W.: *Loc. cit.*, p. 176, 177. (I have not been able to confirm Prof. Mills's experiment with respect to rats. Cf. Morgan, C. L.: *Loc. cit.*, p. 117.)

[2] "Rats are enticed by certain essential oils." Darwin: Descent of Man, p. 530.

[3] Mills, W.: *Loc cit.*

[4] Anecdotes of rats and mice being fascinated by music are so frequent and so well authenticated that this experiment is of peculiar interest. Cf. Weir, Dr. James: The Dawn of Reason, p. 116.

[5] It should be remembered that vision is the least efficient of the white rat's senses. A comparison should be made between the importance of vision and the importance of smell and hearing in the development of the young rats.

What effect in each case? Can you get a winking reflex without touching the eyes?

The experiment upon vision will probably be unprofitable after four or five days, except experiments for the determination of the distance at which the rats can see objects. These may be made at intervals as long as the study continues. These determinations may be made roughly by moving an unfamiliar object in front of the cage, carefully excluding all sound.

5. Observations of the common activities of the rats will yield information in regard to tactual and kinæsthetic sensations, and the sense of equilibrium.

INSTINCTIVE ACTIVITIES. After the eyes and ears are open, observe the gradual disappearance of some activities, the progressive perfection of others, and the appearance of still others.

A. *Vocal.* Even casual observations will show the diminution of vocal activity.

B. *Motor.* 1. Note the slow degeneration of the sucking instinct. 2. Orientation, climbing and washing are rapidly perfected. 3. New activities appear, 17th to 21st days. (a). Gnawing. They nibble at one's fingers, at food, and as early as the 21st day I have seen them gnawing a stick. (b). Digging. (c). Play activities — running, jumping, mock fighting, etc. They may frequently be seen licking each other. It is not apparent whether this is in play or whether they are searching for vermin.

At the end of four or five weeks the student should again " take account of stock " and catalogue the psychic outfit of his subjects. As all our knowledge of the animal mind is inferential, the same observations will serve as basis for conclusions as to instinct, general intelligence and emotion in the rat. For example, the constant investigations of the waking rat will declare his curiosity. The eager expectancy displayed at the usual feeding time,[1] especially when they hear the rattle of the food, is evidence of memory. Fear is apparent at every unusual noise.

---

[1] Rats should be fed in the afternoon.

## II.

### SUGGESTIONS FOR EXPERIMENTAL STUDY OF INTELLIGENCE.

The preceding study of the young rats will have brought out the rat character sufficiently to warrant the setting of a good many tasks. For example: hunger, sociability, and curiosity may safely be appealed to as motives for the performance of tasks; climbing, digging, and gnawing are patently instinctive and persistent activities.[1]

Two practical suggestions for apparatus are appended. In each case aptness for learning, imitation, and memory may be tested. The rats should be at least six or seven weeks old.

1. The apparatus consists merely of an ordinary squirrel revolver. A revolver 10 inches in diameter and one foot long can be used in the cage described above, and it is better to perform the experiments in their accustomed place.

(a). Keeping the door of the revolver open, note the time required for the rats to learn to run the revolver.[2]

(b). After the rats have learned this lesson, a test of imitation may be made by introducing one or two uninitiated rats into the cage. The difference in time required to learn the lesson may be taken as a rough measure of imitation.

(c). Furthermore memory may be tested by removing the drum for a time and noting the results upon its return.

This experiment may be variously complicated. For example, after the rats have learned to run the revolver, the door-way may be closed with a spring door such as is described in connection with the next piece of apparatus.[3]

2. Two pieces of apparatus. In both cases the motive appealed to is hunger. The activity in one case is digging; in the other, gnawing.

(a). Exp. box 1. A box[4] 7 inches square and 6 inches high; sides of wire mesh, $\frac{1}{4}$ inch mesh; top, glass; bottom, wood. At one side of bottom, a hole $3\frac{1}{2}$ by 2 inches is cut. Two strips of wood $1\frac{1}{6}$ inches thick tacked to the bottom raise the box above the floor of the cage. Sand and sawdust are banked about the box just above the level of the floor. Food

---

[1] This enumeration is merely a suggestion; it is not intended to cover the field.

[2] Other interesting things will be observed: *e. g.*, if there is any straw or litter in the cage, they are very likely to carry it into the revolver and make their nest there.

[3] In all these experiments the experimenter must be prepared for individual variations.

[4] The apparatus and the method is more fully described by Dr. L. W. Kline, *Am. Jour. Psychology*, Vol. X, No. 2, p. 277. The diary of a few days' experimentation is given.

of some kind[1] is placed in the box and the top fastened down. At the usual feeding time, Exp. box 1 is placed in the cage and banked up as described. There is nothing to mark the place of entrance. This experiment should be repeated daily till the lesson is completely learned, so that the rats go at once to the right place and dig into the box.[2]

(b). Exp. box 2. The same as Exp. box 1, except that the floor is solid and the entrance is on one side. The entrance is an opening, 2½ inches square. This opening is provided with an inward swinging door of sheet zinc, hung from the top. The door is attached by a spring[3] (an ordinary rubber band) to the top of the cage, so that when free it is held open. The door is held closed by means of narrow strips of stout paper stuck, with sealing wax, to the door and the lower edge of the box. Admission to the food within can be attained only by biting, pulling or scratching off the paper. This experiment, too, should be repeated daily until the habit of getting the food by removing the papers is formed.

The two experiments yield the same results in regard to the determination of instinct, intelligence, and habit.[4] The two should be carried on contemporaneously with two pairs of rats. Some interesting comparisons will in the form of discrimination be apparent.

A further study of intelligence may be made, after the two pairs have mastered their lessons, by interchanging the boxes.

After this new task has been performed, the problem may be complicated still more by alternating the boxes at unequal intervals. If it is desired to test even further the adaptability of the rat, other complications or variations may be devised.

Careful analysis of these experiments will reveal the parts played by the different psychic elements: the instinct feeling of hunger (and curiosity too, perhaps,), the instinctive activities employed, recognition, memory—these all combining to form complex associations.

### THE CAT.

" The cat seems to be a much more intelligent animal than is often supposed."—*Mivart*.

" Indeed no greater contrast in table manners can be observed anywhere than when we turn from the kennel or the pig sty and watch the dainty way in which a cat takes its meals."—*Robinson*.

" In will-power, and ability to maintain an independent existence the cat is superior to the dog."—*Mills*.

---

[1] I use nothing but dog biscuit. The rats must not be over fed.

[2] Not more than two rats should be set to this task at once.

[3] A small hook soldered to the lower part of the door serves to attach the spring to the door.

[4] Kline, L. W.: *Loc. cit.*, p. 279.

A psychological study of the cat,[1] or allied species, will be more profitable and certainly more pleasant to both student and cat if the former bears in mind the dominant cat traits : She is independent of man from a vegetative standpoint ; self-willed, will not brook restraint ; she is slow to forget an injury and often resents it ; enjoys kind treatment ; she is for the most part solitary in her habits.

The senses, instinctive activities, the emotions, the formation of habits, and the growth of intelligence constitute the essential material for observation and investigation.

The *order* in which the senses develop, and likewise the order and the conditions under which the instinctive movements and the expression of the emotions occur, should first engage the attention, and that, too, not later than the second day.[2]

*Sense of Smell.* Cheese, meat, warm milk, the hands after being rubbed over a dog, after handling mice, carbolic acid, etc., may be presented as objects of smell. Can you distinguish between the act of sensing and the motor reactions?

*Sense of Taste.* Solutions of sugar, salt, and aloes may be applied to the tongue by means of a feather or camel's hair brush. Milk, vinegar, and meat juice may be similarly applied.

*Touch.* Reaction to the sense of touch may be solicited by touching the sole of the forepaw, the mouth, inner surface of the nostrils and the ear with a broom straw, or knitting needle.

*Temperature.* Heat an iron rod to an uncomfortable degree to the human skin (not hot enough to burn) and place it against the sole of the kitten's foot.

*Pain.* Pinch different parts with forceps or fingers—note the *latent* time before the response. Does the latent time shorten with age?

*Sense of Support.*[3] (a). Uneasiness manifested by cries, and gripping the supporting surface vigorously with its claws, when it crawls to the edge of the same, is interpreted as a response to a disturbance of the sense of support.[4] If convenient make the same experiment with a turtle, a puppy, an ant, a slug, a chick. (b). Place the kitten on a board 12 x 14

---

[1] Brehm : Thiereleben (Saügethiere, Vol. I, pp. 461-480.) ; J. Hampden Porter's Wild Beasts, pp. 76, 305, contains many significant observations on the habits and traits of Felidæ.

[2] Prof. Wesley Mills is the first scientist to have observed daily the psychic development of the cat from birth to maturity. Many of the above suggestions are founded on Prof. Mills's work. See also Bernard Perez : Mes Deux Chats ; Fragment de Psychologie Comparée, pp. 39-78. Paris, 1881.

[3] See literature under Rat.

[4] Prof. Mills says : "This seems to me as fundamental as anything that is to be found in animal psychology."

inches, the sagittal axis coinciding with the length of the board.  Tip the board slowly by raising one side until the kitten perceives the new position.  Tip the forward end in the same way, then the rear end—note the angle that the board makes with the horizon in each of the positions.[1]

*Reactions to Rotation.*  Place the kitten on a small rotation table—head toward the periphery.  Turn the table at a moderate rate through one rotation—note the direction of the *first* movement after the table stops.

*Hissing.*[2]  This mode of expressing a certain group of emotions is natural only to the *Felidæ*, *Reptilia*, and a few birds. What stimulus provoked the first hissing sound.  How many kinds of hissing sounds can you detect in the kitten?  Note the same points with regard to spitting.

*Tail and Ear Movements.*[3]  The movements of these pendant organs are for the most part instinctive, though in the case of the ear they would seem to be more of the nature of a reflex.  Their *quivering* motion is a curious phenomenon.

*Sight.*  Eyes open about eighth day — note shape, color, the distance at which objects are recognized, when the kitten first follows a moving object by turning the head and by rolling the eyes.

Special directions for observation and experimentation on the kitten after the tenth day are not only useless but a positive hindrance.  No two observers are likely to surround the young cat with the same environment and conditions; therefore, in the matters of habit and intelligence, each place will have its own special problems.  But the appearance of instincts and emotions peculiar to the cat will occur under all favorable conditions, so that it may be helpful to indicate what to expect or look for as the psychic life of the cat unfolds.  Look then for the *first* appearance of spitting, hissing, making its toilet,[4] playing with inanimate objects,[5] chasing moving objects, stretching and yawning, especially after a nap or leaving its nest, enjoying being stroked, setting claws into upright objects, tree-climbing, purring, crouching, "lying in wait," bowing the back in rage, playing "with real living prey," *e. g.*, a mouse,[6] playing "with living mock prey,"[7] *e. g.*, its mother or another

---

[1] "(b)" is not an experiment to test the sense of support, but rather that of "position."

[2] For a probable origin of hissing and tail wagging, see Louis Robinson, "Wild Traits in Tame Animals." London, 1897, pp. 228-264.

[3] Ingersoll, E.: Wild Neighbors. See chap. "The service of Tails."

[4] Robinson, Louis : *Loc. cit.*, pp. 262-264.

[5] Robinson, Louis : *Loc. cit.*, pp. 228-229.

[6] Groos, Karl : The Play of Animals, pp. 121 and 130.

[7] Mills, Wesley : *Loc. cit.*, p. 196.

kitten. How many of these activities can you account for? What is their significance in the economy of cat life? A study in the formation of associations and their consequent habits, may most naturally begin (a) by observing the kitten in learning its name. Make a record of the number of times the name is uttered until it is recognized by the kitten. While teaching it, the name should be used judiciously, and always in immediate connection with a pleasurable reward, e. g., food, stroking, giving it a play object to which it has become attached.

(b). Select from among its play activities, one that the cat may be readily induced to repeat (this the observer must decide), then create conditions that will call forth a second one that has a pleasure giving or satisfying effect. Note the number of times necessary to create the new condition that shall call forth the second act without hesitation. The following account of an actual case will illustrate the point. After the young cat had become accustomed to play with a ball, a long string was attached to the ball by which it was withrawn gently from the cat and dropped into a work-basket. The cat saw the whole performance and immediately took the ball from the basket and continued the play for a few minutes when the ball was jerked away and dropped into the basket with the quickest possible despatch. After two experiences, i. e., at the third time the ball was jerked away, the cat went directly to the basket. The experiment may be varied—basket moved before the ball is jerked into it, a different basket used, etc.

Under this head would come teaching[1] some of the well known

---

[1] A radically different method for studying associative processes from those given in (a) and (b) has been used by Dr. Thorndike. (Thorndike, E. L.: Animal Intelligence, p. 6. New York, 1898.) "It was merely to put animals when hungry in enclosure from which they could escape by some simple act, such as pulling at a loop of cord, pressing a lever, or stepping on a platform. . . . The animal was put in the enclosure, food was left outside in sight, and his actions observed. Besides recording his general behavior, special notice was taken of how he succeeded in doing the necessary act, and a record was kept of the time that he was in the box before performing the successful pull, or clawing, or bite. This was repeated until the animal had formed a perfect association between the sense impression of the interior of that box and the impulse leading to the successful movement." I recommend that the food be put *in the box* and the animal on the *outside*, free, unhampered, and that the several tasks set by Dr. Thorndike for the animal to do in order to escape be accordingly transferred to the outside of the boxes. I have found this method to work admirably well with the white rat, and the cat. See *Am. Jour. of Psychology*, 1899, Vol. X, pp. 277-279. The time required to perform each experiment, and particularly just how it is done, and whether or not experience facilitates the execution of the task, are among the essential items to be noted.

tricks, *e. g.*, rolling over, jumping through the hands, " begging " in upright position, shaking hands, etc.

Full notes are always valuable. While teaching them a task, the notes should be made as near as possible *at the time* of the experiment. It is highly important, too, that every circumstance attending the cat's first successful effort in doing a set task be carefully noted. If convenient, photographs should be taken ; and especially of attitudes expressive of emotions that are usually so difficult to describe.

## 2

Reprinted from *J. Abnorm. Psychol.* **2**:271-279 (1908)

# RECENT PROGRESS AND PRESENT TENDENCIES IN COMPARATIVE PSYCHOLOGY [1]

BY ROBERT M. YERKES, HARVARD UNIVERSITY.

MORE important contributions to our knowledge of comparative psychology, animal behavior, and of certain aspects of the physiology of the nervous system have been made during the past two years than ever before in a like period. And at present there are, on all sides, evidences of deep research impelling, and rapidly increasing interest in the physical and psychical problems of organic development. It is the recognition of these facts that stimulates me to call the attention of psychiatrists and abnormal psychologists to the progress and tendencies in a field of research which is intimately related to their own. I shall not give a *résumé* of all the important articles, monographs, and books on topics of comparative psychology and bordering subjects which have appeared recently, but instead I shall try to indicate by references to a few works those discoveries and tendencies which are of pre-eminent importance for the readers of THE JOURNAL OF ABNORMAL PSYCHOLOGY.

[1] I use "Comparative Psychology" in this connection in the commonly accepted sense of the psychology of all organisms excepting man. It seems to me desirable, however, that it should designate a method of investigation rather than a division of the field of psychology, and that the expression "Animal Psychology," as contrasted with "Human Psychology" should designate that portion of the materials of the science which is usually known as Comparative Psychology.

For our present purposes, investigations which have directly advanced the science of comparative psychology may be arranged in four groups.   1. Studies of the physiology of the central and the peripheral nervous system, in relation to the behavior of organisms and to consciousness.   As representative of this field of research I wish to mention later the work of Sherrington and of Franz.   2. Studies of animal behavior, the goal of which is the accurate and minute description of forms of activity and their explanation in terms of the physiological states and environmental factors which determine them.   In this group fall such investigations as those of Jennings and Bohn.   3. Studies of the mental processes of animals, of sensations, ideas, images, memory types, etc.   The work of Watson, Porter, Cole, and Berry is indicative of the kind of progress which is being made in this direction.   4. Discussions of the basis of the science of comparative psychology, and of the methods by which it may be developed.   Claparède, Washburn, and Yerkes have contributed to the literature of this group.   I shall now describe in a very general way the work which has been referred to above as representative.

Sherrington's[1] book on the integrative action of the nervous system is a masterly summing up of the results of years of well-directed and unusually fruitful research concerning the relations of the nervous system to the reflex activities in certain mammals.   In it he deals in a most illuminative way with the nature and relations of reflexes in the dog and the monkey, and with the control of activity by the nervous system.

The first two lectures of the volume present with unusual clearness the fundamental facts of neural structure and function which concern the integrative action of the nervous system. Simple and compound reflexes are in turn considered in their relations to the essential portions of the nerve arc:  the receptor, the connector, and the effector.   As the author is careful to point out, the simple reflex is probably an abstraction, for it always exists in co-ordination with other reflexes.   This co-ordination is of two kinds:  simultaneous and successive.   The former gives origin to what Sherrington calls the reflex-pattern; and the latter to the chain-reflex.   By these two different types

---

[1] Sherrington, C. S. The Integrative Action of the Nervous System. New York, Charles Scribner's Sons. 1906. Pp. XVI & 411.

of combination of simple reflexes the various parts of the organism are brought into adjustment to one another and to their environment.

After exhibiting the basis of his classification of reflexes as allied and antagonistic, Sherrington shows how the mutual relations of these two sorts of acts provide us with the varied phenomena of inhibition and reinforcement, which are of such great importance to physicians, and especially to those who deal with nervous derangements.

As it is utterly impossible to summarize Sherrington's volume within the limits of this article, I must content myself with this brief and inadequate description of it, and with the suggestion that it is well worth reading and re-reading.

Through his experimental study of the functions of the cerebrum Franz[1] has recently made a notable contribution to comparative psychology. For he has demonstrated that in monkeys and cats the frontal lobes are concerned in the formation of simple associations. Their destruction causes the loss of recently acquired habits, whereas habits of long standing are retained.

Although the work in the field of sense physiology is obviously important for comparative psychology, I cannot do more than call attention to the fact that practically the same investigation may be conducted from any one of the points of view which we may designate as the physiological, the naturalistic, and the psychological. In studying vision, for example, the physiologist is interested in the functioning of the sense-organ or of the central nervous system; the student of behavior, whom for convenience I have termed the naturalist, is interested in what the animal does when the visual organ is functioning; and finally, the psychologist is interested primarily in the phenomena of visual sensation. These three interests cannot be divorced from one another without loss to science. It is partly in view of this fact that I venture to mention, in connection with this comment upon the progress and tendencies of comparative psychology, work in the physiology of the nervous system and in animal behavior.

We may now turn to the investigations of our second group

[1] Franz, S. I.  On the Functions of the Cerebrum : The Frontal Lobes.  Archives of Psychology, Vol. 1, 1907.  Pp. 64.

and examine the work of Jennings.[1]   During the past ten years this indefatigable investigator has published paper after paper on the behavior of the lower organisms, and recently he has brought together under the general title, "Behavior of the Lower Organisms," the chief results of his observation and thought.   His book, which is certainly the most important contribution to the study of animal behavior ever published, consists of three parts. The first is descriptive of the forms of behavior and conditions of activity in certain of the unicellular organisms;  the second deals similarly with the behavior of certain of the lower metazoa, especially the Coelenterata;  and the third presents an analysis of the materials of the first two parts, together with a discussion of the origin of forms of behavior and theories of reaction.

Of prime importance is the fact that Jennings has so thoroughly studied the behavior of many of the lower organisms that he is able to describe their movements accurately and in considerable detail.   He has succeeded in analyzing the apparently complex activities of many organisms into their relatively simple components, and he has thus revealed what he calls their action systems.   To illustrate, I may quote concerning the action system of Paramecium: " Passing in review the behavior of Paramecium, we find that the animal has a certain set of actions, by some combination of which its behavior under all sorts of conditions is made up.   The number of different factors in this set of actions is small, and they are combined into a co-ordinated system, so that we may call the whole set taken together the action system.   The action-system of Paramecium is based chiefly on the spiral course, with its three factors of forward movement, revolution on the long axis, and swerving toward the aboral side.   The behavior under most conditions is determined by variations in these three factors.   Such variations, combined in typical manner, produce what we have called the avoiding reaction.   Other elements in the action-system are the resumption of forward movement, in response to stimulation, and the coming to rest against solid objects in what we have called the positive contact reaction.   Subordinate activities, playing little part in the behavior, are the contractions of the ectosarc and the discharge of trichocysts."   p. 107.

[8] Jennings, H. S.  Behavior of the Lower Organisms.  New York, The Macmillan Company, 1906.  Pp. XIV & 366.

Jennings attention has been devoted chiefly to the investigation of the regulation or adaptation of behavior, and he has sought to discover what principles underlie the phenomena. Incidentally he has discovered that even among simple organisms reaction by trial as well as reaction by definite and precise orientation in accordance with the theory of Verworn or of Loeb, occurs. In other words, he has shown that in the lower organisms, as well as in the higher, there are two fundamentally important types of response: reaction by trial, and reaction by a stereotyped and definite reflex. Trial reaction is a form of behavior—possibly I should say the form of behavior — which is usually accepted as an indication of intelligence. But as Jennings shows, if we accept this criterion of consciousness, practically all organisms are conscious.

In an obviously important manner the "Behavior of the Lower Organisms" supplements "The Integrative Action of the Nervous System." The one deals with units of activity and their relations in the case of the lower organisms; the other deals in a comparable way with the simple act of the higher animal, and with those complex relations of reflexes which we know as behavior.

By Bohn[1] and a number of zoölogical psychologists who are associated with him in the *"Institute génerale psychologique"* a great deal of extremely interesting and valuable work on the problems of animal behavior and animal consciousness has recently been done in France.

In addition to describing many new forms of animal reaction, Bohn has revealed the fact that the influence of any particular environmental factor upon the behavior of an animal is likely to depend upon the presence and relative intensities of other factors which act simultaneously or successively. For example, the reactions of certain shore animals in response to gravity vary with the condition of the tide even after the animals have been removed to a laboratory aquarium. To Bohn, then, we owe the convincing demonstration of the fact that in order to understand any reaction of an organism, we must know the relations of the various environmental factors which have influ-

1 For a list of the papers of Georges Bohn from 1902 to 1905 see a digest entitled "Georges Bohn's Studies in Animal Behavior." Journal of Comparative Neurology and Psychology, Vol. 16, 1906, pp. 231-238. Many of his more recent papers have appeared in the Bulletin and the Monographs of the *Institute génerale psychologique* of Paris.

enced the organism in the past and which are acting upon it at present. In other words, the previous experience of the organism cannot safely be neglected.

The practical importance of such studies of behavior as those of Jennings and of Bohn becomes apparent when we reaize that we cannot deal intelligently and successfully with organlisms which further or hinder human life except in the light of knowledge of how they behave, and by what conditions their activities are determined. Given knowledge of the possible activities of the pathogenic bacterium or amoeba, together with similar knowledge of the conditions which modify these activities, we can discover how to control the relations of the injurious organism to our bodies. Jennings has gone a long way toward giving us a practical working knowledge of certain of the lower organisms, but, better still, he has demonstrated the value and applicability of many methods of investigation, and has given an impetus to research in this field which will undoubtedly have far reaching results. It is desirable, however, that the physician should realize the significance for him of the study of organic activity in relation to the control of life phenomena.

We come now to that group of investigations which is strictly speaking psychological. Watson[1] in his monograph on the role of the senses in the reactions of the white rat has presented a thoroughgoing discussion of this subject from the point of view of a rigorous experimentalist. He has clearly demonstrated that the rat needs none of its special senses, except possibly the kinæsthetic or organic, for the learning or the performing of the act of following a complex maze-path. The form of maze which was used is that known as the Hampton Court Maze.

Although it has long been surmised that animals acquire many, if not most, of their motor habits without much aid from sight, hearing, touch, or smell, Watson is the first investigator to prove experimentally that this is true. His work opens up a field of research which heretofore has been approached rather than entered. Undoubtedly we are now on the way to accurate knowledge of the relations of sense data to modifications in behavior.

[1] Watson. J. B. Kinæsthetic and Organic Sensations : their role in the reactions of the white rat to the maze. Psychological Review, Monograph Supplements, Vol. 8, 1907. Pp. VI & 100.

The psychology of the sparrow, in so far as it is known, we must credit to Porter,[1] who, in two papers which to the true naturalist are more intensely interesting than any "nature fakes" or animal stories, has given a vivid description of the psychological characteristics of this common bird. I shall quote a few sentences from the author's summary by way of illustrating his conclusions. "The scope of his [the sparrow's] attention is probably narrow. Any result of his activity which does not follow closely his definitely directed efforts he seems unable to profit by. He has great power of confining his actions to the matter in hand. His persistency is most striking. Most of the birds tried in the complex maze never rested at all after they were once inside. They also returned again and again to make another attempt to enter the food box. These birds both in the laboratory and outside, have shown the wariness which is popularly attributed to them. Those kept in the laboratory for months failed to show signs of becoming tame. They test by various cautious means any new and strange object. Their fear is by no means a senseless one. Although ideo-motor action plays a rather large role in their movements, they are able to modify their habits readily. They discriminate small differences in the apparatus and adjust their actions accordingly."[2]

The results of Cole's[3] study of the intelligence of the raccoon probably constitute the most important contribution to comparative psychology that has yet been made by a single investigator.

There can be no doubt that Cole was extremely fortunate, so far as psychological results are in question, in his choice of a subject for study, for the raccoon is very intelligent. As the author states, in the rapidity with which it forms associations it stands almost midway between the monkey and the cat, and in the complexity of the associations which it is able to form, it stands nearer the monkey.

Cole has demonstrated the ability of the raccoon to learn by being put through an act, and he has obtained what appears to be excellent evidence of the presence of visual memory. In

[1] Porter, J. P. A preliminary Study of the Psychology of the English Sparrow. American Journal of Psychology, Vol. 15, 1904, pp. 313-346 also, Further Study of the English Sparrow and Other Birds. American Journal of Psychology, Vol. 17, 1906. pp. 248-271

[2] American Journal of Psychology, Vol. 15. p. 346.

[3] Cole, L. W. Concerning the Intelligence of Raccoons. Journal of Comparative Neurology and Psychology, Vol. 17, 1907. pp. 211-261.

view of the results with cats, dogs, and chicks which Thorndike obtained a few years ago, and which since have served to guide comparative psychologists in their estimates of the mental capacities of the higher animals, Cole's results have a value which can scarcely be over-estimated.

Finally, as indicative of the progress in a narrower field of inquiry, I may briefly mention the work of Berry[1] on the imitative tendency of animals.

As the result of careful and long continued observation of white rats and cats under experimental conditions which were especially planned to reveal whatever ability to profit by one another's experience the animals may have, Berry discovered that imitation plays a very important part in the development of activity in these animals.   He experimented only with animals which were thoroughly tamed, accustomed to his presence and to the conditions of the experiment, and which were kept in perfect health.   Possibly his most important conclusion, in view of what has previously been held concerning the imitative ability of cats, is that these animals exhibit a form of voluntary imitation.

Space-limits prevent the examination of additional contributions to the literature of this relatively new line of experimental research, and we must therefore take up the fourth and last group of contributions to comparative psychology.

Claparède[2] and I[3] have attempted to justify the existence of the science by pointing out that our knowledge of the mental life of other animals is a matter of inference, just as is our knowledge of the states of mind of our fellow men;  and I have further argued that inference plays a legitimate part in every science. But after all is said for and against the legitimacy of a science of comparative psychology, or as we might more appropriately call it animal psychology, the real justification of its existence comes from its works.   There is to-day a body of facts whose importance cannot be ignored.

[1] Berry, C. S.   The Imitative Tendency of White Rats.   Journal of Comparative Neurology and Psychology, Vol. 16, 1906, pp.  333-361 ;  also, An Experimental Study of Imitation in Cats.   Journal of Comparative Neurology and Psychology.  Vol. 18, 1908.

[2] Claparède, E.   La psychologie comparée est-elle legitime ?  Archives de Psychologie, Vol. 5, 1905, p. 35.

[3] Yerkes, R. M.   Objective Nomenclature, Comparative Psychology, and Animal Behavior.   Journal of Comparative Neurology and Psychology, Vol. 16, 1906,  pp. 380-389 ; also, Animal Psychology and Criteria of the Psychic.   Journal of Philosophy, Psychology, and Scientific Methods, Vol. 2, 1905.  pp. 141-149.

In a book which she calls "The Animal Mind" Miss Washburn has brought into clear light the chief grounds on which comparative psychology rests, and the materials which at present constitute its right to recognition and pursuit. This book, and my own[2] on "The Dancing Mouse," emphasize aspects of the progress and tendencies of the science, and present critical discussions of methods which should prove useful to investigators.

In concluding this sketch of the progress of comparative psychology I may be permitted to point out that we all have to deal in a practical way with the phenomena of behavior. All of our adjustments to society are made on the basis of inferences concerning the meaning of the actions of our fellow-men. It is extremely important, therefore, that we should acquire scientific knowledge of the forms, generic relations, development, modifying conditions, and values of organic activities. The psychiatrist, and, in fact, every physician, is constantly dealing with modes of behavior which he very imperfectly understands. It is the goal of students of animal behavior and of comparative psychology to render our knowledge of organic activity adequate to our needs. In our investigation of what animals feel, think, imagine, remember, no less than of what they do, or of the structure of their bodies, the comparative method is invaluable. If we approach the study of abnormal mental states in man by way of the study of the mental life and types of reaction in other animals we may escape many errors of interpretation and inference and save ourselves innumerable mistakes of action.

[1] Washburn, Margaret F. The Animal Mind: A text-book of Comparative Psychology. The Animal Behavior Series, Vol. 2. New York, The Macmillan Company, 1908. Pp. X & 333.

[2] Yerkes, R. M. The Dancing Mouse: A study in Animal Behavior. The Animal Behavior Series, Vol. 1. New York, The Macmillan Company. 1907. Pp. XXI. & 290.

# 3

## CONTEMPORARY AMERICAN ANIMAL PSYCHOLOGY
## IN PERSPECTIVE

T. C. SCHNEIRLA

*American Museum of Natural History*
and
*New York University*

At the beginning of the first World War, animal psychology in the United States was in a flourishing condition with promise of continuing the lusty development. There was the *Journal of Animal Behavior,* in its seventh annual volume in 1917 and grow--ing in influence with every number, there were two textbooks *— each an important contribution—and the popularity of the subject in university curricula was increasing. Animal experimental findings were exerting an increasing influence upon general psychology textbooks and courses, especially in discussions of learning. Yet with the last number of their seventh volume the editors of the journal announced its discontinuation " . . . until unfavorable conditions created by the war shall have ceased to exist," papers on animal subjects decreased in number at national meetings, and a decline seemed to have begun that might challenge the possibility of a post-war recovery.

In retrospect, however, that period may be seen as a plateau in the curve of development, as a time of transition and change in the field rather than of arrested development. By examining it in comparison with some of the main aspects of the field in our

---

* WASHBURN, MARGARET F. 1908 (*Rev.*, 1917, 1926, and 1936) The Animal Mind.
  WATSON, J. B. 1914 Behavior: An Introduction to Comparative Psychology.

own times, perhaps light may be cast on our post-war prospects.

In the past two years many animal psychologists have entered military or other federal service, while numerous others have reorganized their experimental and teaching programs in relation to wartime needs.  The number of college courses in the subject has fallen off somewhat, and as an outcome of laboratory reorientations we may expect a decrease in experimental contributions in animal behavior appearing in the *Journal of Comparative Psychology* and the *Journal of Genetic Psychology* within the next year or two.  Yet we may rather confidently describe this as a plateau period rather than one of arrested or declining condition.  Perhaps we may anticipate with equal confidence that as a transition episode this interval will be followed by notable changes when the onward progress of the subject is resumed. To judge from the history of science in general and from the "plateau" phase of animal psychology during the last war in particular, these changes will occur along lines which have been clearly or latently present in pre-war developments.

From the record we learn that the interval of World War I brought many important new developments in this field, notably the investigations on chimpanzee reasoning by Köhler (as an internee on the island of Teneriffe) and the systematic exploration of brain function and learning by Lashley.  Each of these contributions had its foundations in earlier animal work.  In Köhler's bibliography were the names of Hobhouse, Haggerty, Rothmann and Yerkes; in Lashley's, Goltz, Franz, and v. Monakov.  As other examples, the work of Stone on the basis of mammalian reproductive behavior and Richter's investigations, owed a considerable debt to past research in each case.  Also, of course, there was the conditioned-reflex program of Pavlov, which went forward in wartime and even through the critical phases of the revolutionary period in Russia.  All of these lines of investigation brought important new contributions by realizing pre-war potentialities, and all of them have profoundly influenced the further development of animal psychology (and of psychology in general) to the present time.

We may expect this process to repeat itself on a new level

in present and future.   Important programmatic work continues
in many laboratories throughout the world: at the Yerkes Laboratories of Primate Biology in Florida and at the Cornell Experimental Farm, among numerous American institutions which have
continued work, and in numerous laboratories in the warring
and occupied nations of Europe.   Among varied examples, an
interesting program of research on the problem-solving capacities of lower-vertebrate animals goes on in the Beritoff laboratory
at Tbilisi in the U. S. S. R., and we should not be surprised to find
that Kuo in China has kept some important project going even
while devoting his main efforts to administrative responsibilities
in the national defense program.   When conflict ceases there is
every reason to anticipate important developments from research
now in progress.   A glance at the past should prove enlightening
as to events in our own country.

The growth of animal psychology in the United States from
its beginning somewhat more than 50 years ago has been little
short of phenomenal.   A measure of this growth in comparison
with other branches of psychology in America is given in Table 1,
borrowed from Gordon Allport's interesting historical survey.*

## TABLE 1

PERCENTAGES OF INVESTIGATIONS UTILIZING VARIOUS SUBJECTS, REPORTED
IN 14 PRINCIPAL PSYCHOLOGICAL JOUNALS (1888-1938)

| PERIOD | NUMBER OF PUBLICATIONS | SUBJECT | | | |
|---|---|---|---|---|---|
| | | NORMAL HUMAN ADULT | CHILD AND ADOLESCENT | ABNORMAL HUMAN | ANIMAL |
| 1888-1898 | 86 | 48.8 * | 25.6 | 2.3 | 3.5 |
| 1899-1908 | 145 | 24.9 | 13.8 | 8.3 | 4.1 |
| 1909-1918 | 314 | 30.6 | 16.9 | 4.1 | 8.9 |
| 1919-1928 | 346 | 50.18 | 23.8 | 2.9 | 9.0 |
| 1929-1938 | 736 | 42.9 | 15.4 | 3.3 | 15.2 * |

* Percentage of total articles appearing in the given decade.

* BRUNER, J. S., and ALLPORT, G. W.   1940   Fifty years of change in American
psychol. *Psychol. Bull.*, 37, 757-776.

These data on publications show that the amount of animal work has increased steadily, with marked advances occurring in the years following 1908 and 1928. The one interval in which no significant increase occurred was the decade following 1918, when child psychology showed its most prominent advance. In view of the fact that these values are percentages of the total number of psychological publications, which rose moderately after 1918 although more slowly than during the preceding decade (which included the war period), it is apparent that even in this "slack" interval there was a substantial increase in animal work. The degree of overall increase in animal investigations after 1910 is emphasized by G. Allport's finding that at the 1914 meetings of the American Psychological Association 11 per cent of the scheduled papers were based on animal research, in contrast to 25 per cent at the 1939 meetings.* The past decade has been a striking development of animal work. In a special survey, Fernberger found animal psychology the most prolific branch of the field from 1932 to 1937, surpassed in output only by "general experimental psychology." ** At the national meetings in 1934, of the 22 sectional programs 5 were devoted to "Animal Psychology," and two others included animal papers. In 1937, at the national meetings, 4 programs were devoted to "Animal Psychology," and animal papers were given in 5 other sectional programs. The evidence shows that animal psychology has had two principal growth phases, in the decade just preceding World War I and in the years preceding the present war.

A comparison of these phases of marked growth discloses some interesting differences in the field during the two pre-war periods in which they occurred. As a basis for the comparison, Table 2 offers a classification of the kinds of animal subjects used in investigations reported in the *Journal of Animal Behavior* during the pre-War I interval and in the *Journal of Comparative Psychology* during the years just preceding World War II.

* ALLPORT, G. W. 1940 The psychologist's frame of reference. *Psychol. Bull.,* 37, 1-28.
** FERNBERGER, S. W. 1938 The scientific interests and scientific publications of the members of the American Psychological Association. *Psychol. Bull.,* 35, 261-281.

## TABLE 2

SUBJECTS USED IN AMERICAN ANIMAL INVESTIGATIONS DURING TWO
IMPORTANT PERIODS

| PRINCIPAL PUBLICATION | ANIMAL SUBJECT | | | | | | | | | | TOTAL PAPERS |
|---|---|---|---|---|---|---|---|---|---|---|---|
| | PRIMATES | | RAT | | OTHER MAMMAL. | | INFRA-MAMMA-LIAN VER-BRATE. | | INVERTE-BRATES | | |
| | No. | % | No. | % | No. | % | No. | % | No. | % | |
| JOUR. OF ANIMAL BEHAVIOR (v. 1-7) 1911-1917 | 11 | 6 | 37 | 19 | 30 | 15 | 53 | 27 | 66 | 33 | 197 |
| JOUR. OF COMP. PSYCHOL. (v. 35-42) 1938-1941 | 31 | 12 | 167 | 66 | 28 | 11 | 14 | 6 | 12 | 5 | 252 |

The difference is striking. Judging from journal publications, in
the earlier period interest attached to animal behavior widely,
with only 19 per cent of the papers based on the rat as subject
in contrast to 27 per cent on inframammalian vertebrates and 33
per cent on invertebrates. In the late thirties, however, we find
that attention has focussed on the rat as subject, with 66 per cent
of the papers, in contrast to strikingly low percentages for papers
based on inframammalian animals.

It is clear that there must have been some important differences in the outlook of animal investigators in these two periods.
Although the matter is much too involved for adequate treatment
here, it is possible to mention certain influences which were clearly
involved. Further investigation shows that in the earlier period
a large proportion of the work on inframammalian subjects was
contributed by zoologists, prominent among whom were Jennings,
Wheeler, Mast and Holmes. From these and other zoologists
came the largest number of articles on orientation, "instinct," and
general behavior, whereas the main contributions of psychologists
concerned problems in learning and sensory functions in particular, with far less variety in the animal species used. In animal
work at that time the main emphasis was on the qualitative and
descriptive type of approach to behavior study, and on objectivity,
grounds on which there could be a rapprochment of zoologists
and psychologists. Even so, the trend of psychologists toward

quantitative aspects of investigation, toward an emphasis upon methodology, and toward mammalian subjects and the rat in particular, was unmistakeable. The final volume of the *Journal of Animal Behavior*, published in 1917, included nearly twice as many articles involving the rat and the maze as the highest previous total, in the 1915 volume.

Thus the trend toward an increasing emphasis upon methodology and the quantification of results, which became prominent in animal research in the post-war twenties, had reached a fairly advanced point of development prior to the war. The prominence of intelligence testing during the war period, among other wartime influences, served to intensify the emphasis. With this shift toward increased quantification, the descriptive and naturalistic aspects of behavior fell into the background in the animal work of psychologists. An increased specialization of problems and methods augmented the dominance of the rat as the prime subject, and distracted attention from inframammalian forms. In the post-war decade, investigators tended to concentrate on the use of mammalian subjects in specialized investigation of their principal problems, which were early-behavior development, brain function, learning, reproductive behavior, and motivation. All of these specialized projects are readily traceable to a more qualitative research origin in the pre-war period; all of them have continued to the present time as major objects of investigation. Inevitably the specialization of research upon these problems brought animal psychologists into close relationship with mammalian psychologists. Such developments left general behavior studies, and in particular the investigation of inframammalian forms, almost exclusively to zoologists. As one indication of the change from pre-war years, courses in "animal behavior" were offered under Zoology at Chicago, Ohio State, and numerous other institutions,—very different in their content and main program from the "Comparative Psychology" courses of psychologists. The deviation of previously contiguous behavior-study movements in zoology and in psychology was indicated by other changes such as the intensified growth of "ecology" as a special field, prominently involving Shelford, Allee, and others whose early studies had appeared in the *Journal of Animal Behavior*. As the post-war period lengthened, there became increasingly apparent in American animal psychology a characteristic which committed it more fully to a specialization of subjects and quantitative methods. Even a brief inspection of the record shows that this trait was present in psychological research from the beginning, although it was not very influential until post-war developments brought matters to a focus.

The fact is that American animal psychologists always have been dominantly homocentric in their outlook and have become markedly so within the past two decades. Characteristically, they have tended to apply human concepts to the lower animal, although at the same time they have stressed objectivity in their methods. Paradoxically, the homocentricity has been accompanied by a disdain for anthropomorphism, from which animal psychologists generally consider themselves insulated through training and logical precaution. But the insulation process has been faulty. A consideration of the rise and expansion of "Purposive Behaviorism" and "Operationism" in particular would suggest that the bugbear has been hard by right along.

The allergy to anthropocentrism is an important fact about our behavior and perception which accounts to a considerable extent for the popularity of the rat,—and of Operationism. As an example of how this trait appears to scientists capable of viewing the matter objectively, Köhler has cautioned more than once against studying apparatus rather than the animal or the problem, and against making the point of the problem so inaccessible to the subject that the experimenter's traits influence the results more than do the animal's capacities. And recently, Tinbergen has said

"A further characteristic of modern Behaviourism is its restriction to problems, directly derived from human Psychology. The primary aim apparently is to discover the prehuman in the animals. This is done by focussing attention on the higher, more complicated, processes, while neglecting innate behaviour. The same ideal, however, could also be approached in another way, *viz.*, by studying the animals for their own sake, and after that, tracing the animal in Man." . . . A great part of American Psychology is centered around a few methods which have been very fertile in the past and are still doing excellent service, and to which it owes much of its splendid progress.   However, this has led to an undue emphasis on method, giving it a certain priority above the problem itself.   This over-estimation of the value of method finds expression in the centering of problems around mazes, problem boxes and some other methods. . . ." (1942, p. 42).*

This is a fair criticism, and deserves careful consideration.  The principal point of the criticism is simply that American psychologists have become so preoccupied with their own functions in the experimental situation that the psychological distance between experimenter and animal subject has become alarmingly great.

There is no question of the rat's monopoly in American animal-psychology laboratories.   In the four years preceding 1942 (Table 2), about two-thirds of the articles in the *Journal of Comparative Psychology* and more than half of the papers scheduled for national meetings were based on the rat.   The phenomenal growth of the field led to the appearance of four textbooks within five years after 1930, one of them [1] devoted exclusively to the rat and one other [2] dominated by evidence from rat investigations.   (The other two of these books [3][4] adopted a phyletic organization in which the inframammalian animals also received attention.)   Tolman's "Purposive Behavior in Animals and Men" which appeared in 1932 offered a theoretical system based upon the rat almost exclusively, and Skinner's "The Behavior of Organisms," which appeared in 1938, ,based "a science of behavior" upon operant-conditioning experimentation with the rat.[5]   There are reasons to believe that in the last 10 years the

---

* TINBERGEN, N.  1942  An objectivistic study of the innate behaviour of animals.  *Bibliotheca Biotheoretica*, Ser. D, vol. 1, pars. 2: 39-98.

[1] MUNN, N. L.  1933  An Introduction to Animal Psychology.—The Behavior of the Rat.  New York.

[2] MOSS, F. A. (Ed.)  1934 (rev. 1942)  Comparative Psychology.  New York.

[3] WARDEN, C. J., JENKINS, T. N., and WARNER, L. H.  1934  Introduction to Comparative Psychology.  New York.

[4] MAIER, N. R. F., and SCHNEIRLA, T. C.  1935  Principles of Animal Psychology. New York.

[5] A bibliography including the "majority of references" on the rat, which appeared in 1930, numbered 1353 items.—As an indication that the American movement had its influence abroad, Bierens de Haan's book "Labyrinth und Umweg" (Leiden) which appeared in 1937 should be mentioned.  Its subject was maze-learning, and its evidence and discussion centered mainly about the rat.

majority of courses in animal psychology given in American col-
leges have been devoted largely to mammalian evidence.

Of course, the positive contributions from this intensive concentration on the rat and on methodology have been many, and
the influence of the evidence upon psychology in general has been
considerable.    The rat is now a thoroughly explored subject,
through notable contributions on its sensory processes, early development, brain function, reproductive behavior, motivation,
conditioned responses, maze-learning and other problem-adjust-
ments, and its higher processes. —Lately the rat has appeared
as a useful subject for investigation of abnormal behavior patterns.—The contributions which investigations of the rat have
made to general psychological theory of learning and brain function, for example, stand out prominently in most of the contemporary general text-books.    Among other important influences
of intensive mammalian investigations upon psychology in general, results concerning motivation factors in learning and the
objective study of higher processes have been notable.

Progress along these lines has been impressive, yet for the
sake of future development it is highly desirable to avaluate this
trend toward increasingly intensive mammalian specialization in
the light of desirable modifications.    The fact is that at this stage
we do not have a "comparative psychology," for the truly comparative aspects of the science have been progressively minimized
the more investigations have focussed upon mammalian subjects
and upon problems "close to the human level."    As greater emphasis is placed upon instrumentalism in planning experiments
and upon highly quantitative procedures in gathering and in
treating results, the more "personal equation" enters into the investigation and the less the findings are a function of the animal
subject.    Such a discipline becomes highly abstract, but the abstractions are introduced from the human level and not really as
developments arising inductively from study of the animal's behavior and capacities.    Effective experimental control, always
desirable, may well be lost in this way.    Under the domination
of concepts introduced from another level, inductive procedures
are minimized or even excluded, and experimenters tend to work

on animal subjects and under experimental conditions that facilitate deductive patterns of thought. When this process becomes chronic it is involuted and Aristotelian rather than inductive and scientific. Teleology may be avoided in the interpretation of results, but anthropomorphism is introduced on the ground floor.

There are numerous paradoxes in the rise of operationism in psychology. A chief one is that although operationists are presumed to be striving toward a thorough-going empiricism, because their instrumental discriminations are made in terms of extra-experimental criteria they are forced into a subjectivism which is essentially non-empirical. Presumably striving toward a more rigid logical procedure in the science, they introduce fallacy from the beginning by framing problem and method in terms of perceptual processes dominated by a field of experience remote from the zone of the subject to be investigated. When it reaches nominalistic extremes, such methodology inevitably loses its natural-science character, for the properties of the instrument and of statistical procedures become the object of investigation rather than the animal subject. It must be recognized that in the decade preceding the present war a non-naturalistic and even anti-naturalistic movement of this kind has developed in American psychology, and that the influence of this trend will be felt strongly in the post-war decade. However, the movement seems to have recently passed its peak, and there are reasons to believe that the future will bring desirable modifications. More than a few experimenters are beginning to realize that while intensive concentration upon the capacities of a caged animal may have great advantages for experimental control, it is a rather artificial way of studying animal psychology in general and does not lead to a *comparative* psychology.

In the years following the present war we may expect closer international relationships to develop in animal psychology as in other sciences. Such interrelationships are bound to be mutually beneficial. European investigators have much to gain through closer contacts with American laboratory and statistical methodology; Americans much from the naturalistic movement which has been maintained in European animal psychology even through the war period. In the United States, animal psychologists in national service will have been preoccupied for a considerable time with "highly practical" and elementalistic subjects and with statistical (not to speak of military!) procedures. In returning to their laboratories, they will be stimulated in planning new projects by the naturalistic investigations which Continental workers have continued to carry out. On the other hand, the teleological tendencies which have strongly influenced the theorizing of European experimenters should be tempered desirably through closer contact with American objectivism. Along these lines, the organization of an international society of animal psychologists especially to facilitate the exchange of ideas and methods, lecturers and material, is a highly desirable post-war project.

Perhaps the most impressive contribution of the early post-war period of World War I was the great fund of evidence derived through research upon the developmental aspects of behavior and the genesis of behavior patterns. This trend toward a dynamic theory of animal personality led not only to searching out the nature of ontogenetic behavior changes in many animals from the early embryonic stages, but also to special investigations of "native" factors in behavior. This work has continued in many laboratories, with real progress toward clarifying the problems of adaptive behavior. Unfortunately in recent years, with increasing emphasis upon the intensive investigation of adult behavior patterns, there has been a swing away from interest in the genesis of individual behavior. There is however an underlying tendency in American animal psychology to give ontogeny its due, and it may well be that a resurgence of this important factor in the earlier development of the field will account for important post-war metamorphoses. Perhaps through such changes in the coming years animal psychology may at length graduate to the status of "comparative psychology."

# 4

Reprinted from *Am. Psychol.* **5**:115–124 (1950)

# THE SNARK WAS A BOOJUM[1]

FRANK A. BEACH

*Yale University*

THOSE of you who are familiar with the writings of Lewis Carroll will have recognized the title of this address as a quotation from his poem "The Hunting of the Snark." Anyone who has never read that masterpiece of whimsy must now be informed that the hunting party includes a Bellman, a Banker, a Beaver, a Baker and several other equally improbable characters. While they are sailing toward the habitat of their prey the Bellman tells his companions how they can recognize the quarry. The outstanding characters of the genus *Snark* are said to be its taste which is described as "meager but hollow," its habit of getting up late, its very poor sense of humor and its overweening ambition. There are several species of Snarks. Some relatively harmless varieties have feathers and bite, and others have whiskers and scratch. But, the Bellman adds, there are a few Snarks that are Boojums.

When the Baker hears the word, Boojum, he faints dead away, and after his companions have revived him he explains his weakness by recalling for their benefit the parting words of his Uncle.

> If your Snark be a Snark, that is right:
> Fetch it home by all means—you may serve it
>     with greens
> And it's handy for striking a light.
>
> **********
>
> But oh, beamish nephew, beware of the day,
> If your Snark be a Boojum! For then,
> You will softly and suddenly vanish away,
> And never be met with again!

Much later in the story they finally discover a Snark, and it is the Baker who first sights the beast. But by great misfortune that particular Snark turns out to be a Boojum and so of course the Baker softly and suddenly vanishes away.

Thirty years ago in this country a small group of scientists went Snark hunting. It is convenient to personify them collectively in one imaginary

individual who shall be called the Comparative Psychologist. The Comparative Psychologist was hunting a Snark known as Animal Behavior. His techniques were different from those used by the Baker, but he came to the same unhappy end, for his Snark also proved to be a Boojum. Instead of animals in the generic sense he found one animal, the albino rat, and thereupon the Comparative Psychologist suddenly and softly vanished away. I must admit that this description is somewhat overgeneralized. A few American psychologists have done or are doing behavioral research that is broadly comparative. All honor to that tiny band of hardy souls who are herewith excepted from the general indictment that follows.

It is my aim, first, to trace the initial development and subsequent decline of Comparative Psychology in the United States. Secondly, I intend to propose certain explanations for the attitude of American psychologists toward this branch of the discipline. And finally I will outline some of the potential benefits that may be expected to follow a more vigorous and widespread study of animal behavior.

Instead of beginning with the uncritical assumption of a mutual understanding, let me define the basic terms that will be used. Comparative psychology is based upon comparisons of behavior shown by different species of animals including human beings. Comparisons between *Homo sapiens* and other animals are legitimate contributions to comparative psychology, but comparisons between two or more non-human species are equally admissible. Like any other responsible scientist the Comparative Psychologist is concerned with the understanding of his own species and with its welfare; but his primary aim is the exposition of general laws of behavior regardless of their immediate applicability to the problems of human existence. Now this means that he will not be content with discovering the similarities and differences between two or three species. Comparisons between rats and men, for example, do not in and of themselves constitute a comparative psychology although they

[1] Presidential address delivered before the Division of Experimental Psychology of the American Psychological Association, September 7, 1949.

may well represent an important contribution toward the establishment of such a field. A much broader sort of approach is necessary and it is the failure to recognize this fact that has prevented development of a genuine comparative psychology in this country.

PAST AND CURRENT TRENDS

The history of comparative behavior studies in America is reflected in the contents of our journals that are expressly devoted to articles in this field. They have been the *Journal of Animal Behavior* and its successor, the *Journal of Comparative and Physiological Psychology*. Animal studies have, of course, been reported in other publications but the ones mentioned here adequately and accurately represent the general interests and attitudes of Americans toward the behavior of non-human animals. I have analyzed a large sample of the volumes of these journals, starting with Volume I and including all odd-numbered volumes through 1948. I have classified the contents of these volumes in two ways—first in terms of the species of animal used, and second in terms of the type of behavior studied. Only research reports have been classified; summaries of the literature and theoretical articles have been excluded from this analysis.

*Types of animals studied.* Figure 1 shows the number of articles published and the total number of species dealt with in these articles. The number of articles has tended to increase, particularly in the last decade; but the variety of animals studied began to decrease about 30 years ago and has remained low ever since. In other words, con-

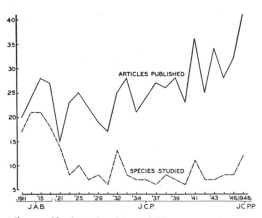

FIG. 1. Number of articles published and variety of species used as subjects.

tributors to these journals have been inclined to do more and more experiments on fewer and fewer species.

Data represented in Figure 2 further emphasize the progressive reduction in the number of species studied. Here we see that the *Journal of Animal Behavior* contained nearly as many articles dealing with invertebrates as with vertebrates; but interest in invertebrate behavior fell off sharply after World War I and, as far as this type of analysis is capable of indicating, it never rose appreciably thereafter. The attention paid to behavior of invertebrates during the second decade of this century is also reflected in the policy of publishing annual surveys of recent research. Each volume of the *Journal of Animal Behavior* contains one systematic review devoted to lower invertebrates, another dealing with spiders and insects with the exception of ants, a third summarizing work on ants and a single section covering all studies of vertebrates.

Figure 2 shows that in the early years of animal experimentation sub-mammalian vertebrates, which include all fishes, amphibians, reptiles, and birds, were used as experimental subjects more often than mammals. But a few mammalian species rapidly gained popularity and by approximately 1920, more work was being done on mammals than on all other classes combined. Now there are approximately 3,500 extant species of mammals, but taken together they make up less than one-half of one per cent of all animal species now living. A psychology based primarily upon studies of mammals can, therefore, be regarded as comparative only in a very restricted sense. Moreover the focus of interest has actually been even more narrow than this description implies because only a few kinds of mammals have been used in psychological investigations. The Norway rat has been the prime favorite of psychologists working with animals, and from 1930 until the present more than half of the articles in nearly every volume of the journal are devoted to this one species.

During the entire period covered by this survey the odd-numbered volumes of the journals examined includes 613 experimental articles. Nine per cent of the total deal with invertebrates; 10 per cent with vertebrates other than mammals; 31 per cent with mammals other than the rat; and 50 per cent are based exclusively upon the Norway rat. There is no reason why psychologists should

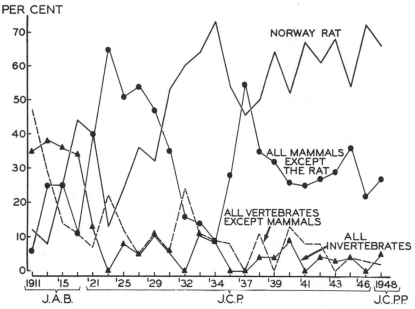

FIG. 2. Per cent of all articles devoted to various phyla, classes or species.

not use rats as subjects in some of their experiments, but this excessive concentration upon a single species has precluded the development of a comparative psychology worthy of the name. Of the known species of animals more than 96 per cent are invertebrates. Vertebrates below the mammals make up 3.2 per cent of the total; and the Norway rat represents .001 per cent of the types of living creatures that might be studied. I do not propose that the number of species found in a particular phyletic class determines the importance of the group as far as psychology is concerned; but it is definitely disturbing to discover that 50 per cent of the experiments analyzed here have been conducted on one one-thousandth of one per cent of the known species.

Some studies of animal behavior are reported in journals other than the ones I have examined but the number of different animals used in experiments published elsewhere is even fewer. The six issues of the *Journal of Experimental Psychology* published in 1948 contain 67 reports of original research. Fifty of these articles deal with human subjects and this is in accord with the stated editorial policy of favoring studies of human behavior above investigations of other species. However, 15 of the 17 reports describing work on non-human organisms are devoted to the Norway rat.

During the current meetings of the APA, 47 experimental reports are being given under the auspices of the Division of Experimental Psychology. The published abstracts show that in half of these studies human subjects were employed while nearly one-third of the investigations were based on the rat.

Is the Experimental Psychologist going to softly and suddenly vanish away in the same fashion as his one-time brother, the Comparative Psychologist? If you permit me to change the literary allusion from the poetry of Lewis Carroll to that of Robert Browning, I will venture a prediction. You will recall that the Pied Piper rid Hamelin Town of a plague of rats by luring the pests into the river with the music of his magic flute. Now the tables are turned. The rat plays the tune and a large group of human beings follow. My prediction is indicated in Figure 3. Unless they escape the spell that *Rattus norvegicus* is casting over them, Experimentalists are in danger of extinction.

*Types of behavior studied.* I trust that you will forgive me for having demonstrated what to many of you must have been obvious from the beginning —namely, that we have been extremely narrow in our selection of types of animals to be studied. Now let us turn our attention to the types of behavior with which psychologists have concerned themselves.

Articles appearing in our sample of volumes of the journals can be classified under seven general headings: (1) conditioning and learning; (2) sensory capacities, including psychophysical measurements, effects of drugs on thresholds, etc.; (3) general habits and life histories; (4) reproductive behavior, including courtship, mating, migration, and parental responses; (5) feeding behavior, including diet selection and reactions to living prey; (6) emotional behavior, as reflected in savageness and wildness, timidity and aggressive reactions; and (7) social behavior, which involves studies of dominance and submission, social hierarchies, and interspecies symbiotic relations.

In classifying articles according to type of behavior studied I have disregarded the techniques employed by the investigator. It is often necessary for an animal to learn to respond differentially to two stimuli before its sensory capacities can be measured; but in such a case the article was listed as dealing with sensory capacity rather than learn-

ing. The aim has been to indicate as accurately as possible the kind of behavior in which the experimenter was interested rather than his methods of studying it.

It proved possible to categorize 587 of the 613 articles. Of this total, 8.6 per cent dealt with reproductive behavior, 3.7 per cent with emotional reactions, 3.2 per cent with social behavior, 3.0 per cent with feeding, and 2.8 per cent with general habits. The three most commonly-treated types of behavior were (1) reflexes and simple reaction patterns, (2) sensory capacities, and (3) learning and conditioning. Figure 4 shows the proportion of all articles devoted to each of these three major categories.

The figure makes it clear that conditioning and learning have always been of considerable interest to authors whose work appears in the journals I have examined. As a matter of fact slightly more than 50 per cent of all articles categorized in this analysis deal with this type of behavior. The popularity of the subject has increased appreciably during the last 15 years, and only once since 1927

FIG. 3. Current position of many experimental psychologists.

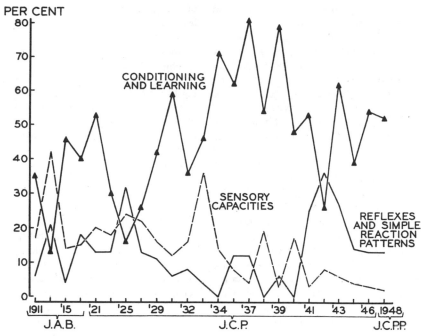

FIG. 4.  Per cent of all articles concerned with various psychological functions.

has any other kind of behavior been accorded as many articles per volume.  This occurred in 1942 when the number of studies dealing with reflexes and simple reaction patterns was unusually large. The temporary shift in relative emphasis was due almost entirely to a burst of interest in so-called "neurotic behavior" or "audiogenic seizures."

Combining the findings incorporated in Figures 2 and 4, one cannot escape the conclusion that psychologists publishing in these journals have tended to concentrate upon one animal species and one type of behavior in that species.  Perhaps it would be appropriate to change the title of our journal to read "The Journal of Rat Learning," but there are many who would object to this procedure because they appear to believe that in studying the rat they are studying all or nearly all that is important in behavior.  At least I suspect that this is the case.  How else can one explain the fact that Professor Tolman's book, "Purposive Behavior in Animals and Men," deals primarily with learning and is dedicated to the white rat, "where, perhaps, most of all, the final credit or discredit belongs." And how else are we to interpret Professor Skinner's 457-page opus which is based exclusively upon the performance of rats in bar-pressing situa-

tions but is entitled simply "The Behavior of Organisms"?

### INTERPRETATION OF TRENDS

In seeking an interpretation of the demonstrated tendency on the part of so many experimentalists to restrict their attention to a small number of species and a small number of behavior patterns, one comes to the conclusion that the current state of affairs is in large measure a product of tradition. From its inception, American psychology has been strongly anthropocentric.  Human behavior has been accepted as the primary object of study and the reactions of other animals have been of interest only insofar as they seemed to throw light upon the psychology of our own species.   There has been no concerted effort to establish a genuine comparative psychology in this country for the simple reason that with few exceptions American psychologists have no interest in animal behavior *per se*.

Someone, I believe it was W. S. Small at Clark University in 1899, happened to use white rats in a semi-experimental study.  The species "caught on," so to speak, as a laboratory subject, and gradually displaced other organisms that were then being examined.  Psychologists soon discovered that rats are hardy, cheap, easy to rear, and well adapted to a laboratory existence. Because of certain resemblances between the associative learning of rats and human beings, *Rattus norvegicus* soon came to be accepted as a substitute for *Homo sapiens* in many psychological investigations. Lack of acquaintance with the behavioral potentialities of other animal species and rapid increase in the body of data derived from rat studies combined to progressively reduce the amount of attention paid to other mammals, to sub-mammalian vertebrates and to invertebrate organisms. Today the trend has reached a point where the average graduate student who intends to do a thesis problem with animals turns automatically to the white rat as his experimental subject; and all too often his professor is unable to suggest any alternative.

To sum up, I suggest that the current popularity of rats as experimental subjects is in large measure the consequence of historical accident. Certainly it is not the result of systematic examination of the available species with subsequent selection of this particular animal as the one best suited to the problems under study.

Concentration of experimental work upon learning seems to stem almost exclusively from the anthropocentric orientation of American psychology. Learning was very early accepted as embodying the most important problems of human behavior; and accordingly the majority of animal investigations have been concerned with this type of activity.

### ADVANTAGES AND DISADVANTAGES
### OF CONCENTRATION

I have no wish to discount the desirable aspects of the course which experimental psychology has been pursuing. There are many important advantages to be gained when many independent research workers attack similar problems using the same kinds of organisms. We see this to be true in connection with various biological sciences. Hundreds of geneticists have worked with the fruitfly, *Drosophila*. And by comparing, combining, and correlating the results of their investigations, it has been possible to check the accuracy of the findings, to accelerate the acquisition of new data, and to formulate more valid and general conclusions than could have been derived if each worker dealt with a different species. Something of the same kind is happening in psychology as a result

of the fact that many investigators are studying learning in the rat, and I repeat that this is a highly desirable objective.

Another valuable result achieved by the methods currently employed in experimental psychology is the massing of information and techniques pertaining to rat behavior to a point which permits use of this animal as a pedagogical tool. A recent article in the *American Psychologist* reveals that each student in the first course in psychology at Columbia University is given one or two white rats which he will study throughout the semester. This, it seems to me, is an excellent procedure. The beginning student in physiology carries out his first laboratory exercises with the common frog. The first course in anatomy often uses the dogfish or the cat as a sample organism. And college undergraduates learn about genetics by breeding fruitflies. But the usefulness of the rat as a standardized animal for undergraduate instruction, and the preoccupation of mature research workers with the same, single species are two quite different things.

Advanced research in physiology is not restricted to studies of the frog and although many geneticists may confine their personal investigations to *Drosophila*, an even larger number deals with other animal species or with plants. As a matter of fact, the benefits that students can derive from studying one kind of animal as a sample species must always stand in direct proportion to the amount of information research workers have gathered in connection with other species. The rat's value as a teaching aid in psychology depends in part upon the certainty with which the student can generalize from the behavior he observes in this one animal; and this in turn is a function of available knowledge concerning other species.

There is another obvious argument in favor of concentrating our efforts on the study of a single animal species. It is well expressed in Professor Skinner's book, "The Behavior of Organisms."

> In the broadest sense a science of behavior should be concerned with all kinds of organisms, but it is reasonable to limit oneself, at least in the beginning, to a single representative species.

I cannot imagine that anyone would quarrel with Skinner on this point and I am convinced that many of the psychologists currently using rats in their investigational programs would agree with him in his implicit assumption that the Norway rat *is* a "representative species." But in what ways is it "representative," and how has this "representativeness" been demonstrated? These questions lead at once to a consideration of the disadvantages of overspecialization in terms of animals used and types of behavior studied.

To put the question bluntly: Are we building a general science of behavior or merely a science of rat learning? The answer is not obvious to me. Admittedly there are many similarities between the associative learning of lower animals and what is often referred to as rôte learning in man. But the variety of organisms which have been studied, and the number of techniques which have been employed are so limited, it is difficult to believe that we can be approaching a comprehensive understanding of the basic phenomena of learning. It may be that much remains to be discovered by watching rats in mazes and problem boxes, but it is time to ask an important question. How close are we getting to that well-known point of diminishing returns? Would we not be wise to turn our attention to other organisms and to devise new methods of testing behavior before we proceed to formulate elaborate theories of learning which may or may not apply to other species and other situations.

Another very important disadvantage of the present method in animal studies is that because of their preoccupation with a few species and a few types of behavior, psychologists are led to neglect many complex patterns of response that stand in urgent need of systematic analysis. The best example of this tendency is seen in the current attitude toward so-called "instinctive" behavior.

The growing emphasis upon learning has produced a complementary reduction in the amount of study devoted to what is generally referred to as "unlearned behavior." Any pattern of response that does not fit into the category of learned behavior as currently defined is usually classified as "unlearned" even though it has not been analyzed directly. Please note that the classification is made in strictly negative terms *in spite of the fact that the positive side of the implied dichotomy is very poorly defined.* Specialists in learning are not in accord as to the nature of the processes involved, nor can they agree concerning the number and kinds of learning that may occur. But in spite of this uncertainty most "learning psychologists" confidently identify a number of complex behavior patterns as "unlearned." Now the obvious question arises: Unless we know what learning is—unless we can recognize it in all of its manifestations—how in the name of common sense can we identify any reaction as "unlearned"?

The fact of the matter is that none of the responses generally classified as "instinctive" have been studied as extensively or intensively as maze learning or problem-solving behavior. Data relevant to all but a few "unlearned" reactions are too scanty to permit any definite conclusion concerning the role of experience in the shaping of the response. And those few cases in which an exhaustive analysis has been attempted show that the development of the behavior under scrutiny is usually more complicated than a superficial examination could possibly indicate.

For example, there is a moth which always lays its eggs on hackberry leaves. Females of each new generation select hackberry as an oviposition site and ignore other potential host plants. However, the eggs can be transferred to apple leaves, and when this is done the larvae develop normally. Then when adult females that have spent their larval stages on apple leaves are given a choice of materials upon which to deposit their eggs, a high proportion of them select apple leaves in preference to hackberry. This control of adult behavior by the larval environment does not fit into the conventional pigeon-hole labeled "instinct," and neither can it be placed in the category of "learning." Perhaps we need more categories. Certainly we need more data on more species and more kinds of behavior.

Primiparous female rats that have been reared in isolation usually display biologically effective maternal behavior when their first litter is born. The young ones are cleaned of fetal membranes, retrieved to the nest, and suckled regularly. However, females that have been reared under conditions in which it was impossible for them to groom their own bodies often fail to clean and care for their newborn offspring. Observations of this nature cannot be disposed of by saying that the maternal reactions are "learned" rather than "instinctive." The situation is not so simple as that. In some way the early experience of the animal prepares her for effective maternal performance even though none of the specifically maternal responses are practiced before parturition.

67

It seems highly probable that when sufficient attention is paid to the so-called "instinctive" patterns, we will find that their development involves processes of which current theories take no account. What these processes may be we shall not discover by continuing to concentrate on learning as we are now studying it. And yet it is difficult to see how a valid theory of learning can be formulated without a better understanding of the behavior that learning theorists are presently categorizing as "unlearned."

### POTENTIAL RETURNS FROM THE COMPARATIVE APPROACH

If more experimental psychologists would adopt a broadly comparative approach, several important goals might be achieved. Some of the returns are fairly specific and can be described in concrete terms. Others are more general though no less important.

*Specific advantages.* I have time to list only a few of the specific advantages which can legitimately be expected to result from the application of comparative methods in experimental psychology. In general, it can safely be predicted that some of the most pressing questions that we are now attempting to answer by studying a few species and by employing only a few experimental methods would be answered more rapidly and adequately if the approach were broadened.

Let us consider learning as one example. Comparative psychology offers many opportunities for examination of the question as to whether there are one or many kinds of learning and for understanding the rôle of learning in the natural lives of different species. Tinbergen (1942) has reported evidence indicating the occurrence of one-trial learning in the behavior of hunting wasps. He surrounded the opening of the insect's burrow with small objects arranged in a particular pattern. When she emerged, the wasp circled above the nest opening for a few seconds in the usual fashion and then departed on a hunting foray. Returning after more than an hour, the insect oriented directly to the pattern stimulus to which she had been exposed only once. If the pattern was moved during the female's absence she was able to recognize it immediately in its new location. Lorenz's concept of "imprinting" offers the learning psychologist material for new and rewarding study. Lorenz (1935) has observed that young

birds of species that are both precocial and social quickly become attached to adults of their own kind and tend to follow them constantly. Newly-hatched birds that are reared by parents of a foreign species often form associations with others of the foster species and never seek the company of their own kind. A series of experiments with incubator-reared birds convinced Lorenz that the processes underlying this sort of behavior must occur very early in life, perhaps during the first day or two after hatching, and that they are irreversible, or, to phase it in other terms, that they are not extinguished by removal of reinforcement.

J. P. Scott's studies (1945) of domestic sheep reveal the importance of early learning in the formation of gregarious habits. Conventional learning theories appear adequate to account for the phenomena, but it is instructive to observe the manner in which the typical species pattern of social behavior is built up as a result of reinforcement afforded by maternal attentions during the nursing period.

The general importance of drives in any sort of learning is widely emphasized. Therefore it would seem worth while to study the kinds of drives that appear to motivate different kinds of animals. In unpublished observations upon the ferret, Walter Miles found that hunger was not sufficient to produce maze learning. Despite prolonged periods of food deprivation, animals of this species continue to explore every blind alley on the way to the goal box.

Additional evidence in the same direction is found in the studies of Gordon (1943) who reports that non-hungry chipmunks will solve mazes and problem boxes when rewarded with peanuts which the animals store in their burrows but do not eat immediately. Does this represent a "primary" drive to hoard food or an "acquired" one based upon learning?

Many experimentalists are concerned with problems of sensation and perception; and here too there is much to be gained from the comparative approach. Fring's studies (1948) of chemical sensitivity in caterpillars, rabbits and men promise to increase our understanding of the physiological basis for gustatory sensations. In all three species there appears to be a constant relationship between the ionic characteristics of the stimulus material and its effectiveness in evoking a sensory discharge. The investigations of Miles and Beck

(1949) on reception of chemical stimuli by honey bees and cockroaches provides a test for the theory of these workers concerning the human sense of smell.

The physical basis for vision and the role of experience in visual perception have been studied in a few species but eventually it must be investigated on a broader comparative basis if we are to arrive at any general understanding of the basic principles involved. Lashley and Russell (1934) found that rats reared in darkness give evidence of distance perception without practice; and Hebb (1937) added the fact that figure-ground relationships are perceived by visually-naive animals of this species. Riesen's (1947) report of functional blindness in apes reared in darkness with gradual acquisition of visually-directed habits argues for a marked difference between rodents and anthropoids; and Senden's (1932) descriptions of the limited visual capacities of human patients after removal of congenital cataract appear to support the findings on apes. But the difference, if it proves to be a real one, is not purely a function of evolutionary status of the species involved. Breder and Rasquin (1947) noted that fish with normal eyes but without any visual experience are unable to respond to food particles on the basis of vision.

I have already mentioned the necessity for more extensive examination of those patterns of behavior that are currently classified as "instinctive." There is only one way to approach this particular problem and that is through comparative psychology. The work that has been done thus far on sexual and parental behavior testifies, I believe, to the potential returns that can be expected if a more vigorous attack is launched on a broader front.

We are just beginning to appreciate the usefulness of a comparative study of social behavior. The findings of Scott which I mentioned earlier point to the potential advantages of using a variety of animal species in our investigation of interaction between members of a social group. Carpenter's (1942) admirable descriptions of group behavior in free-living monkeys point the way to a better understanding of dominance, submission, and leadership.

One more fairly specific advantage of exploring the comparative method in psychology lies in the possibility that by this means the experimentalist can often discover a particular animal species that is specially suited to the problem with which he is concerned. For example, in recent years a considerable amount of work has been done on hoarding behavior in the laboratory rat. The results are interesting, but they indicate that some rats must learn to hoard and some never do so. Now this is not surprising since Norway rats rarely hoard food under natural conditions. Would it not seem reasonable to begin the work with an animal that is a natural hoarder? Chipmunks, squirrels, mice of the genus *Peromyscus,* or any one of several other experimental subjects would seem to be much more appropriate.

And now, as a final word, I want to mention briefly a few of the more general facts that indicate the importance of developing comparative psychology.

*General advantages.* For some time it has been obvious that psychology in this country is a rapidly expanding discipline. Examination of the membership roles of the several Divisions of this Association shows two things. First, that the number of psychologists is increasing at a prodigious rate; and second that the growth is asymmetrical in the sense that the vast majority of new workers are turning to various applied areas such as industrial and clinical psychology.

It is generally recognized that the applied workers in any science are bound to rely heavily upon "pure" or "fundamental" research for basic theories, for general methodology and for new points of view. I do not suggest that we, as experimentalists, should concern ourselves with a comparative approach to practical problems of applied psychology. But I do mean to imply that if we intend to maintain our status as indispensable contributors to the science of behavior, we will have to broaden our attack upon the basic problems of the discipline. This will sometimes mean sacrificing some of the niceties of laboratory research in order to deal with human beings under less artificial conditions. It may also mean expanding the number of non-human species studied and the variety of behavior patterns investigated.

Only by encouraging and supporting a larger number of comparative investigations can psychology justify its claim to being a true science of behavior. European students in this field have justly condemned Americans for the failure to study behavior in a sufficiently large number of representative species. And non-psychologists in this country are so well aware of our failure to develop the field that they think of animal behavior as a province of general zoology rather than psychology. Top-rank professional positions that might have been filled by psychologically trained investigators are today occupied by biologists. Several large research foundations are presently supporting extensive programs of investigation into the behavior of sub-human animals, and only in one instance is the program directed by a psychologist.

### CONCLUSION

If we as experimental psychologists are missing an opportunity to make significant contributions to natural science—if we are failing to assume leadership in an area of behavior investigation where we might be useful and effective—if these things are true, and I believe that they are, then we have no one but ourselves to blame. We insist that our students become well versed in experimental design. We drill them in objective and quantitative methods. We do everything we can to make them into first rate experimentalists. And then we give them so narrow a view of the field of behavior that they are satisfied to work on the same kinds of problems and to employ the same methods that have been used for the past quarter of a century. It would be much better if some of our well-trained experimentalists were encouraged to do a little pioneering. We have a great deal to offer in the way of professional preparation that the average biologist lacks. And the field of animal behavior offers rich returns to the psychologist who will devote himself to its exploration.

I do not anticipate that the advanced research worker whose main experimental program is already mapped out will be tempted by any argument to shift to an entirely new field. But those of us who have regular contact with graduate students can do them a service by pointing out the possibilities of making a real contribution to the science of psychology through the medium of comparative studies. And even in the absence of professorial guidance the alert beginner who is looking for unexplored areas in which he can find new problems and develop new methods of attacking unsettled issues would be wise to give serious consideration to comparative psychology as a field of professional specialization.

### REFERENCES

1. BREDER, C. M. AND RASQUIN, P. Comparative studies in the light sensitivity of blind characins from a series of Mexican caves. *Bulletin Amer. Mus. Natl. Hist.*, 1947, **89**, Article 5, 325–351.
2. CARPENTER, C. R. Characteristics of social behavior in non-human primates. *Trans. N. Y. Acad. Sci.*, 1942, Ser. 2, **4**, No. 8, 248.
3. FRINGS, H. A contribution to the comparative physiology of contact chemoreception. *J. comp. physiol. Psychol.*, 1948, **41**, No. 1, 25–35.
4. GORDON, K. The natural history and behavior of the western chipmunk and the mantled ground squirrel. *Oregon St. Monogr. Studies in Zool.*, 1943, No. 5, 7–104.
5. HEBB, D. O. The innate organization of visual activity. I. Perception of figures by rats reared in total darkness. *J. gen. Psychol.*, 1937, **51**, 101–126.
6. LASHLEY, K. S. AND RUSSELL, J. T. The mechanism of vision. XI. A preliminary test of innate organization. *J. genet. Psychol.*, 1934, **45**, No. 1, 136–144.
7. LORENZ, K. Der Kumpan in der Umwelt des Vogels. *J. f. Ornith.*, 1935, **83**, 137–213.
8. MILES, W. R. AND BECK, L. H. Infrared absorption in field studies of olfaction in honeybees. *Proceed. Natl. Acad. Sci.*, 1949, **35**, No. 6, 292–310.
9. RIESEN, A. H. The development of visual perception in man and chimpanzee. *Science*, 1947, **106**, 107–108.
10. SCOTT, J. P. Social behavior, organization and leadership in a small flock of domestic sheep. *Comp. Psychol. Monogr.*, 1945, **18**, No. 4, 1–29.
11. SENDEN, M. v. *Raum- und Gestaltauffassung bei operierten Blindgeborenen vor und nach der Operation.* Leipzig: Barth, 1932.
12. TINBERGEN, N. An objectivistic study of the innate behaviour of animals. *Biblio. Biotheoret.*, 1942, **1**, Pt. 2, 39–98.

*Received October 24, 1949*

Part II

# FIELD STUDIES

# Editor's Comments
# on Papers 5 and 6

5    **WATSON**
*Recent Experiments with Homing Birds*

6    **CARPENTER**
Excerpts from *A Field Study of the Behavior and Social Relations of Howling Monkeys (Alouatta palliata)*

Comparative psychology is often portrayed as a discipline conducted solely in the laboratory. Indeed, exclusive use of the laboratory approach has been characteristic of the vast majority of studies in comparative psychology. However, most comparative psychologists have been extremely sympathetic to the study of animals in their natural habitats. A surprising number of comparative psychologists, including such workers as Watson, Lashley, Yerkes, Bingham, Nissen, Carpenter, Schneirla, Gottlieb, Hess, Mason, and Bernstein, have conducted important field studies.

Although John B. Watson is generally remembered as a behaviorist who admitted only minimal influences of genotype on behavior, his early career as a comparative psychologist exemplifies the strengths of comparative psychology. In 1907, 1910, and 1913, Watson spent his summers on the Dry Tortugas, off Florida, studying the behavior of birds under natural conditions. During the last summer, Lashley accompanied Watson. Watson studied a wide range of behavioral patterns in true "ethological" fashion (e.g., the nesting cycle, mating behavior, mate and egg recognition, development, orientation, eating, and drinking). His most important work, however, was on bird orientation. In Paper 5 Watson summarizes his research on this subject. He noted with astonishment the observation that birds had returned over open water for distances of up to 900 miles. He concluded that the birds could not possibly be using landmarks but had to use some kind of distance orientation. Although much progress has been made in the study of bird orientation since Watson's research, we still have difficulty in living up to the optimism expressed in his final sentence.

Robert Yerkes was a great facilitator of both field research in particular and of a broadly based approach to the study of behavior in general. Under Yerkes's auspices, Henry Nissen (1931) completed a study of chimpanzees in French Guinea and H. C. Bingham (1932) completed a study of gorillas under field conditions. Perhaps his greatest contribution in this area, however, was his launching of the career of C. Ray Carpenter as a field primatologist. Carpenter would become the true father of field primatology in the twentieth century. In Paper 6 Carpenter reports the results of his classical study of howling monkeys in Panama. Carpenter's work was typified by careful observation and attention to a variety of details of behavior and by a full study of both individual and social behavioral patterns.

Although various other comparative psychologists have conducted field research, the work of T. C. Schneirla deserves special mention. Schneirla made many trips into the field to study ant behavior and did much to apply the methods of careful description and observation to the field. His paper on field methods (Schneirla, 1950) is still a useful guide. It is regrettable that the paper could not be included because of space limitations.

Research under field conditions is difficult and these pioneering comparative psychologists and their families often had to endure trying living conditions. Further, the importance of field studies was seldom recognized by colleagues in the psychology departments providing employment and salaries. Despite these obstacles, however, comparative psychologists carved an important niche in the area of field research.

## REFERENCES

Bingham, H. C., 1932, Gorillas in a Native Habitat, *Carnegie Inst. Washington Publ. No.* **426:**1–65.

Nissen, H. W., 1931, A Field Study of the Chimpanzee: Observations of Chimpanzee Behavior and Environment in Western French Guinea, *Comp. Psychol. Monogr.* **8**(36):1–122.

Schneirla, T. C., 1950, The Relationship Between Observation and Experimentation in the Field Study of Behavior, *Ann. N. Y. Acad. Sci.* **51:** 1022–1044.

## 5

Reprinted from *Harper's* **131**:457–464 (1915)

# Recent Experiments with Homing Birds

BY *JOHN B. WATSON*

Professor of Comparative and Experimental Psychology, Johns Hopkins University

NTIL the advent of telegraphy the most dependable quick bearer of news was the now almost unnoticed bird, the homing - pigeon. Few of us realize the vast influence this bird exercised in its day over the destinies of nations. Historical references show that the pigeon was known and used in very ancient times (500 B.C.). Even as early as A.D. 1200 the "pigeon post" had become a well-established institution over Persia, Servia, and Egypt. The cotes were owned by the government, and attached to each cote was an official post-office and postmaster.

Probably the use of these birds in times of war, and especially in besieged fortresses, is best known. So important was their function in this respect that until 1850 almost every army post and fort had its cote and was supplied with pigeons from other military stations. Indeed, the French army extended the use of the homing pigeon to the field by equipping the cotes with wheels (traveling-cotes) and training the birds to return to these rolling habitations, regardless of their location. The French navy established cotes on board war-vessels, but the experiment was given up, largely because the pigeon does not home well over water from distances greater than two hundred miles. The commercial value of the pigeon post has been very great indeed. Practically all of the boards of trade in the large cities of Europe were supplied with these pigeons. Their use in obtaining advance information concerning crops, local insurrections, rumors of war, etc., can hardly be overestimated. Newspapers likewise were supplied with pigeon posts. After the introduction of the microscope and photography very long messages could be sent. The material was written out and then micro-photographed. Some fifty thousand words could be sent in one despatch, and the total weight of the paper and the carrying-quill was less than 0.5 gram. The recipient of the despatch could read it with an ordinary low-power microscope.

Although the telegraph and the telephone have robbed the homing-pigeon of his utilitarian value, the mystery of how he effects a return over mountain and valley, over trackless waste, forest, and stream, is possibly as unsolved to-day as it was in the twelfth century, when his commercial value was highest.

During the last few years many experiments have been tried which have had. for their purpose the unraveling of the difficult and delicate problems connected with homing. In a previous number of *Harper's* (October, 1909) I gave a brief sketch of some work I had been doing on homing in Dry Tortugas, Florida, under the auspices of the Marine Biological Laboratory of the Carnegie Institution of Washington. The Dry Tortugas group of islands lies well out in the Gulf of Mexico, some seventy-eight miles due west of Key West, about four hundred miles south of Mobile, and nine hundred miles east of Galveston. To Bird Key, one of the tiny islands composing this group, a vast colony of noddy and sooty terns comes annually for its nesting season. These birds are quite similar to the gulls which one sees in almost every harbor. On account of its insular position Bird Key is wonderfully suited for carrying out experiments in homing. The work there has been continued by Dr. K. S. Lashley and the writer.

We have been primarily engaged in testing to what extent the "visual-landmark theory" will account for the facts of homing. It may be mentioned that there are many theories of homing, such as the *magnetic theory* of Thauzies; the *contrepied* ("back-tracking") *theory* of Reynaud, and the *inherited memory theory* of Kingsley, as well as a host of others; but to all of them, with the exception of the visual-landmark theory, there are fatal objections. The visual-landmark theory, on the other hand, has been widely accepted and is to-day the prevailing one. Possibly the best way to give a clear understanding of both the good and the bad points of this theory is to consider it in connection with certain experiments which are now going on.

In all of the work on homing a distinction is made between what is called *proximate orientation* and *distant orientation*. Proximate orientation refers to the method the animal uses to get back to the goal (goal is a general term to cover nest, burrow, cote, etc.) when the goal itself, or objects in its immediate neighborhood, lie within the range of vision or of some other sense organ. This on first sight might seem not to involve any problem of return. It does not in the case of a homing-pigeon which lives in a large and visually prominent cote, but if we consider other birds the problem presents difficulties. In the case of the sooty tern, one of the species of tropical birds nesting in Tortugas, proximate orientation is a life-and-death matter. These birds dig a small round hole in the sand which they use as a nest. These holes are dug usually in the open stretches of the island. The nesting-areas are greatly congested—one nest lying often less than ten inches from its neighbor. During the nesting season the birds are quarrelsome and guard the small areas around their nests jealously. A given bird, having gone out for food, must, on its return, pick out its own nest from a thousand others. To the human observer this seems to be an almost impossible task, yet the birds do it with extreme accuracy and with great rapidity. At first sight there seem to be no guiding signs or landmarks which can aid the birds. In my preliminary study I was not able to find out how the birds accomplished it. I found that I could dig the nest up and then remake it without disturbing the

bird. Yet if I obliterated the old nest and made another only a few inches to the right or left of the old one, the bird invariably went back to the original nest-site, and only by degrees learned to take the nest in its new position.

Recently Dr. Lashley has made a thorough study of this problem. He finds that the birds do not necessarily use the objects immediately around the nest in proximate orientation. When the birds fly in from the sea they direct their flight by the more prominent features of the island, such as the buildings, prominent bushes, etc. This leads them to the general area in which the nest is situated and to a fixed *alighting-place*. Once at the alighting-place, the rest of the journey is made partly through using certain small, inconspicuous visual objects as guides, and partly through the use of the *muscular sense*. Thus in a crowded locality where vision could only lead it astray the bird relies upon the muscular sense somewhat as does the blind man, or as the normal man does in passing through a familiar room in the dark. These experiments of Lashley's seem to show that in short flights the birds do not need any mysterious "sixth sense" to guide them. Vision, aided by the muscular sense, will account for the facts.

Yet it may be asked what bearing such experiments have upon the more distant flights—upon the factors involved in *distant orientation*. The bearing is very close indeed. Many investigators argue that since the birds can form habits of reacting to the nest itself, to proximate landmarks, etc., and can be guided back in this way from short flights, the same process, elaborated, will account for the longer flights, or in general for so-called *distant orientation*. It can be gathered from this that there is in the minds of many a serious doubt as to whether there is any such thing as true *distant orientation*. The adherents of the visual-landmark theory maintain that the method of training the pigeons for long flights finally gives the bird as great familiarity with the whole country as the ordinary animal has with the surroundings of its home; hence, that when a bird is trained and then sent one thousand miles away,

A COLONY OF SOOTY TERNS NESTING IN THE SAND—BIRD KEY

on release it makes for the first familiar landmark, say a mountain-peak one hundred miles away. Arriving there, without breaking the flight, it goes toward the next landmark, say a large city. By following back these landmarks it finally arrives in a neighborhood where it can see the cote. To one familiar only with the flights of the homing-pigeons this theory seems eminently sane and reasonable on first sight; more thorough examination of the flights of the homing-pigeon, however, leads us into difficulties.

We are led into still deeper waters when we consider homing and migration in other birds. Let us glance for a moment at the present world-record flights of homers and at the way in which such birds are trained. In 1901 the world record for time and distance in the case of the pigeon was one thousand miles in about nine days. Since that time the fanciers in Fort Wayne, Indiana, have obtained some startling records.

The present world champion is Bullet D-1872, owned by Mr. O. W. Anderson of the above city. The bird was hatched in 1909. When four and a half months of age, training was begun. She was taken first two, then five, eight, fifteen, twenty-five, forty, and then seventy-five miles away and allowed to return. (This training was distributed, of course, over several weeks.) She was then entered in the one-hundred and two-hundred mile races. In 1910 she was again given the above preliminary training races, and allowed to compete in the two-hundred, three hundred, four-hundred, and five-hundred mile races. In 1911 and 1912 she was given the same amount of training. In 1913, after the preliminary flights, she won the two-hundred and the five-hundred mile races, flying the five-hundred-mile race in about eleven hours. Shortly after this flight the bird was sent to Abilene, Texas, one thousand and ten miles (air-line measure) from Fort Wayne. The bird was liberated at 4.30 A.M., July 11, 1913, and homed at 4 P.M., July 12th, the flying time being one day, eleven hours, thirty minutes, and six seconds. In this same race a bird belonging to Mr. John Schilling homed at 11.30 A.M. the following day (July 13th), and a third bird, belonging to Mr. F. Nahrwald, a half-hour later. All of the above races were flown under the rules of the American Racing Pigeon Union. The best previous record for one thousand miles was made by a pigeon belonging to H. Beech of Fort Wayne, in 1912, the time being two days, nine hours, and some odd minutes. And this record lowered the time made in 1910 by a bird belonging to Mr. L. Gebfert of the same city, this time being three days, eleven hours, and some odd minutes. Such records will probably never be beaten except by happy combinations of strong favorable wind and clear, warm weather.

Even in such amazing flights as these the supporters of the visual-landmark theory find nothing really more wonderful than what we see every day around a pigeon-loft—*viz.*, the bird flying first

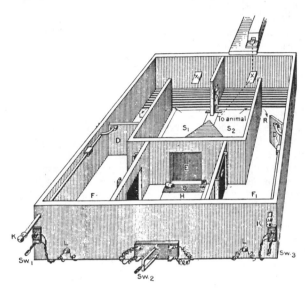

APPARATUS FOR TESTING THE SEN-
SITIVITY OF BIRDS TO LIGHT-RAYS

to one familiar object of sight and then to the next one. Hachet-Souplet, one of the ablest supporters of this theory, has recently made some experiments with the homing-pigeon which lend some slight support to such a view. In order to test whether the birds can return over areas unknown to them he resorted to the use of traveling-cotes. Before any final tests were made, the birds, through experiments in other localities, were made thoroughly familiar with the outside of their own cotes. In a given test the cote was taken first into a strange locality and allowed to remain there for two or three days. We shall call this point A. Several birds were then put into a basket and left at A, while the cote was driven on some four or five miles to a point B. The birds at A were then released. The birds, on release, mounted rapidly in the air and, spying the cote, at once flew to it. Repeated tests showed that the distance between

A and B could be increased up to about seven miles before the birds lost the ability to return. If the distance was increased to *eight miles, none of the birds returned.*

After determining this distance, the experiment was modified: Upon arriving at point A, two birds at a time were tethered to the cote by means of a cord one hundred feet in length and allowed to fly to that height and survey the surrounding country. This was repeated for two or three days, then, as in the test above, these pigeons were left at A while the carriage was sent to B. It was found after many experiments that such birds as were allowed preliminary observation could return to the cote when the distance between A and B was sixty-five miles. Hachet-Souplet believes that the birds' view from the carriage at A gave them a set of "visual memories" which enabled them to fly to the cote even when the latter was not directly visible. The birds probably first flew to one distant familiar point, and then, if the cote itself was not visible, to another, etc., until at some point the cote became visible.

These experiments were made only a short time ago and have not been confirmed by other experimenters. While they were inadequate to bring out the facts for which they were planned, they serve to show quite clearly the method by which the adherents of this theory would attempt to explain even the long flights obtained in the world records.

Some of us, however, are not satisfied that such a theory will account for the facts of homing and migration. Even in advance of actual facts to the contrary, there happen to be obvious theoretical weaknesses in the theory of Hachet-Souplet. In the first place, our laboratory experiments have shown that the bird is exceedingly slow in forming visual habits of a kind to aid him in such flights. Certainly those of us familiar with the laboratory display of ingenuity in this bird can hardly convince ourselves that the few training flights such as we have already witnessed in the case of Bullet, the present world's champion, can give the bird such a rapid command of so vast a territory as would be called for in her later performances. In the second place, convenient landmarks are not always at hand. When we consider the distance at which objects can be seen even by the sharpest human eye (and the human eye is probably much keener than the bird's eye) we become still more skeptical. Mathematical considerations show that if the bird is at a given distance from its cote it must fly to a certain height in order to see it.

To point out the difficulties in the way of this theory, Dr. Lashley and I have recently made a series of calculations to show the height to which the bird, at a given distance from the cote, must fly in order to see the cote. We have made our calculation (allowing for refraction) to suit the conditions at Tortugas. The birds nest there on or near the ground, which is not much above sea-level. On one of the near-by islands, however, there is a lighthouse one hundred and fifty-one feet in height. In order to be fair to the theory we must suppose that the birds use the upper part of this as a landmark. As a result of this calculation we find that when the bird is one hundred miles away it has to fly approximately nine-tenths of a mile high; when two hundred miles away, approximately three miles high; when five hundred miles away, twenty-five miles high; and finally when nine hundred miles away, eighty-five miles high! When we consider how rarefied the air becomes, and how low the temperature of the air is, at even two or three miles above the earth's surface, we may be sure that few birds (certainly few tropical birds) ever reach even a height of one mile. As a matter of fact, the homing-pigeon rarely rises above six hundred to nine hundred feet, and the terns at Tortugas usually fly at a height of less than three hundred feet.

Certain investigators (*e.g.*, Duchâtel), realizing the danger to the visual-landmark theory from this source, have been driven to the extreme position of maintaining the view that the bird does not use ordinary rays of light for vision; but that its retina is sensitive to *infra-*

NESTING AFTER A SUCCESSFUL FLIGHT
The post and attached tag may be seen in the background marking the nest from which the bird was taken.

*luminous* rays and sensitive especially to the long rays (infra-red). They suppose, further, that the infra-red rays follow the surface of the earth. An animal using such rays could see its goal directly from great distances—the curvature of the earth not interfering with the continuity of vision. Such a theory is based upon poor physical grounds. Had it been based upon the assumption that the bird is especially sensitive to the short, or ultra-violet, rays, it would have been physically more defensible. The violet rays undergo greater refraction than the other rays by the earth's atmosphere, and it is conceivable that a bird having a retina very sensitive to such rays might see its goal by rising to a slightly less height than man.

We have recently entered into a somewhat elaborate test of the general question as to whether birds use rays of light to which the human retina is not sensitive. The experiment was carried out with the apparatus shown (page 460), which is used as follows: The apparatus is set up in a dark room; through a small window one allows a beam of colored light (monochromatic) to fall upon the plaster-of-Paris surface X; the other plaster-of-Paris surface, X₁, is not illuminated. The animal is kept in compartment H in darkness. The door E is then raised, and the animal allowed to go either toward X, the lighted side, or toward X₁, the unlighted side. If he goes toward the lighted side he may pass on around through the door D₁ to *food* in compartment F₁. The door D₁ is then closed behind him. After a moment the animal is let through a side-door again into H for another trial. If, on the other hand, the animal goes to the unlighted side, he finds the door D closed. Before obtaining food he must retrace his steps and finally pass through D₁ to the food. The apparatus is so arranged that the light may be made to fall either upon X or X₁. The animal must learn to go *always* to the *lighted* side.

The homing-pigeon and the chick learn to do this very readily after a few trials, rarely making an error. We usually train the animal upon green. When perfect upon this we gradually change the wave-length of the light—*i.e.*, pass successively through yellow, green, orange, red, etc., until we come to the deep red. We finally reach a point where the animal "breaks down"—*i.e.*, goes as often to the dark side as to the light side. This point gives us the limit of spectral sensitivity in the red. We next retrain our animal upon green until he is running perfectly, and then gradually shorten the wave-length—*i.e.*, pass through the blue into the violets, etc. After a long series of such experiments we have found that the pigeon's spectral range almost exactly coincides with man's. Duchâtel's speculation therefore falls to the

A BIRD THAT HOMED NEARLY SIX HUNDRED MILES ACROSS THE GULF OF MEXICO

The markings—three bars across the bird's head — are distinctly visible.

ground. If we are to explain homing in terms of the visual-landmark
theory, we cannot assume any su-
perhuman powers of vision for the
bird.

Such unsatisfactory experimentation
upon distant orientation as we have here
set forth led us to consider possible ways
of making a crucial test as to whether
birds can home from great distances over
a territory which can offer no familiar
landmarks. We decided that under the
ordinary conditions of training and flying homing - pigeons we could never
reach dependable results. If the pigeon
could home over long stretches of water
there would be no difficulty in making
such a test. A moment's consideration,
however, will show that the pigeon cannot possibly home over water for a
period longer than twelve or fourteen
hours, and the distance covered in a
day's flight is rarely more than four to
five hundred miles. This limitation is
forced upon the pigeon by reason of the
fact that it can neither sleep upon the
water nor can it obtain food while flying
over the water. To make such an experiment we must use birds which are as
much at home upon the water as upon
the land. Fortunately, as we have already noted, the conditions at Tortugas
are almost ideal for making such an
experiment. In the first place, the noddy and sooty terns are tropical, spend-
ing their winters along the shores of
the Caribbean Sea. On or about the
25th of April they leave that region in
a body and fly north to Bird Key. They
remain there until the activities connected with nesting, brooding, and the
rearing of the young are complete.
While nesting they rarely leave Bird
Key for distances greater than twenty
miles. Consequently it becomes possible to send the birds anywhere north
into a region never before visited by
them. In the second place, Bird Key
is the last point of land between Key
West and Galveston, which is about
nine hundred miles distant. This gives
us a magnificent opportunity to test
whether the birds can home over a nine-
hundred-mile stretch of water which can
offer apparently no possible visual landmarks. With these birds in this locality
we can realize conditions which cannot

be realized in any homing-pigeon loft at
the present time.

In my previous article in *Harper's* I
gave the results of some successful test
where the birds were sent one thousand
miles north to Cape Hatteras. Three
out of five birds sent to this point homed
with ease and in a time which was then
below the world's record for the homing-
pigeon. These results were found to
be out of harmony with the visual-landmark theory. Several of the adherents
of this theory wrote to me, however,.
and tried to explain the returns by assuming that the birds had been sent into
a country colder than that to which they
were accustomed, and that they instinctively flew along the shores of Florida
toward a warmer region. Arriving in
the neighborhood of Key West, they
were able, in high circling flights, to see
Tortugas (seventy-eight miles distant).
Possibly such a theory of their return is
correct, but it must be said that this
explanation does not lend any support
to the visual-landmark theory.

At that time I had not been able to
get any successful flights over the nine-
hundred-mile water stretch between
Galveston and Bird Key. Our last
season's work in Tortugas was successful
in this respect by reason of the fact that
our early unsuccessful efforts led us to
establish a better technique of capturing
and marking the birds, feeding them *en
route*, etc. In considering these experiments on the terns it must be remembered that we did not have to deal with
a tame pigeon which is used to a ship-
ping-basket and to being fed and wa-
tered by man. The terns are wild birds,
wholly unused to man and to the ways
of civilization in general. Furthermore,
they are water-birds, drinking sea-water,
and getting their food by picking up live
minnows, which, when attacked by large
fish, spring out over the surface of the
water. Methods of capturing the birds,
and especially of caring for them on
their long journeys, had to be learned by
bitter experience. On a given day when
we had made arrangements for shipping
(always a difficult task) we began to
capture the birds. As one passes over
the island the boldest of them stay on the
nests, or, if they do leave, they fly back
while the experimenter is standing close

to the nest. These bold birds are the ones always captured.

Before passing over a given area for the purpose of capture, stakes about twelve inches long and one inch square are made. A large Dennison tag and a small tag are attached to the end of the stake, the small tag being attached loosely. The two tags bear identical legends. The large tag will have written upon it in waterproof ink, *e.g.*, "Sooty, Galveston, removed May 16th, marked with scarlet lake, 3 bars on head and neck." When a sooty is captured the stake is pushed down into the sand; when a noddy is taken the tag is tied to a convenient twig. The small tag, bearing a duplicate of the above legend, is pulled off. The bird and small tag are handed to an assistant, who ties the tag around the bird's neck and puts the animal into a portable cage. When enough birds have been collected the lot is taken back to the house and the birds are marked with oil-paints as indicated by the card attached to each bird's neck. The illustrations (pp. 461, 462), show the clearness with which the markings appear after the return of the birds. The two birds shown in the photographs actually homed from five hundred and eighty-five miles over open water. After the birds are thus captured and marked they are put into a shipping-cage and sent to Key West, where a large supply of minnows is obtained for feeding them *en route*. On the trip in which successful results were obtained Dr. Lashley took the birds in charge, and at Key West boarded the Mallory steamer which sailed directly for Galveston. The birds were released at two points intermediate between Bird Key and Galveston, and also in Galveston Harbor. Ten birds were released when *five hundred and eighty-five miles out;* eight of them returned to the nest.

Two birds were released at night in a driving rain when *seven hundred and twenty miles out*. Both returned. Twelve birds were released in Galveston Harbor, *eight hundred and fifty-five miles from Bird Key*. Only three birds returned. That only three birds returned is not surprising, in view of the fact that by the time Galveston was reached the birds were in poor condition—they had to be forcibly fed. When released they flew at once to the shore to rest, and many were doubtless captured by the hawks which line the Galveston shores.

This is certainly the most astonishing record of returns ever obtained under experimental conditions. *We have here large numbers of birds returning over open water from all distances up to approximately nine hundred miles.* Here there can be no question of flying high enough to see Bird Key directly, nor of an instinctive following of a coast-line into a warmer climate, since Galveston lies in approximately the same latitude as Bird Key. Nor can there be any question of visual landmarks in the customary meaning of that term. That reasonable landmark theory which, if it were true, would explain all of the flights of homing-birds on the ordinary grounds of habit formation seems here to break down completely. We are left apparently with the inference that there is such a thing as *distant orientation*, but without any explanation of how it is effected. Strange as it may seem, this does not discourage us; the mere establishment of the fact that there is a genuine problem in homing will give to scientific investigators a stimulus to further work which has been lacking before. It is unbelievable that the problems connected with homing and migration can long resist the combined attacks of scientific students.

# 6

Reprinted from pages 1–2 and 125–129 of *Comp. Psychol. Monogr.* **10**(48):1–168 (1934)

# A FIELD STUDY OF THE BEHAVIOR AND SOCIAL RELATIONS OF HOWLING MONKEYS (ALOUATTA PALLIATA)

C. R. CARPENTER

*National Research Council Fellow and Research Assistant, Laboratories of Comparative Psychobiology, Yale University*

### TABLE OF CONTENTS

## I. FOREWORD

Doctor Carpenter's is the third in a series of naturalistic studies in primate habitats, planned in supplementation of the experimental studies in the Yale Laboratories of Comparative Psychobiology. The first of the field studies to be reported was that of Doctor Henry W. Nissen, of the laboratory staff, who, with the generous coöperation of the Pasteur Institute of Paris, initiated work on the social and ecological relations of the chimpanzee in French Guinea.[1] Next in sequence appeared Doctor Harold C. Bingham's account of a field study of the mountain gorilla (*G. beringei*) in relation to its habitat in the mountains of the Belgian Congo. His project was conducted with the coöperation of the

[1] See reference at end of this report.

Carnegie Institution of Washington. The present report is the first to deal in strictly naturalistic fashion with a New World primate. In plan, procedures, and results, it differs interestingly and instructively from our studies of Old World forms. But this doubtless is in part due to the fact that it pertains to a type of monkey, whereas the earlier reports are concerned with anthropoid apes.

[*Editor's Note:* Material has been omitted at this point.]

### XII. GENERAL SUMMARY

In this study of the behavior and social relations of howling monkeys an attempt has been made to contribute to a comprehensive psychobiological study of primates. I have sought to present observations with as much objectivity and as little theorizing as possible.

About eight months were spent studying howling monkeys in the Panama Canal Zone and in the Republic of Panama. Carefully planned observational procedures were used to investigate the behavior of *A. p. aequatorialis*, *A. p. palliata*, and *A. p. coi-*

*bensis.* The following generalized statements summarize the findings on these monkeys:

Howlers may behave neutrally toward an observer, they may react defensively or bluffingly, or they may flee and conceal themselves. Apparently the type of reaction shown depends in part on the previous conditioning of the animals. While behaving in a defensive, aggressive manner toward an observer, they may drop objects with reference to him.

The hands show a concentric type of movement toward the palmar surfaces in manipulation, and there is a functional division between the first and second digits. The thumb is not opposable to the other digits. The tail is prehensile and is used almost constantly.

Howlers show considerable variability in posturing during rest, locomotion, and feeding.

Locomotion is typically pronograde with few variations toward an orthograde form. Howlers are awkward in locomotion on the ground. They can swim if necessary.

Howlers feed from the terminal twigs of trees and as a rule pull in with their hands the stems containing the food and eat directly from them. In food preference, they are herbivorous and frugivorous, but primarily the former.

Groups of howlers tend to occupy a definite and limited territory. This region may be shared with other groups and there occurs from time to time some shifting of territorial range. Within their territories groups behave with reference to food and lodge trees. The groups travel at the average rate of about one hundred yards per hour and seldom move more than eight hundred yards per day. The groups move in an irregular column. There is a strong tendency for males to lead the groups and for females carrying infants to travel in the last positions of the column.

Howlers prefer dense, tall primary forests as a habitat and apparently avoid scrub growth.

As determined by carefully made censuses, there were 398 ± 50 howlers on Barro Colorado Island in April, 1932, and 489 ± 25 individuals in April, 1933. The means and standard deviations for the 23 groups counted in 1932 are 17.3 ± 6.8, and for the

28 groups of the following year 17.4 ± 6.8. There were, in both years, 18 animals in the median groups. The groups ranged in size from 4 to 35 individuals in 1932 and from 4 to 29 animals in 1933.

The groups vary in size and constitution from time to time as young are born, as individuals, especially males, join or leave the clan, and as animals die. The composite mean grouping tendency for the howler groups of Barro Colorado Island equals (M 2.8 ± 1.2) + (f4.8 ± 2.5) + (m 2.4 ± 1.5) + (i1.7 ± .7) + (i2 1.4 ± 1.2) + (i3 1.2 ± 1.4) + (j1 1.3 ± 1.0) + (j2 1.8 ± 1.2) + (j3 1.0 ± 1.1) + (M$_I$X). The proportional composition of groups in percentages equals (M 16.4) + (f 27.3) + (m 13.5) + (i1 4.1) + (i2 8.0) + (i3 7.1) + (j1 7.6) + (j2 10.5) + (j3 5.5) + (M$_I$X).

The socionomic sex ratio of adult howlers is approximately 28 per cent males to 72 per cent females.

Within groups there are subgroupings.

Females clean their infants after birth and eat the amniotic fluids.

Mothers carry infants first on their bellies and then on their backs in the sacral and lumbar regions. In general, the infants behave parasitically to the mothers, which are relatively indifferent to them. However, mothers may at times posture for their young to mount them, help the infants over critical crossings, and retrieve young ones when they fall. The social relation between a mother and her infant is a specific one.

The strength of the female-young bond rises and then declines as the infant grows older. About the time of weaning the mothers may even mildly fight their young. Early juveniles continue to associate with their mothers after a sibling is born.

The relations among females of a howler clan are peaceful and communal.

The amount of play shown by young howlers increases until the juvenile 1 stage, and then there is a rather sharp decline to a minimum of play in adult animals. Several rather stereotyped forms of play are shown by young howlers, but especially noteworthy are the wrestling and chasing play patterns.

Female howlers show a rather definite oestrous period during which primary sexual activity occurs frequently. Copulations may occur as frequently as every ten or fifteen minutes during the oestrous period of the female, but there may be several hours be tween copulations.   For 19 copulations the period of adjustment was 9.7 ± 5.7 seconds; the period of intromission in 25 instances was 21.8 ± 2.8 seconds, and the number of thrusts averaged 16.9 ± 4.8.

Characteristically, prior to copulation a female howler postures and rhythmic tongue movements are exchanged between her and the male.   Copulation typically occurs with the male mounting the female.   During the oestrous period of a female, a male associates very closely with her as a sexual consort until he is sexually satiated, and then another male may take his place.   The data indicate that males mate communally with an oestrous female, but they do not show whether particular males consistently become consorts prior to other males.

Howlers reproduce throughout the year, but the frequency of births may vary from season to season.   The observations suggest that there is a higher per cent of infants 1 in the clans in January than in any of the following four months.

In general males behave indifferently to young animals, but they may assist in retrieving fallen infants, protect them from predatory animals, and in unusual situations care for an infant in somewhat the same way as a mother.

The males of a howler clan behave coöperatively in leading and defending the group.   Pugnacity and competition among integrated clan males were not observed.   Clan males behave toward a complemental male which approaches a group as if he were an enemy.

How complemental males come to separate from clans is not known, but these animals, which live temporarily separated from groups, again become parts of a clan either suddenly or by a long process of social adaptation.

The males are dominant in controlling and coördinating the clan. Contact control and distant signalization subserve group coördination.   Posturing, gesticulation, and vocalization are important kinds of distant signalization.

Nine different patterns of vocal behavior were described in this report, although many more actually occur. These patterns vary greatly in the specificity of their stimulating situations and in the specificity of responses stimulated in associated animals. The barking, roaring type of vocalization functions as a means of defense and inter-group control.

New clans may be formed by parental clans dividing, by individuals of a group joining a complemental male, and probably most frequently by subgroupings separating from the parental clan. Groups of howlers when they come near each other engage in vocal battles. Apparently two groups rarely, if ever, become consolidated.

Inter-breeding between groups which are relatively discrete societies occurs through the exchange of complemental males.

The literature and the observational data of this report indicate that there is a high degree of similarity in the behavior and social relations among the different subspecies of howling monkeys. Data on three subspecies of *A. palliata* suggest that the behavior and social relations described in this monograph may be characteristic of the entire *palliata* group.

The indications are that man is the most serious enemy of howlers and that occasionally young animals may be attacked by ocelots.

Howlers are not commensal with any other species of primate living in the same environment. Capuchins and howlers may, however, feed from the same trees for short periods of time.

## BIBLIOGRAPHY

(1) ALLEN, J. A.: Mammals from Venezuela collected by M. A. Carriker Jr. *Bull. Amer. Mus. Nat. Hist.*, 1911, 30: 1-271.

[*Editor's Note:* The remainder of the Bibliography has been omitted.]

Part III

# SOCIAL BEHAVIOR

# Editor's Comments
# on Papers 7 and 8

Although it has been written that comparative psychology differs from ethology in that it has lacked a focus on the study of social behavior (Fremont-Smith in Schaffner, 1955, 131), the study of social behavior has always been important in the field. Early workers such as Wundt, Kline, Small, and Watson had strong interests in social behavior. The topic of imitation, by itself, has been a major source of interest throughout the century. Interest in social behavior continued through the work of such people as Beach, Schneirla, Yerkes, Harlow, and Mason.

Analysis of social behavior requires both observation and experimentation. The former is nicely illustrated in Yerkes's study of a chimpanzee family (Paper 7). In this short paper, Yerkes describes the subtle changes in behavior and social relationships as a chimpanzee family goes through various phases, from early pairing through mating to the development of the young. The objective of the research was to describe the behavioral patterns of chimpanzees under conditions that produce minimal alterations of the behavior typically occurring in the field. This paper is but a small sample of Yerkes's writing on chimpanzees and other nonhuman primates (e.g., Yerkes, 1943).

The other prong of the two-pronged study of social behavior is experimental animal social psychology. The focus here is on the manipulation of independent variables and on the measurement of dependent variables under controlled conditions in an effort to analyze the factors affecting social behavior. Such topics as social facilitation, imitation, cooperation, competition, affiliation, and dominance have been prominent in this approach (Zajonc, 1969). Workers such as Crawford, Bayroff, Lepley, Winslow, Nowlis, Daniel, and Warden made contributions in this area. An early paper from Harry Harlow (Paper 8) has been included in this volume as representative of this approach. In this paper Harlow explores the influence of a 24-hour deprived rat on the eating behavior of satiated companions. An effect of social facilitation is demonstrated and quantified. Harlow concludes that the effect is independent of previous experience, imitation, or envy.

## REFERENCES

Schaffner, B., ed., 1955, *Group Processes,* Josiah Macy Foundation, New York.
Yerkes, R. M., 1943, *Chimpanzees: A Laboratory Colony,* Yale University Press, New Haven, Conn.
Zajonc, R. B., ed., 1969, *Animal Social Psychology,* Wiley, New York.

# 7

## A CHIMPANZEE FAMILY[*][1]

*From Yale Laboratories of Primate Biology*

---

ROBERT M. YERKES

---

Knowledge of the chimpanzee family in freedom is meager and of little value to the student of social behavior. The observations now to be reported and the literature cited refer exclusively to captive individuals. Since its establishment in 1930 the breeding colony of chimpanzees maintained by Yale University at Orange Park, Florida, has offered increasingly varied and favorable opportunities for the study of social phenomena. In the early years of the colony pregnant females were isolated, with intent to minimize the risk of reproductive accidents. But after the possibility of normal reproduction had been sufficiently demonstrated and several infants made available for immediate local use, certain social experiments were arranged. Of these, the first type is the association of two pregnant females; the second, an association of consorts which later became parents and infant.

---

[*]Accepted for publication by Carl Murchison of the Editorial Board and received in the Editorial Office, January 6, 1936.
[1]Acknowledgment is made of the assistance of the Committee for Research in Problems of Sex, National Research Council.
This is one of a series of preliminary reports on such forms or aspects of social behavior in chimpanzee as grooming, suggestibility, avoidance, and sexual, parental, and familial relations. The studies are avowedly exploratory and preparatory to an attempt to apply experimental method to problems of primate social life. The following papers have appeared or are in press.

BINGHAM, HAROLD C. Parental play of chimpanzees. *J. Mammal.*, 1927, **8**, 77-89.
YERKES, ROBERT M. Genetic aspects of grooming, a socially important primate behavior pattern. *J. Soc. Psychol.*, 1933, **4**, 3-25.
————. Suggestibility in chimpanzee. *J. Soc. Psychol.*, 1934, **5**, 271-282.
TOMILIN, MICHAEL I., & YERKES, ROBERT M. Chimpanzee twins: behavioral relations and development. *J. Genet. Psychol.*, 1935, **46**, 239-263.
YERKES, ROBERT M., & TOMILIN, MICHAEL I. Mother-infant relations in chimpanzee. *J. Comp. Psychol.*, 1935, **20**, 321-359.
YERKES, ROBERT M., & YERKES, ADA W. Nature and conditions of avoidance (fear) response in chimpanzee. *J. Comp. Psychol.*, 1936, **21**, 53-56.
SPENCE, KENNETH W. Response of chimpanzee mothers to infants following separation. *J. Psychol.* (in press).

Our mature females Wendy and Josie, and subsequently their infants, constituted the first experimental group in our approach to the study of familial relations. They were known to be intimately acquainted and friendly. When placed together in quarters for this particular experiment Wendy was in her first pregnancy, Josie in her second, having previously suffered a miscarriage in the seventh lunar month.[2] Wendy and Josie were wholly peaceable and congenial throughout their period of companionship, although Wendy tended to dominate Josie and would compel her to surrender food on occasion. Wendy's baby was born about three weeks before Josie's. So far as appears from our records, neither reproductive processes nor infant care were unfavorably affected by the social environment. The mothers cared each for her own infant during the latter's period of helplessness and each resented and thwarted any attempt on the part of the other to touch or in any way to minister to her infant. From the first, proprietary rights were recognized and as a rule respected. Neither during parturition nor subsequently did evidence of interference or undesired and unsolicited mutual aid appear. After the infants, both of which were males, had achieved a considerable degree of independence of their mothers and were able to climb and run about freely and skillfully, social relations in the group became more complex and less stable. Disagreements began to appear. The first quarrel to be recorded which involved all four individuals was observed by Doctors Spence and Spragg when the infants were nearly a year old. As briefly reported, the two babies became rough in their play and presently began to fight. One of them screamed. Instantly their mothers rushed to them, took their respective infants, and exchanged several blows. The mêlée was lively but of short duration, and although excitement was intense no one was visibly injured.

---

[2] For some weeks prior to impregnation these two females had been caged with another female, Mimi, and the mature male Bill. This group was entirely harmonious. Wendy and Josie were continued together, with two brief interruptions, through the gestational period, parturition, and until their infants had been taken from them for weaning at about one year of age. Von Allesch (Bericht über die drei ersten Lebensmonate eines Schimpansen, Sitzber. preuss. Akad. Wiss. Berlin, 1921, p. 679 ff.) has described the behavior of a group of chimpanzees in the Berlin Zoological Garden which included a mother and infant.

93

There is no reason to infer from our data that infant growth and development proceeded less advantageously because of the presence of a second mother and infant.  On the contrary it would appear that the welfare of all members of the social group was enhanced by the increased diversion and recreation which resulted from social stimulation.  In our opinion the social environment was the more nearly natural, normal, and functionally adequate by reason of the presence of the additional female and her infant.

Our second experiment consisted in leaving the male consort with his female following impregnation and throughout gestation, parturition, and the first fifteen weeks of infant-nursing.  This family group eventually was constituted by the male Pan, the female Nana, and their male infant Don.

Pan (*Pan satyrus satyrus*),[3] an exceptionally robust and energetic male, has been used experimentally in these laboratories for ten years.  He is stocky, of medium size, with dark brown skin and rusty brown to gray hair.  His hypothetical birth-date is 1922, his source the Cameroons.  Although rated as relatively dull he is very good tempered, friendly, cooperative, and dependable.

Nana (*Pan satyrus verus*) was brought to the colony in 1930 from French Guinea.  Her hypothetical birth-date is 1921.  Physically and behaviorally she differs extremely from Pan, for she is relatively small, slender, jet black as to skin and coat, shy, timid, gentle, and affectionate.

Early in their acquaintance (1930) Pan occasionally was rough in his treatment of Nana when they were temporarily brought together for mating.  Probably sexual excitement and the strangeness of the female were responsible for this behavior.  Nana never tried to defend herself.  Subsequently, after they had been caged near one another and had several times been together, the pair became friendly and they now (1935) are obviously affectively attached to one another.

Following impregnation of Nana by Pan in September, 1933, it seemed wholly safe to leave them together throughout the reproductive process in order that we might observe especially the behavior of the male as member of the family group.  This was Nana's

---

[3] According to Schwarz, *Ann. Mag. Natural History,* 1934, **13**, p. 576.

second pregnancy, her first infant having been born on September 21, 1932, and separated from her for experimental use in June, 1933. Immediately thereafter she was placed in the cage with Pan and left with him.

The relations of these consorts continued to be amicable throughout the period of the experiment. Mutual grooming, which ordinarily indicates congeniality, was frequently observed. On August 5, 1933, Doctor James H. Elder of the staff recorded in our life-history files: "Pan and Nana are certainly the most affectionate pair of adult chimpanzees I have observed. It is seldom that one comes to greet an attendant without the other. This morning, when making observations of sexual status, I found them lying on the floor grooming each other. My calls did not disturb them for some time. When Nana finally arose Pan grasped her gently with a foot and began to clean her eyes and face." The writer with increasing frequency in the past three years has observed in this pair behavior clearly indicative of mutual attachment and considerateness.

Copulation was not observed during the gestational period. This is not an assertion that it never occurred, although that is the presumption. In this respect our observations contradict those reported by Montané, Tinklepaugh, and Schultz and Snyder.[1] Quite evidently the sexual relationship is variable, presumably due chiefly to the characteristics of the male, his age and developmental status, and the degree of familiarity and the strength of the social bond between the consorts.

Parturition, which was not observed, is known to have occurred about eight o'clock the morning of May 2, 1934. At the time the consorts were together in their small shelter room. When a few minutes later they were admitted by an attendant to the adjoining open-air cage the infant Don was discovered. At 8:20 A.M., father, mother, and infant were carefully observed in the cage, and thereafter during the day verbal and photographic records of their social

[1] MONTANÉ, LOUIS. Un chimpancé Cubano. *El Siglo,* Havana, 1915, **20,** p. 11.
  TINKLEPAUGH, O. L. Sex cycles and other cyclic phenomena in a chimpanzee during adolescence, maturity, and pregnancy. *J. Morphol.,* 1933, **54,** p. 535.
  SCHULTZ, A. H., & SNYDER, F. F. Observations on reproduction in the chimpanzee. *Bull. Johns Hopkins Hospital,* 1935, **57,** p. 197.

FIGURE 1

UPPER

Pan (right) and Nana, with infant Don clinging to her, shortly after his birth, May 2, 1934. She is cleaning him while Pan watches placidly. The umbilical cord is still present.

LOWER

The family (Pan, Nana, and Don) about six weeks after the birth of Don. Nana is grooming her consort.

behavior and relations were made at intervals. The photographic records, reproduced herewith, importantly supplement the following summary verbal description.

When the trio was first observed the mother was intent on her care of infant and self, while the father was quiet, calm, and seemingly interested in the infant and in Nana's actions. Upon the writer Pan's behavior at this time made vivid impression of placid, friendly interest. He appeared ready and eager to help if opportunity offered, but even to us human observers it was entirely clear that Nana neither desired nor needed his assistance. We doubt that she would have tolerated it. For some hours after the birth of Don, Pan was unusually quiet, and he was not observed to molest either mother or infant. On the basis of this favorable relationship, it was immediately decided to keep the three animals together in the hope of establishing a congenial and cooperative, if not also a natural, family group.

On May 7 the group was moved from its restricted livingroom-cage quarters to a more spacious fenced open-air enclosure with a roofed shelter building and sleeping-box. The writer on June 1, 1934, entered the following in the life-history records of the individuals: "Pan, Nana, and Don have been living together contentedly without disturbance in the Enclosure. Pan does not interfere with Nana and the baby. I have not happened to see him giving attention to Don. This is a convincing demonstration of the possibility of housing a family group of chimpanzees together. It opens the way for experimental studies in social behavior which heretofore have been impossible."

Nana, quite commonly in the ensuing weeks, avoided Pan as if in fear of him. When called to the side of the Enclosure to be observed, fed, or petted, she would not approach if Pan did or if he was near at hand. Much of the time she sat, with Don clinging to her, on the timbers of the shelter building in the shade of its roof. That this behavior was due to the hostility of the male might naturally be inferred were it not for the following facts, which are well established by our observations.

As a rule the female chimpanzee with young is suspicious and cautious, constantly protecting her charge from the aggression of other organisms, and also from exposure to direct sunlight. The male of the species is potentially very dangerous to the female with young, both before and after parturition,[5] and it has been discovered in these laboratories that the temperature-regulating mechanism of the infant chimpanzee for several weeks after birth is inadequate to protect it from the injurious effects of over-exposure to sunlight.[6] If Nana had acted as if fearless of her consort and had ignored the sun, her infant probably would have been injured.

We are making our observations available at this time because there is a prevalent superstition, from which we have not been immune, that the male chimpanzee under the spatial limitations of captivity may, either by intent or inadvertently during spells of excitement, injure his pregnant consort or their infant. Consequently it has been common practice to isolate females known to be pregnant. We have scrutinized the few and meager accounts of births in captivity to discover whether support exists for this assumption of hostility on the part of the male. In not a single instance of the few known to us[7] where the male was present either just before or also during parturition is there indication that he in any way interfered with the birth process or disturbed either mother or infant thereafter. The suspicion that the chimpanzee as male parent may on occasion destroy his offspring at present lacks observational support. That he is potentially dangerous, we already have asserted. In the future we shall in this establishment act in accordance with our experimental needs, leaving the consorts together when it is essential. To be sure it is only reasonable to assume that the two animals shall in advance be known as intimately acquainted, wholly accustomed to being together, and friendly, for to bring relative strangers together, even though they had previously mated successfully, would be inexcusably rash, save as crucial experiment.

---

[6]In certain important aspects these interpretative statements are supported by the observations of Bingham (*op. cit.*) on behavior of a chimpanzee family in Cuba which consisted of father, mother, and an infant in its second year.

[6]JACOBSEN, CARLYLE F., JACOBSEN, MARION M., & YOSHIOKA, JOSEPH G. Development of an infant chimpanzee during her first year. *Comp. Psychol. Monog.*, 1932, **9**, 1, p. 22 ff.

BRUHN, JOHN M., & HASLERUD, GEORGE M. Unpublished observations.

[7]BLAIR, W. REID. Notes on the birth of a chimpanzee. *Bull. N. Y. Zool. Soc.*, 1920, **23**, 104-111.

FOX, HERBERT. The birth of two anthropoid apes. *J. Mammal.*, 1929, **10**, 37-51.

There is no evidence in our observations or in the literature that the father chimpanzee aids in the care of his offspring during the months of its dependence upon the mother. Later, however, and especially after the infant has achieved locomotor independence, the male parent may amuse, protect, and defend it as occasion arises.[8]

## Summary

The principal points in this naturalistic study of a captive chimpanzee family may thus be restated.

During early acquaintance of the consorts the male sometimes was rough and hostile toward his female; she, protective, timid, never defensive. Later mutual friendliness developed and the male was consistently gentle and considerate toward this particular female. Finally, during the period of familial relations and subsequently, manifestations of affection and devotion, particularly by the male, were observed. Mutual grooming was common, as well as physical attentions which may be designated as petting.

Sexual intercourse was not observed during the gestational period, nor during lactation to the date of separation of mother and infant from the father. At this time, nearly four months after parturition, the female sexual cycle, with its characteristic features of menstrual bleeding, genital swelling, and ovulation, had not been reestablished.

The male was an interested, passive observer of the parturitional process and of the newly born infant. He in no way interfered with, or aided in, maternal care, but instead was gentle, friendly, and cooperative toward the members of his family. The mother was continuously protective of infant and self, trusting neither her consort nor human males who approached her and her charge. The male seemingly accepted this attitude as a matter of course and without sign of resentment. Familial relations, like the relations of the consorts prior to the birth of the infant, appeared to be favorable to the health and contentment of the parents and to the development of the infant. We eventually characterized them as natural and normal. It is our surmise that this particular family, save in its limitation to a single female and a single offspring, more nearly represents the typical familial relations of the species in freedom than does any other of the descriptions available in the literature.

---

[8]See Bingham (*op. cit.*) for confirmation.

## REFERENCES

1. ALLESCH, G. J. VON. Bericht über die drei ersten Lebensmonate eines Schimpansen. *Sitzber. preuss. Akad. Wiss.* Berlin, 1921, 672-685.

2. BINGHAM, H. C. Parental play of chimpanzees. *J. Mammal.,* 1927, **8**, 77-89.

3. BLAIR, W. R. Notes on the birth of a chimpanzee. *Bull. N. Y. Zool. Soc.,* 1920, **23**, 104-111.

4. BRUHN, J. M., & HASLERUD, G. M. Unpublished observations.

5. FOX, H. The birth of two anthropoid apes. *J. Mammal.,* 1929, **10**, 37-51.

6. JACOBSEN, C. F., JACOBSEN, M. M., & YOSHIOKA, J. G. Development of an infant chimpanzee during her first year. *Comp. Psychol. Monog.,* 1932, **9**. Pp. 94. (See esp. p. 22 ff.)

7. MONTANÉ, L. Un chimpancé Cubano. *El Siglo,* 1915, **20**, 7-17.

8. SCHULTZ, A. H., & SNYDER, F. F. Observations on reproduction in the chimpanzee. *Bull. Johns Hopkins Hospital,* 1935, **57**, 193-205.

9. SCHWARZ, E. On the local races of the chimpanzee. *Ann. Mag. Nat. Hist.,* 1934, **13**, 576-583.

10. SPENCE, K. W. Response of chimpanzee mothers to infants following prolonged separation. (In manuscript.)

11. TINKLEPAUGH, O. L. Sex cycles and other cyclic phenomena in a chimpanzee during adolescence, maturity, and pregnancy. *J. Morphol.,* 1933, **54**, 521-547.

12. TOMILIN, M. I., & YERKES, R. M. Chimpanzee twins: behavioral relations and development. *J. Genet. Psychol.,* 1935, **46**, 239-263.

13. YERKES, R. M. Genetic aspects of grooming, a socially important primate behavior pattern. *J. Soc. Psychol.,* 1933, **4**, 3-25.

14. ———. Suggestibility in chimpanzee. *J. Soc. Psychol.,* 1934, **5**, 271-282.

15. YERKES, R. M., & TOMILIN, M. I. Mother-infant relations in chimpanzee. *J. Comp. Psychol.,* 1935, **20**, 321-359.

16. YERKES, R. M., & YERKES, A. W. Nature and conditions of avoidance (fear) response in chimpanzee. *J. Comp. Psychol.,* 1936, **21**, 53-66.

*Yale University*
*New Haven, Connecticut*

# 8

Reprinted from *J. Genet. Psychol.* **41**:211–220 (1932)

## SOCIAL FACILITATION OF FEEDING IN THE ALBINO RAT*

*From the Psychological Laboratories of Stanford University and the University of Wisconsin*

H. F. HARLOW

The effect of social influences on the drives of the normal human being is quite obvious. We inhibit certain tendencies and reinforce others in the presence of individuals like ourselvves. Eating is influenced, probably not so much as to quantity as to appreciation. A good meal tastes better if we eat it in the company of friends. Likewise, it tastes much worse if we eat it in disagreeable company.

In the study of animals we are reduced to a more quantitative attack on the problem. It is impossible to determine the rat's increased appreciation of food (if any such exists) but we can measure the amount ingested. It has seemed desirable to study the effect of a social situation on this elementary type of response by comparing the amounts of food taken in solitary feeding as compared with the amount eaten by the same animal when feeding in a group.

### PERTINENT LITERATURE

Fischel (2) was able to show that hens, though exhibiting no signs of hunger, were stimulated to begin eating again by the sight of another hen feeding. Bayer (1) completed a series of researches designed to check and extend this observation. In these investigations,

> "The research was carried out as follows: a hungry V-animal (experimental animal) was placed before a large heap of wheat (a food well liked by the hens) and allowed to eat until satiated. Then a hungry A-animal (exciting animal) was introduced."

Two measures of the effect of the social facilitation of the feeding responses which were subsequently obtained were made by Bayer. The first of these was the changed behavior of the hen elicited by the above situation, and the second was the amount of food that the V-animal ate after the A-animal was admitted to the cage.

---

*Accepted for publication by Carl Murchison of the Editorial Board and received in the Editorial Office, January 19, 1932.

Since one of the two hens almost invariably dominated the other, Bayer arranged the situation so that the dominant animal was alternately the V-animal and the A-animal.

The behavior of the hens is described by Bayer as follows:

"As soon as the A-animal was placed in front of the food, it began to eat with great zeal. Now how did the V-animal behave? If it were the dominant animal, it began to attack the A-animal immediately. To one who is not a behaviorist this obviously indicates that the V-animal attempts to prevent the A-animal from eating as a result of envy over the food (*Futterneid*). As soon as the V-animal noticed, however, that it was having little success, and that the A-animal continued to eat in spite of everything, it began once more to eat the food, intermittently striking at the other animal. This behavior was facilitated by the fact that the V-animal no longer ate with its original zeal. If the V-animal was the subordinate animal, it made no effort to hinder the feeding of the other upon its entrance. Instead, it began to eat again in spite of the fact that the dominant animal would strike at it from time to time. The sight of the dominant animal eating was apparently a strong enough stimulus to inhibit the fear which the subordinate animal normally felt. One could note that the subordinate animal behaved cautiously and ate, so to speak, 'behind the back' of the other."

The social increment as measured by the increased amount of food eaten depended somewhat upon the particular situation. Using one V-animal and one A-animal, Baer experimented on eight hens. Social increments (amount of food eaten by the V-animal after the A-animal was admitted to the cage) were obtained in every case and averaged 34%, the lowest being 25%, and the highest 43% of the amount eaten to induce satiation.

Experiments on the same animals in which the situation was altered so that there was always one V-animal and three A-animals gave even greater social increments, averaging 53%, and ranging from 33 to 67%.

Where the situation was reversed so that there was only one A-animal and three V-animals, the effect was very much less. One out of four hens was entirely passive, and no animal showed a social increment in excess of 33%. With the three V-animals eating in the same compartment, results obtained on four animals gave a social increment averaging 10%, and, with the three V-animals eating in separate compartments, results obtained on four animals gave a social increment of 21%.

A fourth experimental situation was so arranged that four hens would eat separately one day and together the next. Two experiments were completed and social increments (increased consumption of food for day 1 over day 2) were obtained in every instance. These ranged in the individual animals from 33 to 200%, and averaged 96%.

Seven experiments have been conducted.[1] In the following study, all have the same purpose but vary slightly in technique. For purposes of convenient understanding, the technique and results will be given for each separately before any attempt is made to compare the results or draw general conclusions.

## TECHNIQUE AND RESULTS

*Experiment 1.* In this experiment the animal was allowed to feed to satiation, an hour period being assumed to meet this requirement. At the end of this time a hungry rat (24-hour food deprivation) was introduced and allowed to feed for an hour. The object was to find if the satiated rat would be stimulated to feed further in the second hour by the presence of the hungry rat. Corn was used as food which made it easy to observe the amount eaten by the satiated animal as the grains seized could be counted. The results were tabulated for eight animals on each of three days, and in no case were they distinctly favorable to the existence of a social facilitation process, as the satiated animal ate no more in the second hour in the presence of the hungry rat than when alone.

*Experiment 2.* In this experiment young rats without previous experience with solid food were used. Tweny rats were weaned at the age of 18 days, and, as the mothers had been fed outside the cage for the three preceding days, they could have had no experience with solid food. They were fed a liquid diet for a certain number of days (2, 7, 12, and 17, respectively, for the four groups of five rats each) so that, on the day of starting the experiment, the groups were 20, 25, 30, and 35 days old. They were then placed in individual cages and fed corn during two one-hour periods per day

[1]Experiments 1-6 were conducted at Stanford University under Dr. C. P. Stone. The work was financed by the Thomas Welton Stanford Fund. Experiment 7 was done at the University of Wisconsin.

TABLE 1

COMPARISON OF AMOUNT OF CORN EATEN AND SPILLED BY ALBINO RATS
FEEDING SEPARATELY AND IN GROUPS OF FIVE

| Group No. | Age days | Individual feeding | | Group feeding | |
|---|---|---|---|---|---|
| | | Grains eaten | Grains spilled | Grains eaten | Grains spilled |
| 1 | 24-25 | 14 | 67 | 21 | 204 |
| 2 | 29-30 | 18 | 59 | 30 | 221 |
| 3 | 34-35 | 21 | 84 | 41 | 242 |
| 4 | 39-40 | 24 | 78 | 49 | 237 |
| Total | | 87 | 288 | 141 | 904 |

for five days.  On the sixth day, all five animals were placed in one cage and allowed to feed.

Objective comparison was made between the fifth day (last individual feeding) and sixth day (first group feeding).  The criteria used were the number of grains eaten and the number of grains spilled on the floor.  The results are summarized in Table 1.

The number of grains eaten by the 20 rats on the last day of individual feeding was 87.  On the first day of group feeding the total number of grains eaten jumped to 141.  This amounts to an increase of about 70%.  The amount of corn spilled was even more strikingly increased.  The 20 rats spilled 288 grains when feeding individually, but when feeding in groups they spilled 904 grains, an increase of about 200%.

The behavior of the rats was even more markedly different. The rat eating alone characteristically fed leisurely and with occasional wandering about the cage.  In the group situation, the performance was hurried and apparently competitive.  Each rat would hasten to a corner, or two rats would eat back to back.  The process of getting grains from the pan occasioned much scrambling and pushing, which was the chief cause of the large amount spilled.  The group performance appeared much more highly motivated than the process of individual feeding.

*Experiment 3.*  In this experiment 20 animals, all males, were reared in isolation from the age of 20 to 40 days.  From the 40th to the 44th day, inclusive, the amount of standard diet eaten by each animal in his two feeding periods was recorded, and on the 44th day they were grouped by weight into ten pairs.  From the 45th to the 49th day they were fed in pairs and the total amount eaten by the pair compared with the sum of the amounts eaten by the two individually. Some of these pairs showed a social increment, some no effect, and some a social decrement. An observation of the behavior of these animals indicated that in many cases the two would spend the feeding hour in play, even though a steady decline in weight indicated that they must be in a state of hunger.

*Experiment 4.* In this experiment 20 males, 40 to 45 days old (with two exceptions, 61 days), were used. The situation was the same as in the third experiment, with the chief exception that previous to the beginning of the individual feeding, they had been housed and fed in groups of four or five, so that they were accustomed to a social feeding situation.

The experiment lasted 25 days, including five individual days, five social, five individual, five social, and a final five individual days. These will be designated control 1, experimental 1, control 2, etc.

The results on amount of food eaten are summarized in Table 2. The differences here are strikingly in favor of the concept of social facilitation. The mean difference between the first control and the first experimental period is 13.35 grams and the *S.D.* of this difference is only 1.69, giving a critical ratio of 7.90. The other differences are even greater, and the critical ratios correspondingly higher.

The amount of gain in weight made by each rat was also computed. These results are given in Table 3. The differences here are all large and reliable except for the comparison of experimental 1 and control 1. The conclusion which is obvious from these two criteria is that social facilitation of feeding responses unquestionably does occur, and that it is important.

*Experiment 5.* This experiment differs from the previous one in that only nine animals were used, and during the two experimental periods they were fed in groups of three. Since the number of cases is so small, the results are not given, but the critical ratios were significant for both food eaten and weight gained, in every comparison of the group and individual situations. The results did not indicate, however, that there was greater facilitation when three animals were feeding together than in Experiment 4 in which they fed in pairs.

*Experiment 6.* Since Bayer (1) claimed that "envy" was one of the factors operating in the social facilitation process, an attempt was made to eliminate the competitive factor. A cage, 7 inches

TABLE 2

AMOUNT OF STANDARD DIET EATEN BY YOUNG ALBINO RATS FEEDING
SEPARATELY AND IN GROUPS OF TWO

| Period | Total grams eaten | Average grams eaten | |
|---|---|---|---|
| Control 1 | 917 | 45.85 | |
| Experimental 1 | 1184 | 59.20 | |
| Control 2 | 794 | 39.72 | |
| Experimental 2 | 1220 | 61.10 | |
| Control 3 | 797 | 39.85 | |
| Mean differences: | Diff. | *S.D. diff.* | *C.R.* |
| E1 — C1 | 13.35 | 1.69 | 7.90 |
| E1 — C2 | 19.50 | 1.67 | 11.67 |
| E2 — C2 | 21.30 | 1.46 | 14.58 |
| E2 — C3 | 21.15 | 1.42 | 14.89 |

TABLE 3

AMOUNT OF WEIGHT GAINED BY YOUNG ALBINO RATS FEEDING SEPARATELY
AND IN GROUPS OF TWO

| Period | Total grams gained | Average grams gained | |
|---|---|---|---|
| Control 1 | 294 | 14.70 | |
| Experimental 1 | 333 | 16.65 | |
| Control 2 | 50 | 2.50 | |
| Experimental 2 | 459 | 22.95 | |
| Control 3 | 75 | 3.75 | |
| Mean differences: | Diff. | *S.D. diff.* | *C.R.* |
| E1 — C1 | 1.95 | 1.41 | 1.38 |
| E1 — C2 | 14.15 | 1.54 | 9.18 |
| E2 — C2 | 20.45 | 1.93 | 10.59 |
| E2 — C3 | 19.20 | 1.48 | 12.97 |

long, 3 inches high, and 1½ inches wide, was used to confine a large adult rat. An opening in the front end allowed him to reach out his head, but he could not escape or turn around. When, thus confined, he was placed in the cage with a feeding rat, the other rat was not stimulated to eat more, whether or not the confined rat was placed near enough to the food to eat from his position. It does not seem likely, then, that "envy" or personal animosity is a factor operative in the social facilitation situation.

*Experiment 7.* The first six experiments were considered as more or less exploratory, and an attempt was made to duplicate Experiment 4 under more carefully controlled conditions. Since we consider this the crucial experiment of the series, the technique is detailed fully.

The rats were weaned at 18 days and reared in individual cages until 30 days old. Their two daily feedings were one-half hour in length, at 9 A.M. and 5 P.M. A double pan was used for feeding, with food only in the inner pan, so that most of the spilled food was collected in the outer. Food falling on the floor of the cage was caught by a sheet of oilcloth placed underneath.

Only the amount of food eaten was taken as a measure of facilitation. Exactly 20 grams of food were furnished the animal daily, and the amount eaten was computed by collecting carefully all spillage and reweighing. The computations were made to 0.1 gram on scales which are accurate to 0.05 gram.

At the beginning of the experimental period, 34 animals were divided into 17 pairs on the basis of weight. On the 31st day of life, they were given their first group feeding, in pairs, and from then on to the 49th day, every odd-numbered day was an experimental period and every even-numbered day (32 to 50) a control day. To avoid any effect of familiarity with surroundings, the animals were alternated between the home cage of one member of the pair and the other.

Table 4 summarizes the results of this experiment. In the social situation the average amount of food eaten was 13.59 grams, while in the individual situation only 12.53 grams were eaten. The difference is 1.058, and is 3.59 times its standard error. It is therefore a statistically "true" difference.

It seems important not only that the group means are significantly differentiated, but also that the difference from day to day is consistent. The differences and critical ratios for each two-day sequence have been computed, but in general (as a result of the small number of cases, no doubt) these ratios are less than three. A definite tendency is shown, however, for group feeding to manifest a significant facilitating influence upon the amount of food ingested.

The behavior of the animals in this experiment (alternating daily between group and solitary feeding) manifested even more excitement than in the previous experiments in which five-day periods had been used.

## DISCUSSION

The results of the several experiments argue clearly for a process of social facilitation of the feeding response in the rat.  If we rely upon differences in food ingested, in food spilled or in weight gained, we see that there is in practically every case a significant superiority of the group situation.

The observations of behavior also indicate a process of facilitation. The animals in the group situation were characteristically highly motivated, displaying an excess of activity in getting food, struggling, crowding other rats from the food dish, etc.   There was a distinct difference in the leisurely feeding of the individual rat, which was frequently interrupted by exploration of the cage, etc.

These generalizations hold true only when the various rats are

TABLE 4

AVERAGE AMOUNT EATEN BY PAIRS OF ALBINO RATS FEEDING TOGETHER AND
SEPARATELY ON ALTERNATE DAYS

| Day of experiment | Group feeding | Individual feeding |
|---|---|---|
| 1 | 10.35 | |
| 2 | | 9.22 |
| 3 | 11.67 | |
| 4 | | 10.43 |
| 5 | 12.57 | |
| 6 | | 11.20 |
| 7 | 12.74 | |
| 8 | | 12.09 |
| 9 | 13.24 | |
| 1C | | 12.24 |
| 11 | 14.08 | |
| 12 | | 13.32 |
| 13 | 13.66 | |
| 14 | | 13.56 |
| 15 | 15.42 | |
| 16 | | 13.83 |
| 17 | 15.84 | |
| 18 | | 14.69 |
| 19 | 16.33 | |
| 20 | | 14.75 |
| Average | 13.59 | 12.53 |
| Difference | 1.057 | |
| S.D. diff. | 0.294 | |
| C.R. | 3.59 | |

free and competing. The experiments in which this condition did not prevail (Experiments 1 and 6) do not show social facilitation.

The observation of the behavior of these animals in the individual and social situations leads to another conclusion which is of considerable importance in the understanding of hunger motivation. It has often been believed that the immediate stimulus for ingestion of food was the stimulation derived from contractions of the stomach. Yet it is well known that struggling and excessive striped muscle activity tend to inhibit the contractions of the smooth musculature. We have, then, in this experiment, the anomalous condition of animals in which the stomach contractions have undoubtedly been inhibited or diminished eating greater quantities of food than they did when under comparable conditions without the external disturbance. We wish to suggest, then, that ingestion of food is determined more by the external situation than by the actual interoceptive stimulation. This conclusion is substantiated by much common knowledge of human behavior, such as the influence of music, pleasant surroundings, the holiday atmosphere, etc.

### Basic Mechanisms of Social Facilitation

1. *Social facilitation does not depend upon learning.* Rats without previous experience with solid food (Experiment 2) and rats without previous experience with food in the presence of other rats (Experiment 7) manifest the effects of facilitation on the first day of the experiment.

2. *The process is not subject to change and adaptation.* Five periods of five days each (Experiment 4) and 20 days of alternate feeding (Experiment 7) showed differences at the end of the experiment equal to or greater than those at the beginning.

3. *It does not depend upon imitation.* A satiated rat watching a hungry rat eating (Experiment 1) is not thereby motivated to eat more.

4. *It does not depend upon "envy."* The presence of a restrained, non-competing rat (Experiment 6) does not motivate the free rat to ingest larger amounts of food.

5. *It is not a function of the size of the group.* Experiment 2 (five rats in group), Experiment 4 (two rats), and Experiment 5 (three rats) show differences of similar size.

6. *It may be related to age.* Table 1 (Experiment 2) indicates that the older rats increase their food intake proportionately more

than the younger rats. Evidence from the individual records of some of the other experiments, however, does not substantiate this finding.

7. *The essential condition for the occurrence of social facilitation is the presence of rats unrestrained and actively competing with each other for food.*

## SUMMARY

1. The effect of social facilitation upon the feeding response in the albino rat has been demonstrated.

2. This social facilitation takes place only between rats that are unrestrained and freely competing.

3. Facilitation is independent of previous experience.

4. It does not depend upon imitation or envy.

## REFERENCES

1. BAYER, E. Beiträge zur Zweikomponententheorie des Hungers. *Zsch. f. Psychol.*, 1929, **112**, 1-53.

2. FISCHEL, W. Beiträge zur Soziologie des Haushuhns. *Biol. Centbl.*, 1927, **47**, 678-696.

*University of Wisconsin*
*Madison, Wisconsin*


[*Editor's Note:* Resumes in French and German have been omitted.]

Part IV

# BEHAVIOR GENETICS

# Editor's Comments
# on Papers 9 and 10

Although an extreme environmentalistic bias has characterized parts of psychology throughout much of the century, the study of genetic influences on behavior has been a recurring theme in comparative psychology. Indeed, comparative psychologists have probably done more than individuals from any other discipline in examining genetic influences on mammalian behavior. An interest in genetic influences on behavior implies neither genetic determinism nor the exclusion of important environmental factors. Rather, genes and environment interact continuously during the process of behavioral development. This interaction cannot be appreciated without an understanding of all factors involved in the interaction.

Yerkes's Yale laboratories produced some of the earliest systematic examples of behavior-genetic analysis. Yerkes and his associates compared inbred and outbred rats and wild and domesticated rats on a variety of behavioral measures. Yerkes's best-known work in this field, however, dealt with "dancing mice," animals displaying a peculiar whirling pattern of repetitive locomotion (Paper 9). In his book, Yerkes adopted a typically broad approach to the study of dancing mice, including discussions of development, the fine structure of behavior, structural peculiarities, sensory function, and learning. In the section reprinted here, Yerkes analyzes the patterns of inheritance of whirling in mice. It is clear that the determinants of whirling are complex, though clearly there is a genetic factor. Yerkes further analyzes the inheritance of learned behavioral tendencies. In contrast to psychologist William McDougall (e.g., McDougall, 1938), Yerkes found no evidence of the inheritance of individually acquired behavioral tendencies.

The method of artificial selection was applied to the study of maze learning by Edward C. Tolman (1924) and was greatly expanded by his student Robert C. Tryon (Paper 10). Tryon's work is a deserved classic, providing clear-cut evidence of a genetic influence on performance in complex mazes. Later research made it clear that the difference may not have been related to learning ability per se (e.g., Searle, 1949). Nevertheless, Tryon's work demonstrated the power and convincingness of the application of the method of artificial selection in the psychology laboratory.

The field of behavior genetics has grown greatly since these pioneering efforts (see Hirsch and McGuire, 1982). The review by Calvin Hall (1951) and the book by Fuller and Thompson (1960) provided organization and cohesion for this developing approach. Today, behavior geneticists have their own journal and society and a flourishing subdiscipline.

## REFERENCES

Fuller, J. L., and W. R. Thompson, 1960, *Behavior Genetics,* Wiley, New York.

Hall, C. S., 1951, The Genetics of Behavior, in *Handbook of Experimental Psychology,* S. S. Stevens, ed., Wiley, New York.

Hirsch, J., and T. R. McGuire, eds., 1982 *Behavior-Genetic Analysis,* Hutchinson Ross, Stroudsburg, Pa.

McDougall, W., 1938, Fourth Report on a Lamarckian Experiment, *Br. J. Psychol.* **18:**321–345.

Searle, L. V., 1949, The Organization of Hereditary Maze-brightness and Maze-dullness, *Genet. Psychol. Monogr.* **39:**279–325.

Tolman, E. C., 1924, The Inheritance of Maze-learning Ability in Rats, *J. Comp. Psychol.* **4:**1–18.

# 9

Reprinted from pages 278–283 of *The Dancing Mouse: A Study in Animal Behavior,*
Macmillan, New York, 1907, 290p.

# THE INHERITANCE OF FORMS OF BEHAVIOR

## Robert M. Yerkes

In a general way those peculiarities of behavior which suggested the name dancing mouse are inherited. Generation after generation of the mice run in circles, whirl, and move the head restlessly and jerkily from side to side. But these forms of behavior vary greatly. Some individuals whirl infrequently and sporadically; others whirl frequently and persistently, at certain hours of the day. Some are unable to climb a vertical surface; others do so readily. Some respond to sounds; others give no indications of ability to hear. I propose in this chapter to present certain facts concerning the inheritance of individual peculiarities of behavior, and to state the results of a series of experiments by which I had hoped to test the inheritance of individually acquired forms of behavior.

My study of the nature of the whirling tendency of the dancer has revealed the fact that certain individuals whirl to the right almost uniformly, others just as regularly to the left, and still others now in one direction, now in the other. On the basis of this observation, the animals have been classified as right, left, or mixed whirlers. Does the dancer transmit to its offspring the tendency to whirl in a definite manner?

Records of the direction of whirling of one hundred individuals have been obtained. For twenty of these mice the determination was made by counting the number of complete turns in five-minute intervals at six different hours of the day. For the remaining eighty individuals the direction was discovered by observation of the activity of the animals for a brief interval at five different times. Naturally, the former results are the more exact; in fact, they alone have any considerable quantitative value. But for the problem under consideration all of the determinations are sufficiently accurate to be satisfactory.

The distribution of the individuals which were examined as to direction of whirling is as follows.

| | RIGHT WHIRLERS | LEFT WHIRLERS | MIXED WHIRLERS | TOTAL |
|---|---|---|---|---|
| Males | 19 | 19 | 12 | 50 |
| Females | 12 | 23 | 15 | 50 |

The frequency of occurrence of left whirlers among the females is unexpectedly high. Is this to be accounted for in terms of inheritance? In my search for an answer to this question I followed the whirling tendency from generation to generation in two lines of descent. These two groups of mice have already been referred to as the 200 line and the 400 line. The former were descended from Nos. 200 and 205, and the latter from Nos. 152 and 151. Individuals which resulted from the crossing of these lines will be referred to hereafter as of mixed descent. There were some striking differences in the behavior of the mice of the two lines of descent. As a rule the individuals of the 200 line climbed more readily, were more active, danced less vigorously, whirled less rapidly and less persistently, and were in several other respects much more like common mice than were the individuals of the 400 line. It is also to be noted (see Table 5, p. 89) that few of the litters of the 200 line exhibited auditory reactions, whereas almost all of the litters of the 400 line which were tested gave unmistakable evidence of sensitiveness to certain sounds. These differences at once suggest the importance of an examination of the whirling tendency of each line of descent.

The results for the several generations of each line which I had opportunity to examine are unexpectedly decisive so far as the question in point is concerned.

### INDIVIDUALS OF THE 200 LINE

| | MALES | FEMALES |
|---|---|---|
| First generation | No. 200, ? | No. 205, ? |
| Second generation | No. 210, Mixed whirler | No. 215, Left whirler |
| Third generation | No. 220, Mixed whirler | No. 225, Mixed whirler |
| Fourth generation | No. 230, Right whirler | No. 235, Mixed whirler |
| Fifth generation | No. 240, Right whirler | No. 245, Left whirler |

### INDIVIDUALS OF THE 400 LINE

| | MALES | FEMALES |
|---|---|---|
| First generation | No. 152, Left whirler | No. 151, Left whirler |
| Second generation | No. 410, Left whirler | No. 415, Right whirler |
| Third generation | No. 420, Left whirler | No. 425, Left whirler |

One line of descent exhibited no pronounced whirling tendency; the other exhibited a strong tendency to whirl to the left. Are these statements true for the group of one hundred individuals whose distribution among the three classes of whirlers has been given? In order to obtain an answer to this question I have reclassified these individuals according to descent and direction of whirling.

### INDIVIDUALS OF THE 200 LINE

| | RIGHT WHIRLERS | LEFT WHIRLERS | MIXED WHIRLERS | TOTAL |
|---|---|---|---|---|
| Males | 7 | 6 | 8 | 21 |
| Females | 5 | 8 | 8 | 21 |
| | 12 | 14 | 16 | 42 |

### INDIVIDUALS OF THE 400 LINE

|  | RIGHT WHIRLERS | LEFT WHIRLERS | MIXED WHIRLERS | TOTAL |
|---|---|---|---|---|
| Males | 4 | 9 | 1 | 14 |
| Females | 6 | 9 | 4 | 19 |
|  | 10 | 18 | 5 | 33 |

### INDIVIDUALS OF MIXED DESCENT

|  | | | |
|---|---|---|---|
| 9 | 10 | 6 | 25 |

Three interesting facts are indicated by these results: first, the inheritance of a tendency to whirl to the left in the 400 line of descent; second, the lack of any definite whirling tendency in the 200 line; and third, the occurrence of right and left whirlers with equal frequency as a result of the crossing of these two lines of descent.

It is quite possible, and I am inclined to consider it probable, that the pure dancer regularly inherits a tendency to whirl to the left, and that this is obscured in the case of the 200 line by the influences of a cross with another variety of mouse. It is to be noted that the individuals of the 200 line were predominantly mixed whirlers, and I may add that many of them whirled so seldom that they might more appropriately be classed as circlers.

## THE INHERITANCE OF INDIVIDUALLY ACQUIRED FORMS OF BEHAVIOR

The white-black discrimination experiments which were made in connection with the study of vision and the modifiability of behavior were so planned that they should furnish evidence of any possible tendency towards the inheritance of modifications in behavior. The problem may be stated thus. If a dancing mouse be thoroughly trained to avoid black, by being subjected to a disagreeable experience every time it enters a black box, will it transmit to its offspring a tendency to avoid black?

Systematic training experiments were carried on with individuals of both the 200 and 400 lines of descent. For each of these lines a male and a female were trained at the age of four weeks to discriminate between the white and the black electric-boxes and to choose the former. After they had been thoroughly trained these individuals were mated,

TABLE 53

THE INHERITANCE OF THE HABIT OF WHITE-BLACK DISCRIMINATION

Number of Errors in Daily Series of Ten Tests

| SERIES | MALES | | | | FEMALES | | | |
|---|---|---|---|---|---|---|---|---|
| | FIRST GENERATION | SECOND GENERATION | THIRD GENERATION | FOURTH GENERATION | FIRST GENERATION | SECOND GENERATION | THIRD GENERATION | FOURTH GENERATION |
| | No. 210 | No. 220 | No. 230 | No. 240 | No. 215 | No. 225 | No. 235 | No. 245 |
| A | 6 | 5 | 6 | 7 | 8 | 4 | 4 | 7 |
| B | 6 | 8 | 8 | 8 | 8 | 7 | 6 | 5 |
| 1 | 6 | 7 | 6 | 5 | 7 | 6 | 5 | 4 |
| 2 | 4 | .3 | 1 | 5 | 5 | 6 | 4 | 5 |
| 3 | 3 | 1 | 4 | 5 | 3 | 4 | 4 | 3 |
| 4 | 5 | 0 | 3 | 4 | 2 | 1 | .3 | 1 |
| 5 | 3 | 0 | 4 | 2 | 1 | 3 | 3 | 0 |
| 6 | 2 | 1 | 4 | 2 | 2 | 1 | 1 | 1 |
| 7 | 1 | 0 | 3 | 1 | 1 | 1 | 2 | 0 |
| 8 | 0 | 0 | 1 | 0 | 0 | 0 | 2 | 3 |
| 9 | 0 | 0 | 0 | 1 | 1 | 0 | 0 | 0 |
| 10 | 0 | | 0 | 1 | 0 | 2 | 1 | 1 |
| 11 | | | 0 | 0 | 0 | 3 | 0 | 0 |
| 12 | | | | 0 | 0 | 0 | 0 | 0 |
| 13 | | | | 0 | | 0 | 0 | 0 |
| 14 | | | | | | 0 | | |

and in course of time a male and female, chosen at random from their first litter, were similarly trained. All the individuals were trained in the same way and under as nearly the same conditions as could be maintained, and accurate records were kept of the behavior of each animal and of the number of errors of choice which it made in series after series of tests. What do these records indicate concerning the influence of individually acquired forms of behavior upon the behavior of the race?

I have records for four generations in the 200 line and for three generations in the 400 line.[1] As the results are practically the same for each, I shall present the detailed records for the former group alone. In Table 53 are to be found the number of errors made in successive series of ten tests each by the various individuals of the 200 line which were trained in this experiment. The most careful examination fails to reveal any indication of the inheritance of a tendency to avoid the black box. No. 240, in fact, chose the black box more frequently in the preference series than did No. 210, and he required thirty more tests for the establishment of a perfect habit than did No. 210. Apparently descent from individuals which had thoroughly learned to avoid the black box gives the dancer no advantage in the formation of a white-black discrimination habit. There is absolutely no evidence of the inheritance of this particular individually acquired form of behavior in the dancer.

---

[1] This experiment was interrupted by the death of the animals of both lines of descent.

# 10

## GENETIC DIFFERENCES IN MAZE-LEARNING ABILITY IN RATS

ROBERT CHOATE TRYON
Associate Professor of Psychology
University of California
Berkeley, California

The experimental geneticist is inclined to be somewhat skeptical of conclusions from nature-nurture studies on human beings. The complex breeding system deriving from the adventitious circumstances of 'young love' and the wide differences in environments into which the progeny of such matings are born and reared present such a complex matrix of determiners of 'mental' differences that it would appear hopeless to endeavor to separate out the relative effects of those termed 'nature' and those termed 'nurture.' Furthermore, the indubitable tendency in the uncontrolled human environment for different genotypes to seek out different environments, and conversely, for different environments to select special genotypes, and all this to an unknown degree, creates a correlation between nature and nurture that confounds any analyst who has neither an hereditary nor an environmental axe to grind. And on top of it all, to make the confusion worse, are the ambiguous psychological omnibus tests of mental ability, about the psychological validity of which the most able psychologists cannot agree.

After several centuries of the type of groping called 'natural history,' the biologist in his rôle as experimental geneticist has discovered that the only way to get definite answers to the nature-nurture question in plants and animals is to establish a pure strain experimentally by means of a controlled selective breeding schedule and then experimentally to vary systematically the milieu for different samples of the strain. The logic is, indeed, very simple: In a given species, (1) hold heredity constant by choosing a pure strain, then study the effects of different environment on it, and (2) hold the environment constant, then vary heredity by studying the development of different pure strains in it, and (3) compare the relative effects of the two types of variations that are, respectively, nature and nurture. Though the logic is simple, its experimental execution is arduous, often requiring many years of work even when investigating only one character in one species.

As the psychologist cannot, of course, perform such experiments on human beings, he must turn to animals. During the last three decades, the animal psychologist has developed techniques for the reliable and valid measurement of individual differences in numerous psychological characters of animals, especially of rats. The securing of definite answers to the question of the relative effects of nature and nurture on psychological characters is thus made possible. An experimental genetics focused on animal *behavior* and ultimately based on studies of numerous species of animals varying in phylogenetic complexity should give us the answers we wish. Only the most egregious 'special creationist' would argue that the findings of such a comparative psychological genetics would have no applications to man.

The attempts of the writer to design and execute such a psychological genetics experiment are outlined below. The essential aims have been to establish under environmental control a maze-bright and a maze-dull strain of rats, to determine the nature of the genetic determiners at work, to discover the constancy of this psychological difference throughout a large range of the rats' life span, and to find important biological and psychological correlates of the differences in this maze ability. Finally, the effects of systematic environmental changes on each strain are to be investigated. Though the work has now been in progress eleven years, it is in many respects still preliminary. Findings are complete with respect to some of the objectives but not to others. A brief summary is presented below under the various types of analyses.

### 1. Proof of the Inheritance of Individual Differences in Maze Ability

An experiment [1] was begun in 1927 that had as its purpose the establishment by selective breeding of a pure line of maze-bright and a pure line of maze-dull rats. Each animal was run nineteen trials through a seventeen-blind T maze. His score was the total number of entrances into blind alleys. The breeding schedule consisted in mating together the brightest rats within each of the brightest litters, the dullest within each of the dullest. Rigorous environmental controls were effected (1) by instituting standard procedure of animal care and of breeding, (2) by using an automatic mechanical device for delivering the animals into the maze without handling, and (3) by employing an electric recorder for the scoring of each rat's maze run. These controls have remained constant for eleven years. Selective breeding has been

[1] Supported by grants from the National Research Council, the Carnegie Corporation of New York, the Research Board of the University of California. Aid in statistical analysis was provided by the Works Progress Administration under Official Project No. 465–03–3–631–A2 at the University of California.

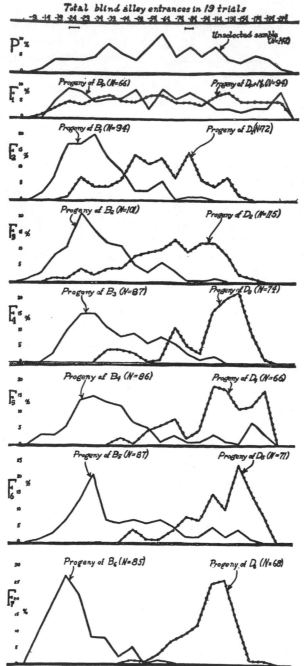

FIG. IV. — EFFECTS OF SELECTIVE BREEDING ON MAZE-LEARNING

Along the top is the scale of brightness as evidenced by the total number of blind-alley entrances made in nineteen trials. All the distributions below use this common top scale. For instance, a bright animal who made from ten to fourteen errors would fall under the scale step, the upper limit of which is marked −14, a dull who made from 195 to 214 errors would fall under −214, etc. The first generation of rats, marked "P" to the left, is shown just below the scale. The total number of P rats was 142, and the percent of them lying at each point on the scale is indicated in the distribution. The brightest of these were bred together, and then the dullest, giving the two $F_1$ groups, as shown. The selective breeding effects are shown down to the $F_7$, where progeny of $B_6$ (bright $F_6$) are markedly different from the progeny of $D_6$ (dull $F_6$).

122

continued for eighteen generations. As success in establishing strains of bright and dull animals is crucial to the proposed project, I present in Figure IV the basic data showing the effects of selective breeding through the $F_7$ generation. For brevity, I have not presented all the later generations, but

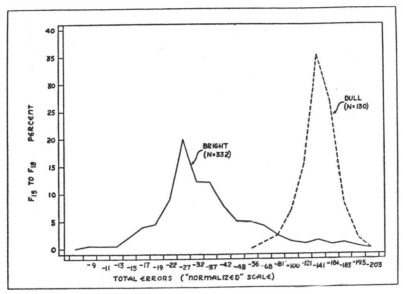

FIG. V. — BRIGHT AND DULL STRAINS OF THE FIFTEENTH TO EIGHTEENTH GENERATIONS

to show the latest results, I have given in Figure V the results in the $F_{15}$, $F_{16}$, $F_{17}$, and $F_{18}$ generations. In this figure the distributions of the two strains are shown for these later generations combined. There appears to be a law of diminishing returns, for after the $F_1$ negligible effects of selective breeding are noted. The results for all generations will be depicted in final form in terms of the improved normalized scale.

## 2. The Genetic Basis of Differences in Maze-Learning Ability

What is the genetic factor basis of differences in learning ability? How many factors must be postulated and what is the nature of their interaction? Geneticists propose a multiple cumulative-factor theory as the genetic explanation of the plant and animal characters that have statistical frequencies similar to those of maze-learning. One crucial experimental test of this theory is the cross between the pure lines at the two extremes of the scale. The $F_1$ progeny of such a cross should show a homogeneous median performance. The next generation progeny of the $F_1$ should vary widely over the whole scale. Figure VI shows the actual results of such a test on our behavior

Genetic Differences in Maze-Learning Ability in Rats   115

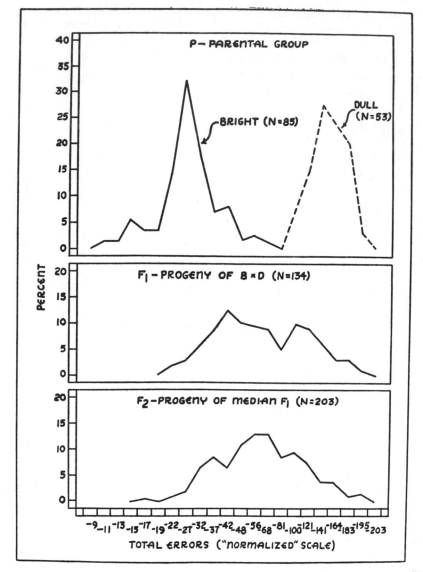

FIG. VI. — $F_1$ AND $F_2$ OF BRIGHT $\times$ DULL

trait.  The $F_2$ progeny of the $F_1$ do *not* vary more than the $F_1$.  Because the going theory was not verified, I repeated this crucial type of cross several years after the first attempt, but the results were the same.  Figure VI combines the findings of both series of experiments.

We need to develop and verify a factor hypothesis consistent with the facts of Figures IV, V, and VI, and with the results of certain back-cross experiments.  One method is that of expressing a given hypothesis concretely in terms of a dice-pattern.  A random parental population is then set up in which the score of each fictitious individual is determined by a dice throw.  These 'individuals' are then 'bred' according to the actual breeding schedule of the rat experiment and the theoretical results compared for fit with the experimental findings.  The hypothesis that gives the best fit and that is most consistent with genetic theory will be the one finally chosen.  I have performed several such artificial experiments, and from these it appears that the most promising hypothesis investigated to date is one that postulates multiple factors, some dominant for bright performance, some (but fewer) dominant for dull, and some cumulative.  The effects of linkage and crossing-over, and of reciprocal crossing — that is, bright male $\times$ dull female vs. dull male $\times$ bright female — must be investigated.

### 3. Biological Correlates of Brightness and Dullness

Large groups of bright and dull animals have been carefully measured in respect to brain size and weight, body weight, and fertility.  Significant differences have been discovered.  The bright animals show physical superiority throughout, except in the one particular of fertility.[1]  Because of the intensive inbreeding that has occurred during the process of selective breeding, the evaluation of these findings is to some extent equivocal.

### 4. The Constancy of Differences in Ability

The extent to which brightness and dullness persist throughout the lives of the animals was investigated.  One hundred and seven animals were measured in maze ability when they were young; then an interval of seven months, amounting to about two-thirds of a rat's life span, was permitted to elapse before remeasurement.  The correlation between the early and late measurements was .80, indicating a high degree of constancy.  For different subgroups that experienced different degrees of environmental variation during the intervening period between measurements, the correlation was the same — a result suggesting that environment as varied in these experiments plays a negligible rôle in this ability.

---

[1] The difference between the $N$'s of the bright and dull groups of Figures IV, V, and VI is a function of the number of matings made by the experimenter and not of differential fertility.

## 5. Psychological Nature of Brightness and Dullness

A variety of experiments were conducted that aimed to provide some insight into the psychological nature of the differences between the bright and dull groups.

*a. Evidence from Ratings of Emotional Characteristics.* Using reliable, objective rating scales, carefully standardized on a large group of preëxperimental animals, three judges independently rated 234 bright, dull, and stock animals on their hiding, avoidance, and escape reactions to controlled handling by the experimenter, and on their reactions to novel inanimate objects in the maze situation. The results show clearly that the bright animals are most adjusted 'emotionally' in the maze-learning situation, whereas in response to handling they are 'neurotic.' Exactly the reverse is the case for dulls.

*b. Evidence from a Cluster Analysis.* In addition to the measures of emotionality, this same group of 234 animals was measured on eleven different aspects of efficiency at different stages of learning the maze; for example, efficiency as measured by errors, speed (rate) of running, hesitation time at choice-points. The significant result from the analysis appears to be that the hereditary difference in maze ability, which was itself discovered by selection on the basis of errors only, is reflected in all the measures of efficiency as well as in those of emotionality.

*c. Evidence from Experiments on the Sensory Nature of Ability Differences.* Are bright animals superior to dull because of superiority in *sense acuity,* or does their superiority reside in a capacity for *abstracting* the spatial relations of the complex maze path? On the sense acuity hypothesis, one would assume that during the 19 trials in the maze the bright animals had learned to follow visual, auditory, kinesthetic, tactual, and olfactory cues by virtue of genetic superiority in their senses. Five experiments were conducted to investigate this hypothesis. In each experiment about 70 bright and 70 dull animals were subjects. Stated briefly, the technique was that of experimentally disrupting cues of the various sense modalities on the trials following the nineteenth. In every experiment the bright animals showed relatively negligible disturbance; many showed no disturbance at all as a consequence of cue disruption. These results fail to support the sense theory, but rather support the view that bright animals are superior to dull in a capacity to *generalize* the spatial pattern.

*d. Evidence from an Analysis of the 'Qualitative' Behavior of Bright and Dull Animals in the Maze Situation.* To investigate further the differences between bright and dull animals in the nonsensory determinants of their maze behavior, I analyzed the frequency pattern of errors made in the 17 blind alleys of the maze by 500 bright and 500 dull animals. As the error patterns of the two types of animals were quite different, especially in the later stages of learning, I attempted to deduce the existence of a number of psychological

gradients of a nonsensory spatial character that theoretically determined
the behavior of brights and dulls.  As the postulation of such gradients constituted being 'wise after the event,' I then attempted to predict the pattern
of errors made by 150 animals in a quite different twenty-blind maze.  The
correlation between the predicted error pattern and the actual error frequencies was .70, and with minor changes in the weights of the gradients, the
correlation was .92.  The hypothesis of nonsensory gradients is therefore supported.

 e. *Evidence from the Study of the Behavior of Maze-Bright and Maze-
Dull Animals in Other Problem-Solving Situations.*  To what degree does
hereditary brightness and dullness represent a *general* capacity to learn?  In
one experiment 150 animals were run through another maze.  In another study,
conducted by Krechevsky, bright and dull groups were studied in a brightness discrimination box.  At the present time Searle is engaged on a program of observing the performance of bright and dull animals in a number
of tasks requiring discrimination of distance, angles, and brightness.  From
the work done and under way, and from published data of other workers
showing the relation between maze-learning and other types of learning, the
evidence clearly supports the view that maze-learning is *specific*.  The doctrine of alleged 'general ability' supported by many psychologists has not
been substantiated in rats.

### 6. Prospectus

Future lines of research are clearly indicated.

One of these, as pointed out earlier, is the study of the effects of experimentally induced environmental variations on the two strains.  The general
question is this: What sorts of environmental variables of a psychological and
biologically pathological character will make hereditarily bright animals dull,
and hereditarily dull animals bright?  No systematic experiments of this
sort have yet been performed.  The only relevant data we have are from
the experiments on constancy and cue variations cited above.  After the
rats had first learned the maze to the best of their capacities, the introduction
of unsystematic though extensive variations in milieu in different groups
during the interval between the original learning and retest did not affect
the test-retest correlations.  In the stimulus disruption tests, extraordinary
variations or deprivations of stimulus (that is, environmental) features did
not significantly affect the bright-dull differences.  But it is to be noted that
these environmental variations occurred *after* the maze had been learned
to the level of capacity.  These observations would seem therefore to verify
the hypothesis that after hereditary capacity has expressed itself in the building up of habits and concepts, the effects of gross environmental changes are
negligible.  On the other hand, we know as yet nothing about the effects of
gross milieu changes before and during learning.

Another problem that calls for study is a systematic examination of the physical growth and behavior development of the *young* of the bright and dull lines. An extensive series of observations was made on the sensory and motor development of 50 progeny of bright and 50 of dull from birth to 30 days of age. These observations were purely exploratory. A program of research in this field, based on this preliminary work, is to be instituted.[1]

[*Editor's Note:* Material has been omitted at this point.]

1. References to previous publications on the experiments described in Section XIII [this paper] are 198, 199, 200, 201, 202, 203, 204, and 205.

## REFERENCES

(198) TRYON, R. C. "Studies in individual differences in maze ability. I. Measurement of the reliability of individual differences." *Jour. Comp. Psychol.,* 11: 1930, 145–170.

(199) TRYON, R. C. "Studies in individual differences in maze ability. II. Determination of individual differences by age, weight, sex and pigmentation." *Jour. Comp. Psychol.,* 12: 1931, 1–22.

(200) TRYON, R. C. "Studies in individual differences in maze ability. III. Community of function between two abilities." *Jour. Comp. Psychol.,* 12: 1931, 95–115.

(201) TRYON, R. C. "Studies in individual differences in maze ability. IV. The constancy of individual differences: Correlation between learning and relearning." *Jour. Comp. Psychol.,* 12: 1931, 303–345.

(202) TRYON, R. C., "Studies in individual differences in maze ability. V. Luminosity and visual acuity as systematic causes of individual differences, and an hypothesis of maze ability." *Jour. Comp. Psychol.,* 12: 1931, 401–420.

(203) TRYON, R. C., *The Genetics of Learning Ability in Rats — A Preliminary Report.* (University of California Press: Berkeley, 1929) University of California Publications in Psychology, Vol. 4, No. 5, 71–89.

(204) TRYON, R. C., "Individual differences." [In] Moss, F. A., editor: *Comparative Psychology.* (Prentice-Hall: New York, 1934) 529pp.

(205) TRYON, R. C., TOLMAN, E. C., and JEFFRESS, L. A. "A self-recording maze with an automatic delivery table." *Univ. Calif. Publ. Psychol.,* 4: 1929, 99–112.

Part V

# DEVELOPMENT OF BEHAVIOR

# Editor's Comments
## on Papers 11 and 12

11  **MILLS**
Excerpts from *The Psychic Development of Young Animals and Its Principal Correlation*

12  **CARMICHAEL**
*The Development of Behavior in Vertebrates Experimentally Removed from the Influence of External Stimulation*

Comparative psychologists have been accused of paying little attention to the study of the development of behavior (Klopfer and Hailman, 1967, 72). However, the study of behavioral development has been a persistent theme throughout the history of the discipline and would be included as an integral part of the definition of comparative psychology of some practitioners (e.g., Adler, 1980).

Perhaps the first great champion of the study of behavioral development in comparative psychology was T. Wesley Mills, one of the earliest members of the American Psychological Association. Mills conducted a series of studies of behavioral ontogeny in a variety of vertebrate species, published them as papers, and collected them in "The Nature and Development of Animal Intelligence," which is excerpted in Paper 11. In this brief segment, Mills describes the rationale behind his research, lists his main objectives, and summarizes his results on dogs. He notes two major epochs in the development of behavior in dogs, that before and after the opening of the eyes, and discusses the transition period that lies between these major epochs. Mills's efforts were followed by substantial contributions to the study of behavioral development from workers such as J. B. Watson (1903) and W. S. Small (1899).

A remarkable program of research in behavioral development was conducted by Leonard Carmichael. In the midst of an antiheredity movement in psychology in the 1920s, Carmichael conducted a series of studies on the development of motor patterns in frogs and sala-manders that led to the conclusion that hereditary factors exerted a strong influence. The first paper in this series in printed here as Paper 12. By comparing the development of behavior of normally developing animals with those developing in the anesthetic chlorotone, Carmichael found that behavior develops during a period when there is no observable response to stimulation. Later, Carmichael (1941) noted that he had been so under the influence of conditioned reflex theory that he initially denied the truth of his own observations. With each experiment, however, Carmichael and others became increasingly convinced.

The study of behavioral development has been a major emphasis of many of the major workers in the field including Lashley and Watson (1913), Schneirla (1957), Beach and Jaynes (1954), Stone (1922), and Yerkes (1927). The field of behavioral development has been repeatedly supported by comparative psychologists, who have taken the lead in pointing to the complexities of ontogeny and the need for careful analyses in dissecting this complexity. The field continues to flourish.

## REFERENCES

Adler, H. E., 1980, Historical Dialectics, *Am. Psychol.* **35:**956–958.

Beach, F. A., and J. Jaynes, 1954, Effects of Early Experience upon the Behavior of Animals, *Psychol. Bull.* **51:**239–263.

Carmichael, L., 1941, The Experimental Embryology of Mind, *Psychol. Bull.* **38:**1–28.

Klopfer, P. H., and J. P. Hailman, 1967, *An Introduction to Animal Behavior,* Prentice-Hall, Englewood Cliffs, N.J.

Lashley, K. S., and J. B. Watson, 1913, Notes on the Development of a Young Monkey, *J. Anim. Behav.* **3:**114–139.

Schneirla, T. C., 1957, The Concept of Development in Comparative Psychology, in *The Concept of Development,* D. B. Harris, ed., University of Minnesota Press, Minneapolis.

Small, W. S., 1899, Notes on the Psychic Development of the Young White Rat, *Am. J. Psychol.* **11:**80–100.

Stone, C. P., 1922, The Congenital Sexual Behavior of the Young Male Albino Rat, *J. Comp. Psychol.* **2:**95–153.

Watson, J. B., 1903, *Animal Education,* University of Chicago Press, Chicago.

Yerkes, R. M., 1927, The Mind of a Gorilla: Part II. Mental Development, *Genet. Psychol. Monogr.* **2:**375–551.

# 11

Reprinted from pages 113–117 and 172–174 of *The Nature and Development of Animal Intelligence,* Macmillan, New York, 1898, 307p.

## THE PSYCHIC DEVELOPMENT OF YOUNG ANIMALS AND ITS PHYSICAL CORRELATION.

### W. Mills

### I.—THE DOG.

#### *Introduction.*

FOR mind and body alike the past determines the present in no small degree; hence it follows that the more perfectly the history of each step in the development of mind is traced, the better will the final product, the mature, or relatively fully-developed mind, be understood. Anatomical researches were long conducted on the bodies of animals before the light thrown on structure by embryology cleared up the obscurities which of necessity hung about parts, the origin and early development of which were unknown.

Comparative anatomy had already done something to give increased significance to anatomy as a whole, but it was only by tracing the animal body back to its primitive germ cells, following these cells in their development into tissues and organs by the naked eye and with the microscope, comparing these changes in one animal with corresponding ones in another, and indeed in plants, and interpreting them all in the light of evolution, that the present status of biology has been reached.

Psychology is as yet in no such position; but it

must be equally clear to those who, guided by facts alone, untrammelled by tradition and dogma of every kind, compare the pyschic status of the young with that of the mature animal, that psychogenesis is a fact; that the mind does unfold, evolve, develop equally with the body. And as with the body so with the mind, each stage in this development can only be understood in the light of all the previous stages.

This truth is apparently as yet only dimly comprehended, for, till recently, studies on psychic history, development or psychogenesis have been all but unknown, and as yet, even in the case of man, are very few and confessedly imperfect.

But just as we have an ontogeny and phylogeny, just as the anatomy, physiology, and pathology of man are clearer from comparative studies on creatures lower in the scale, so must it be in regard to man's psychology.

It follows, then, that all researches in comparative psychology must be as welcome for the general science of mind, and the special study of human psychology, as those in comparative anatomy are to anatomy in general, or the anatomy of man in particular.

Till very recently animals below man seem to have been almost wholly neglected or misunderstood in all that pertains to their psychic nature, one very obvious result of which has been the inability to connect the psychic states of man with others of similar, yet often simpler, character in lower animals, not to mention the impossibility of a science of mind in general, or a true understanding of the psychic side of man's nature. Studies in infant psychology are of comparatively recent date, few in number, and in most instances very incomplete; while, as regards animals lower in the scale, such investigations are still more imperfect.

The relations of mind and body in both health and

disease have been made the subject of considerable speculation and some valuable research, but the subject is vast, and will unfold but slowly till our knowledge of many things is greatly increased.

Much depends on the philosophical or scientific attitude of the worker, as to the views he holds on such a subject, or the interpretations he puts on observed facts.

Nevertheless, to him who can lay aside prejudices—sanctioned, it may be, by ages of belief—it is possible to see that old interpretations fail, and that problems of the mind, which the world has either ignored or grappled with in vain, must be attacked from new standpoints.

### *History and Objects of the Present Research.*

In consequence of the foregoing and many other convictions, some ten years since, I suggested to the students of the Faculty of Comparative Medicine and Veterinary Science of M'Gill University the desirability of forming a Society for the study of Comparative Psychology, more especially for the study of the psychic nature of those animals with which they would be professionally most brought into contact. During this period, more than formerly, I myself bred and reared large numbers of the smaller of the domestic animals and pets with a view of understanding them in all their varied aspects.

The longer, however, I continued my studies, the more I became convinced that, as in every other case to succeed best, one must begin at the beginning. Accordingly I have for a few years kept full, and I hope accurate, notes of the development, psychic and physical, of individuals belonging to several different groups of the above-mentioned animals.

My purpose may be stated about as follows :—

(1) To give a detailed history of the psychic development up to a certain age of representatives of several animal groups.

(2) To compare groups and individuals.

(3) To correlate the psychical and physical—or, at all events, to make some attempt to connect, in time, the psychic and physical development.

The completion of this work will even, so far as I am able to accomplish it, take a considerable time yet, so that I shall be obliged, in the present paper, to confine myself to one group of animals, viz. dogs, of which I have made a study during the greater part of my life, and more especially within the past ten years, as regards their psychic nature and certain other features.

The present paper will be founded chiefly on the notes or diary of three litters of puppies—two of the St Bernard and one of the Bedlington terrier breed.

These histories, then, will concern, it will be observed, only pure-bred dogs, as I have not as yet similar notes on mongrels. As the dog is, after the monkey, more like man psychically than any other animal, I hope to make some comparisons with the development of the young human being, though possibly not in this paper.

Inasmuch as the diary of the last litter of St Bernard puppies studied is more complete, and was written in the light of my past experience, I regard it as much the most valuable. It will therefore be given first of all, as written day by day, with only a few verbal alterations, from which each reader may form his own independent conclusions.

This I purpose to follow by certain remarks. As my work on the brain especially is not yet complete, the physical correlation which has to do chiefly, of course with the nervous system, will be less fully treated than the psychical development.

[*Editor's Note:* Material has been omitted at this point.]

SOME CONCLUSIONS.—The dog is born blind and deaf. He possibly smells and tastes feebly, but this is difficult of demonstration ; but in any case he smells, tastes, has tactile and muscular sensations, the temperature sense, and can experience pain before he can either see or hear.

The eyes are open before the ears, but seeing objects does not correspond in time with the opening of the eyelids, which is gradual, the result of processes of growth and absorption. Hearing follows sooner on complete opening of the ears than seeing on opening of the eyes.

There is progressive improvement in both seeing and hearing.

Both begin about the 17th day, and are in a high state of perfection about the 30th day, hearing being, upon the whole, rather more rapid in development.

Smell and taste are demonstrable on the 13th day, and are well developed about the 30th day.

Newly born dogs are very much affected unfavourably by a temperature below a certain moderate point (50° or 60° F.), and are capable from the first of such movements as enable them to avail themselves of the heat from the mother's body.

They give evidence of feeling hunger, and are capable of making certain slow movements at birth.

They find the teats chiefly, if not wholly, by touch, and continue sucking in consequence of the satisfaction of the appetite for food.

Up to about the 20th day puppies are very readily fatigued, and incapable of attention to anything for more than a very few seconds at one time.

They early show an appreciation of any decided

change in the environment, indicating that experience, even in the earliest days, is not lost on them. In other words, the environment does and must act on the nervous system, with results that manifest themselves if in no more definite way, at least in this : that new experiences (stimuli) cause comfort or discomfort, as evidenced by quiescence or wriggling, cries, etc.

Co-ordinated muscular movements appear in greatest perfection in a certain order, viz. mouth and head parts, fore-limbs, hind-limbs, tail, etc.

These seem to be related to the order of development of the centres of the cerebral cortex.

The epochs most differentiated from each other in the psychic and somatic life of the dog are (1) that prior to the opening of the eyes, and (2) that subsequent to this event.

The former suggests intra-uterine life by its negative character, and is well marked off from the period that follows, the more numerous avenues of knowledge existing, and their utilisation, and in other respects not well understood, of the latter period. In other words, the animal, after this period, can come more fully in contact with environment, with corresponding results in its development. It seems, besides, more impelled to do so ; there is more vim in its whole nature. A transition period between the time when the eyes and ears begin to open, and when the animal actually sees objects and hear sounds, may also be recognised.

The era of most rapid and most important development is subsequent to the period when seeing and hearing are established—when the animal is in possession of all its senses, etc. This extends between the 20th and the 45th day approximately.

Suggestive action, beginning perhaps with the first manifestations of the play instinct, has, especially as time passes, a very important share in determining the direction of development, and what manner of dog the individual becomes. It is education in the more limited sense.

The order of development of the senses and co-ordinated movements as well as reflexes, and the manifestation and perfecting of instincts, have a distinct relation to the needs, as well as the general development of the animal, *e.g.* smell is always more important to the dog than any of his other senses, and it is early developed. The same remark applies to the movements of the jaws and the limbs over those of other parts.

The detailed study of the development of the dog, as recorded in the foregoing pages, illustrates how dependent all subsequent advancement is on the early and full development of the senses and co-ordinated movements. They bring the nervous centres into contact, so to speak, with the environment.

The same is illustrated in the study of the human infant; but in the case of the dog the investigation is not surrounded by the same complications or, at all events, prejudices.

Although it is not possible as yet to determine the physical and psychic correlations down to the minutest details, from what has been accomplished, it seems reasonable to hope that a complete correlation may be ultimately established.

The first sixty days of a dog's existence are of so much more consequence than any later period, that the writer has decided to limit this paper to this period, within which almost all important features in development appear.

[*Editor's Note:* Material has been omitted at this point.]

**12**

Reprinted from *Psychol. Rev.* **33**:51–58 (1926)

# THE DEVELOPMENT OF BEHAVIOR IN VERTE-BRATES EXPERIMENTALLY REMOVED FROM THE INFLUENCE OF EX-TERNAL STIMULATION

BY LEONARD CARMICHAEL

*Princeton University*

The behavior of an adult vertebrate differs radically from the behavior of a young individual of the same species. What are the factors which bring about this differential transformation? Is this modification of activity the result of environmentally conditioned learning or of the maturing of certain innate behavior patterns or 'instincts'? The experiments recorded in this paper were undertaken in an effort to throw some additional empirical light upon certain phases of this question.

## PART I. EXPERIMENTAL

The specific problem of the present investigation was the determination of the nature and the speed of the process by which developing vertebrates first acquire the ability to carry out muscular movements. The work was done upon the embryos of the frog (*Rana sylvatica*) and the salamander (*Amblystoma punctatum*). A relatively short time is required for the development of these embryos from fertilized eggs into larvæ with well-coördinated swimming movements. The fundamental procedure of the investigation consisted in the comparison of the movements of larvæ which were allowed to develop 'normally' with the movements of larvæ which were reared under such experimental conditions that they showed no gross bodily movements until released by the experimenter.

The embryos used in these experiments developed from eggs found in masses in small pools in the neighborhood of Princeton, New Jersey. In all cases the eggs were in very early stages of cell division when they were brought into the

139

laboratory.   The technique of the experiments, save where noted to the contrary, was the same for both the *rana* and *amblystoma* embryos.

In the laboratory the protecting jelly was removed from the individual eggs.   This somewhat tedious process was accomplished by holding a few of the jelly-surrounded eggs upon a piece of very damp paper toweling by means of a wide-mouthed pipette.   Then, by the use of needles, the individual eggs were teased out of the jelly.   The bare eggs were kept at all times in covered glass dishes filled with tap water.   The embryos were allowed to grow in these dishes until the head and tail 'buds' could be observed.   Body movements do not appear in these organisms until a stage much later than this early head and tail bud period; indeed at this stage the peripheral nervous system has not developed.[1]

The embryos in this early head and tail bud stage were, in all of the experiments, divided into two similar groups. One of these sets, the *control group*, was placed in a development dish filled with tap water.   The other set, the *experimental group*, was placed in a development dish filled with a solution of chloretone (chlorbutanol).   Previous work had shown that living organisms placed in a solution containing certain concentrations of this drug continue to grow, but they never exhibit any body movements in response to external stimulation while they are under the influence of the anæs-thetic.[2]   The present experiments confirmed this observation. Some little difficulty was experienced in determining the optimal concentration of the drug in which to raise the experimental groups.   If the solution was too weak the embryos would show some slight movement in response to strong stimulation while still supposedly under the influence of the anæsthetic.   When movement of this sort occurred the

[1] *Cf.* Herrick, C. J. and Coghill, G. E., 'The Development of Reflex Mechanisms in Amblystoma,' *J. Comp. Neur.*, 25, 1915, pp. 67 and 82.

[2] *Cf.* Randolph, H., 'Chloretone (Acetonchloroform): An Anæsthetic and Mascerating Agent for Lower Animals,' *Zool. Anz.*, 23, 1900, pp. 436–439.   Also, *cf.* Harrison, R. G., 'An Experimental Study of the Relation of the Nervous System to the Developing Musculature in the Embryo of the Frog,' *Amer. J. Anat.*, 3, 1904, pp. 197–220.   The writer is indebted to Professor S. R. Detwiler for suggesting the use of this method in the problem reported here.

entire experimental group had to be discarded. On the other hand, if the solution was too strong the embryos developed morphological abnormalities. Typical of such defects was a great bloating of the body which either resulted in death or seriously interfered with later observations on movement. The best concentrations of chloretone for the proper development of the *rana* and *amblystoma* embryos were found to be somewhat different. Good results were obtained with the frog embryos raised in a solution containing, by weight, 3 parts of chloretone in 10,000 parts of water. For *amblystoma* the best results were obtained in a solution containing 4 parts of chloretone in 10,000 parts of water. Acceptable results however were secured in solutions differing slightly from those noted above.

In all cases the experimental and control groups were kept in covered glass dishes on the same table. No especial effort was made to regulate the temperature or the light of the room in which the investigation was carried on. Both the experimental and control groups were thus at all times subject to the same conditions. Morphologically the development of the control and the experimental embryos was, in the best examples, quite similar. In all cases the larvæ in the tap water grew more rapidly in size than did those in the chloretone solution.

At a certain point, as previously noted by Drs. Herrick and Coghill,[1] the developing embryos of the control group began to respond to the stimulation of slight touches of a slender rod. Very soon after such responses had been first elicited, both in the frog and salamander embryos, a coördination of responses was effected which culminated in rapid swimming movements. Similar stimulation elicited no movement in the experimental embryos at this stage or at any other period, so long as the animals lived and were kept in an anæsthetic solution of proper concentration. From day to day these drugged larvæ showed a gradual morphological development; otherwise they were absolutely 'inert.'

In the organisms raised under these experimental con-

[1] *Loc. cit.*

ditions, therefore, bodily movement in response to external stimulation was absent during growth.   Long before muscular response commenced in the normal embryo these experimental larvæ were placed in the chloretone solution, and until released by the investigator they gave no evidence whatsoever of behavior.

The method of liberating each embryo from the influence of the drug consisted in lifting it with a pipette from the chloretone solution and placing it in a large dish of tap water. The time after the organism was placed in the unmedicated water until it elicited the first movement in response to the stimulation of a slender rod was taken by the use of a stop watch.   The tables given below indicate this time to the nearest minute for the frog and salamander embryos.

### Tables Showing the Time After Removing Embryo From Anæsthetic Before First Response to Stimulation Was Observed

#### Table I

##### Amblystoma

| Embryo number | 1 | 2 | 3 | 4 | 5 | 6 | 7 | 8 | 9 | 10 |
|---|---|---|---|---|---|---|---|---|---|---|
| Time in minutes | 14 | 25 | 9 | 7 | 6 | 8 | 8 | 7 | 24 | 13 |

| Embryo number | 11 | 12 | 13 | 14 | 15 | 16 | 17 | 18 |
|---|---|---|---|---|---|---|---|---|
| Time in minutes | 9 | 9 | 12 | 11 | 5 | 5 | 28 | 8 |

#### Table II

##### Rana

| Embryo number | 1 | 2 | 3 | 4 | 5 | 6 | 7 |
|---|---|---|---|---|---|---|---|
| Time in minutes | 10 | 14 | 11 | 7 | 9 | 15 | 15 |

The conclusion of the present preliminary experiments is, therefore, that in a period of time which averages less than twelve minutes, embryos raised under conditions of absolute artificial inactivity are able to respond to external stimulation. In varying lengths of time after this first movement, but in all cases in less than thirty minutes, the previously drugged embryos showed coördinated swimming movements.   In fact a number of the eighteen *amblystoma* embryos swam so well in less than one half hour after they had shown the first sign of movement, that they could with difficulty, if at all, be distinguished from the members of the control group who had been free swimmers for five days.[1]

## PART II.   THEORETICAL

May the results of this experiment be interpreted as giving additional support to the theory that the maturing of innate factors alone accounts for the development of the neuro-muscular mechanism upon which behavior depends?   Certainly the results of the experiments recorded above seem to show that the reflex system of these organisms is able to function in a manner which is biologically useful to the animal in a very short time after the first signs of behavior are noted. But is this rapidity of development a sign that these swimming movements were already determined in the fertilized egg? May we class this behavior with those functions of which Professor Woodworth has written, ". . . the only question, regarding such traits, is whether the environment is going to be such as to enable this young individual to live and mature and unfold what is latent within it"?[2]   It does not seem to the present writer that this 'maturation hypothesis'[3] is necessarily substantiated by the facts discovered in the experiments reported above.   Much recent work upon the development of the neuromuscular system, as I have shown elsewhere,[4] points to the fact that the growth of this system can only be understood in terms of continuous living function.

[1] Due to many imperfections of technique in the rearing of the earlier series, the 25 cases tabulated are the only ones, out of the many hundreds originally studied, in which the conditions of experimentation were sufficiently controlled to assure scientific accuracy.   The writer hopes to make further studies in this problem in subsequent seasons when the material is again available.   The results recorded here upon *amblystoma* as well as upon *rana* confirm in most respects certain observations previously made by Professor Harrison (*loc. cit.*) upon the frog.

[2] Woodworth, R. S., 'Psychology: A Study of Mental Life,' 1921, p. 91.

*Cf.* also Gates, A. I., 'Psychology for Students of Education,' 1924, pp. 110 *ff.*

[3] *Cf.* Allport, F. H., 'Social Psychology,' 1924, p. 44.

[4] Carmichael, L., 'Heredity and Environment: Are they Antithetical'?   *J. Abn. & Soc. Psychol.*, 20, 1925, pp. 245–261.

The intricate development of such interrelated structures as receptors, nerve trunks, central apparatus and motor end-organs appears to be determined by functional stimulation within the organism itself. The excitation and response of the elements of the neuromuscular system is itself a part of the growth process. It may thus be said that during growth these systems are continuously functioning, and yet before a certain stage has been reached they are not able to serve their typical *purpose* in the organism. This of course does not mean that development is a non-functional and a mysteriously teleological event determined alone by certain elements of the original germ.[1] Indeed, as Dr. Child has well said, "The older conception of ontogeny as a process of construction of a machine which, after construction is completed, begins to function seems less and less satisfactory as our knowledge advances. Living protoplasm is functioning at all times and development is a process of functional construction, that is, beginning with a given structure and function, the continuance of function modifies the structural substratum, and this in turn modifies further function and so on." [2]

It should be remembered, too, that in the experiments recorded above, the swimming reaction was not perfect at the first trial. From the initial twitch to the fully coördinated swimming movements, a continuum of increasingly complex responses could be noted in each organism as it developed through the short period indicated above. It is at present impossible to state to what extent this apparent gradual

[1] In passing it should be noted that there is a real difference in meaning between *function* in the sense of activity and *function* in the sense of biological use. Almost always in development the first sort of function is propædeutic to the second. This distinction is not sufficiently emphasized in Sir Charles Sherrington's paper, 'On Some Aspects of Animal Mechanism' (*Science*, 56, 1922, pp. 345–355). In this article he considers nerve regeneration, which is a process similar in many respects to nerve development, and asserts that: 'What is constructed is functionally useless until the whole is complete.' In a similar manner, this distinction might modify the argument of Professor Ogden, based in part upon this paper of Sherrington, that intelligent behavior is analogous to nerve regeneration because it too is based upon a 'functionless procedure.' ("Crossing 'The Rubicon Between Mechanism and Life,'" *J. Phil.*, 22, 1925, pp. 281-293).

[2] Child, C. M., 'The Origin and Development of the Nervous System,' 1921, pp. 114 f.

perfection of behavior was due to a process analogous to very rapid learning, and how much of it was due to the gradual removal of the 'masking' influence of the drug. The observations, however, show no sudden arrival of fitness.

For the reasons given above there is no obligation on the part of the student to assume that behavior in the experimental cases was the result *merely* of the maturation of certain innate factors.

Is it possible, on the other hand, to account for the results of these experiments without any reference to heredity? Dr. Kuo, for example, would dismiss the entire concept of heredity from a behavioristic psychology.[1] May this program be applied to the experimental findings recorded above? It seems to the writer that the facts observed cannot be explained without any reference to heredity. The rapidity and uniformity of the development of the swimming reaction in the experimental larvæ and the unmistakable differences in behavior between the frog and the salamander embryos, even when raised under apparently identical conditions, seems to suggest the basic importance of certain non-environmental influences in the development of responses.

Indeed, it is difficult to see how the facts recorded here, as well as the results of many similar experiments, can be explained save on the assumption that heredity and environment are *interdependently* involved in the perfection of behavior. Is development anything other than a process by which, what is in the last analysis, an hereditary 'given' is transformed by an environmental 'present'?[2]

If this view be true it will appear that any attempted separation of the parts played by heredity and environment in the drama of development can be in logical terms only. Moreover, the sterile products of such verbal analysis are of more than dubious value to science; they may even do much positive harm in education or industry if applications are based upon them.

[1] Kuo, Z. Y., 'A Psychology without Heredity,' PSYCHOL. REV., 31, 1924, pp. 427–448.

[2] As I have suggested before (Carmichael, L., *loc. cit.*, p. 260.) this *interdependence* view of the development of behavior has much in common with the 'convergence theory' of Professor W. Stern. *Cf.* his 'Psychology of Early Childhood,' 1924, p. 51.

In summary, it may be said that the preliminary experiments recorded here successfully demonstrate that in a typical vertebrate form the development of the structures upon which behavior depends may apparently occur during a period when there is no observable response to environmental stimulation. The structures so developed however are not able at their initial appearance to serve the purpose which they ultimately perform in the adult organism.   Theoretically, it is held that these facts do not demonstrate that behavior is alone dependent upon the maturation of certain hypothetical innate factors.   Likewise the results do not show that all behavior may be explained alone in terms of environmental conditioning.   It seems probable indeed that the development of behavior in this typical case, if not in all cases, can only be conceived as resulting from the *interdependent* action of both heredity and environment in determining the functional development of the individual.

Part VI

# THE PROBLEM OF INSTINCT

# Editor's Comments
# on Papers 13 Through 17

Comparative psychologists have directed their attention to many behavioral problems. None, however, has been more pervasive in its history than the problems of instinct and instinctive behavior. I would concur with Hess (1953) that through the history of comparative psychology "Although the term 'instinct' has certainly fallen into ill repute . . . it yet remains as the central problem in comparative psychology" (p. 242). The term has suffered from multiple definitions and interpretations and has come and gone in and out of fashion, but some form of the instinct concept seems always to be with us.

John B. Watson is most noted for his later writings, in which he adopted a strongly environmentalistic and behavioristic approach to behavior, especially human behavior. The work of the early John Watson, however, is as deserving of being regarded as the beginning of ethology as any work that has been published. His early views on instinct (Paper 13) are representative. At times one may confuse Watson with the later writings of Konrad Lorenz. Watson recommends the deprivation experiment as a means of detecting instinctive behavior and distinguishes three classes of instincts according to the degree of environmental input interacting in their ontogeny. Statements like "Experiment shows that young animals without previous tuition from parents or from their mates and without assistance from the human observer can and do perform the correct act the very first time they are in a situation which calls for such an act" (p. 377) could have been written by either John Watson or Konrad Lorenz.

The 1920s was a decade of controversy over instinct. Workers such as Bernard, Dunlap, and Kuo wrote early papers critical of the use of the instinct concept. The critics disagreed among themselves as to how radical a change was needed, but all were critical of the usage of the concept. Psychologists such as McDougall, Tolman, and Carmichael defended the use of various instinct concepts. During the decade, Kuo changed his initial position from one of denying the existence of instincts (e.g., Kuo, 1921) to one in which he questioned even the separability of the hereditary from the learned and the separability of instinct from habit. In 1929 Kuo (Paper 14) summarized the activities of the decade as he perceived them. He was as critical of Watson as of any other writer in making his point not that there is no genetic influence on behavior but that the question really is not accessible.

The concept of instinct has remained taboo for many psychologists for many years. This may have retarded the study of behavioral patterns that might be labeled instinctive by some. Nevertheless, the study of such behavioral patterns did continue. An excellent example of such research can be seen in Karl Lashley's 1938 presidential address to the American Psychological Association (Paper 15). Lashley writes about such behavioral patterns as courtship in birds, the construction of spider webs, and von Frisch's studies of honeybee communication. He proposes a model of instinctive activity free of "finalistic speculations" and emphasizes both the sensory control and physiological bases of instinctive activity. The noted ethologist W. H. Thorpe wrote that this paper "independently of Lorenz, but almost exactly at the same time, expressed almost every point of importance which came to characterize the ethological view of instinct" (1979, 47).

A "Symposium on Heredity and Environment" published in the *Psychological Review* in 1947 featured papers by Beach, Carmichael, Lashley, Morgan, and Stone and was summarized by W. S. Hunter (Paper 16). Hunter reviews progress in empirical research since the great instinct debates of the 1920s. He notes that although the term "instinct" was seldom used, empirical research in comparative psychology continued during this period. This activity occurred at a time when most historians view the field of comparative psychology to have been nearly dead (e.g., Papers 3 and 4).

Soon after Hunter's paper, emphasis on the instinct concept was revived with the increasingly frequent appearances of the work of European ethologists on American shores. This provoked a whole new round of criticism from American psychologists. The most substantial and influential of these criticisms was written by Daniel S. Lehrman and is excerpted as Paper 17. Lehrman's critique was wide ranging, dealing not only with the instinct concept but with various other ethological concepts and the levels at which they were studied. This paper is a true classic in the history of comparative psychology and ethology. By no means, however, does it represent Lehrman's final views on the issues. Like the ethologists, Lehrman continued to develop his ideas throughout his career (e.g., Lehrman, 1970). Lehrman's critique provoked reaction from the ethologists and increasing dialogue occurred. As a result, the gap between ethologists and psychologists, which appeared so large in the 1950s, now seems much smaller. This is as it would have appeared earlier in the history of comparative psychology. The problem of instinct, however, is unlikely to disappear soon.

## REFERENCES

Hess, E. H., 1953, Comparative Psychology, *Ann. Rev. Psychol.* **4:**239–254.

Kuo, Z. Y., 1921, Giving up Instincts in Psychology, *J. Philos. Psychol. Sci. Meth.* **18:**645–664.

Lehrman, D. S., 1970, Semantic and Conceptual Issues in the Nature-nurture Problem, in *Development and Evolution of Behavior,* L. R. Aronson, E. Tobach, D. S. Lehrman, and J. S. Rosenblatt, eds., Freeman, San Francisco, pp. 17–52.

Thorpe, W. H., 1979, *The Origins and Rise of Ethology,* Praeger, New York.

# 13

Reprinted from *Harper's* **124**:376–382 (1912)

# Instinctive Activity in Animals

## SOME RECENT EXPERIMENTS AND OBSERVATIONS
### *BY JOHN B. WATSON*

OWING to the increasing demand on the part of the public for a critical survey and evaluation of existing methods of child instruction, and to the widespread scientific attention to the subject of the development of mental life, there has come renewed interest in the study of the early forms of instinctive activity both in the child and in the animal. The students of experimental evolution, too, becoming more and more dissatisfied with the Darwinian conception of instinct—calling as it does for a belief in the "fitness" or "adaptiveness" of all forms of instinctive action — are asking the comparative psychologists to re-examine the forms of animal activity in the light of recent data which have been gathered by experimentally controlling the process of evolution—data which I may say in passing are revolutionizing our present theory of evolution. Both to bring the work in animal behavior in line with these newer facts on evolution, and to assist the child psychologist in his problems, we need to have more exact knowledge of the different types of "native" or "untutored" activity in child and animal.

To what extent are animals supplied with "true instincts" — that is, inherited fixed modes of responding to definite objects or classes of objects which arise independently of tuition, and to what extent are they equipped with more plastic forms of activity which need to be fixed and made definite by tuition in one form or another? If there are animals, species or individuals, which have a faulty equipment of instincts, how do they overcome the difficulty and supplement a poor inheritance; in other words, to what extent can the process of "habit formation" come to usurp, to displace, and to improve upon the more primitive instinctive functions? We must know more than we do at present about the way instincts unfold themselves: we need to know the age at which instincts appear and the order in which they appear; their complexity on first appearance; their further course of development and the objects and situations which call them into being. This search for the objects and situations which bring out instinctive response is of very great importance, since it leads to means of fostering the growth of desirable tendencies, and to the suppression of those undesired.

In the process of returning answers to these questions and to many others of equal importance, there has grown up a large mass of controversial literature. Discussion in the past, however, has been based too much upon opinion, presupposition, and prejudice, and not enough upon earnest scrutiny of the actions of animals under conditions of experimental control. Naturally we ought to expect such conflicts until students of behavior have had long enough time to watch the daily routine of animals from birth to maturity. The data which will finally solve these various problems will come from the experimental study of young animals whose associations with other animals are known, and whose stock of intelligent habits is known. We must bring up certain members of a given species in isolation from their kind in order to watch the development of activity without tuition, and compare the results with those obtained from a set of similar experiments in which the animals are brought up in social contact with fellows of their own age and with adults of the same species. In this laborious way, and only in this way, will we be able to trace the origin of the various types of action, and put ourselves in a position finally to plan our courses of training for child and animal according to a scientific, yet wholly natural, method.

The start we have made in the laboratory and in the field upon our task is a very modest one. We have reached certain results which bear upon the question of the different types of activity displayed by the young animal during the period of most rapid growth. Incidentally several of the other questions raised a moment ago are touched upon.

Our results in so far as they have been reported seem to show that there are at least three great divisions or classes into which we may provisionally throw the acts of animals: Instincts essentially perfect upon their first appearance; instincts which must be supplemented by habit; and finally, random activity of instinctive origin. It must not be supposed that these three classes are bounded by hard-and-fast lines. As a matter of fact, instincts shade off into one another in such a way that an absolute classification cannot be made.

Experiment shows that young animals without previous tuition from parents or from their mates and without assistance from the human observer can and do perform the correct act the very first time they are in a situation which calls for such an act. In other words, when the animal reaches the proper age and meets with the proper stimulus (object), it will behave in such a way that the uninitiated observer might well believe that the animal has been trained to respond in this highly special way.

The most complete piece of experimental work bearing upon this subject is that of Professor Yerkes and Mr. Bloomfield. These investigators, working jointly in the Harvard Psychological Laboratory, made a test of the question, "Do kittens instinctively kill mice?" This question had been answered in the negative about three years ago by Dr. C. S. Berry, who worked in the same laboratory. Dr. Berry reached the conclusion that "cats are credited with more instincts than they really possess. It is commonly reported that they have an instinctive liking for mice, and that mice have an instinctive fear of cats. It is supposed that the odor of a mouse will arouse a cat, and that the odor of a cat will frighten a mouse. My experiments tend to show that this belief is not in harmony with the facts. When cats over five months old were taken into the room where mice were kept they did not show the least sign of excitement. A cat would even allow a mouse to perch upon its back without attempting to injure it. Nor did the mice show any fear of the cats. I have seen a mouse smell at the nose of a cat without showing any sign of fear." . . . It was not until the manx kittens had seen the mother cat catch and kill the mice and had eaten of the prey that they learned to do likewise. According to Dr. Berry, it is by *imitation* that the average cat learns to kill and eat mice.

Professor Yerkes and Mr. Bloomfield made a much more extensive test upon the more common varieties of cats. They worked with eight kittens belonging to two separate litters. The animals were brought up by hand and were kept free from the influence of older cats. They tested the kittens with mice much more often and more systematically than did Dr. Berry. When first tested the kittens were too young and undeveloped to notice the mice. The instinct was yet "dormant." In succeeding tests it became perfectly clear that as soon as the kittens reached the proper age—as soon as the instinct "ripened," as Professor William James has expressed it—the congenital mode of response appeared. The authors describe in a very clear and interesting way the behavior of one of the kittens in one of the tests: "No. 7 was attracted by the movement of the mouse and touched it with his nose. He then left it. After twelve minutes he happened to be so placed that he could see the mouse as it began to move. For a few seconds he watched as if fascinated by the sight. Then he moved directly and quickly in spite of the shakiness of his legs to the mouse and seized it in his mouth by the middle of the back, at the same time biting hard and bending his head to the floor so that one paw could be placed firmly on the body of the mouse. In a few seconds he had bitten the mouse to death. Without pause the process of eating was begun. It proved a difficult task, notwithstanding the tenderness of the mouse, but after ten minutes of difficult effort and much gagging it was completed." This kitten was only one month old, and was still weak and shaky in its movements. The negative results reached by Dr. Berry were possibly due to the fact that a different variety of cat was used in his experiment; a more probable explanation is that he did not begin his tests with the animals at a young enough age nor make the tests at frequent enough intervals.

From the field observations of young birds and insects we find similar cases of highly perfected modes of response. In my own observations of the development of the young noddy and sooty terns on Bird Key in the Dry Tortugas, it is quite clear that there are many instincts of the congenital type. When first hatched the birds are about as helpless as the chick. No sign of fear is present. If they are allowed to develop normally in the nest, fear, with its complex series of defensive and offensive attitudes, appears in a very few days. By the end of the third day it becomes next to impossible to take them from the nest and rear them, since they steadfastly refuse to eat. On the other hand, if one takes them a few hours after birth one can rear them by hand almost without loss. The instincts connected with fear become suppressed, and habits of responding to the experimenter are formed to take their place. Even on the first day of their life one can notice certain acts connected with the taking of food from the parent which are characteristic of the species. During the first three days many other complex acts appear, such as the choice of sleeping posture, continued "yawning," preening of the feathers; all acts which are carried out after the model of the parent. These acts appear just as clearly in the young reared in isolation from the adult birds. On the sixth and seventh days one can observe the presence of the fighting instinct in the young birds reared by hand. The movements are complicated, involving coordinations of beak and wing muscles, legs, and of the larger trunk muscles. It appears almost full blown and after the exact pattern of the act of the adult. Certain other instincts, such as that of keeping the nest clean, appear even when the birds are taken from the nest and allowed to grow up in a bare room free

from anything which suggests a nest. Others do not show themselves until after the fighting responses appear, such as "sunning" and those connected with fishing, migrating, mating, etc. The field observations of Professor F. H. Herrick on many different species of birds show in an equally clear way the congenital nature of many of these responses. Along with these so-called adaptive responses there are many which are not adaptive; acts which appear without tuition, but which are not of such a nature as to help in the development of the animal.

It is both tempting and convenient to class all of the great life-maintaining acts in animals, such as those connected with reproduction, with the formation of burrows and the building of nests and dams, under this head of perfected congenital responses, but no one has yet made a careful experimental study of them, and we do not therefore know those which are perfect from the first from those which have to be learned, either by a slow "trial-and-error" method or by imitation and other forms of social influence.

The second class of acts contains those instincts which are partially congenital but not completely so. Many of the acts of animals, even of the simplest and most necessary kind, appear at first in a very imperfect and halting way. These acts must be perfected before they become of maximum service to the animal.

Professor Breed, of Michigan University, while working in the Harvard laboratory, undertook to test the accuracy and perfectness of some of the fundamental acts of the chick. He chose for the work the all-important act of pecking. It appears that this act for purposes of exact study must be divided into three separate responses: striking (at small grains, for example), seizing, and swallowing. He measured to what extent each of these divisions is perfect at birth; and since all were imperfect, he made daily tests of the increase in accuracy. Pecking as a whole improved very rapidly for the first two days, then more slowly, until the maximum of efficiency was attained about the twenty-fifth day. Striking improved most rapidly, being almost perfect by the fifth day, while seizing improved most slowly. From

Breed's work it appears that the effect of social influence—of having present older chicks which had already perfected the act—was hardly noticeable. Each chick had to learn the act by his own unaided efforts.

That social influence, in the form of imitation, rivalry, or in whatever other ways social influence may exert its effect, does play a rôle in shaping the early responses of certain other animals comes out clearly in the work of Conradi at Clark University. This investigator reared English sparrows in the presence of canaries, keeping them from birth separate from their own kind. The first sparrow was captured when one day old, and was reared by a canary foster-mother. During the growing period this sparrow was isolated from all other sparrows and placed in a room containing about twenty canaries. The native characteristic "chirp" first developed. As time went on this was given less and less, being gradually replaced by the "peep" which is natural to the canaries. The sparrow improved in his vocal efforts by this kind of training; gaining the confidence finally to chime in when the canaries would burst into song. A second sparrow was captured when two weeks old, and was reared in a room with the canaries. The regular sparrow chirp had, of course, already developed by this time. After being with the canaries for a time he developed a song which more or less resembled that of the canaries—it was certainly something very different from the ordinary song of the sparrow. Dr. Conradi says: "At first his voice was not beautiful; it was hoarse. It sounded somewhat like the voice of the female canaries when they try to sing. He sang on a lower scale; he often tried to reach higher notes, but did not succeed. Later he learned to trill in a soft, musical manner." In both these cases the call notes of the canaries were adopted. These two sparrows were then taken from under the tutelage of the canaries and placed in a room where they could hear the song and call-notes of adult sparrows. For the first two or three weeks the integrity of the song and call-notes learned from the canaries was maintained. At the end of the sixth week, however, they had lost practically every vestige of the acquired canary song.

It is impossible to say just how many of the more complicated acts of animals, which up to the present time have been supposed to be implanted by "nature" in a highly finished form, really belong to this group that has to be supplemented and improved by tuition in one form or another. I strongly suspect that the number of instincts which are really congenitally perfect is very small indeed, and that this second class will be found to be much larger than we have experimental grounds for affirming it to be at the present time.

The third class of responses which may, in lieu of a better name, be called random activity, is one which appears for the first time in the life of the child or animal in a yet more indefinite form. In the former two classes of instincts there is displayed upon the part of the animal the attempt, which is always more or less successful, to respond to some object or class of objects, such as striking and seizing food, picking up sticks, straws, and shells, digging in earth or wood, escape from an enemy, and attack upon prey or enemy. In the present class of acts neither is the muscular response definite, nor is the object calling it forth specific and well defined. I have in mind the random acts of children and all higher animals which are made in response to the indefinite stimulation of warmth and cold, smells and tastes, light and darkness, hunger and thirst. The higher we go in the animal scale the greater is the number of these random movements. It has been said that the human child has no instincts at all comparable with those of the animal, but this is true only with respect to the first two classes of instincts. As regards the presence of the third class of instinctive activity, it is certainly true that the child is sensitive to a wider range of stimuli and can respond to such stimuli by a more varied assortment of movements than any other animal. It is these random movements which are utilized in building up the great store of habits which make the artisan, the musician, the actor, the financier, and the conventional society man.

How habit formation is built upon these random acts shows at its best in the way the very young child learns to control the simple objects in its environment. The bright, noisy rattle if presented to a child only a few months old will almost immediately call forth movements from the hands, the mouth, the feet, and, in fact, from the whole body. None of these acts is especially directed toward this object because of any inherent qualities in it; substitute any small, bright, noisy object and the movements will still be called forth. If we continue to confront the infant with the rattle, however, the hands at some time or other are most likely to come into contact with it, and the child learns slowly and by repeated trials that it can control the article in this way. As soon as the habit of controlling it with the hands is established, the movements in the other parts of the body are no longer called forth, and this one object soon comes to bring out as definite an act from the child as the mouse calls out in the kitten. The more complex habits of eating, speaking, and of reading, writing, and drawing, are built thus by combining these fundamental random acts into systems.

The animals are much like the child in this respect. They also, at least in all the higher forms, are equipped with a wide series of indefinite forms of action. When the hungry puppy is confronted with a puzzle-box containing food, the entrance to which is come at only by pulling out a plug which holds the door, he has no fixed instinctive act which is going to help him out of his difficulty. He attacks the problem as best he can by clawing at the box everywhere, biting, pushing, and pulling everything seen and touched. In this group of random acts some one act will bring success. If the difficulty is presented often enough, the animal forms the habit of reacting with the right movement just as the child learns to act properly when he sees the rattle. The useless random activity dies away, and the useful act or acts become ingrained in the form of a habit. From the casual observer's standpoint there is no difference between a perfect habit and a perfect instinct. We can separate the two only by the "genetic" method I have already described.

Children differ enormously as regards the types of objects, relations, and situations which call forth these random responses. Two children under my close observation developed different tendencies at a very early age. The first, a girl, was surrounded from her second birthday with trains and mechanical toys of several varieties. Almost no kind of real interest was displayed anywhere between the ages of two and six. The boy, on the other hand, early began to attempt to control these toys, taking up the broken and battered fire-engines, wagons, and trains which had been discarded by his sister. By the time he reached his fourth year the greater part of his playtime was given over to these toys and to the use of what tools were allowed him. I am not arguing here for any fundamental differentiation in the early activity of the two sexes—there may or may not be such differences. But certainly it is clearly established that children differ enormously and fundamentally in their modes of response to the various objects, persons, and conditions that surround them.

This brings us to the practical reasons for putting so much time upon the study of animal instincts, and for making us look with interest upon the very preliminary and tentative beginnings which have been made in the field of instinctive control. As adults we are interested in instinctive tendencies because we realize that our whole lives have been influenced in many surprising and unaccountable ways by them. They determine in large measure our choice of companions, occupations, and our pleasures. I doubt though if we go about in any intelligent way the process of getting the most out of our "favorable" tendencies, or that of the suppression of such other tendencies as hamper us through life. In the education of most of us there probably has been as much neglect in eradicating our undesirable tendencies as there has been failure in singling out and encouraging those which would have made for individual fitness. Any instructor who has had long experience with students can clearly see in many otherwise promising men uneradicated traces of secretiveness, shyness, and diffidence, of too great assertiveness, and of other tendencies which produce a lack of balance in the individual, and which put him at a disadvantage in close competition. I feel that these seemingly slight, yet really distressing, drawbacks to a career might have been prevented had there been sufficient care spent in an early singling out of the tendencies which underlie them, and in taking active measures for their eradication.

The recognition of the possibility of selecting a pursuit in life in line with an individual's tendencies has led to the idea of "vocational training," and to the establishment of "vocational bureaus," to which the youth may go for tests as to his probable future in certain lines of work, and for general advice as to the type of work he is best fitted to take up. Indeed, we hear much sounding of trumpets as to our being able at the present time to make such tests and to point out the proper door of commerce or art for our candidate to enter. So far as concerns the possibility of our being able in the years to come to offer helpful guidance along such lines there can be little doubt. But two things must precede any rapid progress in this direction. In the first place we must go much further than we have at present gone in establishing a technique for making such tests. We can make tests upon memory and attention, upon sensory equipment and upon the acquisition of skill; we can tell when a man is color-blind, and naturally we should be able to advise him against taking up railway engineering or piloting as a profession. We should not advise a man who had deficient hearing, poor pitch memory, and deficient contact sensitivity to go in for a musical career. We know a lot about the factors which go to make up a good journalist, a good diplomat, an excellent judge, a powerful tragedian, and an amusing comedian, but we know these things as the common man knows them. They are not susceptible in the present state of our science of exact formulation. Still more difficult is it to seize upon the early manifestations of these tendencies with sufficient clearness to make our predictions safe and to guard against the possibility of doing serious harm. Now that psychologists are breaking away from academic tradition and are willing to admit that psychology has practical outlets, there is no question in my mind but that the next few years will be fruitful in giving us such a technique.

The other serious obstacle our voca-

tional psychologist will still have to combat even after the above technique is established is the way in which elementary instruction is given. Children are grouped and taught in common from the kindergarten through the college course. Yearly and in some cases oftener the child passes into the hands of a new teacher. The new teacher takes the group in entire ignorance of the impulses, tendencies, strains, and aptitudes of the individual members composing it. Some of the necessary evils of such a system are, first, that certain early tendencies are not watched closely enough and checked while incipient—such as exaggerated opinions of one's own capabilities and powers; tendencies toward seclusion; tendencies toward the acquisition of property and ideas belonging to others, leading on the one hand possibly toward paranoia, melancholia, and other functional nervous diseases, and on the other hand toward criminality. I do not doubt but that early scrutiny of tendencies and the prompt enforcement of corrective habits would spare us many a neuropath and many a criminal, even though in such cases the hereditary equipment be poor. Secondly, many incipient tendencies if properly fostered would lead probably to genius, certainly to a higher average of efficiency. These latter under the present system are unnoted, or are at least uncultivated, and soon die away through lack of stimulation. The main result arrived at by the end of the college course through the system of education in vogue is to give us a body of highly respectable young men and young women conforming rather closely to a common standard of attainment and behavior, but lacking in individuality, and relatively at sea as to how to attack the real problems of life. They are more or less unacquainted with their own possibilities and capabilities, and are fearful of what the future may hold in store for them. They are undecided as to what pursuit to follow. If opulent, they choose the line of least resistance, following parent or guardian into commerce, law, or medicine. If in a less fortunate financial status, they seize the first opening, becoming teachers, clerks, and technical assistants. In a few years many of them after attaining a fixed low level of efficiency realize too late their mistake in the choice of pursuit; but habits gained during these years have crystallized about them, and they are too timid to make new ventures.

This condition of affairs makes vocational tests and vocational predictions exceedingly difficult. Something might be gained by educating a new type of teacher—a research, secondary and high-school teacher combined, one capable of taking a small group of children through the formative period from the earliest grammar grades to graduation from the high school. Wouldn't it be a safe experiment to give three such teachers, with their work suitably differentiated, the responsibility of bringing up a squad of twenty children? Under such a system they might carefully note the individual tendencies, impulses, capabilities, and defects in each child, and could shape their methods of training intelligently. The teacher called for in such work would have to be an investigator: he would look upon his task as a special problem requiring all the care exercised by the research man in the universities. In the laboratories the biologists count as nothing the years of toil given over to the study of the inheritance of certain characters in plants and animals. They patiently record the slightest variation in the successive generations of the forms, noting those which are like the parent stock and those which vary from the original stock. Why shouldn't we train our secondary teachers to face the problem of the development of the child's mind in this same patient way? Their body of records bearing upon the course of the development of the children in their charge would be important material for the advancement of child psychology in general, and would serve as a basis for the tests and predictions of the vocational psychologist. The latter with such data at hand and with what other facts he could glean from his laboratory tests would be in a position to help shape the vocational future of the youth with some assurance.

# 14

Reprinted from *Psychol. Rev.* **36**(3):181–199 (1929)

## THE NET RESULT OF THE ANTI–HEREDITY MOVEMENT IN PSYCHOLOGY

BY ZING YANG KUO

*Shanghai, China*

### INTRODUCTION

The controversy on the question of instinct and heredity in psychology was started some seven years ago. At first it was merely an attempt to show that the concept of instinct had been greatly abused in psychology, and that some restriction of its usage was necessary. The usefulness of the concept of instinct in the social sciences was also questioned. Then, there appeared some articles purporting to deny the existence of instincts. This was followed by the attempt on the part of some of the instinct deniers to remove the entire concept of heredity from psychology and the controversy began to assume a broader form than the mere question of instinct. While the whole issue should be finally decided by future experimentation, it seems opportune to sum up critically the salient features of the controversy and to point out the directions toward which the problems of instinct and heredity have been shifted through recent discussions. In this paper I shall try to examine some of the more important contributions to the problem during recent years and to state my final view on the matter. I shall deal with only the more essential points brought forth by recent writers on both sides of the controversy. But as this article is not in the nature of a general review of the recent literature on the subject, no attempt will be made to include in our discussion every writer who has participated in one way or another in the instinct or heredity controversy.

## THE ATTACK OF THE SOCIAL PSYCHOLOGISTS ON INSTINCT

The anti-heredity movement has been participated in by two groups of writers, the social psychologists and the behaviorists. It may be said at the outset that the interest and methods of procedure of the social psychologists in attacking instincts are different from those of the behaviorists, and hence their results are not the same. While the social psychologists attack the problem of instinct from the standpoint of its applicability to social sciences, the behaviorists are interested in it purely as a laboratory problem.[1]

Among the social psychologists who have participated in the attack on the concept of instinct are Allport, Ayers, Bernard, Dunlap, Faris, Josey, Kantor and others. While these writers differ in details, they seem to agree on the following points in their objection to the concept of instinct.

1. The concept of instinct has been misused and abused. This charge every psychologist, even including McDougall, will admit. But the charge does no harm to the concept of instinct whatsoever. If it has been abused, the remedy is to exercise more care in using it; it does not necessitate the abolition of the concept.

2. Classifications of instincts are always arbitrary. This is also true. But to argue that as the classification of instincts is arbitrary, therefore there are no instincts, is to employ false logic. For it is obvious that the arbitrariness of classifying instincts is no evidence against the existence of instincts.

3. The animistic conception of instinct, a concept that defines instinct in terms of inner forces, is unacceptable on

[1] Personally I do not have the slightest interest in such subjects as social psychology. I doubt very much that such a science can be established without assuming some over-individual mind or over-individual behavior. If social psychology deals merely with the responses of the individual to social stimulation, as some recent writers have claimed, it belongs to the domain of the general science of human behavior· For, except the movements of the foetus and of the very young infant, practically every human behavior is social in nature. If social psychology studies the social behavior of the individual, what then, will be left for general psychology?

scientific grounds. But does this point help the case? For note the so-called mechanistic view of instinct which defines instinct in terms of the nervous system has no better scientific ground than the animistic one.[2]

4. Practically all the asserted human instincts are, in the last analysis, acquired habits. The present writer in his earlier writings on the subject also made the same point.[3] This seems to be the great point made by the instinct attackers. But is the point well taken? It must be remembered that this point is based on the sharp distinction between learned and unlearned reactions. Such a distinction is as unsound as the concept of instinct itself.[4] Indeed, to deny instinct without at the same time rejecting the concept of habit is self-contradictory,[5] as we shall see more clearly later on.[6] If the instinct deniers show that the asserted human instincts are acquired habits, the instinct psychologists will demand, with equal justification that the instinct deniers explain those experimental results which have demonstrated unlearnedness in certain activities. In other words, only by accepting the validity of the distinction between the learned and unlearned responses, can the social psychologists deny the entire concept of instinct. Furthermore, most of the leading instinct psychologists have repeatedly asserted that there are no pure instincts in human adults, that is, most of the human instincts are overlapped, modified or superimposed by habits so that it is very difficult to find any pure instincts in human adults. Now if the instinct deniers find no instincts in human adults, it does not weaken the position of the instinct psychologists, for few of them have ever

[2] See Kuo, Z. Y., 'A Psychology without Heredity,' PSYCHOL. REV., 1924, 31, 427–448; also Carmichael, L., 'Heredity and Environment,' *J. Abn. & Soc. Psychol.*, 1925, 20, 245–260.

[3] Kuo, Z. Y., 'Giving up Instincts in Psychology,' *J. Phil.*, 1921, 18, 645–664; also, 'How are our Instincts Acquired'?, PSYCHOL. REV., 1922, 29, 344–365.

[4] See my 'A Psychology without Heredity,' *loc. cit.*

[5] See Woodworth, R. S., 'A Justification of the Concept of Instinct,' *J. Abn. & Soc. Psychol.*, 1927, 22, 3–7.

[6] Dunlap seems to be the only one among the instinct attackers of the social psychology group who does not accept the distinction between the learned and the unlearned or between instinct and habit. See his article on 'The Identity of Instinct and Habit,' *J. Phil.*, 1922, 19, 85–94.

insisted that adult human behavior is instinctive. Indeed we
have made our attacks on the instincts from a wrong angle.
From the very start, we accepted the validity of the concept
of heredity in psychology and emphasized the antithesis
between the inherited and the acquired. We were thus
driven to the absurdity of defining instincts in terms of
smaller units and relegating them to infants and animals.
As long as animals and infants possess instincts, no matter
how simple they may be, the attempt to retain the concept
of instinct is justified. As a matter of fact, the social psychologists have not actually denied instincts at all, they
simply reduced the instincts to smaller units (this is also
true of my own immature articles already referred to). They
have accomplished their purpose in showing that the acceptance of instinct is valueless for the social sciences and for
social psychology, but they have left the concepts of instinct
and heredity in psychology as unvitiated as before. Moreover, in their reconstruction of social psychology, they have
substituted for instinct something just as objectionable as
the instinct concept itself, namely, the concept of habit.
Dunlap's substitution of desires for instincts makes the case
even worse. In fact, judging from Dunlap's conception of
desire one will be inclined to think that Dunlap's objection
to instinct is simply because the instinct concept is not
mysterious enough, that is, not so mysterious as to make it
'conscious' and 'introspectively observable.' [7]  Indeed, those
who have acquired a morbid phobia about 'consciousness'
and 'introspection' will certainly think that the concept of
instinct is really better.

5. These social psychologists not only accepted the validity
of the concept of heredity in general, but also emphasized the
importance of the inheritance of the so-called 'mental' or
behavior traits. Dunlap's 'Social Psychology' serves as the
best example.

6. That most of the social psychologists who have participated in the anti-instinct movement are not interested in
the instincts as a laboratory problem cannot be denied.

[7] See Dunlap, K., 'Instinct and Desire,' *J. Abn. & Soc. Psychol.*, 1925, 20, 170–173.

Their writings are really of what Watson has called the arm-chair variety. Indeed, if these social psychologists ever looked to the laboratory for the solution of the instinct problem, they would not have been so bold as to assert that only infants and animals possess instincts. As a matter of fact, the behavior of animals is much more complex and variable and much less stereotyped than they have imagined at their writing desks. In my recent studies on the behavior of the cat towards the rat, which will soon be reported in the Journal of Comparative Psychology, I have come to the conclusion that neither the concept of instinct nor that of learning nor both together can explain the development of the cat's behavior. We will recur to this matter at the end of this paper. I am merely interested here in pointing out that the problems of instinct and heredity can never be solved by armchair speculations.

7. It is curious to note that in spite of their vigorous attack on the concept of instinct, many of these social psychologists have accepted the notion of inherited nervous disposition without any question. Bernard's conception of heredity is just this sort of thing. I have elsewhere pointed out that the neurological speculations concerning instinct are ungrounded. I shall try in a later section of the paper to make my point clearer.

8. More curious still is the fact that the instinct attackers of the social psychology group have, either explicitly or implicitly, followed the instinct psychologists in accepting the preformation theory. Carmichael has criticized Bernard and Allport in that, in spite of their denial of instinct, their own conceptions of heredity are just as preformistic as the concept of instinct.[8] I think the criticism is well founded. It will be unfair, however, if we make the same charge against Josey, who, to my mind, is the most thorough-going and most consistent among the instinct deniers of the social psychology group.[9]

In brief, my objection to this group of writers is that they

[8] Carmichael, L., *op. cit.*
[9] See Josey's 'Social Philosophy of Instinct.'

are half-hearted, inconsistent, and somewhat insincere in their denial of instincts, that they simply try to push the concept of instinct outside the domain of social psychology and the social sciences without making any further attempt to solve the problem, and that they have paid too little attention to the laboratory side of the problem, being content with pure armchair speculations which have always been the chief characteristic of the instinct psychologists. Now, let us turn to the behaviorists and see how they look at the problem.

## THE ATTITUDE OF THE BEHAVIORISTS

For more than ten years the behaviorists were busily engaged in their quarrel with the mentalists over the questions of consciousness, thinking and introspection. They seemed to be so fully occupied that neither time nor energy was left for them to critically examine the concepts of instinct, heredity, and trial and error. Furthermore, these concepts have been in vogue among the animal workers. And behaviorism is a product of animal psychology. The result is obvious. The behaviorists accept instinct, heredity, habit and trial and error *in toto* without questioning their validity. Thus, we find that such topics as instinct, emotion, and habit occupied the greater part of Watson's earlier books. Even as late as 1924 Watson made no attempt to correct his views on instincts, emotions and habit, when he revised his 'Psychology from the Standpoint of a Behaviorist.' This is also true of the earlier publications of Lashley, M. Meyer and Weiss.[10]

However, after the anti-instinct movement had been started, practically all behaviorists began more or less to realize the necessity of revising their former views on the

[10] In a personal communication Professor Warren informed me that Dr. E. B. Holt rejected the concept of instinct long before any anti-instinctivistic article had appeared. But, unfortunately, so far Dr. Holt has not seen fit to publish his views, although, judging from his comments on my articles through correspondence, I am reasonably sure that he must be classified among the radical instinct deniers. (Professor H. S. Langfeld, in his article on 'Consciousness and Motor Response' has informed us of a forth-coming book by Dr. Holt on 'Animal Drive, Instinct and the Learning Process.' But as these lines are written, I have not been able to ascertain whether or not Dr. Holt's book has appeared.)

matter. The change in Watson's attitude toward instinct is most spectacular and somewhat radical. Since Watson has made a most vigorous attack on instinct during the last two or three years, we may be justified in confining our present discussion to this author alone.

There can be no manner of doubt that Watson has attacked the problem of instinct purely from the laboratory standpoint. He has come to the conclusion that there are no instincts because he could not find them in the nursery. While I am in full agreement with Watson in several aspects of his recent view on heredity, especially his analogy of instinct with the boomerang,[11] I feel compelled to part company with him on the following points:

1. While denying the existence of instincts, Watson still retains the distinction between the learned and the unlearned. Such a retention will make Watson's position very difficult. Are not the instinctive actions always considered as unlearned actions? If there are no instincts, on what ground, then, can we classify responses into the learned and the unlearned? In fact, Watson has accepted the traditional criterion of unlearnedness to measure the existence or nonexistence of instincts. Thus, after he has failed to discover any of the asserted human instincts in the nursery, he comes to deny instincts. But if the instinct psychologists can demonstrate to Watson (and I am sure that they can) that there are certain types of reactions which can be performed without learning, will he not be forced to declare that certain instincts do exist? As a matter of fact, no instinct psychologist will insist that every instinct appears in infancy. They will point out to Watson that there are many delayed instincts which appear rather late in human life and therefore are not easy to be detected, due to modification, or to the overlapping and superimposing of habits. Indeed, the failure of the nursery to discover instincts does not preclude the possibility of their appearance in later life. The instinct psychologists may even go so far as to say that even in infancy habits and instincts are already mixed together, and

---

[11] Watson, J. B., 'Behaviorism,' pp. 78–79.

that it is difficult, if not impossible, to distinguish one from the other.[12]

2. That Watson is still loath to give up the whole concept of heredity is clearly evidenced by his two chapters on emotion in his 'Behaviorism.' While in his 'Psychology from the Standpoint of a Behaviorist,' emotion is defined as an hereditary mode of pattern reactions, in the 'Behaviorism' the word 'hereditary' is purposively avoided. But does it improve Watson's position to substitute for heredity such expressions as 'What Emotions Are We Born With?' or 'The Unlearned Emotional Equipment.' Unless they are metaphysical entities, I do not think that the so-called 'emotions' can 'be born with' or 'acquired.' I even do not agree that the behaviorists are justified in retaining the concept of 'emotion.' Men and animals, under stressing situations, may display chaotic and sometimes violent movements. This, of course, we all admit. But they are the direct results of the stressing situations. They are not emotions either in the mentalistic sense or in the sense of pattern reaction. Nor can they be born with, nor acquired. They are what they are because of the stressing situations, because such situations fail to elicit well organized and well regulated responses. If we were to use the word 'pattern' in this connection, at all, the responses under stressing situations are really characterized by lack of definite patterns. Watson may reply that what he means by emotions is just these chaotic and sometimes violent movements or sometimes momentary paralysis of overt movements. But then, he must not speak of them as pattern reactions. Nor should he include such responses as what he has called 'love,' 'jealousy,' 'attitudes,' etc., under the head of emotions; for, beside the vagueness of these terms, they do not belong to the category of chaotic or disorderly or disrupted responses. And, moreover, he should cease to speak any more of inborn or original or hereditary or acquired emotions. Certainly it is a curious inconsistency

[12] In an article on 'The Behaviorist Looks at Instinct' (*Harp. Mag.*, 1927, 155, 228–235), Watson has been driven to the absurdity of accepting, as did the social psychologists, instincts in animals. This is not to be wondered at in view of Watson's acceptance of unlearnedness as a valid criterion of instincts.

for Watson to admit the inborn or original emotions as against the acquired ones, while denying the inheritance of instincts and 'mental traits.'

3. As I have elsewhere pointed out, one cannot consistently deny instinct and heredity without, at the same time, giving up the concept of habit in its traditional sense. Apparently Watson has committed this error.

My quarrel with Watson is that he has hesitated, that he is not thoroughgoing enough in his denial of heredity, and that he seems to be oscillating and somewhat confused in his treatment of instincts, emotions and habits.

Throughout this paper I have criticized practically every author connected with the anti-instinct or anti-heredity movement. I do not mean to imply that I myself have been free from the above criticisms. In fact, in my first two articles on instincts ('Giving up Instincts in Psychology' and 'How Are our Instincts Acquired?'), I practically took the same position as that now held by Watson and the social psychologists. To be specific, in these two articles, I still accepted the validity of the concept of heredity in psychology as well as the antithesis between the inherited and the acquired. I repudiated the concept of instinct chiefly because the current instincts were, in the last analysis, acquired habits. Like the social psychologists, I reinterpreted instincts in terms of smaller units ('units of reaction' or 'random movements'). I also unscrutinizingly accepted the concepts of purpose, drives, motive, tendency, habit, and trial and error. These are the specific and indefensible flaws I now see in the two articles. Through a more careful reading of biological literature, through more critical thinking, and particularly through my experiments with the cats, I have come to a realization that my former attempt to repudiate instincts in psychology was half-way and inconsistent. The article on 'A Psychology without Heredity' was, in part, intended to remedy some of the defects of my former writings. But the present paper will represent more clearly my present view on the matter.

## THE DEFENSE OF THE CONCEPT OF INSTINCT

Let us now turn to those psychologists who have come to the defense of instinct and heredity during the last few years. Here we come to a very curious fact. The defenders of instinct and heredity have contributed more than did the attackers to the complete breakdown of the concepts of heredity and of instinct in psychology. That is to say that these psychologists have tried to defend instincts by first denying them. Thus, Hocking, McDougall, Tolman and Wells have come strongly to the defense of instincts by ringing a death knell to the traditional view of instincts based as it was on physiological assumptions. McDougall would cast out all instincts as they are ordinarily understood by biologists and psychologists of the Thorndike and Watson school and substitute for them some very genuine ones, instincts that are always unrefutable because they are never scientifically approachable. In a similar way, Professor Tolman gives 'the pure reflex pattern theory its final *coup de grace*' [13] and asserts that instincts must be interpreted in teleological rather than in physiological terms. But as I have elsewhere [14] shown and shall later show, Professor Tolman's objective view of purpose is no better than, or is even inferior to, McDougall's straight-forward animism. Hocking's position is essentially the same as that of McDougall in that they both try to rescue instincts from the attack of the instinct deniers by taking them into the custody of a metaphysician of the Bergsonian school. Wells admits all the faults of the instinct concept which have been pointed out by the instinct deniers, but insists that instinct must be redefined. And he redefines it in terms of 'normal environment.' [15] But the concept of instinct as redefined by Wells is no longer the same as that which the biologists and psychologists have been used to understand.

[13] Tolman, E. C., 'The Nature of Instinct,' PSYCHOL. BULL., 1923, 20, 201–202.

[14] Kuo, Z. Y., 'The Fundamental Error of the Concept of Purpose and the Trial and Error Fallacy,' PSYCHOL. REV., 1928, 35, 414–433.

[15] Wells, W. R., 'The Meaning of Inherited and Acquired in Reference to Instinct,' *J. Abn. & Soc. Psychol.*, 1922, 17, 153–161; also 'The Anti-Instinct Fallacy,' PSYCHOL. REV., 1923, 30, 228–234.

Thus, instincts have been defined not by giving actual evidences but by changing definitions. This clearly shows that instinct has not been a fact, but merely a subject for book and article writing. Perhaps this is the most outstanding result of the whole anti-heredity movement. Perhaps this is the result which instinct deniers who have attacked the problem from the laboratory standpoint can best expect. For if the question of instinct (as well as of heredity) is no longer a question of fact but merely a matter of opinion, as the defenses of the instinct psychologists have most clearly shown, the laboratory student may just as well go ahead with his experimental researches without bothering himself with the mere opinions of psycho-metaphysicians.

Other psychologists who have defended the concepts of instinct and heredity have thought that without these concepts behavior cannot be explained. Why do we behave as we do? Why does not the rat behave like the cat? All these questions, so the argument goes, must be answered by such assumptions as instinct and heredity. I do not think that science has to answer these questions at all. I mean that no science should go beyond the descriptive level. Specific stimuli determine specific responses; given a stimulus, a definite response can be predicated. What else do we need besides this for the scientific description of behavior? Those psychologists who always demand abstract principles for the explanation of behavior may profit by taking a lesson from Watson's boomerang. Certainly no modern physical scientists need to assume instinct and heredity in order to explain why electrons, atoms or molecules behave as they do.

Woodworth has recently tried to justify the concept of instinct by showing that since we cannot repudiate reflex and habits, we must keep instinct as a check or foil to habit.[16] Woodworth seems to think that we are unable to cast out the concept of habit. But this is not true. In my experimental researches as well as in constructing a behavioristic system (which will be first published in the Chinese language) I have found that the concept of habit is just as useless to me as that of instinct; in fact, I have found that no single

[16] Woodworth, *op. cit.*

concept or nomenclature of the traditional psychology is of any use for the scientific description of behavior.

As to the concept of reflex, of course, no one can deny that reflex is a concrete physiological fact. But one who still insists that the reflex mechanism is hereditary pure and simple may be referred to such works as those of Child, Detwiler, Kappers and others in order to appreciate the importance of environmental factors in the development of the nervous system.

There are, however, certain psychologists who in recent years have tried to defend the concept of instinct by demonstrating certain types of activities which can be performed without learning. Such facts demand a more serious attention from the experimental standpoint. We shall discuss the question of unlearnedness more fully in a separate section.

### Vitalism or Preformation?

Through recent discussions on the questions of instinct and heredity in psychology it has become clear that the believers in instinct and heredity are either preformists or vitalists. In going over again and again the literature on the subject I have found that not a single instinct psychologist can escape from this dilemma. If we consider the problems of instinct and heredity as experimental problems, I do not think that we need to go into the discussion of the problem of vitalism at all. Vitalism has its place in metaphysics. But it can hardly demand any serious attention from men of science.

The preformation view of heredity as entertained by the contemporary psychologists really belongs to the Roux-Weismann variety. It is essentially a biological theory of the last century, being outgrown, on the one hand, by the more modern form of preformation as advocated by T. H. Morgan and others, and on the other, being completely repudiated by the contemporary epigeneticists such as C. M. Child and others. The antiquity and crudity of the preformation theory in psychology have been clearly pointed out in a series of articles by Dr. Carmichael.[17] It is not necessary

[17] Carmichael, L., *op. cit.* See also his two articles on 'Study of the Development of Behavior in Vertebrates Experimentally Removed from the Influence of External Stimulation,' PSYCHOL. REV., 1926, 33, pp. 51–58, and 1927, 34, pp. 34–47.

for me to discuss this matter any further. I merely want to mention the fact that this crude psychological preformationism is based on a morphological point of view, hence before the theory can claim any serious attention at all, the psychologists must first show that the so-called hereditary responses are reducible to definite and localizable morphological terms. But this is almost impossible for the psychological preformist to do, as I have shown in my article on 'A Psychology without Heredity.' Thus, the theory of psychological preformation is virtually reduced to mere verbal abstraction besides being outgrown by the more modern biological theories.

Psychological preformationism is already dead in view of the recent advances in developmental physiology and in biological theories of development and heredity and in view of the failure of the psychologist to reduce behavior to definite and fixed morphological facts. And the only course which is left for us to take, if we are still unwilling to abandon the concept of heredity in our science, is vitalism. Vitalism or preformation? Or rather vitalism or no heredity? Can any psychologist avoid this dilemma? Those who are not willing to accept McDougall's hormic theory, certainly cannot make any other choice.

### Is a Third Alternative Possible?

In making the above statement I am fully aware of the recent attempts made by several writers to steer a middle course. We have seen the attempt made by Professor Wells to redefine heredity in terms of normal environment. We have also seen Professor Tolman's attempt to objectify the concept of purpose so that instincts may still be retained. Wells' redefinition is really nothing more than a 'verbal trick,' as Dr. Carmichael has clearly pointed out.[18] As to Professor Tolman's behavioristic view of purpose, I should say that it is really McDougall's animism under disguise. If Professor Tolman merely infers from animal behavior that the animal is purposive without reference to the internal

[18] Carmichael, L., *op. cit.*

striving of the animal, the question will immediately arise: what kind of purpose is it? Is not Dr. Tolman's inference that the animal's behavior indicates purpose a mere analogy derived from human introspection. Does not the statement that the animal is seeking for some goal imply that the animal in question is 'consciously striving' for some end? In other words, Dr. Tolman's behavioristic view of purpose is a true animism plus intolerance, that is, he implicitly assumes purposive striving in the mentalistic sense but does not allow us to speak of it in mental or introspective terms. Indeed, Dr. Tolman's theory is intolerant in practice, as well as inadequate in method of procedure; it is inferior to the method of introspection. For by introspection the purpose can be directly experienced, while by inference from behavior, it can only be indirectly assumed; the reliability of such an assumption can never be tested, since we are not allowed to use introspection. Of course, Dr. Tolman may reply that what he means by purpose is not a mental phenomenon but may be reduced to some physiological facts such as nervous disposition or motor set. I have discussed this motor set concept of purpose more fully in another article on 'The Fundamental Error of the Concept of Purpose and the Trial and Error Fallacy.' To avoid unnecessary lengthening of the present paper I will not restate my arguments already presented there.

Let us now turn to a more important proposal to maintain a middle course in the heredity controversy, namely the proposal of Dr. Carmichael. In a series of articles already referred to, Dr. Carmichael refuted the psychological pre-formationism and its derivative, the hypothesis of 'mere maturation' or 'magic birth.' He says that these theories are not in harmony with more recent views of heredity and development in biology. Thus far, Dr. Carmichael seems to be in complete agreement with me. But here, he pauses and finally refuses to travel with me any further on the same path. He protests against my attempt to dismiss the concept of heredity from psychology. He believes that heredity and environment are not antithetical nor separable, but interdependent. He says that every response is just as hereditary as it is acquired. If I understand Dr. Carmichael correctly, he seems to mean that every response *implies* hereditary potentiality. Without hereditary potentiality no response can be actualized. Therefore, he argues, in understanding behavior, the concept of heredity is indispensable. I need not go so far as to deny the concept of hereditary potentialities in biology. As long as the biochemist has not been able to produce living protoplasms of different species from test tubes, some sort of hereditary potentialities will have to be assumed in order to explain why 'like produce like.' But this is purely a biological problem. Whether we need such an assumption in the science of behavior is an entirely different question. Personally I do not think that in our behavior study we need the concept of hereditary potentialities at all. As I have already pointed out, except very simple reflexes, no response can be reduced to definite, fixed and localizable morphological facts. We must remember that in heredity we deal with definite, concrete and localizable morphological structures. When the Mendelian workers attack an hereditary problem, they point to definite bodily characters. But this is almost impossible for us to do in psychology since behavior is so variable, and has no definite bodily characters or definite and fixed neuromuscular patterns. For this reason I recommend that the problem of heredity be ignored in our behavior study. The Mendelians deal with definite bodily characters, hence they can study heredity in mathematical terms. On the other hand, since in behavior we do not deal with definite and fixed neuromuscular patterns, any study intended to measure either qualitative or quantitative differences in the hereditary factors of behavior is out of question. *Heredity must always be concerned with definite physio-morphological facts. Otherwise, it is beyond any experimental approach, and will always remain as an unverifiable abstraction which serves no scientific purpose whatever.*

Carmichael says that in all hereditary maturation there is learning, while in all learning there is hereditary maturation. From this he concludes that the antithesis between instinct and habit must be abolished. Carmichael here seems to reach a wrong conclusion although he has started from a right premise. If it is assumed that hereditary factors are present in every acquired response, and that every acquired response is an actualization of hereditary factors, our conclusion should not be that the antithesis between instinct and habit be abolished, but that both of these concepts must be cast out altogether. For, note, *since hereditary factors are present in every response, and since the qualitative and quantitative differences in heredity between two responses cannot be measured, we will ask: Of what use is the concept of heredity in our behavior study?* In other words, heredity cannot serve as a *differentia* in behavior study, hence it does no harm for us to ignore it in the science of behavior. The student of behavior ignores heredity as he will ignore gravity. That the factor of gravity is present in every response no one can deny. But since its influence is both qualitatively and quantitatively constant and equal in every behavior (except in some very rare cases), it cannot be a basis upon which responses can be differentiated, and we are justified in not taking gravity into account when we investigate behavior. In short, the argument for a psychology without heredity is not necessarily that heredity has nothing to do with behavior but rather that it is not experimentally approachable and that it cannot be a behavior *differentia*.

Heredity is concerned with definite physio-morphological problems. It is fundamentally a biological problem. But it is negligible in the study of behavior. We can accept the organism as given and start to investigate its behavior in response to environmental stimulation without reference to heredity. We need not ask how the organism comes about, or how heredity determines the organismic pattern. This is a question the biologist must answer. When the biologist delivers us an organism of a given species in a given stage of development, our duty is to find out how and what stimuli can effectively force this organism to behave and in what manner it behaves. Behavior is not a manifestation of hereditary factors, nor can it be expressed in terms of heredity;

it is the direct result of environmental stimulation. Behavior is not inherited, nor is it acquired. It is a passive and forced movement mechanically and solely determined by the structural pattern of the organism and the nature of the environmental forces.

## UNLEARNEDNESS AGAIN

Perhaps the chief difficulty for most of us in getting over the concept of heredity lies in the fact that we do not seem to be able to explain the apparent facts of unlearned behavior without reference to heredity. To those experimentalists, such as Chas. Bird, L. Carmichael, C. P. Stone and others who have demonstrated that there are certain types of behavior which can be performed without learning under controlled conditions, our attempt to make a psychology without heredity seems to be a flight from reality. Indeed, if a psychology without heredity is based on the assumption that all responses are postnatally acquired, the work of these experimentalists should be sufficient to discredit the whole assumption.[19] Fortunately, however, our attempt to dismiss the concept of heredity from psychology has nothing to do with this assumption. It is rather based on the view that the two concepts of heredity and learning, of instinct and habit, *whether they are considered as antithetical or as interdependent,* can no longer be used as behavior categories.

Our objections to the use of unlearnedness as a criterion of inheritance may be summarized as follows:

1. Strictly speaking, except the first movement of the fertilized egg, there is no real unlearned response. Every response is determined partly by the present stimulation and partly by the past history of behavior of the organism. While there may be apparent cases of behavior which can be performed without learning, the indirect influence of the past experiences of the organism on the so-called unlearned behavior cannot be denied. If we can use the term 'learning'

[19] In my recent observations of the behavior of pigeons, I found that there are several types of activity which were performed without learning, but not being satisfied with using the mere verbal concept of heredity or instinct to interpret these observations, I am now endeavoring to discover the exact factors which are responsible for the unlearned responses observed.

at all, it must be conceded that learning takes place immediately after fertilization as many recent embryological works seem to have shown. And if we accept the view (as all of us must accept) that every action in response to stimulation has its effect directly or indirectly upon subsequent responses, we could hardly conceive of any purely unlearned behavior in any stage of development.

2. The concept of unlearnedness is based on two false theories, namely, (1) the theory of maturation, (2) the theory of trial and error. In the first theory it is assumed that the neural pathways for the unlearned response is preformed, their synaptic resistance is low so that upon mere maturation they can function without learning, and that, on the other hand, the neural pathways for the acquired behavior must be formed, and synaptic resistance reduced, by practice. Carmichael has shown that recent discoveries of developmental physiology have definitely given discredit to the maturation theory. Indeed, if the development of the nervous system is the result of living functioning, the result of the excitation-response processes between the organism and its environment, the concept of 'mere' maturation of neural pathways becomes meaningless. As to the formation of new pathways in so-called habit-formation, Watson [20] has pointed out many theoretical difficulties for the concept. Besides, Ulrich's work [21] and especially that of Lashley [22] indicate that the formation of new pathways does not seem to take place in the so-called learning. Moreover, Lashley's work has also made the concept of the reduction of synaptic resistance through practice untenable. The fallacy of the trial and error concept has been fully discussed in another article.[23]

3. I have already pointed out in my article on 'Giving up

[20] Watson, J. B., 'Psychology from the Standpoint of a Behaviorist,' p. 293.

[21] Ulrich, J. L., 'Integration of Movements in Learning in the Albino Rat,' *Psychobiol.*, 1920, 2, 375–447, 455–500, and *J. of Comp. Psychol.*, 1921, 1, 1–95, 155–199, 221–286.

[22] Lashley, K. S., 'Studies of Cerebral Function in Learning,' Psychol. Rev., 1924, 31, 369–375; also *Arch. Neur. & Psychiat.*, 1924.

[23] Kuo, Z. Y., 'The Fundamental Error of the Concept of Purpose and the Trial and Error Fallacy,' Psychol. Rev., 1928, 35, 414–433.

Instincts in Psychology' that while a complex act may be performed without learning its component acts are previously acquired reactions.

4. Unlearned behavior can be better explained by other factors than by heredity. This has been discussed in the article on 'How are our Instincts Acquired'?

5. In the article on 'A Psychology without Heredity' I have pointed out that the distinction between learned and unlearned responses is too crude to be of any use for experimental purpose.

In conclusion, let me mention again my observation concerning the behavior of the cat toward the rat. I have found that some cats kill rats without learning, but some will have to 'learn' it by so-called 'imitation,' others 'learn' it by accident. I have also found that cats could be made to 'fear' the rat. But it may even 'love' and protect the rat. Indeed, so variable is the cat's behavior toward the rat that neither the concept of heredity nor that of learning, nor those of instinct and habit, can be used as adequate explanations. The cat can both 'instinctively' kill and 'instinctively' 'love' and protect the rat, but it can also 'learn' to kill and fear the rat.

A psychology without heredity is a psychology which proposes to do away with not only the concepts of heredity and instinct but also all their related concepts such as habit, trial and error, imitation, insight and purpose. It proposes to study behavior as concrete actualities and refuses to be muddled up with any abstract and teleological concepts. Its view is essentially passivistic in that it considers every action as a 'forced' response to be described solely in terms of the functioning of the environmental stimulation. Indeed, unless we take such a view as this, I do not see how we can explain the conflicting results of my observations on the cat's behavior toward the rat.

## 15

Reprinted from *Psychol. Rev.* **45**(6):445–471 (1938)

# EXPERIMENTAL ANALYSIS OF INSTINCTIVE BEHAVIOR [1]

BY K. S. LASHLEY

*Harvard University*

Some of the most remarkable observations in the literature of comparative psychology are reported in Kepner's study of Microstoma (**21**). This creature, related to the more familiar planaria and liver flukes, is equipped with nematocysts or stinging cells like those of the hydroids, which it discharges in defense and in capture of prey. In discharging, the stinging cell evaginates a threadlike barbed tube through which a poison is ejected. The striking fact about the creature is that it does not grow its own weapons, but captures them from another microscopic animal, the fresh water polyp, Hydra. The Hydras are eaten and digested until their undischarged stinging cells lie free in the stomach of Microstoma. The nettles are then picked up by ameboid processes of the cells lining the stomach and passed through the wall into the mesoderm. Here they are again picked up by wandering tissue cells and carried to the skin. The stinging cells are elliptical sacks with elastic walls, which are turned in at one end as a long coiled tube. In discharging, the wall of the sack contracts and forces out the barbed poison tube, from one end of the sack. The nettle cell can therefore only fire in one direction. When the mesodermal cell carries the nettle to the surface, it turns around so as to aim the poison tube outward. It then grows a trigger, and sets the apparatus to fire on appropriate stimulation.

[1] Presidential Address delivered before the New York meeting of the American Psychological Association on April 2, 1938.

When Microstoma has no stinging cells it captures and eats Hydras voraciously. When it gets a small supply of cells these are distributed uniformly over the surface of the body. As more cells are obtained they are interpolated at uniform intervals between those already present. When a certain concentration of the cells is reached, the worm loses its appetite for Hydras and, in fact, will starve to death rather than eat any more of the polyps, which are apparently not a food but only a source of weapons.

Here, in the length of half a millimeter, are encompassed all of the major problems of dynamic psychology. There is a specific drive or appetite, satisfied only by a very indirect series of activities, with the satisfaction of the appetite dependent upon the concentration of nettles in the skin.

There are recognition and selection of a specific object, through the sensory-motor activities of the animal. Later there is recognition of the undischarged stinging cell by the wandering tissue cells, and some sort of perception of its form, so that it may be aimed. The uniform distribution of the nematocysts over the surface of the body is a splendid illustration of a Gestalt, food for speculation concerning vectors and dynamic tensions.

Actually the phenomena of growth so closely parallel those of behavior, or rather behavior parallels growth, that it is impossible to draw a sharp line between them, and animistic theories of growth have been as numerous as mechanistic theories of behavior. Kepner, in fact, postulates a group mind among the cells of the body to account for the internal behavior of Microstoma, to me a *reductio ad absurdum* of mentalistic hypotheses, whether applied to worms or man.

Nevertheless, the naturalistic literature contains many such descriptions, made by careful and accurate observers, of instinctive behavior so complex and precise in its execution that we can only stand aghast at the inadequacy of our concepts of its mechanism. Its genuine relevance to the problems of psychology is well illustrated by the classical definition of instinct as the faculty which animals have instead of intellect which yet makes their behavior seem intelligent.

I am well aware that instincts were banished from psychology some years ago, but that purge seems to have failed of its chief objective. The anti-instinct movement was aimed primarily at the postulation of imaginary forces as explanations of behavior. It was only incidental that these had also been assumed to be constitutional. The psychology of instincts was a dynamics of imaginary forces and the anti-instinct movement was primarily a crusade against such a conceptual dynamism. Somehow the argument got twisted. Heredity was made the scapegoat and the hypostatization of psychic energies goes merrily on. Desires and aversions, field forces and dynamic tensions, needs and vectors, libidoes and means-end-readinesses have the same conceptual status as had the rejected instincts and, besides, lack the one tie to physiological reality which the problem of genetic transmission gave to the latter. The anti-instinct movement was a critique of logical method which failed of effect because it was aimed at a single group of concepts. Its history is a striking example of the lack of transfer of training or the futility of formal discipline.

Although the distinction of genetic and environmental influences has little importance in many fields of psychology, it is of real significance for problems of the physiological basis of behavior. This is true because information concerning the mechanics of development and the histological organization produced by growth is far more exact than any available data concerning the changes produced by learning. Fundamental principles of neural integration may be inferred from innate structure and the behavior dependent upon it. The plasticity and variability of learned behavior precludes any similar correlations with structural patterns.

In spite of a vast literature, there have been few systematic attempts to carry the study of instincts beyond the descriptive stage. Physiologists have been preoccupied with the mechanism of the spinal reflex and students of behavior either have been content to consider instincts as constellations of reflexes clustering around external stimuli or have neglected this side of the problem entirely and, like von Bechterew (4), considered instinct as synonymous with motivation. There are actually two problems here, whose mutual relations are by no means solved. On the one hand are the more or less precise reactions to definite objects. The primiparous female rat gathers paper or other material and constructs a crude nest, cleans her young of the foetal membranes, retrieves the young to a definite locality, distinguishing them often from quite similar objects, assumes a nursing posture, and the like. These are reactions to specific stimuli. The problems which they suggest are those of neural integration; the nature of the stimulus which elicits the response, the pattern of motor activities by which a given result is achieved and, ultimately, the neurophysiology of the behavior.

In contrast to these precise sensorimotor adjustments is the activity which can only be described as reaction to a deficit. The restless running about of the mother rat deprived of her litter, the homing of the pigeon, or the inhibition of feeding responses in the chick removed from companions presents an entirely different system of reactions from those exhibited in the presence of litter, nest, or companions. This reaction to deprivation of some stimulus presents the typical problem of motivation.

For brevity I shall speak of the specific sensorimotor reactions, such as the spider's construction of a web or the courtship display of birds as the instinctive pattern, in contrast to the deficit reactions. The distinction is not always clear. When the humming-bird builds a nest she reacts specifically to lichens and fibrous material but the building to a definite form also suggests reaction to a deficit. The distinction is not a classification of activities but a suggestion of two different problems, reaction to an obvious stimulus and reaction in a situation where there is no external stimulus, or at least none as yet discovered, which is adequate to account for the observed behavior.

In many instinctive activities a further problem arises from the periodic appearance of both the mechanism and the deficit reaction. The migration of fishes, the seasonal nesting of birds, the receptivity of the female rat during œstrus, all such periodic variations in responsiveness raise the problem of the causes of variation in the excitability of the sensorimotor mechanism and of the reaction to deficit. I shall designate this as the problem of activation of the instinct.

For a number of years we have been trying to discover the mechanisms underlying the reproductive behavior of animals. This activity was chosen for study because it presents the most precise instinctive behavior of mammals which can be brought under laboratory observation and because it exhibits a wide variety of problems, both of integrated behavior and of motivation. The work has developed in several directions. I shall summarize the results and attempt to relate them to some of the more general problems of the mechanism of behavior.

## INNATE COMPONENTS OF SENSORY ORGANIZATION

The majority of studies of instinct have dealt with the motor aspects of behavior or with the products achieved. The honey-dance of the bee (von Frisch, 14, 15), the nest of the oriole, the elaborate procedure by which the spider spaces the radial strands of the web (Peters, 29) are so striking as to attract attention away from the problem of the sensory control of the behavior. The general outcome of such studies is familiar. The end attained, the web, the nest, is fairly constant and characteristic of the species. The series of acts by which it is constructed varies with every new element in the environment. Such stereotyped results attained by diverse means have formed the excuse for interpretations of instinct in terms of purpose or entelechy.

Granting the facts, there is still an alternative to such finalistic speculations, which are meaningless to those of us who ask *how* the result is attained. The apparent working toward a goal, which cannot be foreseen, is very difficult to express in terms of a motor mechanism, since the motor activities are variable and therefore cannot be interpreted as a predetermined sequence, run off automatically like an automatized habit. This variability in motor activity compels a search for some controlling factor and this might lie in the characteristics of the animal's perceptual organization. It is possible that the nest, or other product of activity, presents a sensory pattern which is "closed" for the animal, in the sense in which this term has been applied to visually perceived forms. The nest might then be built by somewhat random activity, modified until it presents a satisfactory sensory pattern.

With this possibility in mind, a number of our experiments have been directed toward a descriptive analysis of the animal's sensory organization, when there has been no opportunity for modification by learning. The visual system is best adapted for such studies. Anatomically the system is very complexly organized, with the different parts of the retina projected with great accuracy upon the optic lobes or visual cortex (23). We have evidence that this precise anatomic pattern develops normally in the absence of any photic stimulation. Structurally it is probably the most elaborate portion of the nervous system so that, if anatomic differentiation has any functional significance, we should expect to find some innate functional organization in the visual system.

Studying the first visual reactions of rats reared to adulthood in total darkness, Hebb (18, 19) has found that the animals respond immediately to objects, as contrasted with background. Something of figure-ground organization is immediately given. They learn readily a differential reaction to figures which cannot be explored in any way except visually. This means that the figures must be distinguished visually before association with motor reactions can occur. The animals show transposition for size and brightness when they have experienced only two absolute units in the series. This demands the immediate perception of relational properties.

Russell and I (25) have found that rats reared in darkness show an accurate discrimination of visual distance and, without training, regulate the force of jumping to the distance to be crossed. This involves a direct control of motor activity through some innate sensory organization.

These experimental results are in accord with the most careful studies of the congenitally blind children who have had vision restored suddenly (Senden, 35). So far as one can interpret the literature, these children distinguish figure from ground, distinguish objects as of different shapes, although they are unable to describe them, and have also some perception of distance.

In a series of experiments on discrimination of visual patterns I have found that the general characteristics of the figure-ground relation, as worked out by Rubin (34) and Wertheimer (49) for man, apply also to the rat. The evidence also points to the conclusion that the formation of the discrimination habit depends upon a perception of relations which is prior to the learning process. When a pair of stimuli is presented, one with positive, the other with negative reinforcement, the positive or negative reactions are associated only with that property of each stimulus which differentiates it from the other. A couple of experiments will illustrate the nature of the evidence. A group of animals was trained for 150 trials to choose an 8 cm. circle opposed to a black card; another group to choose a 5 cm. circle under the same conditions. All were then trained to choose the 8 cm. circle when opposed to the 5 cm. The previous training had no effect whatever upon the learning scores with the pair of figures. The property of size was not associated with the reaction so long as the object was alone. The same result is obtained when animals are trained with a single figure and tested for recognition of its form.

If an animal is trained to choose the larger of two circles he will spontaneously choose the larger of any pair of figures. The reaction is not differentiated for form. If he is trained with two different forms, he is undisturbed by wide variations in the size of the figures. So, in every discrimination habit the response is not to a specific pattern but to some property which distinguishes the two figures and which must be differentiated before the motor responses can be associated with it. Furthermore, when the nature of these differentiating properties is tested, they turn out to be relational; relative size, relative direction, proportions, and the like. Such evidence, I believe, disposes of the theory that reactions to relational properties are due to irradiation of conditioned reactions to absolute properties.

These lines of evidence from the animal work support the conclusion already reached by the members of the Gestalt school, that the fundamental organization in perception is innate. And this organization has very definite characteristics, a preference, as it were, for certain specific arrangements of the physical elements of the stimulus.

## Motor Action Based on Perceptual Organization

In only one of these observations is there a predetermined motor response; that is the regulation of the force of jumping to the distance seen. It is not necessary, however, that specific motor responses be directly elicited by the sensory organization, in order that the latter should be effective in directing the form of activity. Once motor reactions are associated with some aspects of the stimulus, or with an equivalent stimulus, the innate organization may exercise a selective action upon the various associated reactions. Thus the fluctuations of the staircase illusion may determine alternative associated motor responses, which have been built up by experience with three-dimensional situations and which themselves are certainly not responsible for the fluctuations of the illusion. Innate perceptual organization might similarly exercise a selective influence among motor activities not innately associated with the objects eliciting the reactions.

There is good evidence that animals without previous experience may give specific reactions to biologically significant objects and that the recognition or discrimination of these objects may be quite precise. I became interested in this problem first through observations on the brooding of the sooty terns. If these birds were given eggs of a related species to hatch they would invariably reject the foster children within a short time after hatching, throwing the chicks out of the nest and sometimes killing them. Strange chicks of their own species were accepted during the first few days of brooding. The chicks of the two species did not differ greatly in appearance, yet the discrimination was certain. I was unable to discover the sensory basis of the reaction, beyond getting indications that it depended upon a complex of stimuli, not wholly visual. The history of these birds was of course unknown but the number of individuals observed, considered in relation to the death rate of the colony, made it certain that some at least were dealing with their first brood.

Later Stone took up a similar problem, that of sex recognition, under conditions where the history of the animals and the patterns of sensory stimulation could be controlled. His studies of the effective stimulus to sexual activity are the most thorough available. More recently Borovski (7) has reported observations on the recognition of their eggs by gulls and Beach has completed a number of experiments dealing with the sensory control of the rat's reactions to her young. Although the adequate stimulus has in no case been completely defined, certain important general principles have come out of these studies.

When we first began work in the field it seemed probable that the exciting stimulus would turn out to be simple—an odor, a localized tactile stimulus such as that which induces the clasping reflex in the frog, or the like, and that this would initiate a chain of precise reflexes. Sensory controls have made this hypothesis seem untenable. Vision, olfaction, audition, tactile sensitivity of the snout and vibrissæ, of the paws or skin of the ventral surface can be eliminated singly without preventing the appearance of normal patterns of reaction when the stimulus object is first presented. The arousal of sexual excitement by the female in heat or the cleaning and first retrieving of the young is not dependent upon excitation through any one sense modality. The results of the experiments parallel those dealing with the performance of the maze habit, which is little if at all disturbed by the elimination of any single sense modality. Even the elimination of several sensory paths together may not interfere with the reaction. Thus in a familiar experiment Stone (38) observed copulatory activity in a male, reared in isolation, and with vision, olfaction, and tactile sensitivity of the vibrissæ and ventral skin eliminated. Similar results have been obtained by Beach in reactions of females to their young.

These results indicate either that we have missed some simple cue, through inadequacy of technique, or that the same pattern of instinctive behavior may be initiated through different sense modalities and patterns of stimuli. Swann's studies of olfactory discrimination (44) showed that a remnant of the olfactory bulb too small to be identified by gross dissection may mediate olfactory discrimination. This fact might be urged against Stone's conclusions, but Beach has confirmed Stone's observations with animals in which complete destruction of the olfactory bulbs was verified by histological examination. Like sources of error are improbable in experiments dealing with other sense modalities. Beach finds that desensitizing the lips and snout by section of the sensory root of the fifth nerve interferes with the retrieving of young by the female, but it interferes also with the finding and picking up of food, so that this operative control is inconclusive.

The experiments based on sense privation thus point to the conclusion that the exciting stimulus in instinctive recognition of mate or young is not mediated exclusively by any one sense modality.

A second experimental method for analysis of the adequate stimulus has consisted of the successive elimination of properties of the stimulus object in an effort to determine the minimal characters which will elicit the normal pattern of response. Two points have come out clearly in this work. The first is that a wide range of variation in any property of the stimulus is possible, without destroying its effectiveness.

Borovski (7) found that gulls would retrieve eggs to their nests from some distance. He substituted other things for the eggs. The birds retrieved objects of various sizes, weights, textures, and specific heats, ranging from small pebbles to potatoes and billiard balls. But any marked departure from a rounded or oval form led to rejection of the substitute. Cubes, angular stones, and the like were not retrieved. Texture also seemed important, since mudballs were rejected. I have observed that the terns are greatly disturbed by a lump of mud or wax stuck on an egg and distorting its form, although painting or dyeing the eggs in varigated colors is without effect. The adequate stimulus of the egg may thus be defined as a rounded object of certain limited size and texture, and this, in the setting of the nest, elicits specific retrieving, cleaning, and brooding behavior.

Stone (37) could define the stimulus to sexual excitement in the male rat only as an object within certain limits of size, exhibiting a definite jerking movement. The analysis of the female's recognition of her young is still less complete, but size and surface texture seem to provide the chief cues by which the young are identified.

Thus far no investigator has found any single property of the stimulus object which cannot be varied within limits without disrupting the reaction. The stimulus is not a single characteristic color or odor, but seems to be a pattern, having the same characteristics of organization which we have found in studies of visual discrimination of objects. The complete analysis of sensory control of reactions to the mate or young seems scarcely less difficult than the problem of sensory control of homing has proved to be. The experiments thus far carried out have scarcely done more than emphasize the need for exhaustive studies in the field.

It is really imperative that we make a serious effort to define the adequate stimulus, not only in studies of instinct but equally in studies of reflexes and of learning. Psychological theories based upon the relations of stimulus and response remain sheer nonsense so long as the stimulus is defined only as whatever the experimenter puts in front of the animal. We have gone far enough in this work to be sure that the animal rarely reacts to what the experimenter regards as the stimulus. In any complex situation the true basis of reaction can be discovered only by systematic variation of all the parts and properties of the supposed stimulus.

The second point of significance revealed by studies of the stimulus to instinctive behavior is that the effective properties of the stimulus vary with the total situation. The primiparous mother rat will retrieve a number of objects having some resemblance to infants, selecting them from among food objects and nest materials. Temperature, odor, shape, color, surface texture, brightness and size may be somewhat altered without interfering with retrieving. But in the nest the subsequent behavior toward the objects varies with their character. The mother may start to lick a stuffed skin which she has retrieved and discover the stitches in it. She promptly pulls at these, soon removes the sawdust and discards the skin. The nest situation plus the retrieved object calls out new responses and if the sensory pattern of the substitute stimulus does not conform to the requirements of this total situation, the normal course of behavior is disrupted. I have observed that the sooty tern is stimulated to assume the brooding posture by the contact of a chick under the breast but the reaction is only momentary unless the bird is on its own familiar nest.

The accumulated observations suggest that the instinctive behavior is dependent upon a complex of stimuli. Some of the reactions are elicited only by the total integrated pattern. Others may be aroused by single elements of the stimulus and interfering reactions are likely to be excited when the stimulus has abnormal traits which themselves elicit other instinctive or habitual responses.

Such an interplay of specific sensory demands may well form the basis of apparently purposive activities. The nest of the rat is a very primitive affair in comparison with the structures built by many animals. Kinder (22) found that animals which had had no previous experience with any nest materials, collected material as promptly and built nests indistinguishable from those constructed by experienced animals. Sturman-Hulbe (43) found little evidence of a basis for selection of materials beyond ease of manipulation and, possibly, specific heat. The range of materials tested was slight, however.

The actual construction of the nest, that is the determination of its form, seems to meet the requirements of low heat conductivity underneath, contact with the body at the sides, and, less consistently, exclusion of light. The arrangement of optimal conditions in these three respects dictates the form of the nest. The combination of sensory factors is fairly clear and is consistent with the hypothesis of perceptual control that I have suggested. That they are in any sense relational or involve any perception of form is doubtful, in the case of the rat, however.

The available evidence is not sufficient to establish the thesis that the perceptual organization of the animal determines the goal of behavior but the studies of the rat do suggest control by a complex sensory pattern. What the situation is in the case of more elaborate construction, such as the nests of the weaver birds, can only be determined by actual analysis of the process of construction.

## THE DISTINCTION OF REFLEX AND INSTINCT

The changes in the character of the responses and in the nature of the adequate stimulus under different environmental conditions, for example the cleaning of the young in the nest and not during retrieving and the like, are, in a sense, a confirmation of the chain-reflex theory of instinct. It is true that the instinctive behavior creates situations which in turn serve as stimuli to further activities. To dismiss the activity as reflex is, however, to ignore its characteristic features.

Many writers have attempted to differentiate between reflex and instinct, but the final criterion has been only a vague difference in complexity. Our conception of the nature of reflex is derived largely from avoiding reactions elicited by protopathic stimuli and from the muscle-shortening reflexes. These are elicited by a localized group of sensory endings. Locus, intensity and modality of the stimulus are its determining properties. In contrast to this, sexual and maternal behavior seem chiefly determined by the pattern or organization of the stimulus, with locus of incidence upon the sensory surface or sense modality secondary. In this respect the instincts present the organismal problem as the reflexes do not. This difference in the nature of the adequate stimulus justifies, I believe, the retention of the term instinct to stress the importance of the problem of sensory organization.

189

## The Activation of the Sensorimotor System

Many sensorimotor reactions are performed apparently as soon as the growth of essential nervous structures is completed. The pioneer studies of Herrick and Coghill (20) marked the way for the many later investigations correlating the appearance of early reflexes with the growth of nervous connections. In many of the early reflexes the mechanism is capable of functioning as soon as growth is completed. But there are, also, many activities which appear only at some interval after the completion of neuron growth. The work of Tilney and Casamajor (45) suggests that the late appearance of some of the so-called delayed reflexes or instincts may be due to late myelinization of tracts, but the maturation of instinct as studied by Breed (8) and Bird (6) is probably due to a diversity of causes in which neural growth is less important than general development of muscular strength and control.

Reproductive behavior presents a unique situation among instinctive activities in that it is delayed long after the development of the nervous system and is conditioned by the attainment of sexual maturity. Recent studies of hormonal activation of sexual behavior raise important problems, both of neural integration and of motivation. The work of Steinach (36), Stone (37) and a number of more recent investigators shows the dependence of the behavior of the male upon the testicular hormone. Many studies show the importance of endocrine products in the regulation of the œstrus cycle and the relation of the behavior of the female to this cycle. The experiments of Wiesner and Sheard (53), Riddle, (31, 32), and others indicate something of the dependence of maternal behavior upon pituitary secretions.

The interrelations of the hormones are complex and the literature upon this subject is vast. I shall not take time to review the evidence on the physiological action of the various hormones. More important for us who are interested in behavior than the details of the biochemistry and interaction of the endocrine products is the question of how they act to induce the appearance of specific patterns of behavior. The introduction of male hormone into the blood stream somehow sensitizes the animal to the stimuli presented by the female in heat. What is the mechanism of such sensitization?

The difficulty of the problem is enormously increased by the variability of behavior under normal conditions. There seems to be no item of behavior except parturition and the removal of the fetal membranes from the young which is wholly restricted to the mother rat. Norman has found that nests are sometimes built and young retrieved in a manner indistinguishable from that of the best mothers by virgin females and even by males. Stone and others have observed female mating reactions on the part of normal males and Beach the masculine behavior of normal virgin females. The mere observation of such behavior in experiments involving injection of a hormone therefore does not justify the conclusion that the hormone is responsible for the behavior. There are distinguishing characteristics of what we have considered as normal behavior. The parturient female collects her young into the nest immediately or within a few hours after their birth. Virgin females and males show such behavior only after much longer exposure to young, often with an intervening period during which the young are devoured. It is not impossible to establish definite criteria by which hormonal effects may be recognized but the necessary criteria are quantitative rather than qualitative. The validity of the criteria employed by earlier workers is somewhat called in question. We can only consider the problem of activation on the basis of observations which should be checked again with more attention to the range of normal variation.

With this reservation it seems worth while to consider the mechanism of activation, if only to define the problem more clearly.

1. Does the hormone stimulate the growth or formation of new nervous connections, as the chemical organizers in Spemann's experiments stimulate differentiation of structure? A number of observations may be urged as arguments against this possibility. Castration abolishes the male reaction. Injection of the male hormone may restore it promptly and

it may be repeatedly revived by repeated injection of the hormone. It is unlikely that each of these repeated activations involves a renewed growth with intervening degeneration of the mechanism. In the experiments of Wiesner and Sheard retrieving of the young grew less persistent as the young approached weaning age and began to venture from the nest. The retrieving reaction could be restored to its initial vigor, either by injection of pituitary hormones or by giving the mother new-born young to nurse. The responses to the younger infants were apparently immediate. We cannot ascribe the initiation of neuron growth to this stimulus and so have no reason to assume that the hormone produces such an effect. This and other evidence points to the conclusion that the neural mechanism is already laid down before the action of the hormone, and that the latter is only an activator, increasing the excitability of a mechanism already present.

2. Does the hormone act merely by increasing the general excitability of the organism? Reduced sexual activity during starvation or physical illness (Stone, 40) and the fact that male hormone increases the excitability of the sympathetic system as measured by vasomotor reflexes (Wheelon and Shipley, 50) lends plausibility to this assumption. I have found, however, that castration does not alter general activity for a month or so, nor is there other valid evidence for a reduction in general excitability which is common to castrated males, females in the diœstrum, and nonparturient females, which should be the case if the hormones acted as general excitants. Finally, the strongest argument against this hypothesis is the apparent specificity of the different hormones for different patterns of behavior as illustrated by Moore's reversal of sex behavior (27) by interchanging the gonads of the two sexes.

3. The hormones induce specific changes in various organs, such as the vascular changes in the uterine mucosa, the rapid enlargement of the testis, or lactation in the mammary glands. It is possible that these altered states initiate sensory impulses which facilitate the mechanisms of the secondary sexual reactions. This is the mechanism implied in Moll's evacuation theory (26) of the sex drive and in the ascription of

various phases of maternal behavior to lactation. The suppression of the œstrus cycle and of receptivity in the female rat during lactation, and the correlation of sexual behavior with phases of the œstrus cycle suggest an elaborate interplay of such mechanisms.

The evidence against this somatic sensory reinforcement is rather compelling, however. Stone tested the evacuation theory by removing as much as possible of the reproductive system from males and observing their behavior after treatment with male hormone. He found sexual excitability, responsiveness to the female in heat, in castrated animals from which all of the accessory reproductive glands had been removed, leaving no anatomic basis for the tension of accumulated secretions assumed as the source of sensory reinforcement in the evacuation theory. Several investigators (Wiesner and Mirskaia, 52) have reported the hormonal induction of œstrus without the induction of mating behavior. Ball (2) has observed the normal signs of sexual excitement in females from which the uterus and vagina had been removed. Wiesner and Sheard have reported and Norman has confirmed the fact that normal retrieving of young occurs in parturient females from which the mammary glands were removed in infancy. The mechanical stimuli of lactation therefore cannot be an important factor in the induction of this phase of maternal behavior.

In each of these experiments the organs to which the function of sensory reinforcement would naturally be ascribed have been removed without abolishing excitability to the appropriate stimuli. Still more conclusive evidence on this matter comes from instances of reversal of sexual behavior. In gynandromorphic insects with head of one sex, thorax and abdomen of the other, sexual behavior is reported to follow the sex of the head, not that of the reproductive system (Whiting, 51). Reversal of sexual behavior in hens with tumors of the ovary has long been known (Morgan, 28). In the experiments of Moore the gonads were interchanged between male and female rats and corresponding reversal of behavior noted, the feminized males retrieving young and the masculinized females showing male behavior.

Such observations and experiments seem to preclude the evacuation theory of sexual activation and to minimize the importance of any sensory reinforcement from somatic organs in the production of specific reproductive responses. Of course they do not rule out all possible peripheral mechanisms which might provide effective facilitation for specific reflexes. Certain possibilities have not yet been explored, such as that of an altered temperature control during pregnancy which might precipitate nest building, as Kinder (22) has suggested, or localized changes in vasomotor reflexes which might alter local cutaneous sensitivity. Nevertheless, the organs showing greatest structural changes under hormone influences and those to which sensory facilitation has been ascribed have been removed without destroying the secondary sexual reactions and the observations on reversal of sexual behavior make it pretty certain that somatic sensory impulses cannot be the determiners of specific reaction patterns.

4. There remains only the last alternative, that the hormones act upon the central nervous system to increase the excitability of the sensorimotor mechanism specifically involved in the instinctive activity. Direct evidence for this is lacking and we have no conception of the way in which various organic compounds might exercise a selective effect upon specific nervous elements or schemata. There are, however, many instances of the restricted influence of drugs, both upon localized structures, as in the case of strychnine, and upon psychological functions, as in the action of mescal. There is also some slight evidence for the local sensitization of nervous tissue to organic toxins, with a selective action of later doses upon the sensitized tissue. The hypothesis of a specific action of the hormones upon nervous organization is therefore not without parallel in the literature of pharmacology. The problem here is clear enough. Techniques of direct investigation, as by serological tests of the affinity of specific structures for different hormones, are still lacking.

## Neural Structure and Instinct

*Gross localization.*—The probable locus of action of the hormone within the central nervous system leads to the question of the neurological basis of instinct. The notion of a sharp distinction of levels must be abandoned. Zeliony (55) and Culler and Mettler (10) have demonstrated the possibility of conditioning in the decorticate animal, so that the cerebral hemispheres are no longer to be regarded as the exclusive seat of the learning process. Instinctive activities are also not exclusively a function of subcortical structures. In submammalian forms many complicated instincts can be carried out in the absence of the forebrain, as illustrated by Rogers' studies of the reproductive activities of decerebrate pigeons (33). In these birds such complex learning as is required by differential reaction to visual forms is also independent of the forebrain (Gemelli e Pastori, 16) so that these animals do not provide evidence for a separate localization of instinct and learning. In mammals instinctive activities may suffer severely from total or partial decortication. I have found that the rat's reactions to visual distance are disturbed by injuries to the visual cortex but are unaffected by extensive destruction of the optic centers of the thalamus and midbrain. Mating behavior has not been observed in male rats lacking more than half of the neocortex. It is difficult to keep such animals at a normal level of general vigor and their impotence might be ascribed to lowered vitality. They usually fail, however, to show any specific reactions to cage mates and in this respect are quite different from animals which are under-nourished or ill. Stone (41) has found normal mating behavior in male rabbits with large cortical lesions and Brooks (9) in completely decorticate male and female rabbits, so long as the olfactory system remains intact. The difference between the rat and rabbit thus seems to correspond to the degree of specificity of the adequate stimulus in the two genera. Brooks has reported normal mating in rabbits deprived of olfactory bulbs and with the neocortex intact. This confirms our conclusion concerning alternative effective stimuli.

The studies of Beach (3) show the dependence of many aspects of maternal behavior upon the cortex. Using such criteria as the time of initiation of nest-building before parturition, the removal of the fœtal membranes, grade of nest, retrieving, and the removal of the nest and young from unfavorable conditions, he has compared the performance of normal mothers with that of others having various cerebral lesions. Practically every item of the behavior showed deterioration in proportion to the extent of cerebral injury.

None of the primary reactions dropped out as a result of the cerebral lesions. Collecting nest material, nest building, cleaning the young, retrieving were observed in all animals, but in case of those with extensive lesions the activities were not fitted together into an effective organization. Nests were poorly constructed and inadequate as protection to the young. One or two of the litter might be cleaned, the rest left to die in the fœtal membranes. In retrieving tests the young were carried about but not collected into a single group, and so on.

The results of this study are of especial importance in emphasizing, by contrast, the degree of integration of activities in the normal pattern. Dunlap (13) has averred that there are no instincts, although there is instinctive behavior, meaning by this that such categories as maternal behavior are created by the observer out of an aggregate of activities which, in themselves, have no physiological coherence. The analysis of cerebral function in maternal behavior favors an opposite interpretation. The partially decerebrate mother shows all of the component activities which are revealed by the maternal behavior of the normal animal, but these elements are so poorly coordinated that she cannot rear her litter. The normal pattern of maternal behavior involves a total integration of the component activities which makes it a functional unit and in mammals this unity is given by the activity of the cerebral cortex.

*Histologic structure.*—In the visual system there is a high degree of precision in the topographic arrangement of the fibers. A statistical study of the distribution of normal cells in the lateral geniculate nucleus shows after lesions in the visual cortex that the axons which reach the cortex reproduce exactly the relative spacial positions of the cells in the nucleus; that is to say, the concentration of cells is uniform, right up to the edge of a degenerated area in the nucleus. But this accuracy of growth is apparently rare and it constitutes in the visual system not a precise set of sensorimotor connections, but a cortical field in which the spatial relations of retinal excitation are reproduced and whose parts are still equipotential for the integrative processes.

Experimental studies of nerve growth and regeneration seem to establish the fact that in general there is little specificity in the connections of individual fibers. The transplantation experiments of Detwiler (11) and of Weiss (47, 48) show that the distribution of the fibers to the muscles may be quite random and yet coordinated movements are effected as soon as growth is completed, without any opportunity for the intervention of practice to establish the patterns of integration. This, rather than the precision of the afferent visual pathway, must represent the usual state of affairs in the growth of nerves and tracts. No exact sensorimotor connections are established, yet the instinctive reactions may have a high degree of precision.

In general the neurological problems which have arisen in the study of instincts are identical with those of cerebral function in learning. The same questions of equivalence of stimuli, of substitute responses, and of similar effects of various cerebral lesions appear, whether the activities are innate or learned. We are no nearer to an answer to such questions in one case than in the other, but I believe that there is more hope of solution of these problems through the study of instincts than of learning.

## The Physiology of the Drive

I have reviewed the evidence that the endocrines must act directly upon the central nervous system to activate the instinctive pattern. The same evidence may be applied to the problem of reactions to deficit. The experimental studies have in fact dealt with gross activities such as retrieving or mating which involve both reaction to deficit and specific sensorimotor patterns, both preparatory and consummatory activity. This means that the various motivational factors observed in maternal behavior cannot be ascribed to somatic sensory reinforcement, any more than can the hormonal activation of the reactions.

Most of the current theories concerning the nature of primitive drives have been derived by analogy with the hunger mechanism and assume some continued visceral activity, comparable to the contractions of the empty stomach, as the source of masses of excitation whose irradiation in the nervous system increases the general responsiveness of the animal. This analogy has certainly been overworked, especially as it is by no means assured that hunger motivation is itself synonymous with the hunger pangs. The work of Richter (30) and Wada (46) shows a correlation between rhythmic bodily activities and hunger contractions, but the activities of the animal under hunger motivation are not rhythmic. The rat in the maze does not stop running between hunger pangs. Even for hunger motivation we must assume, I believe, some source of continued excitation which is no more than activated by the hunger contractions.

When the theories of motivation by somatic sensory facilitation were developed, there was little evidence that activity could be sustained within the central nervous system. The maintenance of tension or activity through some form of circular reflex was more in accord with the conception that all excitation must pass over immediately into motor response, as first formulated by Dewey (12). The recent demonstration of recurrent nervous circuits, perhaps capable of indefinite reverberation, by the anatomic and physiologic studies of Lorente de No, relieves us from the necessity of finding a peripheral mechanism to account for the maintenance of activity or for the dynamic tensions which are implied by the phenomena of motivation. The studies of the sexual and maternal motivation strongly suggest a central nervous mechanism which is merely rendered excitable by hormone action.   What this means is that the seeking activities or reactions to a deficit, such as are measured by the obstruction method, are not a reaction to a continuous peripheral stimulus, such as is assumed in the evacuation theory, but are the expression of some central nervous activity or state.

The relation between the reactions to deficit and the excitability of the specific patterns of behavior is obscure. It is generally stated that the drive is first aroused, as by endocrine action, and that this, in turn, causes the appearance of the instinctive sensorimotor reactions.   An increase in the excitability of sexual reactions is accepted as evidence for intensification of the drive.   But the phenomenon actually observed is only a more ready excitation of specific responses. There is no need to postulate an extraneous drive to account for the fluctuations in the threshold of such reactions.   The mechanism is present and under the influence of the hormone or of excitation by an adequate stimulus its excitability is increased.

Only in cases of reaction to a deficit is there any justification for introducing the notion of a drive as a source of facilitation.   An increase in general activity or in exploratory behavior indicates an increased responsiveness to stimuli not obviously related to the specific sensorimotor patterns of the instinctive behavior.   There is also inhibition of reactions to other stimuli, as when the chick removed from companions refuses to eat.   This is a selective facilitation of activity and the facilitation originates with the organism.   Does it call for the postulation of some source of energy apart from that of the specific sensorimotor patterns?   The evidence indicates that the facilitation is probably independent of somatic stimulation and is of central nervous origin.   Stimulation of an instinctive pattern will increase the intensity of the apparent drive.   Thus sexual excitement in the male rat is aroused only by the very specific pattern of the female in heat, but once the animal is so excited, he will respond to less definite patterns of stimulation.   The waning retrieving activity of the female is intensified by supplying her with a younger litter.   Motivation of the hungry animal in the maze is really effective only after the maze has been associated with the getting of food. In these cases the apparent motivation seems to derive from a specific sensorimotor mechanism.

I suspect that all cases of motivation will turn out to be of this character; not a general drive or libido, or disturbance of the organic equilibrium, but a partial excitation of a very specific sensorimotor mechanism irradiating to affect other systems of reaction. In his dynamic psychology Woodworth (54) suggested that habits might acquire dynamic functions, that a mechanism might become a drive, as he expressed the matter. I should carry this notion a step further and suggest that physiologically all drives are no more than expressions of the activity of specific mechanisms.

## Summary

I have reviewed the material on reproductive behavior chiefly to illustrate what seem to me the fundamental problems of instinct. Practically the whole of physiological theory concerning the integration of behavior, whether of spinal reflex or of speech, is based upon inference from the relations of stimulus and response. Instinctive behavior raises questions of the nature of the adequate stimulus which seem to differentiate such activities sharply from spinal reflexes. An essential first step toward an understanding of the mechanism of instinct is the analysis of the properties of the stimulus situation which are really effective in arousing the behavior. This has proved to be a very difficult task, ramifying into all of the problems of perception. Understanding of the motor activities seems to hinge upon these perceptual problems. Little of the behavior can be described in terms of stereotyped movements; rather the whole repertoire of learned and reflex movements may be elicited until some definite sensory pattern is produced. The phenomena are identical with those from which I have inferred the equivalence of reactions and Bethe (5) the principle of "sliding coupling."

I feel that the problem of motivation is also closely identified with the problem of the specific patterns of instinctive response. Hormone action, or reinforcement by sensory impulses from the viscera, seems to do nothing more than activate some central nervous mechanism which maintains excitability or activity. There is no good reason to assume that this mechanism is distinct from the sensorimotor organization which is later active in the consummatory reaction. The current trend in social psychology and psychopathology is to elevate the drive to the position formerly occupied by instinct, as some general motivating force apart from specific sensorimotor systems. Actually the term is nothing more than a general designation of reactions to deficit and its hypostatization as a real force can only blind us to the fact that each such reaction constitutes a special problem involving, perhaps, a unique mechanism.

## REFERENCES

1. AVERY, G. T., Notes on reproduction in guinea pigs, *J. Comp. Psychol.*, 1925, **5**, 373–396.
2. BALL, J., Sex behavior of the rat after removal of the uterus and vagina, *J. Comp. Psychol.*, 1934, **18**, 419–422.
3. BEACH, F. A., The neural basis of innate behavior. I. Effects of cortical lesions upon the maternal behavior pattern in the rat, *J. Comp. Psychol.*, 1937, **24**, 393–434.
4. BECHTEREW, W. v., *La psychologie objective*, Paris: Alcan, 1913, iii + 478.
5. BETHE, A. UND FISCHER, E., Die Anpassungsfähigkeit (Plastizität) des Nervensystems, *Handb. d. norm. u. path. Physiol.*, 1931, **15** (zweite Hälfte), 1045–1130.
6. BIRD, C., The effect of maturation upon the pecking instinct of chicks, *Ped. Sem.*, 1926, **33**, 212–233.
7. BOROVSKI, V. M., The relation of the gull to its nest, eggs, and young (Russian), *Reflexksi, Instinkti, Naviki*, 1936, **2**, 139–174.
8. BREED, F. S., Maturation and use in the development of instinct, *J. Animal Behav.*, 1913, **3**, 274–285.
9. BROOKS, C. M., The role of the cerebral cortex and of various sense organs in the excitation and execution of mating activity in the rabbit, *Amer. J. Physiol.*, 1937, **120**, 544–553.
10. CULLER, E. AND METTLER, F. A., Conditioned behavior in a decorticate dog, *J. Comp. Psychol.*, 1934, **3**, 291–303.
11. DETWILER, S. R., *Neuroembryology*, New York: Macmillan, 1936, x + 218.
12. DEWEY, J., The reflex arc concept in psychology, PSYCHOL. REV., 1896, **3**, 357–370.
13. DUNLAP, K., Are there any instincts?, *J. Abn. Psychol.*, 1919, **14**, 307–311.
14. FRISCH, K. v., Über die "Sprache" der Bienen, *Zool. Jahrb., Abt. f. zool. u. Physiol.*, 1923, **40**, 1–186.
15. —— UND RÖSCH, G. A., Neue Versuche über die Bedeutung von Duftorgan und Pollenduft für die Verständigung im Bienenvolk, *Zsch. f. vergl. Physiol.*, 1926, **4**, 1–21.

16. GEMELLI, A. E PASTORI, G., Sulla rieducabilita di animali scerebrati, *Bol. d. Soc. Ital. di Biol. Sper.*, 1930, 5, 1–6.

17. GIERSBERG, H., Gehirntransplantationen bei Amphibien, *Zool. Anz.*, 1935, 8, Suppl. Bd., 160–168.

18. HEBB, D. O., The innate organization of visual activity. I. Perception of figures by rats reared in total darkness, *J. Genet. Psychol.*, 1937, 51, 101–126.

19. ——, The innate organization of visual activity. II. Transfer of response in the discrimination of brightness and size by rats reared in total darkness, *J. Comp. Psychol.*, 1937, 24, 277–299.

20. HERRICK, C. J. AND COGHILL, G. E., The development of reflex mechanisms in Amblystoma, *J. Comp. Neurol.*, 1915, 25, 68–86.

21. KEPNER, W. A., *Animals Looking into the Future*, New York: Macmillan, 1925, pp. 197.

22. KINDER, E. F., A study of the nest-building activity of the albino rat, *J. Exper. Zool.*, 1927, 47, 117–161.

23. LASHLEY, K. S., The mechanism of vision. VIII. The projection of the retina upon the cerebral cortex of the rat, *J. Comp. Neurol.*, 1934, 60, 57–79.

24. ——, The mechanism of vision. XV. Preliminary studies of the rat's capacity for detail vision, *J. Gen. Psychol.*, 1938, 18, 123–193.

25. —— AND RUSSELL, J. T., The mechanism of vision. XI. A preliminary test of innate organization, *J. Genet. Psychol.*, 1934, 45, 136–144.

26. MOLL, A., *Handbuch der Sexualwissenschaften*, Leipzig: F. C. W. Vogel, 1926, 2 vol.

27. MOORE, C. R., On the physiological properties of the gonads as controllers of somatic and psychical characteristics. I. The rat, *J. Exper. Zool.*, 1919, 28, 137–160.

28. MORGAN, T. H., *Heredity and Sex*, New York: Columbia University Press, 1914, pp. 284.

29. PETERS, H., Studien am Netz der Kreuzspinne (Aranea diadema, L.). II. Über die Herstellung des Rahmes, der Radialfäden, und der Hilfsspirale, *Zsch. f. Morphol. u. Ökologie d. Tiere*, 1937, 1, 126–150.

30. RICHTER, C. P., Animal behavior and internal drives, *Quart. Rev. Biol.*, 1927, 2, 307–343.

31. RIDDLE, O., LAHR, E. L. AND BATES, R. W., Maternal behavior induced in virgin rats by prolactin, *Proc. Soc. Exp. Biol. Med.*, 1935, 32, 730–734.

32. ——, Aspects and implications of hormonal control of the maternal instinct, *Proc. Amer. Phil. Soc.*, 1935, 75, 521–525.

33. ROGERS, F. T., An experimental study of the corpus striatum of the pigeon as related to various instinctive types of behavior, *J. Comp. Neurol.*, 1922, 35, 21–59.

34. RUBIN, E. J., *Visuell wahrgenomene Figuren*, Kopenhagen: Gyldendalske, 1921, pp. 1–244.

35. SENDEN, M. v., *Raum- und Gestaltauffassung bei operierten Blindgeborenen vor und nach der Operation*, Leipzig: 1932, ix + 305.

36. STEINACH, E., Geschlechtstrieb und echt sekundäre Geschlechtsmerkmale als Folge der inneresekretorischen Funktion der Keimdrüsen, *Zentbl. f. Physiol.*, 1910, 24, 551–566.

37. STONE, C. P., The congenital sexual behavior of the young male albino rat, *J. Comp. Psychol.*, 1922, 2, 95–153.

38. ——, Further study of sensory functions in the activation of sexual behavior in the young male albino rat, *J. Comp. Psychol.*, 1923, 3, 469–473.
39. ——, A note on 'feminine' behavior in adult male rats, *Amer. J. Physiol.*, 1924a, 68, 39–41.
40. ——, Delay in the awakening of copulatory ability in the male albino rat incurred by defective diets. I. Quantitative deficiency, *J. Comp. Psychol.*, 1924b, 4, 195–224; II. Qualitative deficiency, *J. Comp. Psychol.*, 1925a, 5, 177–203.
41. ——, The effects of cerebral destruction on the sexual behavior of rabbits. I. The olfactory bulbs, *Amer. J. Physiol.*, 1925b, 71, 430–435; II. The frontal and parietal regions, *Amer. J. Physiol.*, 1925c, 72, 372–385; III. The frontal, parietal, and occipital regions, *J. Comp. Psychol.*, 1926, 6, 435–448.
42. —— AND BARKER, R. G., Spontaneous activity, direct and indirect measures of sexual drive in adult male rats, *Proc. Soc. Exper. Biol. Med.*, 1934, 32, 195–199.
43. STURMAN-HULBE, M. AND STONE, C. P., Maternal behavior in the albino rat, *J. Comp. Psychol.*, 1929, 9, 203–238.
44. SWANN, H. G., The functions of the brain in olfaction. II. The effects of destruction of olfactory and other structures upon the discrimination of odors, *J. Comp. Neurol.*, 1934, 59, 175–201.
45. TILNEY, F. AND CASAMAJOR, L., Myelinogeny as applied to the study of behavior, *Arch. Neurol. Psychiat.*, 1924, 12, 1–66.
46. WADA, T., An experimental study of hunger in its relation to activity, *Arch. Psychol.*, 1922, No. 57.
47. WEISS, P., Das Resonanzprinzip der Nerventätigkeit, dargestellt in Funktionsprüfungen an transplantierten überzähligen Muskeln, *Arch. f. d. ges. Physiol.*, 1931, 226, 600–658.
48. ——, Further experimental investigations on the phenomenon of homologous response in transplanted amphibian limbs, *J. Comp. Neurol.*, 1937, 66, 181–209; 481–535; 537–548; 1937, 67, 269–315.
49. WERTHEIMER, M., Untersuchungen zur Lehre von der Gestalt. I, *Psychol. Forsch.*, 1921, 1, 47–58; II, *Psychol. Forsch.*, 1923, 4, 301–350.
50. WHEELON, H. AND SHIPLEY, J. L., The effects of testicular transplants upon vasomotor irritability, *Amer. J. Physiol.*, 1915, 39, 395–400.
51. WHITING, P. W. AND WENSTRUP, E. J., Fertile gynandromorphs in Habrobracon, *J. Hered.*, 1932, 23, 31–38.
52. WIESNER, B. P. AND MIRSKAIA, L., On the endocrine basis of mating in the mouse, *J. Exper. Physiol.*, 1930, 20, 273–279.
53. —— AND SHEARD, N. M., *Maternal Behavior in the Rat*, Edinburgh: Oliver, 1933, xi + 245.
54. WOODWORTH, R. S., *Dynamic Psychology*, New York: Columbia Univ. Press, 1918, pp. 210.
55. ZELIONY, G. P., Observations sur des chiens auxquels on a enlevé les hémisphères cérébraux, *C. r. soc. de biol.*, 1913, 74, 707–709.

# 16

Reprinted from *Psychol. Rev.* **54**:348–352 (1947)

## SUMMARY COMMENTS ON THE HEREDITY–
## ENVIRONMENT SYMPOSIUM

BY W. S. HUNTER

*Brown University*

It will come as a surprise to many psychologists that all five of the distinguished contributors to this Symposium have emphasized the role of heredity in the determination of behavior. Not one has insisted that environmental factors are of primary significance in shaping the psychological characteristics of the individual. I am sure that all of them acknowledge the importance for behavior of the environmental factor whether it is called learning, practice, or the modification of the internal milieu. Historically, the interesting thing is that all of the speakers place their stress on heredity.

Twenty-five years ago, the situation was quite different. Such writers as J. B. Watson and Z. Y. Kuo were conducting a great offensive against the accepted belief that inherited patterns of behavior existed in man and animals. Kuo (1924) entitled one of his papers 'A psychology without heredity' (4) and proceeded essentially to deny even reflexes as inherited patterns of response. Watson (1914 and 1919) originally made much use of the concept of instinct in his books on *Behavior* (7) and *Psychology from the Standpoint of a Behaviorist* (8). However, in the 1924 volume entitled *Behaviorism*, after listing such responses as love, rage, fear, sneezing, feeding, and sex, which were termed unlearned behavior, Watson continues as follows: "In this relatively simple list of human responses there is none corresponding to what is called an 'instinct' by present-day psychologists and biologists. There are then for us no instincts—we no longer need the term in psychology.

Everything we have been in the habit of calling an 'instinct' today is a result largely of training—belongs to man's *learned behavior*. As a corollary from this we draw the conclusion that there is no such thing as an inheritance of *capacity, talent, temperament, mental constitution* and *characteristics*" (9, p. 94).

The anti-instinct movement came not only from some of the behaviorists but also from numerous writers on social psychology like Bernard, Dunlap, Faris, and Kantor. I believe that a prime basis for the origin of this anti-heredity movement was the violent reaction against the presentation of the topic of instinct in William McDougall's (1908) *Introduction to Social Psychology* (5). This book reached at least the 22nd revised edition (1931), and few psychologists whose professional careers occupy only the last twenty years have any appreciation of the tremendous influence exercised earlier by this work. The primary instincts and emotions as well as the innate tendencies there described, however, offered a too facile means of describing social behavior, and thus they were wide-open to the type of attack later made on them by the critics. Nevertheless, I should like partly to counteract the neglect from which McDougall's psychology currently suffers by giving a brief quotation from the *Social Psychology* bearing principally on human behavior: "Now, the afferent or receptive part and the efferent or motor part [of the instinct] are capable of being greatly modified, independently of one another and of the central part, in the course of the life history of the individual; while the central part persists throughout life as the essential unchanging nucleus of the disposition." ". . . the actual bodily movements by which the instinctive process achieves its end may be complicated to an indefinitely great extent; while the emotional excitement, with the accompanying nervous activities of the central part of the disposition, is the only part of the total instinctive process that retains its specific character and remains common to all individuals and all situations in which the instinct is excited" (5, pp. 33–34). That I agree with the gist of these quotations will be apparent in the concluding sentences of this discussion.

The net result of the anti-instinct movement was to all but purge the term instinct from the psychological vocabulary. And it will have been noted that the term is not conspicuous in the present Symposium. Articles on instinct which appeared during the period, for example my own paper in 1920 on 'The modification of instinct from the standpoint of social psychology' (2), received far less attention and exercised for less influence than should have been the case! And writers whose experiments, I think, justified a clear-cut conclusion on the influence of hereditary factors on behavior, for example Leonard Carmichael's article in 1926 on 'The development of behavior in vertebrates experimentally removed from the influence of external stimulation' (1), were led to minimize such an influence.

One should not assume from the foregoing that there have been no excellent studies of instincts and inherited capacities during the past twenty-five years. The contrary is the case. The following are a few examples of such studies, many of them conducted by members of this Symposium: (1) studies of the pecking behavior of chicks; (2) hoarding and maternal behavior of rats; (3) the neurological and hormonal factors controlling emotional behavior; (4) patterns of sexual behavior; (5) the establishment by selective breeding of strains of bright and dull rats; (6) co-twin and race studies of intelligence; (7) unlearned pattern organization of the afferent neural centers; (8) fetal and neonate behavior; and (9) the study of tropisms.

The type of investigation which is conspicuously missing from the above list is the one dealing with the genetics of behavior crosses, work of the character published by Yerkes (10) as far back as 1913 on the inheritance of savageness and wildness in rats. Although the biologist does not limit his discussion of heredity to those cases where the genetics of the transmission of traits has been worked out, it is clear that the understanding of heredity in general rests largely on the experiments in breeding various genetic strains. There is a great dearth of material on the genetics of behavior patterns; and, so far as I can find, no one has brought together in critical summary such studies as do exist.

It is true that there are many genealogical studies of human behavior and behavior capacities, but by and large these do not inspire confidence in the critically minded student unless they deal with the inheritance of such characteristics as color blindness where training and social factors can have but little influence. By contrast the genealogical evidence presented for the inheritance of feeblemindedness, behavior disorders, musical talent, and general eminence is far from convincing support for the conclusion that these aspects of human nature are essentially gene determined. Educational influences, social ostracisms and rewards, and intra-familial relationships may well be the prime factors producing a run of such traits in specific families.

The late Charles R. Stockard in his *Genetic and Endocrine Basis for Differences in Form and Behavior* (6) contributed extensively to the problem of genetics in various breeds of dogs. This work was oriented primarily toward the inheritance of endocrine structure and function and gave little attention to patterns of behavior not hormonally controlled. The results showed typical variations in the histological structure of the glands and typical ratios of glandular to bodily weight for the various dog hybrids. Associated with these variations in endocrine function went certain emotional or temperamental dispositions in the standard dog breeds and in their hybrids. W. T. James and O. D. Anderson, working at the Cornell Dog Farm on Stockard's animals, were able to show the influence of these temperamental traits on conditioning. Anderson comments on the work in part as follows: "The inherited pattern of the internal secretions may differ but slightly between one 'normal' individual and another and, consequently, behavior may deviate but little from one to the other. But when the pattern is a markedly distorted one, the individual's behavior may show correspondingly great deviation from the normal. The glands may thus be found to play a significant role, not only in the production of the various 'normal' types and patterns of behavior, but also in the production of the abnormal types" (6, p. 747).

If it is correct, as it is customary, to say that by behavior we mean motor and glandular responses, then we can say that there is evidence from genetics for the inheritance of glandular behavior. Endocrine secretions are well known for their effects upon brain functioning, as in cretinism, as well as upon the growth and functioning of many other organs. To the extent that the degree of endocrine activity is gene determined, to that extent the genes may be said to determine the above mentioned functions. There is a growing body of evidence which also indicates that one function of the hormones is to sensitize neural centers and thus to make possible the arousal of rare or unsuspected patterns of motor behavior. Drs. Stone and Beach have both contributed to the study of this problem in the field of sex behavior. It is well known even to the lay observer that in many species an individual of either sex may manifest a partial pattern of the sex behavior of the other even without any abnormality of the gonads, although males predominantly exhibit male reactions and females, female reactions. Dr. Beach in particular has clarified this problem in his studies of mating behavior in pre-pubertally castrated male and female rats. Thus he finds that females treated with testosterone show a very greatly increased percentage of essentially completed male sex responses. The total picture is very complex; but the important points to make in the present context are: (1) patterns of sex behavior do appear in essentially unlearned form and in a style typical of the species; (2) the degree of hormonal activity itself may be a gene determined trait; and (3) the existence of male and female behavior patterns in the same individual may be shown or their occasional appearance accentuated by the action of hormones probably acting as sensitizers of neural centers.

I believe that it is important in considering the role of heredity in the determination of behavior to distinguish between direct and indirect effects— between the inheritance of receptors, effectors, or other organs which may indirectly affect behavior on the one hand and the inheritance of those neural patterns which directly control behavior on the other hand. Thus there is no question but that human behavior may be different from what it would otherwise be if the individual has hereditary color blindness, or polydactyly, or dwarfism, or even red hair. However, it is not so clear, due to the lack of data on the genetics of behavior crosses, that there are even in animals inherited patterns of neural activity. Of course neural patterns as structures are as open to inheritance as are bone structures. And the widespread existence in animals below man of essentially stereotyped unlearned responses is enough to satisfy many students of the reality of inherited neural patterns. Nevertheless, the situation would be very much more satisfying if it were possible to point to genetic results where the inherited behavior patterns could not be due to receptor, effector, or other non-neural structure differences. Two illustrations will help make clear the kind of data that I hope some one will secure. Most birds appear to have the sensory and motor equipment for nest building, but not all of these birds build nests nor, where they do, do they build nests of equal complexity. Since the behavior runs true to the variety of bird, since it is not due to imitation of the parents and has no learning history in the individual's lifetime, it is surely an instinct, a behavior pattern fundamentally controlled by inherited neural connections. By contrast we may consider the voice of the mule which is more like that of the ass than that of the horse. This difference may be due to inherited vocal structures rather than to inherited neural patterns which control what the vocal structures do.

It is man's lack of elaborate, unlearned stereotyped forms of externally observable behavior which has led to the denial of the importance of heredity in human behavior and which has led specifically to the denial of human instincts. If man periodically manifested an elaborate unlearned courtship and mating ritual, if the human female came into heat at stated intervals and then performed a fairly fixed pattern of behavior, if man did not need to learn to build houses and yet did build them periodically and always essentially to the same plan, then there would only be a few recalcitrant souls to deny the direct role of heredity in determining human behavior. However, the evolutionary development which culminated in the primates did not proceed by merely continuing the type of behavioral organization found in lower animals. To have done so would have meant primate dominance by insect-like instinctive behavior with a relative neglect of learning, symbolic processes, and other plastic modes of adjustment. In the primates there is not only a marked cephalization in the organization of neural and behavioral controls; there is also, as has been pointed out today, a partial independence of external behavior from hormonal control. Thus, I may say, as McDougall recognized, evolutionary development has largely freed man from a dependence upon directly inherited behavior patterns except for those controlling reflex responses, emotions, drives, and certain general capacities.

## REFERENCES

1. CARMICHAEL, L. The development of behavior in vertebrates experimentally removed from the influence of external stimulation. PSYCHOL. REV., 1926, 33, 51–58.

2. HUNTER, W. S. The modification of instinct from the standpoint of social psychology. PSYCHOL. REV., 1920, 27, 247–269.

3. ——. The nature of instinct and its modification. Psychosom. Med., 1942, 4, 166–170.

4. KUO, Z. Y. A psychology without heredity. PSYCHOL. REV., 1924, 31, 427–448.

5. MCDOUGALL, W. An introduction to so-

352     W. S. HUNTER

*cial psychology.* (4th ed.) Boston:
Luce, 1911.

6. STOCKARD, C. R. *The genetic and endocrine basis for differences in form and behavior.* Philadelphia: Wistar Institute, 1941.

7. WATSON, J. B. *Behavior: an introduction to comparative psychology.* New York: Holt, 1914.

8. ——. *Psychology from the standpoint of a behaviorist.* Philadelphia: Lippincott, 1919.

9. ——. *Behaviorism.* New York: Norton, 1924.

10. YERKES, R. M. The heredity of savageness and wildness in rats. *J. animal Behav.,* 1913, 3, 286–296.

# 17

Reprinted from pages 337, 340–346, and 358–363 of Q. Rev. Biol. **28**(4):337–363 (1953)

# A CRITIQUE OF KONRAD LORENZ'S THEORY OF INSTINCTIVE BEHAVIOR

By DANIEL S. LEHRMAN

*The American Museum of Natural History and Rutgers University*

BEGINNING about 1931, Konrad Lorenz, with his students and collaborators (notably N. Tinbergen), has published numerous behavioral and theoretical papers on problems of instinct and innate behavior which have had a widespread influence on many groups of scientific workers (Lorenz, 1931, 1932, 1935, 1937a; Lorenz and Tinbergen, 1938; Lorenz, 1939; Tinbergen, 1939; Lorenz, 1940, 1941; Tinbergen, 1942, 1948a, 1950; Lorenz, 1950; Tinbergen, 1951). Lorenz's influence is indicated in the founding of the *Zeitschrift für Tierpsychologie* in 1937 and in its subsequent development, and also in the journal *Behaviour*, established in 1948 under the editorship of an international board headed by Tinbergen.

Lorenz's theory of instinctive and innate behavior has attracted the interest of many investigators, partly because of its diagrammatic simplicity, partly because of its extensive use of neurophysiological concepts, and partly because Lorenz deals with behavior patterns drawn from the life cycle of the animals discussed, rather than with the laboratory situations most often found in American comparative psychology. These factors go far toward accounting for the great attention paid to the theory in Europe, where most students of animal behavior are zoologists, physiologists, zoo curators or naturalists, unlike the psychologists who constitute the majority of American students of animal behavior (Schneirla, 1945).

In recent years Lorenz's theories have attracted more and more attention in the United States as well, partly because of a developing interest in animal behavior among American zoologists and ecologists, and partly through the receptive audience provided for Lorenz and his colleague, Tinbergen, by American ornithologists. The ornithologists were interested from the start, especially because a great part of the material on which Lorenz based his system came from studies of bird behavior, but the range of interest in America has widened considerably. Lorenz and his theories were recently the subject of some discussion at a conference in New York at which zoologists and comparative psychologists were both represented (Riess, 1949), and are prominently represented in the recent symposium on animal behavior of the Society of Experimental Biologists (Armstrong, 1950; Baerends, 1950; Hartley, 1950; Koehler, 1950; Lorenz, 1950; Tinbergen, 1950), and extensively used in several chapters of a recent American handbook of experimental psychology which will be a standard sourcebook for some years to come (Beach, 1951a; Miller, 1951; Nissen, 1951).

*[Editor's Note: Material has been omitted at this point.]*

## PROBLEMS RAISED BY INSTINCT THEORIES

Even this brief summary brings to light several questions which ought to be critically examined with reference to the theory. These are questions, furthermore, which apply to instinct theories in general. Among them are: (1) the problem of "innateness" and the maturation of behavior; (2) the problem of levels of organization in an organism; (3) the nature of evolutionary levels of behavioral organization, and the use of the comparative method in studying them; and (4) the manner in which physiological concepts may be properly used in behavior analysis. There follows

209

an evaluation of Lorenz's theory in terms of these general problems.

### "Innateness" of behavior

#### The problem

Lorenz and Tinbergen consistently speak of behavior as being "innate" or "inherited" as though these words surely referred to a definable, definite, and delimited category of behavior. It would be impossible to overestimate the heuristic value which they imply for the concepts "innate" and "not-innate." Perhaps the most effective way to throw light on the "instinct" problem is to consider carefully just what it means to say that a mode of behavior is innate, and how much insight this kind of statement gives into the origin and nature of the behavior.

Tinbergen (1942), closely following Lorenz, speaks of instinctive acts as "highly stereotyped, coordinated movements, the neuromotor apparatus of which belongs, in its complete form, to the hereditary constitution of the animal." Lorenz (1939) speaks of characteristics of behavior which are "hereditary, individually fixed, and thus open to evolutionary analysis." Lorenz (1935) also refers to perceptual patterns ("releasers") which are presumed to be innate because they elicit "instinctive" behavior the *first time* they are presented to the animal. He also refers to those motor patterns as innate which occur for the first time when the proper stimuli are presented. Lorenz's student Grohmann (1938), as well as Tinbergen and Kuenen (1939), speak of behavior as being innately determined because it matures instead of developing through learning.

It is thus apparent that Lorenz and Tinbergen, by "innate" behavior, mean behavior which is hereditarily determined, which is part of the original constitution of the animal, which arises quite independently of the animal's experience and environment, and which is distinct from acquired or learned behavior.

It is also apparent, explicitly or implicitly, that Lorenz and Tinbergen regard as the major *criteria* of innateness that: (1) the behavior be stereotyped and constant in form; (2) it be characteristic of the species; (3) it appear in animals which have been raised in isolation from others; and (4) it develop fully-formed in animals which have been prevented from practicing it.

Undoubtedly, there are behavior patterns which meet these criteria. Even so, this does not neces-sarily imply that Lorenz's *interpretation* of these behavior patterns as "innate" offers genuine aid to a scientific understanding of their origin and of the mechanisms underlying them.

In order to examine the soundness of the concept of "innateness" in the analysis of behavior, it will be instructive to start with a consideration of one or two behavior patterns which have already been analyzed to some extent.

#### Pecking in the chick

Domestic chicks characteristically begin to peck at objects, including food grains, soon after hatching (Shepard and Breed, 1913; Bird, 1925; Cruze, 1935; and others). The pecking behavior consists of at least three highly stereotyped components: head lunging, bill opening and closing, and swallowing. They are ordinarily coordinated into a single resultant act of lunging at the grain while opening the bill, followed by swallowing when the grain is picked up. This coordination is present to some extent soon after hatching, and improves later (even, to a slight extent, if the chick is prevented from practicing).

This pecking is stereotyped, characteristic of the species, appears in isolated chicks, is present at the time of hatching, and shows some improvement in the absence of specific practice. Obviously, it qualifies as an "innate" behavior, in the sense used by Lorenz and Tinbergen.

Kuo (1932a-d) has studied the embryonic development of the chick in a way which throws considerable light on the origin of this "innate" behavior. As early as three days of embryonic age, the neck is passively bent when the heartbeat causes the head (which rests on the thorax) to rise and fall. The head is stimulated tactually by the yolk sac, which is moved mechanically by amnion contractions synchronized with the heartbeats which cause head movement. Beginning about one day later, the head first bends *actively* in response to tactual stimulation. At about this time, too, the bill begins to open and close when the bird nods—according to Kuo, apparently through nervous excitation furnished by the head movements through irradiation in the still-incomplete nervous system. Bill-opening and closing become independent of head-activity only somewhat later. After about 8 or 9 days, fluid forced into the throat by the bill and head movements causes swallowing. On the twelfth day, bill-opening always follows head-movement.

In the light of Kuo's studies the "innateness" of the chick's pecking takes on a different character from that suggested by the concept of a unitary, innate item of behavior. Kuo's observations strongly suggest several interpretations of the *development* of pecking (which, of course, are subject to further clarification). For example, the head-lunge arises from the passive head-bending which occurs contiguously with tactual stimulation of the head while the nervous control of the muscles is being established. By the time of hatching, head-lunging in response to tactual stimulation is very well established (in fact, it plays a major role in the hatching process).

The genesis of head-lunging to visual stimulation in the chick has not been analyzed. In *Amblystoma*, however, Coghill (1929) has shown that a closely analogous shift from tactual to visual control is a consequence of the establishment of certain anatomical relationships between the optic nerve and the brain region which earlier mediated the lunging response to tactual stimulation, so that visual stimuli come to elicit responses established during a period of purely tactual sensitivity. If a similar situation obtains in the chick, we would be dealing with a case of intersensory equivalence, in which visual stimuli, because of the anatomical relationships between the visual and tactual regions of the brain, became equivalent to tactual stimuli, which in turn became effective through an already analyzed process of development, which involved conditioning at a very early age (Maier and Schneirla, 1935).

The originally diffuse connection between head-lunge and bill-opening appears to be strengthened by the repeated elicitation of lunging and billing by tactual stimulation by the yolk sac. The repeated elicitation of swallowing by the pressure of amniotic fluid following bill-opening probably is important in the establishment of the post-hatching integration of bill-opening and swallowing.

### Maternal behavior in the rat

Another example of behavior appearing to fulfil the criteria of "innateness" may be found in the maternal behavior of the rat.

Pregnant female rats build nests by piling up strips of paper or other material. Mother rats will "retrieve" their pups to the nest by picking them up in the mouth and carrying them back to the nest. Nest-building and retrieving both occur in all normal rats; they occur in rats which have been raised in isolation; and they occur with no evidence of previous practice, since both are performed well by primiparous rats (retrieving may take place for the first time only a few minutes after the birth of the first litter of a rat raised in isolation). Both behavior patterns therefore appear to satisfy the criteria of "innateness" (Wiesner and Sheard, 1933).

Riess (pers. com.), however, raised rats in isolation, at the same time preventing them from ever manipulating or carrying any objects. The floor of the living cage was of netting so that feces dropped down out of reach. All food was powdered, so that the rats never carried food pellets. When mature, these rats were placed in regular breeding cages. They bred, but did *not* build normal nests or retrieve their young normally. They scattered nesting material all over the floor of the cage, and similarly moved the young from place to place without collecting them at a nest-place.

Female rats do a great deal of licking of their own genitalia, particularly during pregnancy (Wiesner and Sheard, 1933). This increased licking during pregnancy has several probable bases, the relative importance of which is not yet known. The increased need of the pregnant rat for potassium salts (Heppel and Schmidt, 1938) probably accounts in part for the increased licking of the salty body fluids as does the increased irritability of the genital organs themselves. Birch (pers. com.) has suggested that this genital licking may play an important role in the development of licking and retrieving of the young. He is raising female rats fitted from an early age with collars made of rubber discs, so worn that the rat is effectively prevented from licking its genitalia. Present indications, based on limited data, are that rats so raised eat a high percentage of their young, that the young in the nest may be found under any part of the female instead of concentrated posteriorly as with normal mother rats, and that retrieving does not occur.

These considerations raise some questions concerning nativistic interpretations of nest-building and retrieving in the rat, and concerning the meaning of the criteria of "innateness." To begin with, it is apparent that practice in carrying food pellets is partly equivalent, for the development of nest-building and retrieving, to practice in carrying nesting-material, and in carrying the young. Kinder (1927) has shown that nest-building activity is inversely correlated with environmental temperature, and that it can be stopped by raising the temperature sufficiently. This finding, together with Riess's experiment, suggests that the nest-building activity arises from ordinary food (and other object) manipulation and collection under conditions where the accumulation of certain types of manipulated material leads to immediate satisfaction of one of the animal's needs (warmth). The fact that the rat is generally more active at lower temperatures (Browman, 1943; Morgan, 1947) also contributes to the probability that nest-building activity will develop. In addition, the rat normally tends to stay close to the walls of its cage, and thus to spend much time in corners. This facilitates the collection of nesting material into one corner of the cage, and the later retrieving of the young to that corner. Patrick and Laughlin (1934) have shown that rats raised in an environment without opaque walls do not develop this "universal" tendency of rats to walk close to the wall. Birch's experiment suggests that the rat's experience in licking its own genitalia helps to establish retrieving as a response to the young, as does its experience in carrying food and nesting material.

#### Maturation-vs.-learning, or development? The isolation experiment

These studies suggest some second thoughts on the nature of the "isolation experiment." It is obvious that by the criteria used by Lorenz and other instinct theorists, pecking in the chick and nest-building and retrieving in the rat are not "learned" behavior. They fulfil all criteria of "innateness," i.e., of behavior which develops without opportunity for practice or imitation. Yet, in each case, analysis of the developmental process involved shows that the behavior patterns concerned are not unitary, autonomously developing things, but rather that they emerge ontogenetically in complex ways from the previously developed organization of the organism in a given setting.

What, then is wrong with the implication of the "isolation experiment," that behavior developed in isolation may be considered "innate" if the animal did not practice it specifically?

Lorenz repeatedly refers to behavior as being innate because it is displayed by animals raised in isolation. The raising of rats in isolation, and their subsequent testing for nesting behavior, is typical of isolation experiments. The development of the

chick inside the egg might be regarded as the ideal isolation experiment.

It must be realized that an animal raised in isolation from fellow-members of his species *is not necessarily isolated from the effect of processes and events which contribute to the development of any particular behavior pattern*. The important question is not "Is the animal isolated?" but *"From what is the animal isolated?"* The isolation experiment, if the conditions are well analyzed, provides at best a negative indication that certain specified environmental factors probably are not directly involved in the genesis of a particular behavior. However, the isolation experiment by its very nature does not give a positive indication that behavior is "innate" or indeed any information at all about what the process of development of the behavior really consisted of. The example of the nest-building and retrieving by rats which are isolated from other rats but not from their food pellets or from their own genitalia illustrates the danger of assuming "innateness" merely because a *particular* hypothesis about learning seems to be disproved. This is what is consistently done by Tinbergen, as, for example, when he says (1942) of certain behavior patterns of the three-spined stickleback: "The releasing mechanisms of these reactions are all innate. A male that was reared in isolation . . . was tested with models before it had ever seen another stickleback. The . . . [stimuli] . . . had the same releaser functions as in the experiments with normal males." Such isolation is by no means a final or complete control on possible effects from experience. For example, is the "isolated" fish uninfluenced by its own reflection from a water film or glass wall? Is the animal's experience with human handlers, food objects, etc., really irrelevant?

Similarly, Howells and Vine (1940) have reported that chicks raised in mixed flocks of two varieties, when tested in a Y-maze, learn to go to chicks of their own variety more readily than to those of the other variety. They concluded that the "learning is accelerated or retarded . . . because of the directive influence of innate factors." In this case, Schneirla (1946) suggests that the effect of the chick's experience with its own chirping during feeding has not been adequately considered as a source of differential learning previous to the experiment. This criticism may also be made of a similar study by Schoolland (1942) using chicks and ducklings.

Even more fundamental is the question of what

is meant by "maturation." We may ask whether experiments based on the assumption of an absolute dichotomy between maturation and learning ever really tell us *what* is maturing, or how it is maturing? When the question is examined in terms of *developmental* processes and relationships, rather than in terms of preconceived categories, the maturation-versus-learning formulation of the problem is more or less dissipated. For example, in the rat nest-building probably does not mature autonomously—and it is *not* learned. It is not "nest-building" which is learned. Nest-building develops in certain situations through a developmental process in which at each stage there is an identifiable interaction between the environment and organic processes, and within the organism; this interaction is based on the preceding stage of development and gives rise to the succeeding stage. These interactions are present from the earliest (zygote) stage. Learning may emerge as a factor in the animal's behavior even at early embryonic stages, as pointed out by Carmichael (1936).

Pecking in the chick is also an emergent—an integration of head, bill, and throat components, each of which has its own developmental history. This integration is already partially established by the time of hatching, providing a clear example of "innate" behavior in which the statement "It is innate" adds nothing to an understanding of the developmental process involved. The statement that "pecking" is innate, or that it "matures," leads us *away* from any attempt to analyze its specific origins. The assumption that pecking grows *as* a pecking *pattern* discourages examination of the embryological processes leading to pecking. The elements out of whose interaction pecking emerges are not originally a unitary pattern; they *become* related as a consequence of their positions in the organization of the embryonic chick. The understanding provided by Kuo's observations owes nothing to the "maturation-versus-learning" formulation.

Observations such as these suggest many new problems the relevance of which is not apparent when the patterns are nativistically interpreted. For example, what is the nature of the rat's temperature-sensitivity which enables its nest-building to vary with temperature? How does the animal develop its ability to handle food in specific ways? What are the physiological conditions which promote licking of the genitalia, etc.? We want to know much more about the course of establishment of the connections between the chick's head-lunge and bill-opening, and between bill-opening and swallowing. This does *not* mean that we expect to establish which of the components is learned and which matured, or "how much" each is learned and how much matured. The effects of learning and of structural factors differ, not only from component to component of the pattern, but also from developmental stage to developmental stage. What is required is a continuation of the careful analysis of the characteristics of each developmental stage, and of the transition from each stage to the next.

Our scepticism regarding the heuristic value of the concept of "maturation" should not be interpreted as ignorance or denial of the fact that the physical growth of varied structures plays an important role in the development of most of the kinds of behavior patterns under discussion in the present paper. Our objection is to the *interpretation* of the role of this growth that is implied in the notion that the *behavior* (or a *specific* physiological substrate for it) is "maturing." For example, the post-hatching improvement in pecking ability of chicks is very probably due in part to an increase in strength of the leg muscles and to an increase in balance and stability of the standing chick, which results partly from this strengthening of the legs and partly from the development of equilibrium responses (Cruze, 1935). Now, isolation or prevention-of-practice experiments would lead to the conclusion that this part of the improvement was due to "maturation." Of course it is partly due to growth processes, *but what is growing is not pecking ability*, just as, when the skin temperature receptors of the rat develop, what is growing is not nest-building activity, *or anything isomorphic with it*. The use of the categories "maturation-vs.-learning" as explanatory aids usually gives a false impression of unity and directedness in the growth of the behavior pattern, when actually the behavior pattern is not primarily unitary, nor does development proceed in a straight line toward the completion of the pattern.

It is apparent that the use of the concept of "maturation" by Lorenz and Tinbergen as well as by many other workers is not, as it at first appears, a reference to a process of development but rather to ignoring the process of development. To say of a behavior that it develops by maturation is tantamount to saying that the obvious forms of learning do not influence it, and that we therefore do not consider it necessary to investigate its ontogeny further.

### Heredity-vs.-environment, or development?

Much the same kind of problem arises when we consider the question of what is "inherited." It is characteristic of Lorenz, as of instinct theorists in general, that "instinctive acts" are regarded by him as "inherited." Furthermore, inherited behavior is regarded as sharply distinct from behavior acquired through "experience." Lorenz (1937a) refers to behavior which develops "entirely independent of all experience."

It has become customary, in recent discussions of the "heredity-environment" problem, to state that the "hereditary" and "environmental" contributions are both essential to the development of the organism; that the organism could not develop in the absence of either; and that the dichotomy is more or less artificial. [This formulation, however, frequently serves as an introduction to elaborate attempts to evaluate what part, or even what percentage, of behavior is genetically determined and what part acquired (Howells, 1945; Beach, 1947a; Carmichael, 1947; Stone, 1947).] Lorenz does not make even this much of a concession to the necessity of developmental analysis. He simply states that some behavior patterns are "inherited," others "acquired by individual experience." I do not know of any statement of either Lorenz or Tinbergen which would allow the reader to conclude that they have any doubts about the correctness of referring to behavior as simply "inherited" or "genically controlled."

Now, what exactly is meant by the statement that a behavior pattern is "inherited" or "genically controlled"? Lorenz undoubtedly does not think that the zygote contains the instinctive act in miniature, or that the gene is the equivalent of an entelechy which purposefully and continuously tries to push the organisms's development in a particular direction. Yet one or both of these preformistic assumptions, or their equivalents, must underlie the notion that some behavior patterns are "inherited" as such.

The "instinct" is obviously not present in the zygote. Just as obviously, it is present in the behavior of the animal after the appropriate age. The problem for the investigator who wishes to make a causal analysis of behavior is: How did this behavior come about? The use of "explanatory" categories such as "innate" and "genically fixed"

obscures the necessity of investigating developmental *processes* in order to gain insight into the actual mechanisms of behavior and their interrelations. The problem of development is the problem of the development of new structures and activity patterns from the resolution of the interaction of *existing* structures and patterns, within the organism and its internal environment, and between the organism and its outer environment. At any stage of development, the new features emerge from the interactions within the *current* stage and between the *current* stage and the environment. The interaction out of which the organism develops is *not* one, as is so often said, between heredity and environment. It is between *organism* and environment! And the organism is different at each different stage of its development.

Modern physiological and biochemical genetics is fast destroying the conception of a straight-line relationship between gene and somatic characteristic. For example, certain strains of mice contain a mutant gene called "dwarf." Mice homozygous for "dwarf" are smaller than normal mice. It has been shown (Smith and MacDowell, 1930; Keeler, 1931) that the cause of this dwarfism is a deficiency of pituitary growth hormone secretion. Now what are we to regard as "inherited"? Shall we change the name of the mutation from "dwarf" to "pituitary dysfunction" and say that dwarfism is not inherited as such—that what is inherited is a hypoactive pituitary gland? This would merely push the problem back to an earlier stage of development. We now have a better understanding of the origin of the dwarfism than we did when we could only say it is "genically determined." However, the pituitary function developed, in turn, in the context of the mouse as it was when the gland was developing. The problem is: What was that context and how did the gland develop out of it?

What, then, is inherited? From a somewhat similar argument, Jennings (1930) and Chein (1936) concluded that only the zygote is inherited, or that heredity is only a stage of development. There is no point here in involving ourselves in tautological arguments over the definition of heredity. It is clear, however, that to say a behavior pattern is "inherited" throws no light on its *development* except for the purely negative implication that *certain types* of learning are not directly involved. Dwarfism in the mouse, nest-building in the rat, pecking in the chick, and the "zig-zag dance" of the stickleback's courtship (Tinbergen, 1942) are all "inherited" in the sense and by the criteria used by Lorenz. But they are not by any means phenomena of a common type, nor do they arise through the same kinds of developmental processes. To lump them together under the rubric of "inherited" or "innate" characteristics serves to block the investigation of their origin just at the point where it should leap forward in meaningfulness. [Anastasi and Foley (1948), considering data from the field of human differential psychology, have been led to somewhat the same formulation of the "heredity-environment" problem as is presented here.]

### Taxonomy and Ontogeny

Lorenz (1939) has very ably pointed out the potential importance of behavior elements as taxonomic characteristics. He has stressed the fact that evolutionary relationships are expressed just as clearly (in many cases more clearly) by similarities and differences in behavior as by the more commonly used physical characteristics. Lorenz himself has made a taxonomic analysis of a family of birds in these terms (Lorenz, 1941), and others have been made by investigators influenced by him (Delacour and Mayr, 1945; Adriaanse, 1947; Baerends and Baerends-van Roon, 1950). This type of analysis derives from earlier work on the taxonomic relations of behavior patterns by Whitman (1898, 1919), Heinroth (1910, 1930), Petrunkevitsch (1926), and others.

Lorenz's brilliant approach to the taxonomic analysis of behavior characteristics has had wide influence since it provides a very stimulating framework in which to study species differences and the specific characteristics of behavior. However, it does not necessarily follow from the fact that behavior patterns are species-specific that they are "innate" as patterns. We may emphasize again that the systematic stability of a characteristic does not indicate anything about its mode of development. The fact that a characteristic is a good taxonomic character does not mean that it developed autonomously. The shape of the skull bones in rodents, which is a good taxonomic character (Romer, 1945), depends in part upon the presence of attached muscles (Washburn, 1947). We cannot conclude that because a behavior pattern is taxonomically stable it must develop in a unitary, independent way.

In addition it would be well to keep in mind that the species-characteristic nature of many behavior patterns may result partly from the fact that all members of the species grow in the same environment. Smith and Guthrie (1921) call such behavior elements "coenotropes." Further, it is not at all necessary that these common features of the environment be those which seem a priori to be relevant to the behavior pattern under study. Lorenz's frequent assumption (e.g., 1935) that the effectiveness of a given stimulus on first presentation demonstrates an innate sensory mechanism specific for that stimulus is not based on analysis of the origin of the stimulus-effectiveness, but merely on the fact that Lorenz has eliminated the major alternative *he* sees to the nativistic explanation.

Thorpe and Jones (1937) have shown that the apparently innate choice of the larvae of the flour moth by the ichneumon fly *Nemerites* as an object in which to deposit its eggs is actually a consequence of the fact that the fly larva was *fed* on the larvae of the flour moth while it was developing. By raising *Nemerites* larvae upon the larvae of *other* kinds of moth Thorpe and Jones caused them, when adult, to choose preponderantly these other moths on which to lay their eggs. The choice of flour-moth larvae for oviposition is quite characteristic of *Nemerites* in nature. In view of Thorpe and Jones' work, it would obviously be improper to conclude from this fact that the choice is based on innately-determined stimuli. Yet, before their paper was published, the species-specific character of the behavior would have been just as impressive evidence for "innateness" as species-specificity *ever* is.

Taxonomic analysis, while very important, is not a substitute for concrete analysis of the ontogeny of the given behavior, as a source of information about its origin and organization.

[*Editor's Note:* Material has been omitted at this point.]

## CONCLUSION

We have summarized the main points of Lorenz's instinct theory, and have subjected it to a critical examination. We find the following serious flaws:

1. It is rigidly canalized by the merging of widely different kinds of organization under inappropriate and gratuitous categories.

2. It involves preconceived and rigid ideas of innateness and the nature of maturation.

3. It habitually depends on the transference of concepts from one level to another, solely on the basis of analogical reasoning.

4. It is limited by preconceptions of isomorphic resemblances between neural and behavioral phenomena.

5. It depends on finalistic, preformationist conceptions of the development of behavior itself.

6. As indicated by its applications to human psychology and sociology, it leads to, or depends on, (or both), a rigid, preformationist, categorical conception of development and organization.

Any instinct theory which regards "instinct" as immanent, preformed, inherited, or based on specific neural structures is bound to divert the investigation of behavior development from fundamental analysis and the study of developmental problems. Any such theory of "instinct" inevitably tends to short-circuit the scientist's investigation of intraorganic and organism-environment developmental relationships which underlie the development of "instinctive" behavior.

## ACKNOWLEDGMENTS

I am greatly indebted to Dr. T. C. Schneirla (who originally suggested the writing of this paper) and to Dr. J. Rosenblatt for many stimulating and helpful discussions of the problems discussed here. Dr. Schneirla in particular has devoted much attention to criticism of the paper at various stages.

The following people also have read the paper, in part and at various stages, and have made many helpful suggestions and comments: Drs. H. G. Birch, K. S. Lashley, D. Hebb, H. Klüver, L. Aronson, J. E. Barmack, L. H. Hyman, L. H. Lanier, and G. Murphy. Since these scientists differ widely in the extent of their agreement or disagreement with various points of my discussion, I must emphasize that none of them is in any way responsible for any errors of omission or commission that may appear.

Present address: Rutgers University, Newark 2, N. J.

[*Editor's Note:* Only those references cited in the preceding article are included here.]

## LIST OF LITERATURE

ADRIAANSE, M. S. C., 1947. *Ammophila campestris* Latr. und *Ammophila adriaansei* Wilcke. Ein Beitrag zur vergleichenden Verhaltensforschung. *Behavior*, 1:1–34.

ANASTASI, A., and J. P. FOLEY, JR. 1948. A proposed reorientation in the heredity-environment controversy. *Psychol. Rev.*, 55:239–249.

ARMSTRONG, E. A. 1950. The nature and function of displacement activities. *Symp. Soc. exp. Biol.*, 4:361–384.

BAERENDS, G. P. 1950. Specializations in organs and movements with a releasing function. *Symp. Soc. exp. Biol.*, 4:337–360.

BAERENDS, G. P., and J. M. BAERENDS-VAN ROON. 1950. An introduction to the study of the ethology of cichlid fishes. *Behaviour,* suppl. 1:1–242.

BEACH, F. A. 1947a. Evolutionary changes in the physiological control of mating behavior in mammals. *Psychol. Rev.*, 54:297–315.

———. 1951a. Instinctive behavior: reproductive activities. In *Handbook of Experimental Psychology* (S. S. Stevens, ed.) pp. 387–434. John Wiley & Sons, New York.

BIRD, C. 1925. The relative importance of maturation and habit in the development of an instinct. *Pedagog. Semin.*, 32:68–91.

BROWMAN, L. G. 1943. The effect of controlled temperatures upon the spontaneous activity rhythms of the albino rat. *J. exp. Zool.*, 94:477–489.

CARMICHAEL, L. 1936. A re-evaluation of the concepts of maturation and learning as applied to the early development of behavior. *Psychol. Rev.*, 43:450–470.

———. 1947. The growth of the sensory control of behavior before birth. *Psychol. Rev.*, 54:316–324.

CHEIN, I. 1936. The problems of heredity and environment. *J. Psychol.*, 2:229–244.

COGHILL, G. E., 1929. *Anatomy and the Problem of Behavior.* Cambridge University Press, London.

CRUZE, W. W. 1935. Maturation and learning in chicks. *J. Comp. Psychol.*, 19:391–409.

DELACOUR, J., and E. MAYR. 1945. The family Anatidae. *Wilson Bull.*, 57:3–55.

GROHMANN, J. 1938. Modifikation oder Funktionsreifung? Ein Beitrag zur Klärung der wechselseitigen Beziehungen zwischen Instinkhandlung und Erfahrung. *Z. Tierpsychol.*, 2:132–144.

HARTLEY, P. H. T. 1950. An experimental analysis of interspecific recognition. *Symp. Soc. exp. Biol.*, 4:313–336.

HEINROTH, O. 1910. Beiträge zur Biologie, namentlich Ethologie und Psychologie der Anatiden. *Int. orn. Congr.*, 5(Berlin): 589–702.

———. 1930. Ueber bestimmte Bewegungsweisen bei Wirbeltieren. *S. Ges. naturf. Fr., Berl.*, 1929:333–342.

HOWELLS, T. H. 1945. The obsolete dogmas of heredity. *Psychol. Rev.* 52:23–34.

———, and D. O. VINE. 1940. The innate differential in social learning. *J. abnorm. (soc.) Psychol.*, 35:537–548.

JENNINGS, H. S. 1930. *The Biological Basis of Human Nature.* Norton & Co., New York.

KEELER, C. 1931. *The Laboratory Mouse.* Harvard University Press, Cambridge.

KINDER, E. F. 1927. A study of the nest-building activity of the albino rat. *J. exp. Zool.*, 47:117–161.

KOEHLER, O., 1950. Die Analyse der Taxisanteile instinktartigen Verhaltens. *Symp. Soc. exp. Biol.*, 4:269–303.

KUO, Z. Y. 1932a. Ontogeny of embryonic behavior in Aves. I. The chronology and general nature of the behavior of the chick embryo. *J. exp. Zool.*, 61:395–430.

———. 1932b. Ontogeny of embryonic behavior in Aves. II. The mechanical factors in the various stages leading to hatching. *J. exp. Zool.*, 62:453–489.

———. 1932c. Ontogeny of embryonic behavior in Aves. III. The structure and environmental factors in embryonic behavior. *J. comp. Psychol.*, 13:245–272.

———. 1932d. Ontogeny of embryonic behavior in Aves. IV. The influence of embryonic movements upon the behavior after hatching. *J. comp. Psychol.*, 14:109–122.

LORENZ, K. 1931. Beiträge zur Ethologie sozialer Corviden. *J. Orn., Lpz.*, 79:67–127.

———. 1932. Betrachtungen über das Erkennen der arteigenen Triebhandlungen der Vögel. *J. Orn., Lpz.*, 80:50–98.

———. 1935. Der Kumpan in der Umwelt des Vogels. *J. Orn. Lpz.*, 83:137–213, 289–413.

———. 1937a. Ueber den Bergriff der Instinkthandlung. *Folia biotheor., Leiden*, 2:17–50.

————. 1939. Vergleichende Verhaltensforschung. *Zool. Anz.*, 12 (Suppl. band): 69–102.

————. 1940. Durch Domestikation verursachte Störungen arteigenen Verhaltens. *Z. angew. Psychol. Charakterkunde* 59:2–81.

————. 1941. Vergleichende Bewegungsstudien an Anatinen. J. Orn., Lpz., 89 (Sonderheft): 194–294.

————. 1950. The comparative method in studying innate behavior patterns. *Symp. Soc. exp. Biol.*, 4:221–268.

————, and N. TINBERGEN. 1938. Taxis und Instinkthandlung in der Eirollbewegung der Graugans. I. *Z. Tierpsychol.*, 2:1–29.

MAIER, N. R. F., and T. C. SCHNEIRLA. 1935. *Principles of Animal Psychology.* McGraw-Hill Co., New York.

MILLER, N. E. 1951. Learnable drives and rewards. In *Handbook of Experimental Psychology* (S. S. Stevens, ed.), pp. 435–472. John Wiley & Sons, New York.

MORGAN, C. T. 1947. The hoarding instinct. *Psychol. Rev.*, 54:335–341.

NISSEN, H. W. 1951. Phylogenetic comparison. In *Handbook of Experimental Psychology* (S. S. Stevens, ed.), pp. 347–386. John Wiley & Sons, New York.

PATRICK, J. R., and R. M. LAUGHLIN. 1934. Is the wall-seeking tendency in the white rat an instinct? *J. genet. Psychol.*, 44:378–389.

PETRUNKEVITSCH, A. 1926. The value of instinct as a taxonomic character in spiders. *Biol. Bull., Wood's Hole*, 50:427–432.

RIESS, B. F. 1949a. A new approach to instinct. *Sci. & Soc.*, 13:150–154.

————. 1949b. The isolation of factors of learning and native behavior in field and laboratory studies. *Ann. N. Y. Acad. Sci.*, 51:1093–1102.

ROMER, A. S. 1945. *Vertebrate Paleontology.* University of Chicago Press, Chicago.

SCHNEIRLA, T. C. 1945. Contemporary American animal psychology in perspective. In *Twentieth Century Psychology.* (P. Harriman, ed.) pp. 306–316. Philosophical Library, New York.

————. 1946. Problems in the biopsychology of social organization. *J. abnorm. (soc.) Psychol.*, 41:385–402.

SCHOOLLAND, J. B. 1942. Are there any innate behavior tendencies? *Genet. Psychol. Monogr.*, 25:219–287.

SHEPARD, J. F., and F. S. BREED. 1913. Maturation and use in the development of an instinct. *J. Anim. Behav.*, 3:274–285.

SMITH, P. E., and E. C. MacDOWELL. 1930. An hereditary anterior-pituitary deficiency in the mouse. *Anat. Rec.*, 46:249–257.

SMITH, S., and E. R. GUTHRIE. 1921. *General Psychology in Terms of Behavior.* Appleton, New York.

STONE, C. P. 1947. Methodological resources for the experimental study of innate behavior as related to environmental factors. *Psychol. Rev.*, 54:342–347.

THORPE, W. H., and F. G. W. JONES. 1937. Olfactory conditioning in a parasitic insect and its relation to the problem of host selection. *Proc. roy. Soc.*, B, 124:56–81.

TINBERGEN, N. 1939. On the analysis of social organization among vertebrates, with special reference to birds. *Amer. Midl. Nat.*, 21:210–234.

————. 1942. An objectivistic study of the innate behaviour of animals. *Bibl. biotheor., Leiden*, D, 1:39–98.

_____. 1948a. Physiologische Instinkforschung. *Experientia*, 4:121–133.

_____. 1950. The hierarchical organization of nervous mechanisms under-lying instinctive behaviour. *Symp. Soc. exp. Biol.*, 4:305–312.

_____. 1951. *The Study of Instinct*. Oxford University Press, Oxford.

_____, and D. J. KUENEN. 1939. Ueger die auslosenden und die richtungge-benden Reizsituationen der Sperrbewegung von jungen Drosseln (*Tur-das m. merula* L. und *T. e. ericetorum* Turton). *Z. Tierpsychol.*, 3:37–60.

WASHBURN, S. L. 1947. The relation of the temporal muscle to the form of the skull. *Anat. Rec.*, 99:239–248.

WHITMAN, C. O. 1899. Animal Behavior. *Biol. Lect. mar. biol. Lab. Wood's Hole*, 1898:285–338.

_____. 1919. The behavior of pigeons. *Publ. Carneg. Inst.*, 257:1–161.

WEISNER, B. P., and N. M. SHEARD. 1933. Maternal Behaviour in the Rat. Oliver & Boyd, London.

Part VII

# LEARNING

# Editor's Comments
# on Papers 18 Through 22

In the view of various authors, comparative psychology in the twentieth century became nothing but the study of learning in artificial situations. Hopefully, it is already apparent to the reader that the field is much more diverse and multifaceted than implied by such authors. Nevertheless, the study of learning and of the evolution of learning ability has been a major topic in comparative psychology throughout its history and remains so today.

Many of the issues that would later dominate debate on the study of behavior in general and learning in particular can be seen in an early exchange between E. L. Thorndike and T. Wesley Mills (Papers 18, 19, and 20). Thorndike's dissertation (1898a), *Animal Intelligence, An Experimental Study of the Associative Processes in Animals,* is a classic and was summarized in *Science* (Paper 18). Thorndike studied dogs, cats, and chicks, but is best known for his work on cats learning to escape from puzzle boxes. Thorndike found that his animals learned many tasks, but concluded that they did so via the gradual formation of many small connections and not via complex processes of insight or consciousness. He believed that these processes were essentially identical in all vertebrates, a conclusion that did little to foster comparative study of learning in later years. Further, Thorndike believed that animals failed to learn through imitation. Thorndike's research was in controlled situations and he emphasized quantitative measurement of behavior.

In the same year, Thorndike (1898b) wrote in *Science* a review of Mills's "Animal Intelligence" (excerpted as Paper 11) and was highly critical of Mills's methodology. Mills (Paper 19), in turn, wrote a scathing review of Thorndike's work. Mills accused Thorndike of neglecting prior literature in comparative psychology and of ignoring individual differences. Mills's major criticism, however, was that Thorndike tested animals under unnatural conditions that would not permit the full expression of the animals' potentially complex behavior. He noted, "As well enclose a living man in a coffin, lower him, against his will, into the earth, and attempt to deduce normal psychology from his conduct" (p. 266). Mills regarded imitation as widespread among higher vertebrates.

In his reply (Paper 20), Thorndike repeated his pleas for methodological rigor. He noted his awareness of the problem of unnatural conditions; however, he proposed that unnaturalness per se is not a sufficient problem to invalidate his research.

The archetypical study in animal psychology of which ethologists and others have been critical is the analysis of rats learning to negotiate mazes. It is generally agreed that the animals and tasks were chosen arbitrarily and without regard to the naturally occurring behavior of the animals under study. W. S. Small and Linus Kline were primarily responsible for initiating research on rats learning various tasks under laboratory conditions. In 1930 both Carl Warden (1930) and Walter Miles (Paper 21) attempted to reconstruct the events surrounding the beginnings of this research through published correspondence with its imitators. It is apparent in reading this correspondence that Kline and Small were very much aware of the importance of matching the task to the animal's abilities and behavioral tendencies and that the choice of neither animal nor task was arbitrary.

The comparative study of animal learning was addressed throughout the century. The subjects varied and included both invertebrates and vertebrates. Few meaningful species differences were found with respect to the learning of simple tasks. Therefore, psychologists devised more complex problems with which to confront their animals: reversal learning, delayed response, oddity learning, alternation, delayed alternation, and double alternation. One task that became quite popular was the "learning set," promulgated especially by Harry F. Harlow (Paper 22). In the learning set procedure, animals are presented with a series of different discrimination, and one determines whether the experience of solving the earlier tasks aids them in "learning to learn." Harlow contends that this task is especially useful in detecting meaningful differences in complex learning ability. It became widely used in comparative analyses of learning, although critics (e.g., Warren, 1973) have noted various difficulties in interpreting species differences.

Problems in interpreting quantitative differences in learning ability are so great that Bitterman (1965) proposed an emphasis on qualitative comparisons. The dominant contemporary trend, however, appears to be toward analysis of the specific ways in which individual species have become adapted to learn particular tasks relevant to their success in nature (e.g., Seligman, 1970). We may be winding up very close to the positions of Mills, Kline, and Small, but with the advantages of greater methodological rigor as promulgated by Thorndike, Harlow, and Bitterman.

## REFERENCES

Bitterman, M. E., 1965, Phyletic Differences in Learning, *Am. Psychol.* **20:**396–410.

Seligman, M. E. P., 1970, On the Generality of the Laws of Learning, *Psychol. Rev.* **77:**406–418.

Thorndike, E. L., 1898a, Animal Intelligence: An Experimental Study of the Associative Processes in Animals, *Psychol. Rev. Monogr. Suppl.* **2**(4): 1–109.

Thorndike, E. L., 1898b, Review of W. Mills's *Animal Intelligence, Science* **8:**520.

Warden, C. J., 1930, A Note on the Early History of Experimental Methods in Comparative Psychology, *J. Genet. Psychol.* **38:**466–471.

Warren, J. M., 1973, Learning in Vertebrates, in *Comparative Psychology: A Modern Survey,* D. A. Dewsbury and D. A. Rethlingshafer, eds., McGraw-Hill, New York.

# 18

Reprinted from *Science* **7**:818–824 (1898)

# SOME EXPERIMENTS ON ANIMAL INTELLIGENCE

**Edward Thorndike**
*Psychological Laboratory*
*Columbia University*

THE results of a recent investigation on animal intelligence, the details of which are about to be published,* seem to be of sufficient general interest to deserve an independent statement here. The experiments were upon the intelligent acts and habits of a considerable number of dogs, cats and chicks. The method was to put the animals when hungry in enclosures from which they could escape (and so obtain food) by operating some simple mechanism, *e. g.*, by turning a wooden button that held the door, pulling a loop attached to the bolt, or pressing down a lever. Thus one readily sees what sort of things the animals can learn to do and just how they learn to do them. Not only were the actions of the animals in effecting escape observed, but also in every case an accurate record was kept of the times taken to escape in the successive trials. The first time that a cat is put into such an enclosure, some minutes generally elapse before its instinctive struggles hit upon the proper movement, while after enough trials it will make the right movement immediately upon being put in the

box. The time records show exactly the method and rate of progress from the former to the latter condition of affairs. A graphic representation of the history of six kittens that learned to get out of a box $20 \times 15 \times 12$ inches, the door of which opened when a wooden button $3\frac{1}{2}$ inches long, $\frac{7}{8}$ inch wide, was turned, is found in the curves in Figure 1. These curves are formed by joining the tops of perpendiculars erected along the abscissa at intervals of 1 mm. Each perpendicular represents one trial in the box; its height represents the time taken by the animal to escape, every 1 mm. equalling 10 seconds. A break in the curve means that in the trials it stands for, the animal failed in ten minutes to escape. Short perpendiculars below the abscissa mark intervals of twenty-four hours between trials. Longer intervals are designated by figures for the number of days or hours. The small curves at the right of the main ones are, as the figures beneath them show, records of the skill of the animal after a very long interval without practice. This process of associating a certain act with a certain situation is the type of all the intelligent performances of animals, and by thus recording the progress of a lot of animals, each in forming a lot of each kind of associa-

---

* Animal Intelligence ; An Experimental Study of the Associative Processes in Animals ; *Psychological Review*, Supplement No. 8.

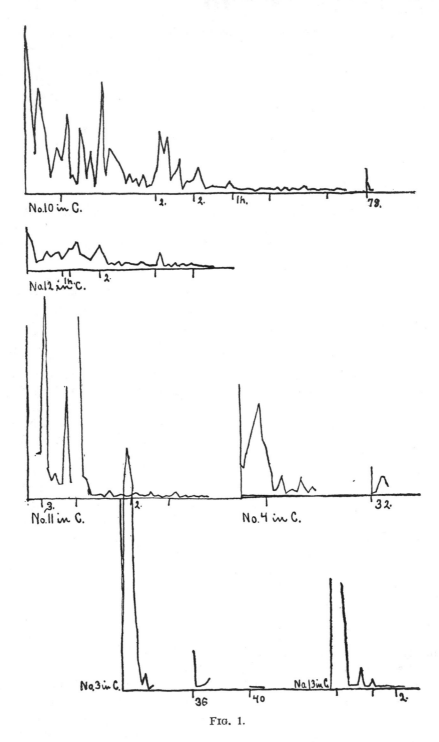

Fig. 1.

tion, one gets a quantitative estimate of what animals can learn and how they learn it.

What happens in all these cases is this: The animal on being put into the box, and so confronted with the situation 'confinement with food outside,' bursts forth into the instinctive activities which have in the course of nature been connected with such a situation. It tries to squeeze through any openings, claws and bites at the walls confining it, puts its paws through and claws at things outside trying to pull itself out. It may rush around, doing all this with extraordinary vehemence and persistence. If these impulsive activities fail to include any movement which succeeds in opening the door, the animal finally stops them and remains quietly in the box. If in their course the animal does accidentally work the mechanism (claw the button round, for instance), and thus win freedom and food, the resulting pleasure will stamp in the act, and when again put in the box the animal will be likely to do it sooner. This continues; all the squeezings and bitings and clawings which do not hit the vital point of the mechanism, and so do not result in any pleasure, get stamped out, while the particular impulse, which made the sucessful clawing or biting, gets stamped in, until finally it alone is connected with the sense-impression of the box's interior, and it is done at once when the animal is shut in. The starting point for the formation of any association is the fund of instinctive reactions. Whether or not in any case the necessary act will be learned depends on the possibility that in the course of these reactions the animal will accidentally perform it. The progress from accidental performance to regular, immediate, habitual performance depends on the inhibiting power of effort without pleasure and the strengthening by pleasure of any impulse that leads to it.

Although it was of the utmost importance to them to get out of the various boxes and was, therefore, certain that they would use to the full all their mental powers, none of the animals gave any sign of the possession of powers of inference, comparison or generalization. Moreover, certain of the experiments seem to take the ground from beneath the feet of those who credit reason to animals. For it was found that acts (e. g., opening doors by depressing thumb-latches and turning buttons) which these theorizers have declared incapable of performance by mere accident *certainly can be so done*. It is, therefore, unnecessary to invoke reasoning to account for these and similar successes with mechanical contrivances; and the argument based on them falls to the ground. Moreover, besides destroying the value of the evidence which has been offered for the presence of reason in animals, the time-records give us positive evidence that the subjects of these experiments could not reason. For the slopes of the curves are *gradual*. Surely if a cat made the movement from an inference that it would open the door, it ought, when again put in, to make the movement *immediately*. If its first success was due to an inference, all trials after the first should take a minimum time. And if there were any slightest rudiment of a reasoning faculty, even if no real power of inference, the cat ought at least sometime, in the course of ten or twenty successful trials, to realize that turning that button means getting out, and thenceforth make the movement from a decision, not a mere impulse. There ought, that is, to be a sudden change from the long, irregular times of impulsive activity to a regular minimum time. The change is as a fact very gradual.

Finally, experiments made in another connection show that these animals could not learn to perform even the simplest acts by seeing another do them or by being put through them by the experimenter. They were thus unable to infer that since another by pulling a string obtained fish, they might, or that since fish were gained when I pushed round a bar with their paws it would be gained if they pushed it round themselves.

Experiments were made on imitation by giving the animals a chance to see one of their fellows escape by clawing down a string stretched across the box, and then putting them in the same box alone. It was found that, no matter how many times they saw the act done, they could not thereby learn anything which their own impulsive activity had failed to teach them, and did not learn any more quickly what they would have sooner or later learned by themselves. One important consequence of these results is the resulting differentiation of the Primates from the other orders of mammals. If the Primates do imitate and the rest do not, we have located a definite step in the evolution of mind and given a new meaning to the line of human ancestry. I do not, however, hold that these results eliminate the possibility of an incipient faculty of imitation among mammals in general. They do deny the advisability of presupposing it without proof, and emphatically deny its presence in anything equivalent to the human form. Finally many actions which seem due to imitation may be modifications of some single instinct, such as that of following.

Perhaps the most valuable of the experiments were those which differentiate the process of association in animals from the ordinary 'association by contiguity' of human psychology. A man, if in a room from which he wishes to get out, may think of being outside, think of how he once opened the door, and accordingly go turn the knob and pull the door open. The *thought* of opening the door is sufficient to arouse the act of opening the door, and in most human

association-series the *thoughts* are the essential and sufficient factors. It has been supposed that the same held true of animals, that if the thought *of doing* a thing were present an impulse *to do* it would be readily supplied from a general stock. Such is not the case. *None of these animals could form an association leading to an act unless there was included in the association an impulse of its own which led to the act.* Thus cats who had been induced to crawl into a box as the first element in a pleasurable association-series soon acquired the habit of crawling in of their own accord, while cats who had been *dropped in* did not. In the second case the *idea of being in* would be present as strongly as in the first, but the particular *impulse to go in* was not. So also cats who failed of themselves to learn certain acts could not be taught to do them by being put through them, while cats who were thus put through acts which accident would of itself alone have taught them, learned them no more quickly and often made the movement in a way quite different from that which they were shown. Their associations are not primarily associations of ideas with ideas, but associations of sense-impressions and ideas *with impulses to acts, muscular innervations.* The impulse, the innervation, is the essential.

This does not mean that the animals can have no representations or images at all. Another set of experiments show that they probably can. It means that they have no stock of free-floating impulses which can be called on at will; that the elements of their associations occur chiefly just in their particular connections; that their ideational life consists not of a multitude of separate ideas, but of a number of specific connections between ideas and impulses.

Having thus denied that animal association is homologous with human association, as the latter is ordinarily conceived, we find the true homologue of animal association in the mental process involved when a man learns to play tennis or billiards or to swim. Both contain sense-impressions, impulses, acts, and possibly representations. Both are learned gradually. Such human associations cannot be formed by imitation or by being put through the movement. Nor do its elements have any independent existence in a life of free ideas apart from their place in the associations. No tennis player's stream of thought is filled with representations of the tens of thousands of sights he has seen or movements he has made on the tennis-court, though his whole attention was on them at the time.

The great step in the evolution of human intellection is then not a jump to reason through language, but a change from a consciousness which equals a lot of specific connections to a consciousness which includes a multitude of free ideas. This is the prerequisite of all the human advance. Once get free ideas in abundance, and comparison, feelings of transition or relation, abstractions and 'meanings' of all sorts may emerge. In this respect, as in imitation, the monkeys bear the marks of their relationship.

Besides the experiments resulting in this new analysis of the mental processes of animals, others were made to discover the delicacy, complexity, number and permanence of their associations. It was found that naturally they discriminate very little, that what they react to is a vague, unanalyzed total situation. Thus, cats that had learned to climb up the front of a cage on hearing the words, 'I must feed those cats,' would climb up just as readily if you said, 'What time is it?' or any short sentence. By associating only the right reaction with pleasure, however, you can render the association delicate to any degree consistent with their sense powers. For instance, a cat was taken that was just

beginning to form the association between the words, 'I must feed those cats,' and the act of climbing up the front of the cage (after she climbed up she was given a bit of fish). She was now given a lot of trials, some as just described, some with the signal changed to, 'I will not feed them.' At these trials she got no fish. The purpose was to see how many trials would be required before she would learn always to climb up at the "I must feed" and always stay down at the "I will not." The two sorts of trials were mixed indiscriminately. 60 of the "I must feed"'s were, in addition to its previous training, enough to make the proper reaction to it inevitable. 380 of the 'I will not''s were required before perfect discrimination between it and the former signal was attained.

It was found that complex associations (such, e.g., as the way to escape from a box where the door fell open only after a platform had been pushed down, a string clawed and a bar turned around) were very slowly formed and never really formed at all. That is, the animals did not get so that they went through the several acts in a regular order and without repeating uselessly one element. In respect to delicacy and complexity, then, we see a tremendous difference between association in animals and association in man.

Equally great is the difference in number. A practised billiard player has more associations due to just this one pastime than a dog has for his whole life's activity. The increase in the number of associations is a sign, and very likely a cause, of the advance to a life of free ideas. Yet, small as it is, in comparison with our own, the number of associations which an animal may acquire is probably much larger than previous writers have fancied.

A great many experiments were made on the permanence of associations after from 10 to 70 days. Samples of the results will be found in the figure given. What an animal once acquires is long in being lost, and this power of retention thus renders the power of acquisition a big factor in the struggle for existence. But these experiments give better information than this quantitative estimate of the value of past experience, for they demonstrate conclusively that the animals have no real memory. The cat or dog that is put into a box from which he has escaped thirty or forty times, after an interval of fifty days without any experience with it, will escape quicker than he did in his first experience and will reach a perfect mastery of the association in much fewer trials than he did before, but he will reach it *gradually*. If he had true memory he would, when put in the box after the interval, after a while think, " Oh, yes! pulling this string let me out," and thenceforth would pull the string *as soon as dropped in the box*. In the case of genuine memory you either know a thing and do it or forget it utterly and fail to do it at all. So with a man recalling the combination to a safe, for instance. But the memory of the animal is only that of a billiard player who hasn't played for a long interval and who gradually recovers his skill. No billiard player keeps thinking, "Two years ago I hit a ball placed like this in such and such a way." And the cat or dog does not think, " When I was in this box before, I got out by pulling that string." Not only the gradual recovery of skill, but also the actions of the animal show this. In case of an association only partially permanent the animal claws around the vital spot, or claws feebly and intermittently, or varies its attacks on the loop or what not, by instinctive bitings and squeezings. Memory in animals is permanence of associations, not conscious realization that a certain event or sequence occurred in the past.

So much for some of the experiments and what theoretical consequences they seem directly to involve. The general view which the entire investigation has forced upon me is that animals do not think *about* things at all, that consciousness is for them always consciousness in its first intention, 'pure experience,' as Lloyd Morgan says. They feel all their sense-impressions as we feel the sky and water and movements of our body when swimming. They see the thumb-latch as the ball-player sees the ball speeding toward him. They depress the thumb-piece, not because they think about the act, but just because they feel like doing so. And so their mental life never gets beyond the limits of the least noticeable sort of human intellection. Conception, inference, judgment, memory, self-consciousness, social consciousness, imagination, association and perception, in the common acceptation of the terms, are all absent from the animal mind. Animal intellection is made up of a lot of specific connections, whose elements are restricted to them, and which subserve practical ends *directly*, and is homologous with the intellection involved in such human associations as regulate the conduct of a man playing tennis. The fundamental phenomenon which I find presented in animal consciousness is one which can harden into inherited connections and reflexes, on the one hand, and thus connect naturally with a host of the phenomena of natural life ; on the other hand, it emphasizes the fact that our mental life has grown up as a mediation between stimulus and reaction. The old view of human consciousness is that it is built up out of elementary sensations, that very minute bits of consciousness come first and gradually get built up into the complex web. It looks for the beginnings of consciousness to *little* feelings. This our view abolishes, and declares that the progress is not from little and simple to big and complicated, but from direct connections to indirect connections in which a stock of isolated elements plays a part ; is from 'pure experience' or un-differentiated feelings to discrimination, on the one hand, to generalizations, abstractions, on the other.   If, as seems probable, the Primates display a vast increase of associations, and a stock of free-swimming ideas, our view gives to the line of descent a meaning which it never could have so long as the question was the vague one of more or less 'intelligence.'   It will, I hope, when supported by an investigation of the mental life of the Primates and of the period in child life when these directly practical associations become overgrown by a rapid luxuriance of free ideas, show us the real history of the origin of human faculty.

# 19

Reprinted from *Psychol. Rev.* **6**:262–274 (1899)

## THE NATURE OF ANIMAL INTELLIGENCE AND THE METHODS OF INVESTIGATING IT.

### BY PROFESSOR WESLEY MILLS.

*McGill University, Montreal.*

Those interested in this subject may be classified in the main somewhat as follows perhaps :

1. Those who see in the animal mind only a sort of weaker human intellect; who look chiefly for evidences of intelligence and take no account of the failures and stupidity of animals.

2. Those who recognize that the animal mind is not the equivalent of the human mind in all its qualities as it exists in men of superior development in the highest civilization, but who nevertheless recognize the resemblance up to a certain point to man.

3. Those who approach more or less closely to the view that animals are automata, or at all events consider animal consciousness as utterly different from human consciousness, except in a few of its lowest states. With regard to investigation or material of knowledge we recognize a class who, while suspicious with reference to the conclusions of the anecdotal school, do not consider anecdotes worthless, much less meriting the supreme contempt some writers manifest for such evidence. They believe that there is no more reason to set aside reliable anecdotes of animals than of men. Anecdotes may illustrate a normal, sub-normal or super-normal mental condition or development; but if they set forth facts it is for the psychologist to explain, not to ignore them. Another class of investigators see little or no good in anything in comparative psychology or psychology in general, except experiment, which is for them the sole key to a reliable knowledge of the mind.

Among psychologists as among biologists there are those who are willing to shut themselves up in the narrow lane of experiment—a lane with high walls on each side cutting off all view of the surrounding domain open to general observation and experience. As these people see so little themselves yet ever behold that little before them, they come to interpret everything in the light of their own limited observations. They insist on others believing as they do; they would have others wear the fetters they have put on themselves; all thinking must conform to the rigid conditions in which they are content to live and move and have their intellectual being.

The only hope of safety for the man who engages in experiment is ever to check his observations, and, above all, his conclusions, by other wider observations and those broad general principles which are like the points of the compass to the mariner; and I venture to suggest that it is the failure to do this which accounts for the greater part of the wrecks scattered along the shores and over the bottom of those seas traversed by the experimenter in biology and psychology.

As we have had what I cannot but think a recent conspicuous example of the sort of neglect referred to, I propose to criticise the methods pursued and the conclusions drawn, the more especially as this investigator claims to have swept away, at one fell swoop, almost the entire fabric of comparative psychology.[1] He appears to believe that he has razed the old structure to its very foundations and settled once and forever the weightiest problems with which others have been long struggling in vain.

Dr. Thorndike has not been hampered in his researches by any of that respect for workers of the past of any complexion which usually causes men to pause before differing radically from them, not to say gleefully consigning them to the psychological flames. For Dr. Thorndike the comparative psychologists are readily and simply classified—they are all insane—the only difference being the degree, for he speaks of one of them as being 'the sanest' of the lot.

Having thus cleared the way, this investigator proceeds to set forth, in no uncertain terms, what we should believe, and his creed is very brief and easily remembered. Animals neither

[1] ANIMAL INTELLIGENCE, by Ed. L. Thorndike. (Monograph Supplement to the PSYCHOLOGICAL REVIEW, Vol. II., No. 4, whole No. 8.)

imitate, feel sympathetically, reason nor remember, though about the latter point he is not quite so dogmatic.[1] He comes very near to the belief that they are automata pure and simple, though this he does not assert in so many words. The above mentioned views he thinks he has deduced from experiments. If so, the present writer thinks so much the worse for the experiments. At all events, with the exception of reasoning about which I wish to reserve judgment, I have come to widely different conclusions and from experiments also as well as from other sources of information.

Dr. Thorndike in criticising my book[2] has given the impression that I have not made experiments, or ' crucial experiments.' Now, I think it can be shown from my publications that I have recorded more experiments (not to mention scores which have not been described) than all other investigators together, if we except those working on insects. Moreover, these experiments have been invariably conducted under natural conditions, the absence of which seems to be almost a recommendation with some, but which I consider a fatal objection to Dr. Thorndike's work. Incidentally, I may remark that a laboratory as ordinarily understood is not well suited for making psychological experiments on animals.

When Dr. Thorndike charges that most of the books do not give us a psychology, but rather a eulogy of animals; that they have all been about animal intelligence, never about animal stupidity, I recognize a certain amount of truth in the imputation. But I beg to suggest that to a certain extent the same applies to works on human psychology. To what extent has the mind of the savage or semi-barbarous man been investigated? Yet to make comparisons between man and the lower animals parellel such a study is essential. I do not find Dr. Thorndike's publication any freer than others from the fallacies aris-

[1] In an account of his own work given by Dr. Thorndike in *Science* (Vol. VII., p. 823) he goes still further in his negations. " Conception, inference, judgment, memory, self-consciousness, social consciousness, imagination, association and perception, in the common acceptation of the terms, are all absent from the animal mind."

[2] The Nature and Development of Animal Intelligence. London, T. Fisher Unwin; New York, The Macmillan Company. 1898.

ing from considering the superior class of human minds or the civilized and educated man, and comparing him with the lower animals. Dr. Thorndike considers his experiments crucial; that individual peculiarities have been eliminated; that hunger is an adequate stimulus or condition; that no personal factor need be considered; that "the question of whether an animal does or does not form a certain association requires for an answer no higher qualification than a pair of eyes"—all of which I consider fallacious and to a large degree explanatory of the misleading psychology which he has constructed. With dogs I found several stimuli stronger than hunger, as any one really acquainted with the nature of animals must know, and such stimuli may, and frequently do, lead animals so to deport themselves that they become a perfect revelation to those who have long been associated with them.

I had that well illustrated in the case of a tame fox (vixen) that I reared. When a certain critical period (œstrum) was reached her whole nature took on a new character, and it became practically impossible to control her as formerly; and, unless I had ocular demonstration of the facts, I would not have believed it possible for any animal to have accomplished what this fox did. Nevertheless, in order to learn her methods of procedure it was necessary to observe unawares to her, and that I may say applies to very many studies of animals. That a pair of eyes is not all that is requisite for a complete outfit as an observer, Dr. Thorndike's work but too pointedly exemplifies. I venture to think that in all cases it is a question of whose eyes, or, in other words, the training those eyes have had, and still more of the intellect that passes judgment on what is seen.

I have all along endeavored to emphasize the importance of individual differences. They do somewhat disturb statistics, and they rather spoil curves, it is true, and experimenters have always been prone to ignore them; but they exist in nature, and when adequately recognized our explanations for many things will be found altogether too simple, and, therefore, delusive, rather than real and adequate.

Dr. Thorndike admits that ' an act of the sort likely to be attended to will be learned more quickly.' Undoubtedly, yet this investigator has practically ignored this in his tests, for he placed cats in boxes only 20×15×12 inches, and then expected them to act naturally. As well enclose a living man in a coffin, lower him, against his will, into the earth, and attempt to deduce normal psychology from his conduct.

The present writer has pointed out distinctly that when animals are removed from even their usual, not to say natural, surroundings they may be so confused or otherwise diordered that they fail to act normally, and this I have illustrated by experiments. Dr. Thorndike found that dogs when placed under similarly improper and disturbing conditions, as I deem them, behaved in a like panicky way, except that they gave up sooner, which he attributes in part to their being insufficiently hungry. But dogs have not as much perseverance as cats, as my experiments abundantly prove. However, had Dr. Thorndike witnessed the resources of my dogs when let loose in the yard after some of their companions, which had already been set free in the adjoining fields and woods, I can believe that even one so fast bound in the grip of his experiments as he would have altered his opinions on this and many other subjects. In dogs under such circumstances we have illustrated not alone an adequate motive or stimulus, but it is shown that they have memory—can conjure up exciting pictures of the pleasure-giving scenes of the past, re-experience in some fashion the delights associated with that past, make a sort of generalized abstract of the whole—in a word, have very much the same experiences as the human being who accompanies them and delights in such things.

When the contrary is proved by adequate observations or experiments, I am ready to alter my opinions, but not on such evidence as seems to go directly counter to all that one has borne in upon him by daily observation. To do otherwise is, indeed, to bid adieu to common sense as well as to science, and to accept as proof what seems to me of no more value than counterfeit coins, but which, nevertheless, like bogus money, deceives the unwary, even among psychologists.

The experiments on chicks I consider the least misleading and most valuable part of Dr. Thorndike's work. Not only are birds much lower in the psychological scale; not only does free association explain more in their case, but the conditions of the experiments were rather more natural. A pen 16 × 14 × 10 makes for a chick a very different thing from one 20 × 15 × 12 for a cat. Even those curves which in the case of the cats and dogs only serve to stereotype error are possibly of some value when applied to the chicks. Says Dr. Thorndike: "I hate to burden the reader with the disgusting rhetoric which would result if I had to insist on particularizations and reservations at every step." If anything, just such particulars might have somewhat redeemed these experiments. They might at least have proved helpful in some way. At the present stage of comparative psychology we are in need of observations down to the minutest details. We can better spare the rhetoric.

When we consider how widespread—indeed, almost universal—is imitation among animals of the middle and higher grades, that it is difficult so to separate it from the general psychic life of the animal as to be able fairly to analyze their mental processes and determine how much is due to independent development *per se* and how much to imitation, one cannot but marvel at the degree to which that magic word of modern science 'experiment' can blind the mind to facts thick as the leaves of the forest, and all pointing to the importance of imitation in animal life. So obvious an example of imitation as the talking of parrots is set aside or twisted out of all recognition. It is, moreover, a case of heads I win, tails you lose. Much that Dr. Thorndike has said when discussing this subject is valuable as suggesting a basis for observation and on the genesis of imitation, though this applies also to human psychology. There is one fallacy that underlies the whole of Dr. Thorndike's experimenting and vitiates his conclusions, namely, this: that he overlooks the many possible and actual inhibitions to response to a stimulus. One would have thought that the case of the cat mentioned by him (p. 59) would have given him pause. The conduct of that cat, like all the rest, only proves to him that animals do not imitate.

I find myself ever disposed to imitate in certain cases, yet do not. To illustrate—when I read a chapter on psychology written in the fascinating style of James, one exemplifying the profundity of a Ladd or a Hall, the bold constructive character of a

Baldwin, or a vigorous plea on behalf of modern psychology by Cattell—the list might be much enlarged—I am filled with admiration, and there is an impulse to imitate, but I have not as yet taken the first step. Having thus been the subject of experiment in this way over and over again, I should, according to the logic of Dr. Thorndike, be characterized as a non-imitating creature—not only as regards the subject in question, but generally. The truth is far from this. There is a strong tendency on my part to imitate, but there are stronger forces acting to inhibit the process, and, moreover, these forces are not always the same nor is each always equally potent. In truth, the whole matter is very complex even in animals. I find no difficulty whatever in explaining why the animals did not respond to the stimuli Dr. Thorndike used.

When one meets the *questionaires* he seems at last to strike the rock bottom of common sense. The author of the experiments referred to has no high opinion of the trainers. " I would first adjust all things in connection with the surroundings of the cat so that they would be applicable to the laws of nature, and then proceed to teach the trick." I see much saving sense in this remark, and believe that had Dr. Thorndike grasped its significance he would have given us a very different psychology. The writer seems to have totally neglected the methods and experience of the trainers of dogs for field work, and has also I believe failed to make use of the lessons the trainers of trick animals can teach us. Even to witness a performance of trick animals is enough to enable one to see how at one time the tendency to imitate assists and at another mars the performance. To be sure, there is a sort of deliberate, studied, high-class imitation possible to man, but beyond the reach of animals, but this is, after all, comparatively rarely employed in the lives of the great mass of men.

A student of McGill University has communicated to me the fact that a kitten which could not be induced to jump over an object placed before it did so only after seeing the mother do it, and after that there was no more trouble in getting it to perform the trick. The young hounds of the Montreal Hunt Club are taught by being actually put through the performance, *i. e.,* they are attached to an old and strong dog while hunting, so that Dr. Thorndike's contention as to the uselessness of an animal's being put through a performance breaks down. Indeed, that was to be expected even from his own teaching as to the genesis of associations, to go no further. As to the inability of animals to have memory images for which Dr. Thorndike contends I find myself, in the light of my experience with animals, quite unable to agree. I believe that their memory is like our memory of the same things so far as image, etc., are concerned, but that there may be with man, owing to the complexity of his mental condition, a more varied fringe around that memory core which latter will be much alike in both the man and the animal.

To refer to but a single experiment to illustrate this : I had a greyhound that was very prone to chase cats, a habit which became with him more and more pronounced, I presume, from his success in consequence of his speed. On the occasion I wish to emphasize I had taken the dog in a certain direction, and, as a result, a cat crossing the street was so hotly pursued by him that she took to a tree. Many months after I brought the dog along this same way, but approached the scene of the exciting chase from the opposite direction. Long before the exact spot was reached the dog was all attention. It was perfectly plain that he remembered the long-past incident, and that certain feelings (which accompanying feelings Dr. Thorndike denies to animals) were also aroused; but great was my astonishment when the dog stopped at a certain tree, looked up and behaved otherwise in such a manner as left no doubt in my mind that he remembered the identical tree and every detail of the whole incident. This cannot be explained by the sort of consecutive association that Dr. Thorndike would substitute for 'memory' as ordinarily understood, for the locality was approached from the opposite direction.

The central phenomena of memory were in this case the same with the dog and his master, but the feelings and the mental fringe or associated ideas were not identical. In the one case they were appropriate to the dog, in the other to the man, his master, who was in this instance trying to draw some psychological conclusions, so the difference was considerable ; but had it been a hunting expedition in which both dog and man took an active part, the resemblance even in revival would have been altogether greater.

One finds in the end, however, that Dr. Thorndike does allow representation to animals within very narrow limits. Along with this writer's " I never succeeded in getting the animal to change its way for mine," a quotation from a recent interesting and instructive publication seems timely : " One must be familiar with the normal conditions of the insects in question before he is able to note those slight changes in the environment that offer some opportunity for an adaptation of means to ends, or before he is competent to devise experiments which test their powers in this direction."[1]  The above seems to the present writer to be applicable in the widest sense to investigations in comparative psychology.

The experiments to which Dr. Thorndike refers under the heading 'Association by Similarity and the Formation of Concepts' only really show that animals may react to a vague stimulus, and this is quite sufficient to meet the ends of their existence in many cases; but neither these experiments nor any others show conclusively that this alone is the best of which animals are capable.  The comparison of animal consciousness to human consciousness during swimming is open to the same objection.  Such a mental state is possible to both man and animals, but neither is confined within such narrow limits of almost pure sensation.

I must object to Dr. Thorndike's analysis of human consciousness in playing open-air games as being inadequate.  It does not correspond with my own experience nor with the accounts I have heard persons of different degrees of skill give as to what was going on in their minds during the playing of games.  No doubt Dr. Thorndike's account does fit a certain portion of the mental phenomena, but the whole matter is much more complex than he seems to think, and is worthy of an analysis more accurate and comprehensive than has ever been given to it.  Such views of animal consciousness as Dr. Thorndike presents seem

[1] Instincts and Habits of the Solitary Wasps, by Geo. W. Peckham and Elizabeth G. Peckham, p. 234.

to me altogether too narrow to meet the actual mental condition of, say, a dog when engaged in a fowling expedition.

From certain experiments which I made with my dogs in play, taken along with scores of others, I find myself utterly unable to agree with many of the views of the destructive or narrowly restrictive school of comparative psychologists. We should surely be very cautious in denying wholly to animals what Dr. Thorndike terms ' free floating ideas.' The believer in evolution will demand that, in this and other cases in which qualities man possesses are denied to animals, there be the clearest proofs given. The burden of proof lies with those who deny them, and this remark applies to feelings as well as intellectual processes, though to a less degree. Nor can I agree with those who maintain that we must always adopt the *simplest* explanation of an animal's action. Such does not apply to man, and why should it meet every case among animals? Though in this regard Professor C. Ll. Morgan with others seems to me to be in error, I fully agree with the views of this writer as quoted in the publication under consideration (p. 86) : " Lastly, before taking leave of the subject of the chapter, I am most anxious that it should not be thought that in contending that intelligence is not reason I wish in any way to disparage intelligence," etc. But Professor Morgan is more and more in sympathy with the destructive school, so that he now seems willing to surrender anything to all and sundry who may ask him to stand and deliver. I have been myself classed by one of my reviewers[1] with Romanes. While I agree with much in Romanes' attitude in regard to animal intelligence, nevertheless, since this writer preferred to work upon second-hand material rather than make observations and experiments for himself, and had, moreover, a tendency to speculation rather than the accumulation and weighing of facts, I prefer to be myself considered an humble follower of Darwin, who, so far as he went in animal psychology, best illustrates the method and especially the spirit that will, I think, prove most fruitful.

The one point about which I feel like withholding an opinion till many more observations have been made is that of reasoning.

[1] *Science*, Vol. VIII., p. 520.

That animals can reach C by some mental process when A and B are given, and that this is to be explained either by some process of inference or by one as yet unexplained, I have little doubt. Unquestionably, association explains much in the mental structure of man and still more in animals, but that this is the whole story when we get beyond elementary chapters in instinct I cannot for a moment believe, unless the meaning of the word is greatly and unwisely extended. The subconscious must enter largely into the psychic life of animals, as of men, and one who observes animals long and closely must believe that no such naked skeleton as Dr. Thorndike presents to us can represent the animal mind.

The mental processes of an animal are generally not comparable to pure tones, but rather like those tones that abound in overtones, though this applies still more to man. Our age will probably be looked back upon as one characterized intellectually by great destructive and constructive activity, but also as one readily satisfied with unduly simple explanations put forward with a confidence and rashness that will be astounding to a later age. As showing, however, a different spirit and tendency I quote the following [1] with much gratification, coming, as it does, from two most patient, sympathetic and successful observers: " Our study of the activities of wasps has satisfied us that it is impossible to classify them in any simple way. The old notion that the acts of bees, wasps and ants were all varying forms of instinct is no longer tenable and must give way to a more philosophical view. It would appear to be quite certain that these are not only instinctive acts, but acts of intelligence as well, and a third variety also—acts that are probably due to imitation, although whether much or little intelligence accompanies this imitation is admittedly difficult to determine. Again, acts that are instinctive in one species may be intelligent in another, and we may even assert that there is considerable variation in the amount of intelligence displayed by different individuals of the same species."

The same may, I believe, be affirmed for animals generally; and it is work of the character described in the monograph

[1] Op. cit., p. 228.

from which I quote which really advances comparative psychology.

Were it possible to observe an animal, say a dog, from the moment of its birth onward continuously for one year, noting the precise conditions and all that happens under these conditions, the observer being unnoticed by the creature studied, we should, I believe, be in possession of one of the most valuable contributions it is possible to make to comparative psychology. This would imply not one, but several persons giving up their whole time, day and night, by turns, to such a task. As yet, but very imperfect approaches have been made to anything of the kind; nevertheless, such as they have been, they are the most valuable contributions thus made, in the opinion of the present writer, and the more of such we have the better.

If to such a study another were added, in which the effect of altering conditions from time to time with the special object of testing the results on an animal or animals similarly closely observed from birth onward, we should have another most valuable contribution to comparative psychology; but experiment on animals whose history is unknown must, in the nature of the case, be very much less valuable than in such an instance as that just supposed.

As Professor Groos has suggested in a private communication to me, it is important to make observations on wild animals, and there seems to be room for the worker in comparative psychology in zoological gardens as well as in the field or forest. But I must again maintain that it is fact rather than theory—observation, as ordinarily understood, and experiment—that are more needed than anything else as yet.

### Résumé.

Comparative psychology is advanced rather by systematic observations and experiments than by anecdotes; nevertheless, the latter, when strictly true, are not valueless.

The study of the development of the animal mind (genetic psychology) is of the highest importance.

Insufficient attention has been paid to distinguishing between normal, subnormal and super-normal comparative psychology;

an objection, however, which applies with a certain degree of force to human psychology.

In making experiments on animals it is especially important that they should be placed under conditions as natural as possible. The neglect of this is a fatal objection to the work of the author of 'Animal Intelligence,' published as a monograph supplement to the PSYCHOLOGICAL REVIEW, Vol II., No. 8, 1898.

The portion of this research referring to chicks is the most reliable, and the suggestions as to pedagogics, etc., valuable.

This investigator's experiments show that certain associations may be formed under conditions highly unnatural, which associations bear about the same relation to the normal psychic evolution of animals as the behavior of more or less panic-stricken or otherwise abnormal human beings does to their natural conduct.

It is not proved, as asserted in the publication referred to, that animals do not imitate, remember, have social consciousness, imagination, association, and perception; nor that their consciousness is only comparable to that of a human being during swimming or when playing out-door games, as understood by this writer.

It is highly probable that animals, even the highest below man, have only rarely and at the best but a feeble self-consciousness, if it exist at all.

But on this point and on the question of inference, reasoning, etc., the time is not yet ripe for positive assertions.

It seems more than probable that the mental processes of the highest animals are not radically different from those of men so far as they go, but that the human mind has capacities in the realms both of feeling and intellection to which animals cannot attain. While it is desirable to push analysis as far as possible it is safer to remain in the region of the indefinite, to refrain from making very precise and positive statements as to whether the animal mind does or does not possess certain powers, till we are in possession of a larger storehouse of facts, especially of the nature of exact and systematic observations (or experiments). *Festinate lente* is a good rule to observe in regard to *conclusions* in comparative psychology.

# 20

Reprinted from *Psychol. Rev.* **6**:412-420 (1899)

## A REPLY TO "THE NATURE OF ANIMAL INTELLI-GENCE AND THE METHODS OF INVESTI-GATING IT."[1]

### Edward Thorndike

My first duty is to beg the reader's pardon for a certain personal tone in this discussion. As Professor Mills has mentioned Dr. Thorndike twenty-nine times in his article, this reply will of necessity contain the word ' I ' oftener than one would wish.

There are two sorts of assertions in Professor Mills' article : first, a number of important objections to a certain method of studying animal psychology ; second, a number of attacks on my ' Experimental Study of the Associative Processes in Animals.'[2] The former I am glad to have the opportunity to discuss, because they should be of real interest to all comparative psychologists. The latter can be safely left to the judgment of anyone who has read the monograph itself, and will be taken up here only because that monograph has probably been seen by only a few of the many who have read the attack upon it.

Let us turn first to the important objections to my method of studying the formation of associations in animals. I say my method, because it seems likely to be thought of chiefly in connection with my experiments, though Lubbock used practically the same method with insects. It is, in fact, odd that Lubbock's recommendation as to insects was not sooner followed with mammals. He says, " In order to test their intelligence, it has always seemed to me that there was no better way than to ascertain some object which they would clearly desire, and then to interpose some obstacle which a little ingenuity would enable them to overcome " (Ants, Bees and Wasps, N. Y., 1896, p. 247). He used food as the ' object,' as I did, and interposed mechanical obstacles as I did.

Professor Mills' weightiest objection is that, when confined while hungry in such boxes and pens as I used, the dogs and cats were in a ' panic-stricken ' condition and, therefore, temporarily lost their normal wits. Now, it is true that in many of the trials with cats and chicks, notably the first ten or twenty trials with each animal, there is often, as I fully noted, great violence and fury of activity. And this *might* be the result of mental panic, and so might be a sign of a loss of normal mentality. But the animals (the dogs and some of the cats) which did not display this excitement and fury did not display any variation in the results toward more intelligence. Nor did the animals

[1] By Professor Wesley Mills, pp. 262-274 of the May number of THE PSYCHOLOGICAL REVIEW.

[2] *Animal Intelligence*, Monograph Supplement, No. VIII., to THE PSYCHOLOGICAL REVIEW.

which showed certain results in the experiments of which confinement in small boxes was an essential feature show any variation from those results in the experiments (see pp. 87–91 and 96 of the monograph already cited) in which there was no excitement, no different activity from that shown all the time. In these experiments the cats were in the big cage which had been their home for weeks.

Furthermore, it seems unlikely that in the case of the animals which had already been the subjects of two or three experiments, and which had been in such boxes a hundred or more times, the violence and fury of activity could have been the result of fear or in any way a sign of its presence. For, as was stated in the monograph, such animals which have been made during a number of trials to crawl into these boxes which Professor Mills supposes were so disturbing to them, *habitually of their own accord went into them again and again.* Nor did they try to escape when I picked them up to drop them in. In the experiments in which I moved the animal's limbs, putting him through the movements, there was after from 0 to 12 trials no fear of my handling. (See p. 68 of the monograph.)

In short, all evidences of panic may be absent without any change in mental functioning, and the only cause of mental panic which would seem probable, namely, *fear*, was certainly not present in the greater number of the experiments. So I feel bound still to maintain the account given in the monograph, and attribute the animal's fury of activity not to mental panic, but to a useful instinctive reaction to confinement. It should be remembered that even in the midst of the utmost activity the cats would take instant advantage of any chance to escape which appealed to their instinctive equipment (*e. g.*, the widening of an orifice). It should further be remembered that the most violent animals did the most pseudo-intelligent acts. If any one of the eight or ten psychologists and biologists who saw the experiments in progress had seen signs of mental panic in the animals I should have inserted this discussion in the monograph. But I venture to think that if Professor Mills had repeated five or six of my experiments he would have discarded this mental panic objection.

The next important objection is that the surroundings were unnatural. I myself long since criticised my method on these grounds,[1] and I am and always have been ready to admit that an animal may be able to reason with certain data, to imitate certain acts, and yet be unable to reason with the data with which you confront him or imitate the act you present as a model. For that reason I chose varied acts,

[1] See *Science*, Vol. VIII., No. 198, p. 520.

very simple acts, trying each with different animals and making many of them approach very closely to acts common in animal life, and making others practically identical with acts which have been recorded as proofs of high mental ability in animals (vide the experiments with boxes C, D and G). We have seen that so far as the mere being in boxes is concerned the animals soon got used to it, did not fear it, and presumably could and did use their mental powers while in that situation. If Professor Mills had specified some particular situation as unnatural, and argued in concrete terms that its remoteness from the ordinary conditions of animal life made it unfit to call forth what mental functions the animal had, I should here either try to show that it was fit to call them forth or confess that from the animal's conduct in it no conclusion could be drawn save the one that the animal's mentality was such as was not aroused thereby. Even this one conclusion would be valuable. Even if we had to say, ' all that these experiments prove is that these circumstances will not cause the animal to manifest memory, imitation, etc.,' we should be saying a good deal, for the advocates of the reason theory have pretty uniformly given as evidence the reactions of animals to novel mechanical continuances.

Professor Mills does not argue in concrete terms, does not criticise concrete unfitness in the situations I devised for the animals. He simply names them unnatural. Moreover, it would seem that he makes this word face two ways. When talking of my experiments, he uses the word in the sense of novel, unfamiliar to the animal. When arguing that my conclusions are wrong, he uses the word in the sense of beyond the limits of their mental functions, abhorrent to their normal intellection. Of course, the former may be true and the latter false. The fact that cats are not ordinarily treated as mine were does not imply that my cats could not and did not come to be at home in the life I imposed on them to such an extent that they could use therein all the general intellectual functions they possessed. Professor Mills himself has based statements about the presence of certain mental functions on the conduct of a kitten in gaining a certain resting-place (in a bookcase, if I remember rightly), in spite of mechanical obstacles interposed. The situation here coped with is as 'unnatural' as that in a majority of my experiments.

The general argument of the monograph is used in all sorts of scientific work and is simple enough. It says: " If dogs and cats have such and such mental functions, they will do so and so in certain situations and will not do so and so; while, on the other hand, the absence of the function in question will lead to the presence of certain things and the absence of certain other things." To provide the ' certain situations' was the task my experiments undertook. It is mere rhetoric to damn the whole argument with a word, 'unnatural.' The thing to do is to show the error in the logic or the disturbing factor in each experiment, to repeat the experiment minus that factor, get opposite results, and so refute my claims. Dr. Kline has in one slight case gained results by the use of more ' natural' surroundings and his results agree with mine. (See *Am. J. of Psy.*, Vol. X, pp. 277–8.) I may say here that Dr. Kline has in this article treated of fear and novel surroundings as disturbing features in my experiments more discriminatingly, perhaps, than Professor Mills, and that this paper is intended to be an explanation which will satisfy his criticisms as well as those of the latter.

Observational records are, as I said in the review in *Science* which has already been quoted, of very great value; but the fact remains that the host of observations so far collected, including the large number of Professor Mills' own to which he refers on page 264, had not provided us with agreement about the presence of a single general function in animal consciousness that was in dispute. I tried, therefore, to devise-situations in which the conduct of the animals might be really illuminating. It would seem that Professor Mills allows that if the experiments were only free from the disturbing factors we have been talking about, the conclusions reached would be probably true, for he does not criticise the logic of the deductions. Now these conclusions are so far reaching that I am reviled for even pretending to have made such important ones. But this goes to show just that the method will, if we can show that these factors are not present, or can modify the method so as to exclude them, get us somewhere psychologically. So my general plea for experiments in animal psychology is that they at least pretend to give us an explanatory psychology, and not fragments of natural history.

Finally, just as in experiments like mine you may miss the truth by some mistake you make in picking the circumstances, the situation to test the presence of a function, so in the mere observation of the habitual life of animals or the experimental regulation of their ordinary activities, you may miss the truth by mistaking instinctive for imitative acts, associative for rational acts, permanent associations for memories. For instance, Professor Mills offers in his article, as a proof of the presence of an imitative faculty, an act (p. 268) which might very possibly have been the result of the instinct to follow common to so many young animals, so far as one can judge from his account—

248

"a student of McGill University has communicated to me the fact that a kitten which could not be induced to jump over an object placed before it, did so only after seeing the mother do it, and after that there was no more trouble in getting it to perform the trick." We shall see that another observation, that of the dog and the tree, which Professor Mills quotes to refute me, may have suffered in the interpretation.

Of course, it is clear that the psychological story told by correct experimentation will not conflict with the story told by correct observations reported correctly at first, second or tenth hand. But I am not yet sure that any trustworthy observation about the interpretation of which there is general agreement, conflicts with the results of my observations under test conditions in such a way as to render necessary the presupposition that in them there was some vital flaw. Such refutation of them may come, but Professor Mills does not seem to have brought it.

So much in general defence of the methods I used. It may now be permitted to mention some matters of detail: Professor Mills finds in the printed report of my experiments signs of conceit and of lack of 'respect for workers of the past of any complexion.' For psychological interpretations of the sort given by Romanes and Lindsay I certainly had and have no respect, though, of course, I esteem them for their zeal. But I cannot see that the presence or absence of megalomania in me is of any interest to comparative psychology. The monograph in question was not a presentation of personal opinion, but of certain facts, the accuracy of which, and of certain impersonal inductions and deductions, the logic of which, should be attacked impersonally. The question is whether certain facts exist and what they mean, and does not concern the individual psychology of any person.

Professor Mills' humor in making believe that because I characterize Lloyd Morgan as the 'sanest' of comparative psychologists, I think of them all as insane (p. 263), seems a bit disingenuous in view of the fact that his article will probably be the sole source of information about my book to a large number of people. Of course, when I wrote 'sanest,' I meant sanest. Had I meant 'least insane' I should assuredly have so written. On page 264 our author says, 'He' (Dr. Thorndike) 'comes very near to the belief that they are automata pure and simple, though this he does not assert in so many words.' This, I may be permitted to say, is an absolute misrepresentation. In every associative process discussed in the book I find present as an important element, *impulses*, and impulse I expressly define as 'the consciousness accompanying,' etc. (p. 14). Again, I speak everywhere of the *pleasure* resulting from the attainment of freedom, food, etc., as stamping in the connection between sense-impression and impulse. So, also, I speak everywhere of the sense-impression as the starting-point of the mental association.  As a fact, *mental* processes are mentioned throughout the whole discussion.  The one place where I frankly offered opinion in addition to fact was where I also attributed *representations* to animals: ' my opinion would be that animals *do* have representations, and that such are the beginning of the rich life of ideas in man' (p. 77).  Again, after an attempt to ' describe graphically * * * the *mental* fact we have been studying,' I say (p. 89) : " Yet there is consciousness enough at the time, keen consciousness of the sense-impressions, impulses, feelings of one's bodily acts.  So with the animals.  There is consciousness enough, but of this kind."

On page 264 Professor Mills talks as if I were trying to answer the question as to whether the animal mind was comparable to the human mind, and to answer it in the negative for the sake of exalting the human mind above the realm of natural evolution.  The reader of the monograph will remember that one of the results of the study was the attainment of a possible mental evolution of an entirely natural sort. I never tried to answer the question, ' How far does the mentality of a dog or cat equal that of man in general, genus homo,' for such a question seems to me fruitless.  It is like asking how far is 2 like x. The mentality of man *in general* is an unknown quantity, has a lot of possible values and so cannot be well used as a measure of anything. Any answer to it will be partially false and partially meaningless. Whether cats infer and compare, whether they imitate as present day adult human beings known to psychologists do, whether they form associations minus impulses of their own, are clear, answerable questions.  Such I tried to answer.  To say or to prove that the human mind of Europeans of to-day comes by continuous evolution from the animal mind does not make the latter any higher, endow it with a single new function nor alter it one whit.  The protozoa are not at all different from what they were before after we call them the ancestors of the vertebrates.  And one is free, it seems to me, to find out about questions of descriptive psychology, as well as of morphology, without meddling with questions of classification.

On page 265 Professor Mills rebukes me for considering hunger the strongest stimulus to animals.  Of course, I did not so consider it, and I am not aware of anything in the monograph which even looks as if I did.

Again, on this same page he misrepresents me by quoting a sentence without its context and, indeed, with comments which positively give a wrong notion of the context. The sentence is: 'the question of whether an animal does or does not form a certain association requires for an answer no higher qualification than a pair of eyes.' This sentence, as anyone may see by reading pages 5, 6 and 7 of the monograph, refers to the particular associations involved in learning to escape from boxes. And whether an animal does or does not learn to escape from a box certainly can be observed by anyone with a pair of eyes. And as the text clearly states, it was just because I did not wish to impose on any one my own opinions or even observations, because I wanted to use a method which any one else could employ and gain results which any one else could verify or refute, that I planned experiments which depended, so to speak, on impersonal eyes, eyes in general, for many of their results. I unhesitatingly affirm that so far as the facts of escape or non-escape and the time records (and the sentence concerns nothing else), Professor Mills or any one else would have kept just the same records as I myself did—that his eyes would have seen no more nor less than mine.

On page 267 I am accused of sacrificing particulars about facts for the sake of rhetoric, again on the basis of an entirely misrepresented quotation. On pages 38 and 39 of the monograph I say that henceforth I shall frequently use the word 'animal' or 'animals' when I mean to make statements only about the particular score of animals which were the subjects of my experiments, as "really I claim for my animal psychology only that it is the psychology of just these particular animals." After giving one reason for this verbal usage I add, "my second reason is that I hate to burden the reader with the disgusting rhetoric which would result if I had to insert particularizations and reservations at every step." Professor Mills quotes, omitting the first five words, and giving the impression that I generally omitted details so as to have good paragraphs or something of that sort, whereas the only 'particularizations' to which I objected were such as saying, Cats 1 (8–10 months), 2 (5–7 months), 3 (5–11 months) etc., up to cat 13; Dogs etc., etc., did not do so and so every page or two, when by means of this little note upon verbal usage the reader could on each occasion interpret the word 'animals' to mean "the particular animals which he observed, not necessarily all animals." The rhetorical excellence thus gained requires absolutely no sacrifice of fact of any sort.

If I were sure that Professor Mills would enjoy a bit of jocularity, I should reply to his explanation of the failure of my animals to imitate, by his own failure to imitate Professors James, Ladd, Hall and

Cattell, by saying that it was a good explanation, that they, like him, did not imitate because they could not. His whole discussion of my views on imitation should, in fairness, be accepted only after a careful reading of what the monograph said on that subject. There is room in this reply for only one more comment, on another matter.

To prove that dogs have memory in the sense of the ability to " refer the present situation to a situation of the past and realize that it is the same" (the meaning taken in the monograph), Professor Mills tells us of a dog which stopped at a certain tree, up which he had, months ago, chased a cat, " looked up and behaved otherwise in such a manner as left no doubt in my mind that he remembered the identical tree and detail of the whole performance." I suppose this description of the effect on Professor Mills, beginning with the words ' behaved otherwise,' means that the dog barked at or jumped at the tree, or behaved as he would if the cat were there. It must be confessed that to a hardened disbeliever the argument, " the dog remembered because he behaved so that I know he remembered," seems hardly scientific; but supposing that the description means what we have suggested, it still does not prove that the dog felt a memory of previous incident. At the table this morning I took hold of a cup, raised it to my lips and drank, acted toward the cup just as I did a month ago, but I had absolutely no memory in connection with the act. Indeed, if the dog really remembered the previous chase, he would have good reasons *not* to stop at the tree and act as if a cat were there. Let us suppose that Professor Mills and his dog were both out for cats; that they chased a cat to a tree; that the dog barked, etc., at the foot; and that Professor Mills, running up, shot his gun at the cat. Next month they come along toward the tree. Now, suppose that Professor Mills should run up and shoot his gun as he did the other time. Would we think he remembered his chase of a month before? No! we would think that he had gone daft, or had *forgotten* that the cat was there a month ago. Such an act would be the natural result of a permanent association between the sight of that tree and certain impulses, or of an ill-defined representation; but it would be one of the last things to expect as a result of a memory of the previous occasion.

This reply should close with an apology. Discussions of method and argument over results are likely to be less profitable and much less interesting than new constructive work. This reply was, however, necessary because of Professor Mills' eminence as an observer of animals, and because of the importance of getting at the truth about the

420   E. Thorndike

possible disturbing influence of fear and novel surroundings in certain convenient and, if legitimate, illuminating experiments.

[NOTE.—On page 268 Professor Mills has put 'to the laws of nature' instead of 'to the laws of its nature,' which means something rather different.]

# 21

## ON THE HISTORY OF RESEARCH WITH RATS AND MAZES: A COLLECTION OF NOTES

Walter R. Miles

It is now several years since the rat was adopted as a laboratory animal, and maze studies were begun. The literature is already quite large and there are doubtless a number of individuals who are interested in the early history of this research field. In February, 1928, letters were addressed to Professor Linus W. Kline, Dean Willard S. Small, and Dr. Adolf Meyer requesting early data or memoranda in reference to the use of the white rat. These gentlemen very courteously replied and sent material. Later, similar requests were made of professors Colin C. Stewart, Irving Hardesty, C. F. Hodge, J. R. Slonaker, H. H. Donaldson, John B. Watson, and others. In most cases these requests resulted in replies containing discussion which seems worth preserving.

The first reply came from Professor Kline who, on February 18, 1928, informed us as follows:

"I am writing L. N. Wilson, Librarian at Clark, to check some of my references to old books at Clark containing wood cuts of various sorts of mazes and from which I made drawings of the first mazes used at Clark in 1898-1899."

Five weeks later, at the time of communicating his notes, he sent a prefatory letter which may be quoted in part:

Farmville, Virginia
March 27, 1928

My dear Professor Miles:—

I am sending you by parcel post the promised manuscript on the early history of the use of boxes and of mazes in studying white-rat-learning. This is my vacation and I am a bit late in getting the work to you.

I have had drawings made of the two boxes. These drawings are with the manuscript. The original drawings of box #1 appear on page 28 of my old note book which I have taken the liberty to send along. Figure (c) is added to make clear the exact structure of the inward swinging of the door. Figure (b) in the drawing of box #2 is also added, otherwise the drawings are similar to the pencil sketches made in 1898.

You will notice on pages 20-21 and on page 42 entries made in a new hand. This was done by Dr. W. S. Small and I merely mention it to show that we were good fellows together working in the same laboratory mutually sharing each others plans and ideas. But even so I fail to recall at this distance his use of my boxes but I know he did as described in his published reports. Nor do I recall how or when he decided to adapt the Hampton maze to his work but it must have been the later part of 1898.

I do not think Adolf Meyer had anything to do with the introduction of the use of white rats in the Psychol. Laboratory at Clark. Both Colin C. Stewart and H. F. Hodge and others had used these rats before Meyer came to America, and I know I got my idea of using white rats from observing Stewart's work. It is true I had conferences with Meyer but they related to other problems and the question of using white rats never arose. I trust I have cleared up the early study of the white rat at Clark and made it clear that the idea of the Hampton maze came from Professor Sanford. I have enjoyed going over this ancient history and trust that I have put it in shape to be used.

Very truly yours,

(Signed) Linus W. Kline

### KLINE'S EARLY PSYCHOLOGICAL WORK WITH ANIMALS

In attempting to answer your inquiry about the early history of maze work with animals at Clark University, it may be in order to say that I entered Clark in 1896 with the intention of studying "zoological psychology." In shaping a problem for the doctorate thesis I was steered to a compromise and began work on "The Migratory Impulse *vs.* the Love of Home," believing that this problem offered legitimate grounds for experimenting on the effect of certain physical factors on the migration of animals.

During the fall and winter of 1896-97 I studied the effect of temperature on the movements of tadpoles, adopting the method used by Verworn in a similar study on paramaecium. Also with children I studied the effect of hunger and bad social conditions on truancy. The other half of the problem, "The Love of Home," also called for experimental observation. Problems like the "homing" of pigeons and of the honey bee, of the persistence and directness of domestic animals in returning home, and the effect of confinement upon animal life naturally arose. The latter problem prompted a study, during the summer of 1897, on the effect of solitude on the rate of the growth of chicks (results unpublished). I had hoped to find methods that might be applied to the study of the dark problem of nostalgia, "sickness for home." It was during this work on chicks and while reading the chapter on "Association in Animals" in C. Lloyd Morgan's *Introduction to Comparative Psychology*, that the idea occurred of using little boxes somewhat as harmless traps to study the ways by which rats search for food in out-of-way places. The notion of using rats came from observing an extended investigation conducted by Colin C. Stewart in the Department of Biology at Clark, 1895-97. Stewart's methods, apparatus, and technique were both interesting and instructive and made a decided impression upon me. He justified the use of rats and mice on the grounds that "They are small, cheap, easily fed and cared for; and best of all, when placed in revolving cages they spend most of their time, when not eating or sleeping, in running." (See Colin C. Stewart: "Variations in Daily Activity Produced by Alcohol and by Changes in Barometric Pressure and Diet, etc." June 19, 1897, p. 41. Thesis for the Degree of Doctor of Philosophy, Department of Biology, Clark University.)

It was not until the fall of 1898, however, that opportunity occurred for beginning a psychological study of the formation of "association" in rats. In planning the first series of experiments, I was guided chiefly by two ideas: (1) that the rat is a "gnawer"! and (2) that the gnawing must be done under the hunger impulse, free from fear, and, as far as possible, under natural conditions. At that time I was impressed with the importance of working with animals in as natural moods as conditions permitted. For this purpose, mouse box No. 1 was constructed. This box, although *made first,* is described as No. 2 on page 426, by L. W. Kline, *Amer. J. Psychol.,* 1899, **10**, April, and is also referred to by W. S. Small in a footnote to the same journal vol. **11**, pp. 29-30. There occurred in the same footnote an abbreviated account of the experiments given herewith in Table 1. (The reader may be referred to Linus W. Kline, "Methods in Animal Psychology," *Amer. J. Psychol.,* 1898-99, **10**, 256-279, section on "The White Rat," pp. 277-279; and W. S. Small, "Suggestions Toward a Laboratory Course in Comparative Psychology," *Amer. J. Psychol.,* 1898-99, **10**, 399-430, section on "The White Rat," pp. 419-424 for other details. Ed.) This box was 7 inches square and 6 inches high; sides of wire mesh; top of glass; bottom of wood. The side view is here shown in Plate 1, Figure *a*; the entrance and front view in Figure *b*. The entrance is an opening 2½ inches square, provided with an inward swinging door of sheet zinc hinged at the top

# MOUSE BOX NUMBER 1·

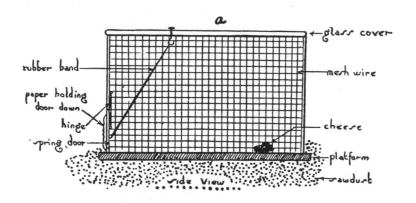

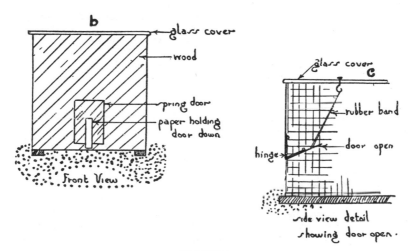

**PLATE 1**
THE DETAILS OF THE FIRST MOUSE BOX MADE BY KLINE IN 1898 AT
CLARK UNIVERSITY

of the opening. The lower end of the door was caught by a rubbei band stretched from a hook fastened in the glass top. Figure *c* shows this arrangement in detail.

While the first series of observations, seven in number, were cut short by the death of the animal, yet because they mark the first attempt to investigate the learning of the white rat they are here transcribed in tabular form as recorded at the time in my notes of 1898 which are still preserved.

TABLE 1

KLINE'S FIRST LEARNING EXPERIMENT ON THE WHITE RAT

| No. of exper. | Date | Hour | Time for opening door —minutes | Remarks |
|---|---|---|---|---|
| 1 | Dec. 3, 1898 | 9:10 A.M. | 10 | Marked desire to get in box. Tore paper loose in 9 min. |
| 2 | Dec. 3, 1898 | 9:45 A.M. | | Worked 20 min. and gave it up. |
| 3 | Dec. 3, 1898 | 3:50 P.M. | 45 | Opened door by butting with head. |
| 4 | Dec. 4, 1898 | 3:55 P.M. | 5 | Tore paper with mouth. |
| 5 | Dec. 4, 1898 | 4:03 P.M. | 3 | Localized place but did not recognize paper. |
| 6 | Dec. 4, 1898 | 4:08 P.M. | 2½ | Food taken from rat in 4th, 5th, and 6th experiments. |
| 7 | Dec. 4, 1898 | 4:17 P.M. | .. | Rat appeared stolid or sick, refused to work. |
| .. | Dec. 5, 1898 | 9:00 A.M. | .. | Rat found dead. |

This first series of observations developed the fact that the white rat was a "digger" as well as a "gnawer" and perhaps more so. To test this point, I made box No. 2 (see Plate 2) described in *Amer. J. Psychol.*, **10**, p. 277. The box was 8 inches long, 7 inches wide, 6 inches deep; sides of wire, top of glass, bottom of wood. Plate 2, Figure *a* shows the box raised above the level of the floor by resting on two strips 1½ inches thick. Figure *b* of the same box shows a bottom view with a piece 3½" x 2" sawed out at one end. This small experimental box, like box No. 1, was placed in a large home box 18 inches long, 14 inches wide and 14 inches deep; one side was wire, one end glass, the rest wood. The rats to be used in the experiment knew practically no other home as they had been reared in much the same sort of box. They were then placed in the home box along with box No. 2 several days before the time of the experiment in order to become familiar with their surroundings. A series of 13 observations using this box were made on two rats beginning January 9, 1899, and ending January 23. The first five observations are described in *Amer. J. Psychol.*, **10**, p. 277 and are also referred to by Small in the same journal, **11**, pp. 25-26.

# MOUSE BOX NUMBER 2·

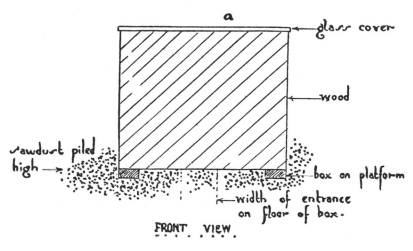

**a**

glass cover

wood

sawdust piled high →

box on platform

← width of entrance on floor of box.

FRONT VIEW

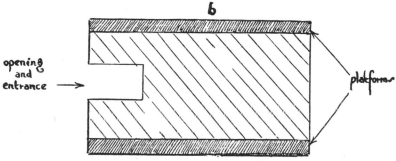

**b**

opening and entrance →

platforms

BOTTOM VIEW

PLATE 2

ARRANGEMENT OF MOUSE BOX USED BY KLINE IN 1899 TO STUDY THE DIGGING AND GNAWING OF RATS

TABLE 2

A SERIES OF EXPERIMENTS IN WHICH TWO RATS WERE JOINTLY ENGAGED IN
SECURING FOOD FROM BOX NO. 2

| No. of exper. | Date | Hour | Time to dig into box |
|---|---|---|---|
| 1 | Jan.  9, 1899 | 2:00 P.M. | 1 hour, 30 minutes |
| 2 | Jan. 10, 1899 | 3:45 P.M. | 8 minutes |
| 3 | Jan. 11, 1899 | 2:12 P.M. | 2 minutes, 30 seconds |
| 4 | Jan. 12, 1899 | 4:17 P.M. | 3 minutes |
| 5 | Jan. 13, 1899 | 4:15 P.M. | 3 minutes, 30 seconds |
| 6 | Jan. 14, 1899 | 4:30 P.M. | 2 minutes, 30 seconds (observation incomplete) |
| 7 | Jan. 16, 1899 | 5:30 P.M. | 1 minute |
| 8 | Jan. 17, 1899 | 5:30 P.M. | 5 minutes (rats disturbed by noise in room) |
| 9 | Jan. 18, 1899 | 4:30 P.M. | 1 minute, 30 seconds |
| 10 | Jan. 19, 1899 | 5:30 P.M. | 1 minute, 45 seconds |
| 11 | Jan. 20, 1899 | 2:30 P.M. | 1 minute, 30 seconds |
| 12 | Jan. 21, 1899 | 5:30 P.M. | 30 seconds |
| 13 | Jan. 22, 1899 | 5:00 P.M. | 45 seconds |

The complete record taken from my notes is given here in Table 2 for the first time.

The complete protocol for the experiment, January 9, 1899, is as follows: "Food (dog biscuit and cheese) was placed in the box at 2:00 P.M. The rats attacked the box at once, crawled up its side, over its top and round and round until it grew quite monotonous watching them. At 3:00 P.M. their activities abated—their movements less quick and more haphazard, one began playing at the side of the box where the piece had been sawed out. The hole scratched was about the size of the head, it immediately poked its head in the excavated place and seemed to be frightened; it ran away to a hiding place. Rat came out in two minutes, smelled around the hole and dug at some sawdust, then ran away as before. This was repeated several times until a hole quite too large had been excavated. It then ventured cautiously up into the box, snatched the food and made way with it at 3:30 P.M." The total time for the two rats to solve the problem was therefore 1 hour, 30 minutes. (It is not stated whether both rats actually engaged in the digging. Ed.) Protocol for January 10, 1899, 3:45 P.M. "The two rats behaved much like on the preceding day except they spent more time about the place where they had excavated the day before—as if they located the place, although this seemed very indefinite. They walked and fidgeted about for 4 minutes then one began digging away the sand and sawdust and at the end of the fifth minute the work was completed. As before they hesitated to go straight in, they frisked about nervously for another minute and at about 3:53 P.M. or after 8 minutes work they secured their dinner." January 16, 5:30 P.M. "Came out at sight of box—went at once to work and in *one minute* had secured the food, the quickest record yet made."

The 13th experiment was the last made in this series owing to other pressing work, but I felt that the rat had not reached its maximum speed which at that stage of learning appeared to depend upon *intensity* of hunger and upon absence of distraction. The former surmise has since been investigated by Professor Washburn. The two types of boxes figured were later used more extensively by W. S. Small.

The idea of using a maze for studying the "home-finding" capacities of the rat came from Professor Edmund C. Sanford during a conversation I had with him about the burrowing and digging activities of the rat. This conversation occurred in the spring of 1898 before I had finished work on my doctorate thesis. I had described to him runways which I had observed several years ago made by large feral rats to their nests under the porch of an old cabin on my father's farm in Virginia. These runways were from three to six inches below the surface of the ground and when exposed during excavation presented a veritable maze. Sanford at once suggested the possibility of using the pattern of the Hampton Court maze for purposes of constructing a "home-finding" apparatus. That was my first acquaintance with mazes. I looked up the Hampton Court pattern and made a copy of it, but from what source I am now unable to determine, perhaps it was from the 9th edition of *Encyclopedia Britannica*. It is not claimed that my account of the burrowing rats was an initial suggestion to Professor Sanford. In fact the readiness with which he directed my attention to the Hampton maze is presumptive evidence that he had thought of its use before. I should say that my interest in the maze at the time related to its fitness to study the "home-finding" or "food-box–finding" capacity of animals and not as an apparatus for the study of animal learning as it was used later by Small. My interests and experiments with rats in box-learning as above described came later. Other work prevented the use of the maze in my problem and prevented my making any further study in that direction.

As I recall, my attention was again directed to the Hampton maze in January, 1899, by observing W. S. Small constructing his first maze in the hallway in front of an entrance to the laboratory machine shop of Clark University. Small now began extended series of experiments on maze learning with the white rat which not only marked the first use of the maze in the study of animals, and determined its experimental value but also by his published reports gave to comparative psychology a model for painstaking, judicial procedure and for conservative interpretation of results.

(Signed) Linus W. Kline

Skidmore College
March 27, 1928

SMALL'S ACCOUNT OF EARLY WORK WITH MAZES AND RATS[1]

University of Maryland
College Park, Md.
March 29, 1928

My dear Professor Miles:

About the time I received your letter I received one from Dr. Warden asking for similar information for use in a book he is writing on the History of Comparative Psychology. I am sending you a copy of my letter to him, as it covers the information you seek. One question in your letter is not covered in my letter to Warden. The maze pattern I used was the Hampton Court pattern, corrected to rectangular form. No other maze pattern was tried.

I shall be very glad to have you make a "note" for the *Journal of General Psychology* if the material I am sending seems significant.

Yours very truly,
(Signed) W. S. Small, Dean

March 29, 1928

Professor C. J. Warden,
Department of Psychology,
Columbia University,
New York City, N. Y.

My dear Professor Warden:

I have finally got a line on a photograph and will send the print in a few days. It is quite recent.

I have been unable to find any contemporary notes, so I must depend upon my memory for the facts you desire. As nearly thirty years have elapsed—years in which Rat Psychology has been a gradually vanishing item in my mental furniture, I cannot be sure that my memory is exact.

I. So far as I know I did first make use of the albino rat as a psychological subject; and so far as I can recall, the work was begun in the spring of 1898. Three factors in the matter, I think I recall with reasonable certainty. (1) I had been working a little with Kline on insects—chiefly study of tropisms. (2) I had, that year, been carrying on with Dr. C. F. Hodge, a minor study on transmission of acquired characters using the albino rats for experimental purposes. I had kept a fairly large number and had become rather familiar with their "manners and customs" and had developed a liking for the animal. (3) At the same time, I had been making a preliminary study on the Development of Altruism and had dipped into Darwin, Morgan and others for possible material in the sub-human species. In particular, I read thoroughly Sutherland's "Origin and Growth of the Moral Instinct." (Reviewed it for the *American Journal of Psychology*).

These three factors tended to focus my interest upon a study in compara-

---

[1]Dr. Small's first reply was under date of February 23, 1928, when he said:

"Thirty years is a long time and I find that most of the specific items of fact that you ask about in your letter of February 10th are very hazy in my mind.

"It is possible that I have packed away somewhere the original notes in regard to the use of the maze in my old study of the rats. I shall have to do a little "house cleaning" to determine whether I still have those notes or whether they have been destroyed. In either event I will write you very soon as nearly as I can recall, the facts that you desire."

tive psychology as a probable thesis project. My familiarity with the albino rat was, I believe, what determined that animal as my special object of study.

II. I am not very clear as to the origin of the idea of using Hampton Court pattern as the main experimental device. As nearly as I can remember, the suggestion came from Dr. E. C. Sanford after I had done some of the preliminary work reported in my first paper. I was working under Dr. Sanford's direction. I recall that we had a number of consultations relative to methods of procedure and that I discussed with him the characteristic activities of the rat and the necessity of devising apparatus that would conform with those characteristic activities. I feel quite certain that Dr. Sanford responded with the maze suggestion. Memory is not clear on this point, but the "feeling" is so insistent that I have no doubt that the "guilt" was his.

III. As to the boxes used in my work, I cannot remember clearly but my impression is that Kline and I thought those out together, though it is possible—probably even—that Kline devised both of them. I shall be glad to have the credit go to him, as I know he was more resourceful in such matters than I was.

IV. My early work was in no way influenced by Thorndike as I did not know of his work when I made my approach to the problem. His study was published soon after I began my experimental work. I studied it carefully and thoroughly—and with profit. The chief advantage I derived from it was to make me more certain that I was on the right track in seeking to conform experimental procedure to the native tendencies of my animals and to sharpen criticism of my own methods and results.

V. I am unable to say "whence came the interest at Clark in Animal Psychology from the experimental standpoint"; but my judgment is that it had no specific *locus in quo*. Dr. Hall's insistent interest in evolutionary psychology was surely one element in the situation, but it may interest you to know that he did not give me, at first, much encouragement in my project. He doubted whether laboratory methods could be devised that would yield returns of much value. Dr. Sanford was just developing an interest at the time I began my work. My belief is that Kline was the instigator of Sanford's interest. He preceded me and I feel rather certain that he really opened up the matter to Sanford. At any rate it was Kline's work that first enlisted my interest and made clear to me the possibilities of laboratory study of animal psychology.

I hope this rather discursive narrative will enable you to pick out the facts you need. Of course, I shall be glad to give other items of information if you wish—and my memory is not too treacherous.

Yours very truly,
(Signed) W. S. Small, Dean

MEYER ON THE FIRST LABORATORY RAT COLONIES

The Johns Hopkins Hospital
Baltimore, Md.
October 1, 1928

Dr. Walter R. Miles
Dept. of Psychology
Stanford University
California
My dear Dr. Miles:

The only person that remains to be asked is Colin Stewart of Dartmouth. From all I have been able to reconstruct white rats must have been in use through Hodge and others at Clark and elsewhere.

My own share lies in the fact that I raised large numbers in Worcester and urged Donaldson to make the white rat the standard animal (May, 1897), and furnished him with a large lot, handled by Hardesty.

The use for maze work was evidently independent, and based largely on the use of these animals in Hodge's laboratory—and on good sense in choosing a reasonably *manageable* animal.

The Wistar Colony on the other hand had an impetus through Donaldson and it has done a good job.

Sincerely yours,

(Signed) Adolf Meyer

STEWART ON THE EARLY EXPERIMENTAL USE OF THE RAT

Dartmouth College
Hanover, N. H.
October 7, 1928

Dr. Walter R. Miles
Stanford University
My dear Dr. Miles:

I have been much interested in your letter and in one received from Dr. Meyer, with reference to the early work with white rats. My work at Clark University during the years 1894-1897 was undertaken at the suggestion of Dr. Hodge. At his suggestion the wild gray rat was used as the experimental animal. The difficulty of handling the gray rats (1894-95) was the reason for changing to albino rats for the remaining two years of my stay at Clark (1895-1897). No one was in any way associated with me in the animal activity work. There were no white rats in the department before 1895, and there were none but those employed in my experiments during the years 1895-1897. I do not recall receiving any white rats from Dr. Adolf Meyer, but it is entirely possible that I did as he came to the Worcester Hospital in 1895. Albino rats were on sale in bird and animal stores and I know that I purchased some in Worcester.

I should say that whatever credit there is in having suggested the use of *rats* as experimental animals, belongs to Dr. C. F. Hodge. If anyone wants to know why I changed from wild gray rats to *white rats* in 1895, let him work with gray rats for a year. I don't deserve any credit for the change. Whether I gave white rats to Dr. Meyer or he gave some to me I do not recall, but he alone was responsible for any that were sent to Prof. Donaldson at the Wistar Institute.

'Prof. Kline's work with white rats was done, probably under Dr. Sanford, after I left Clark University in 1897, and probably with the lineal descendants of my "animal activity" stock.

Dr. A. M. Cleghorn used white rats and the same recording methods in Boston in 1897-98, in testing the effects of orchitic extracts on voluntary activity.

Yours sincerely,

(Signed) Colin C. Stewart

SLONAKER ON THE EARLY USE OF THE RAT

Stanford University, Calif.
January 15, 1929

Dear Dr. Miles:

I have read with much interest the data you have collected in regard to the early history of the use of the albino rat in animal experimentation. I will add some notes and suggestions which may be of assistance to you.

I entered Clark the fall of 1893 and entered at once into an investigation of the comparative anatomy of the point of acute vision in vertebrates under the direction of Dr. C. F. Hodge. This I pursued continuously for the three years I was there, taking my degree the spring of 1896. During the first year I have no recollection of any rats or mice being used in any of the departments. Stewart entered the fall of 1894 and, working under Hodge, began his work with the gray rat as stated in his letter to you. During this year I made use of the gray rat in a fatigue experiment as a minor problem, but never published the results. This, however, was after Stewart had begun his work as I used one of his spare cages in my experiment. I feel confident that Stewart was the first to use the rat at Clark.

I would suggest that you communicate with Dr. H. H. Donaldson at Wistar Inst. and with Dr. Irving Hardesty, Tulane University, New Orleans. Donaldson had left Clark and gone to Univ. Chicago before I went to Clark. Hardesty was associated with him in Chicago and is a very dear friend of mine. If Meyer sent Donaldson some rats it must have been to Chicago for he was not in this country after until Donaldson had gone to Chicago. I was associated with Donaldson in Chicago during the years 1901-1903. At that time they had a well established colony which both Watson and myself made use of. The nucleus of this colony may have come from Meyer. Donaldson or Hardesty can inform you.

I do not know of any published account of the origin of the Wistar Colony. However, when I took lunch with Donaldson while in Philadelphia some three years ago, I asked him or Dr. King, if the original stock did not come from the Chicago colony and was informed that it did. Our colony here at Stanford also came from the same source.

If there is anything more I can give please let me know and I will comply.

Very sincerely,

(Signed) J. R. Slonaker

HARDESTY ON THE EARLY LABORATORY ADOPTION OF THE RAT

Tulane University
New Orleans
January 24, 1929

Dr. Walter R. Miles
Department of Psychology
Stanford University
Dear Prof. Miles:

In reply to your inquiry of Jan. 17, I am sorry to say that as to personal experience I know little of the use of the white rat prior to 1897. I am quite sure that in the latter part of this year Prof. Donaldson in Chicago, after deliberation, decided to try out the white rat with a view to replacing the frog as the general laboratory animal in his projected program for his laboratory, namely, problems dealing with the Embryology, Growth and Functional Development of the Nervous System. Though a few papers from his laboratory after this year used the frog, my thesis included, we were beginning to use the rat, and I remember that in 1898 one of our regular class laboratory exercises in his course on the growth of the nervous system was to measure the internodes of the freshly taken nerves of rats of different ages.

Dr. Donaldson's laboratory had a small supply of rats in 1896 and maybe prior to 1896. I think it was in 1898 that Dr. Adolf Meyer sent us two or three dozen adults and these were chiefly those from which the Donaldson colony started, later so elaborately developed into the Wistar Colony. I remember Donaldson advocating the white rat for general use both with the Chicago staff and with men from other laboratories in the year '96-'97.

He may have begun it earlier. I taught in the University of Missouri in '95-'96, having had to drop out for a year to make some "Pin money." I had thought all along that the idea originated with Donaldson till learning from Dr. Meyer's statement that he had urged Donaldson to make the rat the standard animal. I have no reason, however, to doubt Dr. Meyer's statement.

The first use of the white rat as a maze animal that I know of was in the work of Slonaker and then Watson. I did not know of Dr. Stewart's work till reading the copy of his letter you sent me.

I went to the Department of Anatomy of the University of California from Chicago in 1901 and have not been closely associated with the matter since. My memory may not be wholly trustworthy as to the dates. I wish I could be of more definite help. I am sure that the present general use of the rat is due more to Donaldson's advocacy and use of it in the papers done under him than to any other man.

Yours very truly,

(Signed) Irving Hardesty

DONALDSON ON THE HISTORICAL RAT PROBLEM

Wistar Institute of Anatomy
Philadelphia, Pa.
January 29, 1929

Dr. Walter R. Miles
Department of Psychology
Leland Stanford University
Stanford University, Calif.

Dear Dr. Miles:

Yours of the 17th, with enclosures, reached me duly and I regret the tardiness of my response. To do what I can I am sending this to you by air mail.

Your primary question relates to the use of the rat in maze studies. I have nothing to add to the information contained in the documents save to note that in his book published in 1903 bearing the title of "Animal Education", John B. Watson figures several mazes and refers to the work of Small. Watson's study was begun in the fall of 1901 and has an interest merely as the first study employing the maze made at the University of Chicago. It is, of course, several years later than the pioneer investigations.

As I see our historical rat problem there is the one in which you have an interest, then comes the first use of the rat in my laboratory as a general experimental animal and the employment of the rat for nutritional studies at Wisconsin and New Haven. There are, roughly, three separate topics and as you note by the correspondence I am taking up the one that relates to my laboratory at Chicago, with Dr. Meyer and others concerned.

I am much interested in this little investigation and hope you will let me know when it is put in final form.

Yours sincerely,

(Signed) Henry H. Donaldson

So far as we may judge from the foregoing letters the laboratory use of the white rat began in 1895. In that year we are informed by Professor Stewart that he secured and used albino rats in Hodge's laboratory at Clark University, following a previous experimental experience with the wild rat which had been undertaken at the suggestion of Professor Hodge. It appears that Donaldson and perhaps also Meyer began work with the white rat at Chicago almost if not quite as early as did Hodge at Clark. The relationships of these two centers as regards the adoption of the animal are not perfectly clear. Probably Professor Hardesty's statement is correct that Donaldson's continuous work with the rat has done much to bring about its present general acceptance for laboratory use. We judge from the evidence submitted that Sanford was the first to conceive the idea of using the maze as an implement for studying the behavior of the rat and to bring about the completion of investigations of this character.

*Stanford University*
*California*

# 22

Reprinted from *Psychol. Rev.* **56**:51–65 (1949)

## THE FORMATION OF LEARNING SETS [1,2]

BY HARRY F. HARLOW

*University of Wisconsin*

In most psychological ivory towers there will be found an animal laboratory. The scientists who live there think of themselves as theoretical psychologists, since they obviously have no other rationalization to explain their extravagantly paid and idyllic sinecures. These theoretical psychologists have one great advantage over those psychological citizens who study men and women. The theoreticians can subject their subhuman animals, be they rats, dogs, or monkeys, to more rigorous controls than can ordinarily be exerted over human beings. The obligation of the theoretical psychologist is to discover general laws of behavior applicable to mice, monkeys, and men. In this obligation the theoretical psychologist has often failed. His deductions frequently have had no generality beyond the species which he has studied, and his laws have been so limited that attempts to apply them to man have resulted in confusion rather than clarification.

One limitation of many experiments on subhuman animals is the brief period of time the subjects have been studied. In the typical problem, 48 rats are arranged in groups to test the effect of three different intensities of stimulation operating in conjunction with two different motivational conditions upon the formation of *an isolated* conditioned response. A brilliant Blitzkrieg research is effected—the controls are per-

fect, the results are important, and the rats are dead.

If this *do and die* technique were applied widely in investigations with human subjects, the results would be appalling. But of equal concern to the psychologist should be the fact that the derived general laws would be extremely limited in their application. There are experiments in which the use of naive subjects is justified, but the psychological compulsion to follow this design indicates that frequently the naive animals are to be found on both sides of the one-way vision screen.

The variety of learning situations that play an important rôle in determining our basic personality characteristics and in changing some of us into thinking animals are repeated many times in similar form. The behavior of the human being is not to be understood in terms of the results of single learning situations but rather in terms of the changes which are affected through multiple, though comparable, learning problems. Our emotional, personal, and intellectual characteristics are not the mere algebraic summation of a near infinity of stimulus-response bonds. The learning of primary importance to the primates, at least, is the formation of learning sets; it is the *learning how to learn efficiently* in the situations the animal frequently encounters. This learning to learn transforms the organism from a creature that adapts to a changing environment by trial and error to one that adapts by seeming hypothesis and insight.

The rat psychologists have largely ignored this fundamental aspect of learning and, as a result, this theoretical

[1] This paper was presented as the presidential address of the Midwestern Psychological Association meetings in St. Paul, May 7, 1948.

[2] The researches described in this paper were supported in part by grants from the Special Research Fund of the University of Wisconsin for 1944–48.

52 HARRY F. HARLOW

domain remains a *terra incognita*. If learning sets are the mechanisms which, in part, transform the organism from a conditioned response robot to a reasonably rational creature, it may be thought that the mechanisms are too intangible for proper quantification. Any such presupposition is false. It is the purpose of this paper to demonstrate the extremely orderly and quantifiable nature of the development of certain learning sets and, more broadly, to indicate the importance of learning sets to the development of intellectual organization and personality structure.

The apparatus used throughout the studies subsequently referred to is illustrated in Fig. 1. The monkey responds by displacing one of two stimulus-objects covering the food-wells in the tray before him. An opaque screen is interposed between the monkey and the stimulus situation between trials and a one-way vision screen separates monkey and man during trials.

The first problem chosen for the investigation of learning sets was the object-quality discrimination learning problem. The monkey was required to choose the rewarded one of two objects differing in multiple characteristics and shifting in the left-right positions in a predetermined balanced order. A series of 344 such problems using 344 different pairs of stimuli was run on a group of eight monkeys. Each of the first 32 problems was run for 50 trials; the next 200 problems for six trials; and the last 112 problems for an average of nine trials.

In Fig. 2 are presented learning curves which show the per cent of correct responses on the first six trials of these discriminations. The data for the first 32 discriminations are grouped for blocks of eight problems, and the remaining discriminations are arranged in blocks of 100, 100, 56, and 56 problems. The data indicate that the subjects progressively improve in their ability to

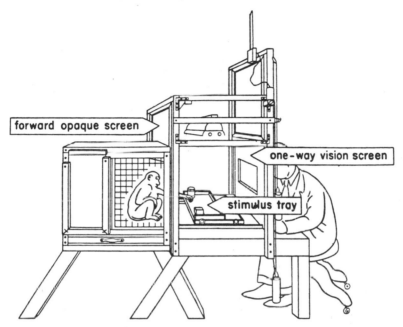

FIG. 1. Wisconsin general test apparatus.

learn object-quality discrimination problems. The monkeys *learn how to learn* individual problems with a minimum of errors. It is this *learning how to learn a kind of problem* that we designate by the term *learning set*.

The very form of the learning curve changes as learning sets become more efficient. The form of the learning curve for the first eight discrimination problems appears S-shaped: it could be described as a curve of 'trial-and-error' learning. The curve for the last 56 problems approaches linearity after Trial 2. Curves of similar form have been described as indicators of 'insightful' learning.

We wish to emphasize that this *learning to learn*, this *transfer from problem to problem* which we call the formation of a learning set, is a highly *predictable, orderly* process which can be demonstrated as long as controls are maintained over the subjects' experience and the difficulty of the problems. Our subjects, when they started these researches, had no previous laboratory learning experience. Their entire discrimination learning set history was obtained in this study. The stimulus pairs employed

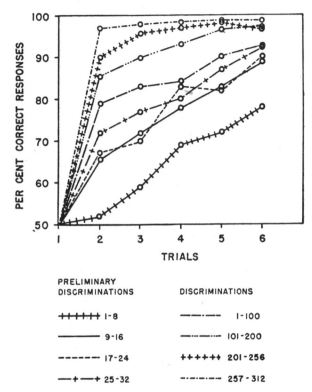

FIG. 2. Discrimination learning curves on successive blocks of problems.

had been arranged and their serial order determined from tables of random numbers. Like nonsense syllables, the stimulus pairs were equated for difficulty. It is unlikely that any group of problems differed significantly in intrinsic difficulty from any other group.

In a conventional learning curve we plot change of performance over a series of *trials;* in a learning set curve we plot

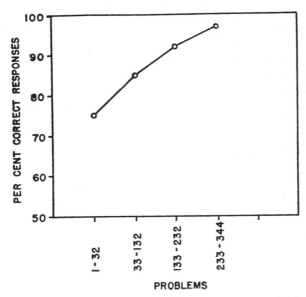

FIG. 3. Discrimination learning set curve based on Trial 2–6 responses.

change in performance over a series of *problems*. It is important to remember that *we measure learning set in terms of problems* just as *we measure habit in terms of trials*.

Figure 3 presents a discrimination

learning set curve showing progressive increase in the per cent of correct responses on Trials 2–6 on successive blocks of problems. This curve appears to be negatively accelerated or possibly linear.

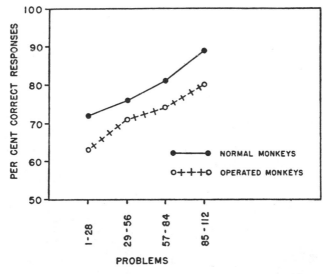

FIG. 4. Discrimination learning set curves based on Trial 2–6 responses: normal and operated monkeys.

Discrimination learning set curves obtained on four additional naive normal monkeys and eight naive monkeys with extensive unilateral cortical lesions, are shown in Fig. 4. Brain-injured as well as normal monkeys are seen to form effective discrimination learning sets, although the partial hemidecorticate monkeys are less efficient than the normal subjects. Improvement for both groups is progressive and the fluctuations that occur may be attributed to the small number of subjects and the relatively small number of problems, 14, included in each of the problem blocks presented on the abscissa.

Through the courtesy of Dr. Margaret Kuenne we have discrimination learning set data on another primate species. These animals were also run on a series of six-trial discrimination problems but under slightly different conditions. Macaroni beads and toys were substituted for food rewards, and the subjects were tested sans iron-barred cages. The data for these 17 children, whose ages range from two to five years and whose intelligence quotients range from 109 to 151, are presented in Fig. 5. Learning set

curves are plotted for groups of children attaining a predetermined learning criterion within differing numbers of problem blocks. In spite of the small number of cases and the behavioral vagaries that are known to characterize this primate species, the learning set curves are orderly and lawful and show progressive increase in per cent of correct responses.

Learning set curves, like learning curves, can be plotted in terms of correct responses or errors, in terms of responses on any trial or total trials. A measure which we have frequently used is per cent of correct Trial 2 responses— the behavioral measure of the amount learned on Trial 1.

Figure 6 shows learning set curves measured in terms of the per cent correct Trial 2 responses for the 344-problem series. The data from the first 32 preliminary discriminations and the 312 subsequent discriminations have been plotted separately. As one might expect, these learning set curves are similar to those that have been previously presented. What the curves show with especial clarity is the almost unbelievable

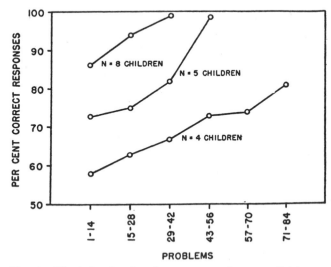

FIG. 5. Discrimination learning set curves based on Trial 2–6 responses: children.

change which has taken place in the *effectiveness of the first training trial.* In the initial eight discriminations, this single paired stimulus presentation brings the Trial 2 performance of the monkeys to a level less than three per cent above chance; in the last 56 discriminations, this first training trial brings the performance of the monkeys to a level *less than three per cent* short of perfection. Before the formation of a discrimination learning set, a single training trial produces negligible gain;

which is initially difficult for a subject into a problem which is so simple as to be immediately solvable. The learning set is the mechanism that changes the problem from an intellectual tribulation into an intellectual triviality and leaves the organism free to attack problems of another hierarchy of difficulty.

For the analysis of learning sets in monkeys on a problem that is ostensibly at a more complex level than the discrimination problem, we chose the discrimination reversal problem. The pro-

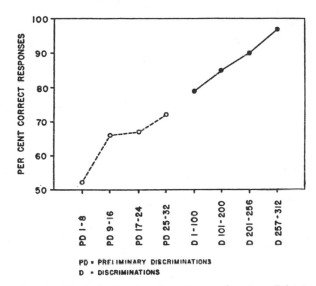

FIG. 6. Discrimination learning set curve based on Trial 2 responses.

after the formation of a discrimination learning set, *a single training trial constitutes problem solution.* These data clearly show that *animals can gradually learn insight.*

In the final phase of our discrimination series with monkeys there were subjects that solved from 20 to 30 consecutive problems with no errors whatsoever following the first blind trial,—and many of the children, after the first day or two of training, did as well or better.

These data indicate the function of learning set in converting a problem

cedure was to run the monkeys on a discrimination problem for 7, 9, or 11 trials and then to reverse the reward value of the stimuli for eight trials; that is to say, the stimulus previously correct was made incorrect and the stimulus previously incorrect became correct.

The eight monkeys previously trained on discrimination learning were tested on a series of 112 discrimination reversal problems. Discrimination reversal learning curves for successive blocks of 28 problems are shown in Fig. 7. The

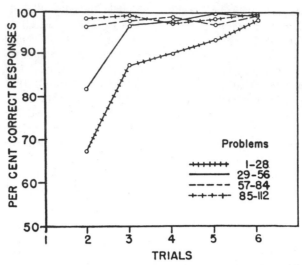

Fig. 7. Discrimination reversal learning curves on successive
blocks of problems.

measure used is per cent of correct responses on Reversal Trials 2 to 6. Figure 8 presents data on the formation of
the discrimination reversal learning set
in terms of the per cent of correct responses on Reversal Trial 2 for successive blocks of 14 problems. Reversal
Trial 2 is the first trial following the
'informing' trial, i.e., the initial trial
reversing the reward value of the stimuli.

Reversal Trial 2 is the measure of the
effectiveness with which the single informing trial leads the subject to
abandon a reaction pattern which has
proved correct for 7 to 11 trials, and to
initiate a new reaction pattern to the
stimulus pair. On the last 42 discrimination reversal problems the monkeys
were responding as efficiently on Reversal Trial 2 as they were on comple-

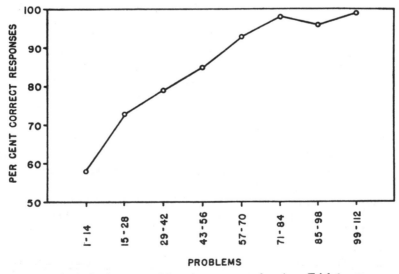

Fig. 8. Discrimination reversal learning set curve based on Trial 2 responses.

mentary Discrimination Trial 2, *i.e.*, they were making over 97 per cent correct responses on both aspects of the problems. The eight monkeys made from 12 to 57 successive correct second trial reversal responses. Thus it becomes perfectly obvious that at the end of this problem the monkeys possessed sets both to learn and to reverse a reaction tendency, and that this behavior could be consistently and immediately elicited with hypothesis-like efficiency.

This terminal performance level is likely to focus undue attention on the one-trial learning at the expense of the earlier, less efficient performance levels. It should be kept in mind that this one-trial learning appeared only as the end result of an orderly and progressive learning process; insofar as these subjects are concerned, the insights are only to be understood in an historical perspective.

Although the discrimination reversal problems might be expected to be more difficult for the monkeys than discrimination problems, the data of Fig. 9 indicate that the discrimination reversal learning set was formed more rapidly than the previously acquired discrimina-

tion learning set. The explanation probably lies in the nature of the transfer of training from the discrimination learning to the discrimination reversal problems. A detailed analysis of the discrimination learning data indicates the operation throughout the learning series of certain error-producing factors, but with each successive block of problems the frequencies of errors attributable to these factors are progressively decreased, although at different rates and to different degrees. The process might be conceived of as a learning of response tendencies that counteract the error-producing factors. A description of the reduction of the error-producing factors is beyond the scope of this paper, even though we are of the opinion that this type of analysis is basic to an adequate theory of discrimination learning.

Suffice it so say that there is reason to believe that there is a large degree of transfer from the discrimination series to the reversal series, of the learned response tendencies counteracting the operation of two of the three primary error-producing factors thus far identified.

The combined discrimination and dis-

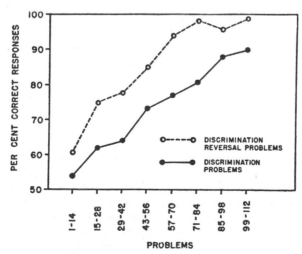

FIG. 9.  Discrimination reversal and discrimination learning set curves based on Trial 2 responses.

crimination reversal data show clearly how the learning set delivers the animal from Thorndikian bondage. By the time the monkey has run 232 discriminations and followed these by 112 discriminations and reversals, he does not possess 344 or 456 specific habits, bonds, connections or associations. We doubt if our monkeys at this time could respond with much more than chance efficiency on the first trial of any series of the previously learned problems. But

We believe that other learning sets acquired in and appropriate to the monkey's natural environment would enable him to adapt better to the changing conditions there. We are certain, moreover, that learning sets acquired by man in and appropriate to his environment have accounted for his ability to adapt and survive.

Before leaving the problem of discrimination reversal learning we submit one additional set of data that we feel

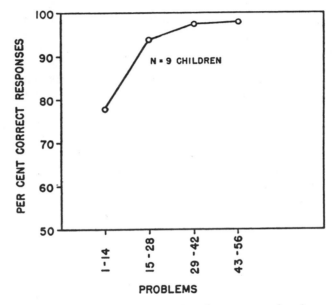

FIG. 10. Discrimination reversal learning set curve based on Trial 2 responses: children.

the monkey does have a generalized ability to learn *any* discrimination problem or *any* discrimination reversal problem with the greatest of ease. Training on several hundred specific problems has not turned the monkey into an automaton exhibiting forced, sterotyped, reflex responses to specific stimuli. These several hundred habits have, instead, made the monkey an adjustable creature with an *increased capacity* to adapt to the ever-changing demands of a psychology laboratory environment.

merits attention. Nine of the children previously referred to were also subjected to a series of discrimination reversal problems. The outcome is partially indicated in Fig. 10 which shows the per cent of correct Reversal Trial 2 responses made on successive blocks of 14 problems. It can be seen that these three to five-year-old children clearly bested the monkeys in performance on this series of problems. Trial 2 responses approach perfection in the second block of 14 discrimination reversal problems. Actually, over half of the total Trial 2 errors were made by one child.

These discrimination reversal data on the children are the perfect illustration of set formation and transfer producing adaptable abilities rather than specific bonds. Without benefit of the monkey's discrimination reversal set learning curves we might be tempted to assume that the children's data indicate a gulf between human and subhuman learning. But the *extremely rapid* learning on the

mediately by ten right-position discrimination trials with the same stimuli continuing to shift in the right-left positions in predetermined orders. In the first 7 to 11 trials, a particular object was correct regardless of its position. In the subsequent 10 trials, a particular position—the experimenter's right position—was correct, regardless of the object placed there. Thus to solve the problem the animal had to respond to object-quality cues and disregard position cues in the first 7 to 11 trials and,

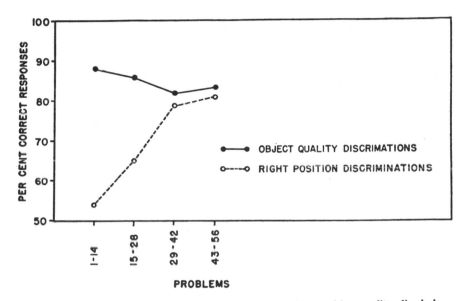

FIG. 11. Learning set curves for problem requiring shift from object-quality discrimination to right-position discrimination.

part the children is not unlike the *rapid* learning on the part of the monkeys, and analysis of the error-producing factors shows that the same basic mechanisms are operating in both species.

Following the discrimination reversal problem the eight monkeys were presented a new series of 56 problems designed to elicit alternation of unequivocally antagonistic response patterns. The first 7, 9, or 11 trials of each problem were simple object-quality discrimination trials. These were followed im-

following the failure of reward of the previously rewarded object, he had to disregard object-quality cues and respond to position cues.

The learning data on these two antagonistic tasks are presented in Fig. 11. It is to be noted that the object-quality curve, which is based on Trials 1 to 7, begins at a very high level of accuracy, whereas the position curve, plotted for Trials 1 to 10, begins at a level little above chance. This no doubt reflects the operation of the previously well-established object-quality discrimination learning set. As the series continues, the object-quality curve shows a drop until the last block of problems, while the position curve rises progressively. In the evaluation of these data, it should be noted that chance performance is 50 per cent correct responses for the object-quality discriminations and 45 per cent for the position discriminations, since each sequence of 10 position trials includes an error "informing" trial. It would appear that the learning of the right-position discriminations interferes

the last 14 problems is indicated in Fig. 12. Since the right-position part of the problem was almost invariably initiated by an error trial, these data are limited to those problems on which the first trial object-quality discrimination response was incorrect. The per cent of correct Trial 7 responses to the 'A' object, the correct stimulus for the object-quality discriminations, is 98. The initiating error trial which occurs when the problem shifts without warning to a right-position problem, drops this per cent response to the 'A' object to 52—a level

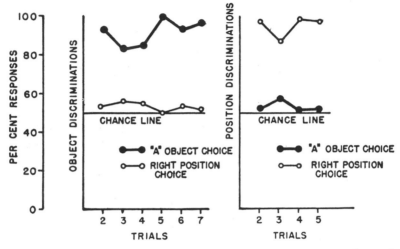

FIG. 12. Object and position choices following initial errors on both phases of object-position shift series, based on problems 42–56.

with the learning of the object-quality discriminations to some extent. In spite of this decrement in object-quality discrimination performance for a time, the subjects were functioning at levels far beyond chance on the antagonistic parts of the problems during the last half of the series. We believe that this behavior reflects the formation of a right-position learning set which operates at a high degree of independence of the previously established object-quality discrimination learning set.

The precision of the independent operation of these learning sets throughout

barely above chance. The per cent of Trial 7 responses to the right position during the object-quality discriminations is 52. The single error trial initiating the shift of the problem to a right-position discrimination is followed by 97 per cent right-position responses on the next trial. In other words, *it is as though* the outcome of a single *push of an object* is adequate to switch off the 'A'-object choice reaction tendency and to switch on the right-position choice reaction tendency.

The cue afforded by a single trial produces at this point almost complete discontinuity of the learning process. The only question now left unsettled in the controversy over hypotheses in subhuman animals is whether or not to use this term to describe the behavior of a species incapable of verbalization.

Again, it should be remembered that both the object-quality discrimination learning set and the right-position discrimination learning set developed in a gradual and orderly manner. Only after the learning sets are formed do these

position and left-position problems presented alternately. The remaining five blocks of problems continued the alternate presentation of 14 object-quality discrimination problems and 14 right-left positional discrimination problems. Figure 13 presents curves showing the per cent of correct responses on total trials on these alternate blocks of antagonistic discriminations. The complex positional discrimination learning set curve shows progressive improvement

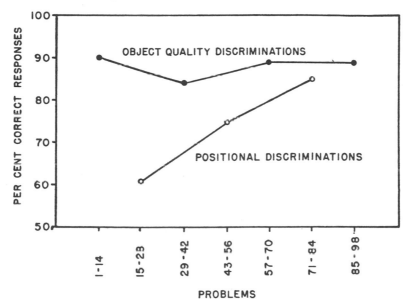

FIG. 13. Learning set curves for problem series with alternating object-quality and positional discriminations, based on total trial responses.

phenomena of discontinuiy in learned behavior appear.

Further evidence for the integrity of learning sets is presented in an additional experiment. Six monkeys with object-quality discrimination learning experience, but without training on reversal problems or position discriminations, were given seven blocks of 14 problems each, starting with a block of 25-trial object-quality discriminations, followed by a block of 14 25-trial positional discriminations composed of right-

throughout the series, whereas the object-quality discrimination curve begins at a high level of accuracy, shows decrement on the second block, and subsequently recovers. By the end of the experiment the two basically antagonistic learning sets had 'learned' to live together with a minimum of conflict. These data are the more striking if it is recalled that between each two blocks of object-quality discriminations there were 350 trials in which no object was differentially rewarded, and between each two blocks of 14 positional discriminations there were 350 trials in which no position was differentially rewarded.

In Fig. 14 we present additional total-trial data on the formation of the positional learning set. These data show the change in performance on the first and last seven positional discriminations in each of the three separate blocks of positional discriminations. The interposed object-quality discrimination problems clearly produced interference, but

112 six-trial discriminations. The lower curves show total errors on an additional group of 56 discriminations presented one year later. In both situations the full-brained monkeys make significantly better scores, but one should note that the educated hemidecorticate animals are superior to the uneducated unoperated monkeys. Such data suggest that half a brain is better than one if you compare the individuals having appropriate learning sets with the individuals lacking them.

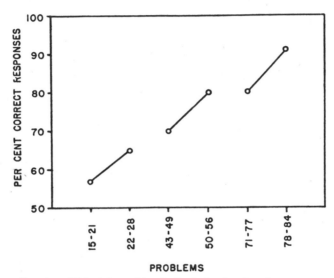

FIG. 14. Right-left positional discrimination learning set curve based on total trial responses. (Data on antagonistic object-quality discrimination problems omitted.)

they did not prevent the orderly development of the positional learning sets, nor the final attainment of a high level of performance on these problems.

We have data which suggest that the educated man can face arteriosclerosis with confidence, if the results on brain-injured animals are applicable to men. Figure 15 shows discrimination learning set curves for the previously described groups of four normal monkeys and eight monkeys with very extensive unilateral cortical injury. The upper curves show total errors on an initial series of

More seriously, these data may indicate why educated people show less apparent deterioration with advancing age than uneducated individuals, and the data lend support to the clinical observation that our fields of greatest proficiency are the last to suffer gross deterioration.

Although our objective data are limited to the formation of learning sets which operate to give efficient performance on intellectual problems, we have observational data of a qualitative nature on social-emotional changes in our animals. When the monkeys come to us they are wild and intractable but within a few years they have acquired, from the experimenter's point of view, good personalities. Actually we believe that one of the very important factors in the development of the good personalities of our monkeys is the formation of social-emotional learning sets organized in a manner comparable with the intellectual learning sets we have previously described. Each contact the monkey has with a human being represents a single specific learning trial. Each person rep-

freedom. Actually a learning set once formed determines in large part the nature and direction of stimulus generalization. In the classic study in which Watson conditioned fear in Albert, the child developed a fear of the rat and generalized this fear, but failed to develop or generalize fear to Watson, even though Watson must have been the more conspicuous stimulus. Apparently Albert had already formed an affectional social-emotional learning set to people, which inhibited both learning and simple Pavlovian generalization.

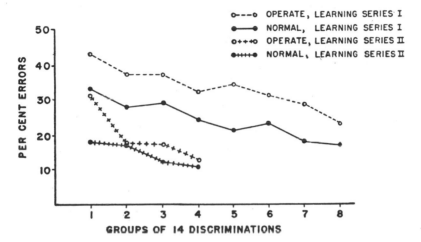

FIG. 15. Discrimination learning set curves based on total error responses: normal and operated monkeys.

resents a separate problem. Learning to react favorably to one person is followed by learning favorable reactions more rapidly to the next person to whom the monkey is socially introduced. Experience with additional individuals enables the monkey to learn further how to behave with human beings, and eventually the monkey's favorable reactions to new people are acquired so rapidly as to appear almost instantaneous.

The formation of social-emotional learning sets is not to be confused with mere stimulus generalization, a construct applied in this field with undue

Our observations on the formation of social-emotional learning sets have been entirely qualitative and informal, but there would appear to be no reason why they could not be studied experimentally.

The emphasis throughout this paper has been on the rôle of the historical or experience variable in learning behavior—the forgotten variable in current learning theory and research. Hull's Neo-behaviorists have constantly emphasized the necessity for an historical approach to learning, yet they have not exploited it fully. Their experimental manipulation of the experience variable has been largely limited to the development of isolated habits and their generalization. Their failure to find the phenomenon of discontinuity in learning may stem from their study of individual as opposed to repetitive learning situations.

The field theorists, unlike the Neo-behaviorists, have stressed insight and hypothesis in their description of learning. The impression these theorists give is that these phenomena are properties of the innate organization of the individual. If such phenomena appear independently of a gradual learning history, we have not found them in the primate order.

Psychologists working with human subjects have long believed in the phenomenon of learning sets and have even used sets as explanatory principles to account for perceptual selection and incidental learning. These psychologists have not, however, investigated the nature of these learning sets which their subjects bring to the experimental situation. The determining experiential variables of these learning sets lie buried in the subjects' pasts, but the development of such sets can be studied in the laboratory as long as the human race continues to reproduce its kind. Actually, detailed knowledge of the nature of the formation of learning sets could be of such importance to educational theory and practice as to justify prolonged and systematic investigation.

In the animal laboratory where the experiential factor can be easily controlled, we have carried out studies that outline the development and operation of specific learning sets. We believe that the construct of learning sets is of importance in the understanding of adaptive behavior. Since this is our faith, it is our hope that our limited data will be extended by those brave souls who study *real* men and *real* women.

[MS. received June 23, 1948]

Part VIII

# SENSORY-PERCEPTUAL FUNCTION

# Editor's Comments
# on Papers 23 and 24

**23   WASHBURN and BENTLEY**
*The Establishment of an Association Involving*
*Color-Discrimination in the Creek Chub,*
Semotilus atromaculatus.

**24   WATSON**
Excerpt from *Comparison of the Psychical Development of the*
*White Rat at Different Ages*

One key to an understanding of the factors affecting an animal's behavior is an understanding of the sensory-perceptual processes of that animal. It is these systems that provide the animal's "windows on the world" and determine the nature of the environmental influences that can alter behavior. This fact has been widely appreciated within comparative psychology, and material on animal sensory function has been prominent in virtually all reviews and textbooks in the field. Among the prominent comparative psychologists of the century, Yerkes (Yerkes and Eisenberg, 1915) studied color vision in ringdoves, Watson and Lashley (1915) studied spectral sensitivity in birds, Yerkes and Watson (1911) detailed methods for the study of color vision, Lashley published eighteen papers on the mechanisms of vision in rats (e.g., Lashley, 1948), Warden (Warden and Baer, 1929) studied the Müller-Lyer illusion in ringdoves, Stone and Beach examined the influence of sensory modalities on reproductive behavior, Schneirla examined sensory function in orientation, Kellogg studied sensory function in dolphins, and Hess wrote several general chapters on sensory function. This is but a small sample of the research by prominent comparative psychologists on sensory-perceptual systems in animals.

In the first of two papers reprinted here, Washburn and Bentley (Paper 23) present a representative early study of animal sensory function. The issue addressed is that of the sensory capacity of the animal, in this case the ability of fish to discriminate colors. The authors conclude that the fish can discriminate colors in a manner that is independent of brightness variations. This paper is typical of many experiments of animal sensory function. It also provides an introduction to the work of two psychologists with strong influences on comparative psychology. Margaret Floy Washburn's *The Animal Mind* (1908) went through four editions and was the dominant textbook in the field for several decades. Washburn's coauthor, Madison Bentley, exerted his influence primarily through writing and editorial work. Both Washburn and Bentley were representatives of the structural school of psychology established by E. B. Titchener at Cornell University.

Along with research designed to assess the sensory capacities of animals, such as the Washburn and Bentley study, there has been much interest in just which sensory cues are used in particular situations. An excerpt from J. B. Watson's doctoral dissertation, "Animal Education," illustrates this endeavor. This is one of the earliest studies of chemical communication in rodents conducted under the controlled conditions of the laboratory. In his first studies, Watson found no evidence that his rats used odor cues to track each other through a maze. In the later study, however, Watson concluded that adult rats prefer entrances containing the odor of animals of the opposite sex. Watson then turned his attention to visual cues influencing his rats in the mazes. Because the main thrust of his dissertation was developmental and because his name has become synonymous with an extremely environmentalistic brand of behaviorism, Watson's influences on the study of sensory systems in general and olfactory communication in particular have often been overlooked.

## REFERENCES

Lashley, K. S., 1948, The Mechanism of Vision, XVIII. Effects of Destroying the Visual "Association Areas" of the Monkey, *Genet. Psychol. Monogr.* **37:**107–166.

Warden, C. J., and J. Baer, 1929, The Müller-Lyer Illusion in the RingDove, *Turtor risorius, J. Comp. Psychol.* **9:**275–292.

Washburn, M. F., 1908, *The Animal Mind: A Text-Book of Comparative Psychology,* Macmillan, New York.

Watson, J. B., and K. S. Lashley, 1915, Homing and Related Activities of birds, *Publ. Carnegie Inst.* **7**(211):1–104.

Yerkes, R. M., and A. M. Eisenberg, 1915, Preliminaries to a Study of Color Vision in the Ringdove *Turtor risorius, J. Anim. Behav.* **5:**25–43.

Yerkes, R. M., and J. B. Watson, 1911, Methods of Studying Vision in Animals. *Behav. Monogr.* **1**(2):1–90.

## 23

Reprinted from *J. Comp. Neurol. Psychol.* **16**(2):113-125 (1906)

## THE ESTABLISHMENT OF AN ASSOCIATION INVOLVING COLOR-DISCRIMINATION IN THE CREEK CHUB, SEMOTILUS ATROMACULATUS.

BY

MARGARET F. WASHBURN AND I. MADISON BENTLEY.

The only experimental evidence hitherto existing, so far as we have been able to learn, that fish possess the power to discriminate colors is contained in the work by VITUS GRABER, published over twenty years ago and entitled *Grundlinien zur Erforschung des Helligkeits- und Farbensinnes der Tiere.*[1] GRABER experimented on a large number of animals, including two species of fish, Cobitis barbatula and Alburnus spectabilis. His method was to offer the animals the choice between two compartments differently illuminated, and at the end of a given period to count the number in each compartment. The results thus tested light-preferences rather than light-discrimination merely. GRABER himself points out that the two do not coincide, inasmuch as an animal may be quite capable of distinguishing between two colors and yet find them so nearly equal in feeling-value that it seeks them equally often. There must also be reckoned with the possibility that apparent color-preferences are really brightness-preferences, due to the difference in brightness between the two stimuli employed. This latter difficulty GRABER avoided in the following manner: If an animal showed itself to be, in our modern phrase, positively

---

[1] Rough experiments performed some years later by W. BATESON (*Jour. of the Marine Biol. Assoc. of the United Kingdom*, N. S., Vol. I, 1889-90, p. 225) gave, as the author says, "chiefly negative results." BATESON fed young mullet with minced worms sprinkled on tiles of various colors and noticed that the light-colored tiles were first cleared of food. It is to be remarked that BATESON was working for *preference* and not for discrimination of color and also that he neglected to control the element of brightness.

or negatively phototropic to a marked degree, and also showed a preference for one color or another, the preferred color was taken much darker than the other, if the animal was positively phototropic, or lighter if negatively phototropic. The persistence of the preference under these conditions showed it to be a true color-preference. GRABER'S results for the two species of fish were approximately the same and showed decided preference for white over black, a lesser degree of preference for blue without the ultra-violet rays over blue with the ultra-violet rays, for red over green, and for green over blue (ultra-violet). The last-mentioned could hardly be called a preference at all, and the difference between red and green was so slight as to be reversed when the green was made decidedly dark. In fact, the color-preferences proper, as distinguished from the cases involving ultra-violet rays, are scarcely marked enough to allow one to conclude from the experiments that the fish tested had the power of discriminating colors.

The subject of the following study was a female of the common species, Semotilus atromaculatus, the creek chub or horned dace. Our general plan upon beginning the investigation was to test color-discrimination by establishing, if possible, an association between a certain color and food. This method has a two-fold advantage over that employed by GRABER. First, it is a true test of discrimination as distinguished from preference; and, second, involving, as it does, "associative memory," the truly psychic nature of the phenomena resulting will be admitted by the most conservative biologists, whereas the "preference" method, which involves reaction to present stimulation only, establishes the existence merely of a tropism which may or may not have a mental aspect. Of course, in the case of fish, where intelligence has been shown to exist, by the experiments of MÖBIUS, THORNDIKE, TRIPLETT and others,[1] the presumption would be for consciousness.

The fish was kept throughout the experiments in a circular glass tank 50 cm. in diameter and 45 cm. deep. The apparatus used for feeding it consisted of two like pairs of dissecting forceps which were faced on the outer surfaces with four-cornered strips

---

[1]Zeitschr. d. gesammt. Naturwiss., Bd. 42, p. 89; Amer. Naturalist, Vol. 33, p. 923; Am. Jour. of Psych., Vol. 12, p. 354.

of wood 5 x 5 mm. across and 70 mm. long.   In all the earlier
experiments the strips of wood attached to one pair of forceps
were painted red, while those attached to the other pair were
green of a shade—to the experimenter's eye—somewhat brighter
than the red.   The strips were fastened to the forceps by small
rubber bands and projected in both cases about 5 to 10 mm.
beyond the metallic points.   The first attempt to apply our
general method may be described as follows:

*I.   The Method of Inhibition.*—When the fish reached a certain position at the bottom of the tank, a young live grasshopper,
held in one of the two pairs of forceps, was quickly thrust under
the surface of the water.   *The fish was allowed to take the food
from the red forceps, but when it snapped at the green pair the food
was quickly withdrawn.*   For one day, the red forceps only were
used and for the succeeding four days (six feedings) the red and
green were used in irregular sequence.   One of us applied the
stimulus while the other recorded, by means of a stop-watch, the
time of reaction—from the instant the food touched the water till
it was snapped at by the fish.   At the second red-green feeding,
we noticed that the reactions seemed, at times, to be prematurely
released by the sight of the approaching hand that held the forceps.   In order to eliminate the possibility of reaction to a warning
signal, the side of the tank next the experimenter was enveloped
with a black cloth screen and half the top was covered with  heavy
gray cardboard.   In the subsequent tests, the baited forceps were
slipped over the edge of the cardboard top and directly into the
water at the center of the tank.   In this way, the fish saw no movement until the object appeared at the surface of the water.

The recorded times were, of course, too inaccurate to be considered as "reaction times"; but it was not with reaction times
that we were primarily concerned, but rather with the discrimination of color-tones.   It seemed probable, however, that a discrimination of red and green—if it occurred—might be expected to
lead, in time, to an inhibition, or at least to a retardation, of the
green (unsuccessful) reaction.

In  the  last four days (six feedings) one hundred and thirty-one
trials were made, sixty-two with red and sixty-nine with green.
The longest reaction was five seconds, and one hundred and thirteen of the whole number fell within one to three seconds.   The
average time for red and for green was the same, 1.4 seconds.

The total times for the first ten tests were red, fourteen seconds, green, thirteen seconds; and for the last ten, red, ten seconds, green, eleven seconds.

Neither the times nor the observed behavior of the fish indicated any constant difference in the response to the two colors used. The results do not, however, prove a lack of color-discrimination. They are inconclusive. They simply show that even if color-vision existed and if colors were "associated" with success or failure in procuring food, the discrimination and the "association" were insufficient to cause an inhibition of the "green reaction." The outcome is not unaccountable, since brook fish have, at least during a part of the year, a varied diet, and they may therefore be expected to react positively and persistently to a wide range of objects that offer the possibility of food.

Although the result of the inhibition experiments was, for our purposes, largely negative, the method was valuable both because it made us acquainted at first hand with the behavior of our subject and because it suggested a second method which offered a *choice* of stimuli without, at the same time, demanding the actual inhibition of an old and firmly-rooted mode of response to stimulation.

*II. The Method of Choice.*—In the second set of experiments, *both pairs of forceps were presented at the same time, the red baited and the green empty.* In order still further to eliminate movement of the stimulus the tank was divided by a thin wooden partition into two like compartments. An opening about three inches wide was left at either side of the partition, allowing the fish to swim freely around the tank. These openings could be closed by wooden gates, thus making it possible to confine the fish in either half of the tank. With the subject in compartment A, the forceps were suspended side by side in the middle of compartment B and about two inches from the partition. They were held in place by being slipped vertically into narrow grooves sawed in a horizontal strip which ran across the tank just above the surface of the water, parallel with, and attached to, the upper edge of the partition. After the forceps had been set into position, one of the gates, right or left, was opened and the fish allowed to swim to compartment B and to secure the food from the forceps.

The procedure involves two constant errors of space, one of position of stimulus and one of direction of movement. The first was eliminated by setting the red forceps as often on the right as on the left of the green, and the second was canceled by using both gates and allowing the subject to enter half the time on the same side as the bait and half the time on the opposite side. Both of these compensatory changes occurred in irregular sequence, but an equal number of "right" and "left," of "same" and "opposite" settings were taken at each feeding. The following sample protocol for a series of experiments will serve to make this clear. "Right" and "Left" refer to the position of the forceps in the horizontal support; "Same" means that the fish was allowed to enter compartment B on the same side as the forceps with food in it, and "Opposite" means that it entered on the opposite side from the baited forceps. "R" and "G" refer to the red and green forceps, respectively.

| RIGHT. | | LEFT. |
|---|---|---|
| G. | Same | R. |
| R. | Same | G. |
| R. | Opposite | G. |
| G. | Opposite | R. |
| G. | Same | R. |
| R. | Opposite | G. |
| R. | Same | G. |
| G. | Opposite | R. |
| R. | Opposite | G. |
| G. | Same | R. |

In all these experiments, numbering two hundred and twenty-six exclusive of trials without bait, the red forceps held the food and the green forceps were empty. After August 3 mealworms were used for bait instead of grasshoppers, on account of their greater uniformity of appearance. In each case record was made of the forceps at which the fish *first* bit. The accompanying table (I) shows the results in the columns headed "Food." It will be seen that in the first series, of fifteen experiments (food), made on July 31, the fish bit first at the red eleven times and four times at the green; that in the second series of ten experiments it bit eight times at the red and twice at the green, and that after this point biting at the green was very infrequent; in the last seventy-four experiments, from August 5 on, the green was bitten at only once, on which occasion, as our notes show, the fish was ravenously hungry and chancing to come straight against the green forceps on entering, snapped at them.   The exceptional results of August 3, where the fish touched the green first three times and the red first five times, should be accompanied by the statements that the

TABLE I.  FOOD IN RED FORCEPS.

| Date. | No. Exp. | Food. | | No Food. | | Remarks. |
|-------|----------|-------|---|---------|---|----------|
|       |          | Dk. Red. | Green. | Lt. Red. | Green. |          |
| July 31 | 16 | 11 | 4 | 1 |   | Grasshoppers. |
| Aug. 1 | 12 | 8 | 2 | 1 | 1 |   |
| Aug. 1 | 14 | 10 |   | 4 |   | Partition added. |
| Aug. 2 | 16 | 11 | 1 | 3 | 1 | Space errors corrected. |
| Aug. 2 | 12 | 9 | 1 | 2 |   |   |
| Aug. 3 | 8 | 5 | 3 |   |   |   |
| Aug. 3 | 12 | 10 |   | 2 |   |   |
| Aug. 4 | 14 | 10 |   | 4 |   | Mealworms. |
| Aug. 4 | 14 | 10 |   | 4 |   | Light red sticks on green forceps. |
| Aug. 5 | 16 | 11 | 1 | 4 |   | Grasshoppers and mealworms. Sluggish. |
| Aug. 5 | 14 | 12 |   | 2 |   | Grasshoppers and mealworms. Sluggish. |
| Aug. 6 | 16 | 12 |   | 4 |   | Mealworms. |
| Aug. 6 | 7 | 7 |   |   |   | Red, daubed with green, and green with red.  Sluggish. |
| Aug. 7 | 10 | 10 |   |   |   | Not feeding well.  Grasshoppers and mealworms. |
| Aug. 8 | 16 | 11 | 1 | 4 |   | Ravenous.  Grasshoppers and mealworms. |
| Aug. 8 | 15 | 12 |   | 3 |   | Mealworms. |
| Aug. 9 | 14 | 10 |   | 4 |   |   |
| Totals | 226 | 169 | 13 | 42 | 2 |   |
|       |          | Dk. Red. | Blue. | Lt. Red. | Blue. | Blue strips substituted for green. |
| Aug. 10 |   | 7 |   | 2 |   |   |
| Aug. 10 |   | 3 |   |   |   |   |
| Aug. 11 |   | 10 |   | 4 |   |   |
| Aug. 12 |   | 10 |   | 4 |   |   |
| Totals |   | 30 |   | 10 |   |   |

subject was in an abnormal condition on that day, languid and sluggish, and that two of the green "bites" were the merest touches with the nose.   The fish's indifference to food on this day was so marked that only eight experiments could be made, as it wholly refused to rise after the eighth.

The obvious source of error which would wholly invalidate the results if they stood alone is that food was actually in the red forceps and not in the green, so that both sight and smell might have led the fish in the right direction. It demanded some care to eliminate this error, for, on the one hand, it was impossible, with the forceps fixed in the support, to have them both baited and, at the same time, to prevent the fish's getting food from the green as well as from the red pair; and, on the other hand, we could not perform a large number of tests where neither fork should be baited without weakening the association between red and food. We adopted the plan of performing each day a certain number of experiments, usually eight or ten, with the red fork baited and then making two tests with both forks empty. If the fish's appetite was good, we would give it two more tests with the baited fork and finish with two "unbaited" tests, again. In this way, without greatly weakening the association, we accumulated forty-four experiments where both forks were empty. In two only of these did our subject bite at the green. These two occurred in the first four days of experimenting, and in the second case the fish merely touched the green, then swam to the red and bit vigorously. The results thus show that the sight of the red forceps came to be connected with the impulse to bite, quite independently of the sight of the food. As a matter of fact, the fish's behavior throughout indicated that the sight of the food played little part in setting off the biting impulse. It seldom bit directly at the food, but nearly always at the ends or sides of the sticks, and if by accident the food became detached and floated in the water half an inch or so away, the chub still ignored the morsel and bit persistently at the stick.

The possibility that the smell of the food might have guided the subject remained uneliminated by merely testing the animal with unbaited forceps; for, since food was so often in the red pair and never in the green, the odor of the food might be supposed to linger about the former. Further, we still had the brightness error to deal with. It was possible that the fish distinguished between the red and the green forceps not as different in color but as different in brightness. To avoid this, we took a suggestion from GRABER, and prepared a pair of sticks exactly like the others in size but painted a light red, of the same color-tone as the previous red—so far as our discrimination went—but considerably brighter to ordinary vision than the green, which was, it will be remembered itself a little brighter than the red hitherto used. In all the unbaited test experiments made on and later than the afternoon of August 4, the following procedure was adopted: While the dark red sticks were still used on the baited forceps in the experiments where the fish was fed, when it was tested without bait we removed the dark red sticks and substituted for them the green sticks on the same forceps, using the same rubber bands that had previously fastened the dark red ones. Thus all the apparatus that could have the odor of food about it was now attached to the green sticks. On the forceps that had previously carried the green sticks were fastened, with the rubber bands that had been used for the green, the pair of light red sticks. When the forceps thus arranged were put into position, the fish had the choice between two unbaited forks, one, the green, having about it whatever food odor was present, the other, the light red, having in common with the pair from which it was usually fed only shape, size and color, not smell or brightness. If, then, the creature persisted in biting first at the red pair, it would show that the impulse to bite was "associated" with the color red, not with smell or brightness. It will be seen from the table that in the twenty-five tests made under these conditions the subject never once failed to bite first at the red.

One last, very remote possibility of error lay in the chance that the green and red paints might have had different odors. Inasmuch as the sticks were all covered with the same varnish, the chance was slight, but it was guarded against by putting, where they would not show, daubs of green paint on the red sticks and daubs of red paint on the green sticks. The results were wholly unaffected by this precaution.

In the work from August 10 to August 12 inclusive, comprising forty experiments in all, we substituted for the green sticks on the empty forceps a pair painted a light blue, lighter than the green and approximately equal in brightness to the light red. The last-named were still used and the forceps exchanged as before in the unbaited test experiments, and food was placed in the forceps carrying the dark red sticks in the ordinary feeding experiments. The fish made not a single error in distinguishing either dark or light red from blue, invariably biting first at the red (Table I).

How firmly rooted the association between the color red and the biting impulse was by this time we learned when from August 16 to August 18, in a series of about seventy experiments, we undertook to break it up and form a new association between food and green. The same procedure in every respect was employed as before, except that in the feeding experiments the food was always placed in the green forceps. Dark red was still used on the other pair, in these experiments, and light red in the unbaited tests, and the forceps were again exchanged in such a way as to eliminate error from smell. Because of the light which its behavior threw on the strength of the acquired impulse, we allowed the fish to bite as many times as it would at the red (empty) forks and recorded the number and order of the bites, in each experiment. In the preceding series, the single experiment practically never lasted beyond two or three bites, for if the fish bit first at the red it usually got the food, and in the few cases where it bit first at the green it bit but once and then either went down to the bottom of the tank or swam over to the red. Not so in these final series. The first time the subject entered compartment B, when the food was in the green forceps, it bit fourteen times in succession at the empty red sticks. It then bit once at the green, but not hard enough to get the food, and, returning to the red, bit thirteen more times at it. The fish then tried the green once more, came back to the red for four bites, and then, when it went down to the bottom of the tank, we considered the experiment over. At the second test, the fish bit three times at the red, then went to the green and got the bait at the third bite. In the next test, it bit ten times at the red, then twice at the green, getting the food on the second bite. At the fourth trial, the subject bit four times, but feebly, at the red, came up once from the bottom between the two forceps, "hesitated" and went down again, then came up, bit at the green and got the food. In the fifth test, it came up toward the red, seemed to look at it, swam to the green, nibbled, bit, and got the bait. The sixth time, it bit first at the green but failed to seize the food, turned to the red and bit once, then to the green and got the mealworm in two bites. The seventh time, the chub bit only at the green, taking four bites to obtain the food. The eighth time, it bit first at the red, then at the green, securing the bait in two bites. We then made two tests with unbaited forks, the usual arrangement of apparatus being maintained. The first of these rather indicated that, in this new order of things, the fish was being somewhat influenced by the sight or smell of the food, for in the absence of food it relapsed and bit ten times at the red before it tried the green. In the second "no-food" test, however, the subject barely touched the red, swam to the green and bit three times. And in three more baited experiments it bit first every time at the green; while in the first of the final two tests without food the subject swam past the red, turning away from it, snapped at a small object floating in the water near the red, then at the red, and then, more vigorously, at the green; and in the last unbaited test it bit first at the green, then at the red, then twice more at the green. The fish's behavior throughout this entire series was of the utmost interest as illustrating the process of animal learning. On the following day, the older habit reasserted itself, at the first trial, and the fish bit three times, vigorously, at the red before it tried the green; the second time, it swam straight as an arrow to the green, although it entered on the opposite side and had to pass the red. From this time on, with occasional rather marked relapses, the new "association" between green and the biting impulse shows growth, until in the last series, made on August 18, and consisting of eight experiments with food and four without, our subject bit first at the green every time, except in the first experiment of the series. The following table (II) shows, like the preceding one, the color first bitten at in each test.

We had some difficulty, in this latter part of our work, on account of the fish's diminishing appetite. The confinement of its life undoubtedly told upon its digestive powers. The series of August 14 and 15 were, for this reason, incomplete, and after that we attempted only one feeding a day, instead of a morning and an afternoon feeding as had been our custom. The "no-food" experiments of August 16 and 17 again furnished some indication that the sight of the food in the green forceps had partly influenced the fish in the feeding experiments and that when both forceps were empty it had a tendency to relapse into the old "red-food" habit. On August 16, after six feeding experiments in which the animal had only once bitten first at the red, when confronted with the two pairs of empty forceps, it bit nine times at the red, went down to the bottom of the tank, rose, and bit five more times at the red, sank, rose to the red without biting, and went down again. And on August 17 there still remained a tendency to bite first at the red when both forceps were empty. Also, we observed, at this time, that the biting movements were made less at random than before, that they were aimed less at the sticks and more definitely at the bait; that there was, in other words, a more precise and delicate adjustment to the food-situation.

TABLE II. FOOD IN GREEN FORCEPS.

| Date. | No. Exp. | Food. | | No Food. | | Remarks. |
|---|---|---|---|---|---|---|
| | | Dk. Red. | Green. | Lt. Red. | Green. | |
| Aug. 13 | 15 | 5 | 6 | 2 | 2 | |
| Aug. 14 | 6 | 3 | 3 | | | Sluggish; refuses to bite. |
| Aug. 15 | 7 | 4 | 3 | | | |
| Aug. 15 | 1 | | 1 | | | Refuses to bite after first exp. |
| Aug. 16 | 14 | 3 | 7 | 3 | 1 | |
| Aug. 17 | 14 | 2 | 8 | 3 | 1 | |
| Aug. 18 | 12 | 1 | 7 | | 4 | |
| Totals | 69 | 18 | 35 | 8 | 8 | |

Another factor, without perceptible effect when the connection between a given color and the impulse to bite was fully established, seems to have had some influence, for a time, during the breaking up of the association, "red-food," and the formation of the association, "green-food." This influence, which appeared about the middle of the process, when we may suppose the tendencies to have been about equally balanced, consisted in the position of the fork with reference to the fish's entrance. If these "food-in-green" experiments be divided into three groups, with regard to the temporal order of their performance, the proportion of right cases, i. e., where the green was bitten at first, is for the first third, comprising twenty-three experiments, 52 per cent. The wrong cases are 48 per cent., of the total number. Of the right cases, 58 per cent. occurred when the fish came up on the same side as the correct fork; 42 per cent. when it came up on the opposite side. Of the wrong cases, 45 per cent. occurred when it came up on the same side, 45 per cent. for the opposite side, and in 10 per cent.

it rose from straight below, midway between the forks. In the first third, then, the position of the forks seems to have made little difference with the results.

In the second third, the percentages of right and wrong cases were as before, 52 per cent. and 48 per cent. But 75 per cent. of the right cases happened when the fish was on the same side as the green fork, and only 25 per cent when it was on the opposite side; while of the wrong cases 64 per cent. occurred when the subject was on the opposite side, 18 per cent. when it was on the same side, and 18 per cent. when it rose from below, between the two forks. In the last third of the experiments, 81 per cent. were right and 19 per cent. wrong. Of the right cases, 50 per cent. were from the same side and 50 per cent. from the opposite side; of the wrong cases, 50 per cent. were from the same side, 25 per cent. from the opposite side and 25 per cent. from the middle. In the previous experiments, where the food was in the red fork, the association was pretty well established before the final method was adopted, which allowed the place of the fish's entrance and the position of the forks to be regularly varied. Of the few errors that occurred after the adoption of this method, half were made when the fish entered on the same side as the red fork, and half when it entered from the opposite side; while, of the right cases, $50\frac{1}{2}$ per cent. happened when the fish was on the same and $49\frac{1}{2}$ per cent. when it was on the opposite side. It looks, then, as if the association once formed was wholly independent of the subject's position, but that, at a critical period, when the animal was not strongly drawn to either fork, the fact that it happened to come upon one of them first was in some degree an influence leading it to bite at that one.

In summary, the experiments indicate the following conclusions:
1. Semotilus atromaculatus distinguishes red from green and from blue pigments, the discrimination being independent of the relative brightness of the colors. It must be borne in mind that owing to the great physical complexity of pigment colors, the existence of specific visual qualities in the fish's consciousness cannot be inferred with as great certainty as if pure (homogeneous) colors had been used.
2. An individual of this species is capable of forming with considerable rapidity an "association" between the impulse to

bite and an object of a particular color, thus displaying in the service of the nutritive instinct a fair degree of "intelligence."

3. Experience involving pleasurable consequences in connection with one object and the absence of such consequences in connection with another object may be powerful enough to guide an animal in the performance of an instinctive action, but not powerful enough to suppress the performance of such an action.

4. An influence, such as the actual presence of food in one pair of forceps, or the fact that the fish entered the compartment on the side nearest a particular pair of forceps, may be completely swamped when the association between a color and the biting impulse is fully formed, but may have some effect while the association is non-existent or incomplete.

One or two comments may be added. The rapidity with which the fish learned was a surprise to us. In general, it may be prophesied that the more deep-rooted and essential the instinct appealed to by the "experience" to which an animal is subjected, the more rapidly will the animal profit by that experience. It is quite probable that the maximal "intelligence" of which such a fish as Semotilus is capable is enlisted in the service of the feeding instinct. The third conclusion seems to us of great interest. When we began the experiments by the Method of Choice we were impressed with the probability that the fish's previous experience by the Method of Inhibition, though it had failed to influence the animal's behavior under that method, was making itself felt in the very rapid learning to choose rightly between red and green. Although this cannot be dogmatically asserted as a fact, yet the speed of the creature's acquisition in this case, together with its apparent entire failure to learn by the other method, affords a very pretty illustration of the truth that the chief function of experience is to guide rather than to inhibit instinct.

# 24

Reprinted from pages 48–56 of *Animal Education: An Experimental Study on the Psychical Development of the White Rat, Correlated with the Growth of Its Nervous System,* The University of Chicago Press, Chicago, 1903, 122p.

# COMPARISON OF THE PSYCHICAL DEVELOPMENT OF THE WHITE RAT AT DIFFERENT AGES

## J. B. Watson

[*Editor's Note:* In the original, material precedes and follows this excerpt.]

### SOME SUPPLEMENTARY TESTS ON THE INSTINCTS OF THE WHITE RAT.

In the above tests with the three groups of young rats certain questions came up relating to their instinctive life. In some of the tests, such as that of the labyrinth,[1] it was desirable to know whether or not these young rats showed a tendency to go into an entrance that another rat had just gone through.

From mere observation of the rats at work, it seemed to me that each discovered the entrances for himself independently of any rat that might have preceded him. For instance, I have seen one rat go into the true entrance, while another, coming up an instant later, would enter a blind opening situated near by the true entrance. In all these experiments I have seen the rats sniffing in the air, but it seemed to be at the food rather than at another rat's tracks. They very rarely stopped at an entrance to smell it, but if it suited their fancy would dash into it.

However, it must be remembered that rats have a keen sense

[1] P. 22.

of smell in detecting the odor of a strange rat when it enters their home. In the "rat quarters" at the University of Chicago we have a general runway where all the rats not kept in cages dwell harmoniously together; if a strange male rat is put in with these, the "boss rat" of the runway singles him out at once and "the best man wins."

The apparatus used for finding out whether or not rats track one another into entrances by the sense of smell was as follows: Four rectangular boxes, with wooden sides and wire netting at

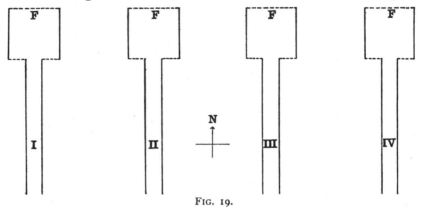

FIG. 19.

Tubes II and IV are kept always smelling of the rat odor. Tubes I and III are kept free from such odor. For the first test each rat from the three groups was put in at the south side of the cage containing the apparatus.

the two ends, were constructed. Through one of the wire ends of each box a pasteboard mailing tube, three inches in diameter, was admitted (marked by Roman numerals in Fig. 19). Strips of paper were then cut one inch longer than this mailing tube. These strips of paper were used to line the tube. The method of conducting the experiment was as follows: The tubes were all lined with paper; two of the tubes were kept always smelling of the odor of a rat and two were kept always free from any such odor. The two last-named tubes were kept free from the odor of the rat by changing the paper in them each time a rat entered. The stimulus used was fresh light-bread (F, Fig. 19). The four boxes were arranged side by side and a large cage was placed over all.

First   rat from Group II, entered Tube II*[1]
Second "   "   "   "   "   "   I
Third "   "   "   "   "   "   II* came out and entered I
Fourth "   "   "   "   "   "   II*
Fifth "   "   "   "   "   "   III
First   rat from Group III entered Tube II*
Second "   "   "   "   "   "   I
First   rat from Group I entered Tube II*
Second "   "   "   "   "   "   I
Third "   "   "   "   "   "   II*
Fourth "   "   "   "   "   "   I

Thinking that the rats might be influenced by reason of their being put into the cage on the south side, I determined to test each rat four times, putting him in first west, then east, then north, and finally south.

| | West | East | North | South |
|---|---|---|---|---|
| First rat from Group II entered....... | II* | IV* | I | III |
| Second " " " " " ....... | III | IV* | II* | I |
| Third " " " " " ....... | II* | IV* | II* | II* |
| Fourth " " " " " ....... | I | II* | IV*+III | I |
| Fifth " " " " " ....... | I | III+IV* | IV* | III |
| First rat from Group III entered ...... | II* | III | II* | I |
| Second " " " " " ....... | II* | IV* | IV* | I |
| First rat from Group I entered....... | I | IV* | III | II*+I |
| Second " " " " " ....... | III | IV* | III | III |
| Third " " " " " ....... | II* | II* | I+IV* | IV* |
| Fourth [2] " " " " " ....... | IV* | IV* | IV* | IV* |

Total number of tubes entered containing odor of rat......34
Total number of tubes entered free from odor of rat.......28

This gives a balance of six out of sixty-two tests in favor of their tracking, which means that we have no good evidence for assuming that there is a tendency in these young rats to follow

[1] In the following tables the asterisk marks the tubes containing the rat odor.

[2] The fourth rat from Group I entered Tube IV every time he was tried. Thinking that he had perhaps associated the getting of the food by going into that particular tube, I took out the paper smelling of the rat odor and put fresh paper in its place, changing it each time he entered Tube IV. When put in on the west side, he entered IV, at the east side IV, at the north side IV, and at the south side III.

one another through entrances in the sense of tracking by the sense of smell.

In order that the above test might be made more conclusive, all four of the tubes were moistened at the entrance with damp sawdust. The damp sawdust retains the odor better than the dry paper. In the following test only Group II was used. The reason for this was that where different groups are used, differences in odor are left in the tubes; thus there was a possibility in the above test of the element of fear entering in. The odor of Group II is the same for all members of it, since they live in the same cage. To further eliminate any element of fear, each rat, just before experiments were begun with him, was rubbed around the entrances of the two tubes designed to be kept smelling of the odor of the rat. This procedure was repeated for each rat.

The arrangement of the apparatus was the same as on p. 49.

| | West | South | East | North |
|---|---|---|---|---|
| First rat from Group II entered....... | I | I | I | I |
| Second " " " " " ........ | I | IV* | IV* | IV* |
| Third " " " " " ........ | I | IV* | III | IV* |
| Fourth " " " " " ........ | I | II* | IV* | IV* |
| Fifth " " " " " ........ | I | II* | IV* | IV* |

The arrangement of the apparatus was then changed—I and III being kept "saturated" with the rat odor.

| | West | South | East | North |
|---|---|---|---|---|
| First rat from Group II entered....... | IV | II | IV | I* |
| Second " " " " " ........ | III* | IV | I* | I* |
| Third " " " " " ........ | I* | IV | II | II |
| Fourth " " " " " ........ | IV | IV | I* | II |
| Fifth " " " " " ........ | IV | IV | II | III* |

Total number of tubes entered smelling of rat's own odor......18
Total number of tubes entered free from rat's own odor.......22

The results obtained from this test unquestionably support those obtained from the previous test.

It was thought worth while to continue this test with the four adult rats used in the experiments cited in this paper.

I determined to conduct this experiment a little more carefully than the preceding one had been conducted. Thinking that perhaps the element of sex would make the test more conclusive, I separated the males from the females for several days.

The males were then starved for two or three days, so that they would enter the tubes more quickly. The method of conducting this test was as follows: The four tubes were lined with paper, and damp sawdust was kept in the entrance. Two tubes, as in the preceding test, were kept smelling of the rat odor, but in this test the odor was always of a female.

The two tubes designed to contain the odor of the female were taken from the table, where the experiment was to be conducted, to the floor, and the female was then driven through them and rubbed around the entrance. This procedure was repeated after each test. The other two tubes were kept free from rat odor, just as in the previous test. After handling a rat the hands were always washed before picking up another.

In place of putting the rat into the cage at four different places, as was done on the test with the young rats, the position of the two tubes smelling of the rat odor was changed six times, while the rats were placed always in the center of the cage. In this table X and Y represent the two tubes that contain the rat odor.

Arrangement of
Apparatus.

I  X  Y  IV—Male A entered IV; male B entered X.
I  II  X  Y—Male A entered X; male B entered X.
X  Y  III  IV—Male A entered IV; male B entered X.
X  II  III  Y—Male A entered X; male B entered II.
X  II  Y  IV—Male A entered X; male B entered X.
I  X  III  Y—Male A entered X; Male B entered III.

Total number of tubes entered smelling of odor of female..................8
Total number of tubes entered free from odor of female....................4

The females were then tested in the same way.

I  X  Y  IV—Female A entered Y; female B entered Y.
I  II  X  Y—Female A entered X; female B entered II.

X  Y  III  IV—Female A entered Y; female B entered Y.
X  II  III  Y—Female A entered Y; female B entered X.
X  II  Y  IV—Female A entered Y; female B entered Y.
I  X  III  Y—Female A entered Y; female B entered Y.

Total number of tubes entered containing odor of male...................11
Total number of tubes entered free from odor of male.................... 1
Total number of tubes entered containing odor of opposite sex.............19
Total number of tubes entered free from odor of opposite sex.............. 5

We concluded from this test that adult rats show a preference for entrances that contain the odor of the opposite sex.

Another question that came up in the work of the rats was whether or not, other conditions being the same, they showed any preference between light and dark entrances. This question likewise arose from experiments with the labyrinth.[1] In this labyrinth the blind pathways are light, while the true pathway is dark.

Before I saw them at work on the labyrinth I would have said unhesitatingly that, if a rat showed any preference at all, it would have been for the dark entrances. Small animals in escaping from their pursuers instinctively seek some place to hide, and in the case of these rats, although perfectly domesticated, it was at least reasonable to suppose that they had not entirely lost this tendency.

To test this question, four boxes somewhat like those used in the previous experiment on tracking were constructed. The backs of two of these boxes were made opaque (A and B, Fig. 20); the backs of the other two were made of wire netting. In the middle of each of the four boxes a board partition was nailed. The front ends of all four boxes were made of wire netting. The pasteboard mailing tubes (I, A, III, and B in Fig. 20) were fitted both through the wire netting on the front end and through the partition in the middle of the box. We have each box, then, divided into two compartments, front and back. The front ends of all four boxes are exactly alike, but at the back end we have two of the boxes opaque and two that permit the entrance of light.

[1] P. 22.

Food (F, Fig. 20) was put into both compartments of each box. Since a rat was not permitted to see the backs of the four boxes, the front view of all four boxes appeared alike to him, *except that two of the tubes were light and two were dark.*

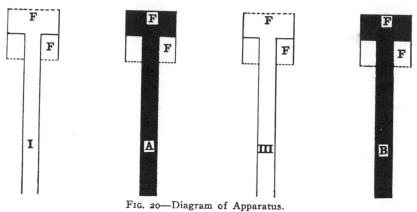

FIG. 20—Diagram of Apparatus.

In the following description of this test A and B show the position of the two dark entrances. The Roman numerals mark the position of the two light tubes. The position of the boxes was changed six times; the rats were put into the cage always at the same place.

Tubes arranged as in diagram.
1st rat from Group II entered tube III.
2d rat from Group II entered tube A, but came out at once.
3d rat from Group II entered tube I.
4th rat from Group II entered tube I.
5th rat from Group II entered tube I.
1st rat from Group III entered tube III.
2d rat from Group III entered tube I.
1st rat from Group I entered tube I.
2d rat from Group I entered tube A.
3d rat from Group I entered tube III.
4th rat from Group I entered tube III.

A  II  B  IV—Arrangement for second trial.
1st rat from Group II entered tube II.
2d rat from Group II entered tube A, but brought out the bread.
3d rat from Group II entered tube A, but came out and entered II.

4th rat from Group II entered tube II.
5th rat from Group II entered tube B, but brought out the bread.

1st rat from Group III entered tube II.
2d rat from Group III entered tube B.

1st rat from Group I entered tube II.
2d rat from Group I entered tube II.
3d rat from Group I entered tube B.
4th rat from Group I entered tube IV.

A   II   III   B—Arrangement for third trial.

1st rat from Group II entered tube A, but came out and entered II.
2d rat from Group II entered tube II.
3d rat from Group II entered tube II.
4th rat from Group II entered tube II.
5th rat from Group II entered tube A.

1st rat from Group III entered tube II.
2d rat from Group III entered tube B, but brought out the bread.

1st rat from Group I entered tube A.
2d rat from Group I entered tube II.
3d rat from Group I entered tube B.
4th rat from Group I entered tube B.

I   A   B   IV—Arrangement for fourth trial.

1st rat from Group II entered tube A.
2d rat from Group II entered tube I.
3d rat from Group II entered tube I.
4th rat from Group II entered tube I.
5th rat from Group II entered tube I.

1st rat from Group III entered tube B, but came out and entered I.
2d rat from Group III entered tube B, but came out and entered I.

1st rat from Group I entered tube A.
2d rat from Group I entered tube B.
3d rat from Group I entered tube B.
4th rat from Group I entered tube IV.

A   B   III   IV—Arrangement for fifth trial.

1st rat from Group II entered tube A.
2d rat from Group II entered tube III.
3d rat from Group II entered tube III.
4th rat from Group II entered tube III.
5th rat from Group II entered tube III.

1st rat from Group III entered tube III.
2d rat from Group III entered tube IV.

1st rat from Group I entered tube B.
2d rat from Group I entered tube III.
3d rat from Group I entered tube III.
4th rat from Group I entered tube A.

  I   II   A   B—Arrangement for sixth trial.

1st rat from Group II entered tube II.
2d rat from Group II entered tube I.
3d rat from Group II entered tube I.
4th rat from Group II entered tube I.
5th rat from Group I entered tube B.

1st rat from Group III entered tube I, then entered B.
2d rat from Group III entered tube I, then entered B.

1st rat from Group I entered tube I.
2d rat from Group I entered tube I.
3d rat from Group I entered tube A.
4th rat from Group I entered tube A.

Total number of dark tubes entered......................................24
Total number of light tubes entered......................................44

These results show that the young rats show a preference for light entrances. The young rats were used for this test because we have already shown that they do not track one another through entrances. If the adult rats had been used, tracking would doubtless have entered in, and the results of such a test as this would not have been so trustworthy as the present one.

Part IX

# EVOLUTION

# Editor's Comments
# on Papers 25 and 26

**25  ANGELL**
*The Influence of Darwin on Psychology*

**26  STONE**
*Multiply, Vary, Let the Strongest Live and the Weakest Die—
Charles Darwin*

The perceptions of various authors of the role of evolutionary theory in comparative psychology vary from one extreme, in which it is held that evolutionary theory exerted little or no influence, to another wherein the evolutionary approach forms a part of the very definition of the field. It is true that comparative psychologists at various times in the history of their discipline have paid less overt attention to evolutionary principles than might have been the case. Nevertheless, evolutionary theory played a major role in stimulating the very initiation of a comparative psychology in the efforts of such scientists as Charles Darwin, George John Romanes, and C. Lloyd Morgan. Psychologists played a major role in proposing a mechanism whereby behavioral patterns that appeared to be inherited via a pattern of Lamarckian inheritance of acquired traits could be explained using established principles of evolutionary change. The principle is named after the comparative psychologist James Mark Baldwin and is called the "Baldwin effect" (Baldwin, 1896; Morgan, 1896; Osborn, 1986).

The profound influence of Darwin and evolutionary theory has been generally appreciated within psychology even if it has not always been apparent outside of it. In 1909 psychologist James Rowland Angell (Paper 25) reviewed the influence of Darwin on psychology. As Angell notes, the issue is not why evolutionary theory exerted so little influence on psychology but why it succeeded in gaining such easy access. Angell emphasizes three main influences: (1) the evolution of instinct and the role of intelligence, (2) the evolution of mind, and (3) the expression of emotion.

In his presidential address prepared for the American Psychological Association, Calvin Stone (Paper 26) reviewed various studies and principles related to the evolution of instinctive behavior. Today it may seem remarkable that an APA President should present an address so heavily devoted to evolution, particularly at a time in the history of comparative psychology that many feel represented a low point for the discipline. However, it should be remembered that such workers as Lashley, Yerkes, Beach, Nissen, Carpenter, Schneirla, and others were extremely active during this period; it was not a period of inactivity. Also remarkable is Stone's last paragraph. The APA President in 1943 anticipated the development of Behavioral Ecology, a major development in the study of animal behavior in recent years. Stone alerted young comparative psychologists to adopt an attitude of "constant vigilance for opportunities to study the instincts as they are related to the subject of behavioral ecology" (p. 24).

Some comparative psychologists took Stone's advice. More and more are being directly influenced by evolutionary principles in their research, and are, in turn, making substantial contributions to our understanding of the evolution of behavior. The understanding and study of evolution is and generally has been an integral part of the broadly based, biologically oriented field that has been, is, and will continue to be comparative psychology.

## REFERENCES

Baldwin, J. M., 1896, A New Factor in Evolution, *Am. Nat.* **30:**441–451, 536–553.

Morgan, C. L., 1896, *Habit and Instinct,* Arnold, London.

Osborn, H. F., 1896, A Mode of Evolution Requiring Neither Natural Selection nor the Inheritance of Acquired Characteristics, *N. Y. Acad. Sci. Trans.* **15:**141–148.

# 25

Reprinted from *Psychol. Rev.* **16**:152–169 (1909)

## THE INFLUENCE OF DARWIN ON PSYCHOLOGY.

BY PROFESSOR JAMES ROWLAND ANGELL,
*The University of Chicago.*

### I.

Darwinism has never been a really vital issue in psychology. Occasionally a theologian or a naturalist has inveighed against the Darwinian theory of mental evolution, but the psychologists as such have rarely uttered a protest. In view of the storm of vituperative scientific criticism precipitated by the publication of the *Origin of Species*, this fact is distinctly significant. Indeed, so much a matter of course have the essential Darwinian conceptions become, that one is in danger of assuming fallaciously that Darwinism has no important bearing on psychology. How Darwin's radical theories succeeded in gaining such easy access to the psychological sanctuary is a matter of distinct interest upon which a few speculative comments may be made.

It must be borne in mind, then, that Darwin's most revolutionary ideas on mental evolution did not appear until the publication of the *Descent of Man* in 1871. This was nearly thirty years after Weber's epoch-making experiments on sensations, almost a score of years after the appearance of Lotze's medical psychology, sixteen years after the issuance of Spencer's evolutionary psychology and Bain's work on the *Senses and Intellect*, with its excellent presentation of the facts of nervous organization, eleven years after Fechner's publication of the *Psychophysik*, nine years after the first edition of Helmholtz's *Sensations of Tone* and seven years after his *Physiological Optics*. It was only three years in advance of the first edition of Wundt's *Physiological Psychology*. There had thus been rapidly growing during the preceding thirty years a disposition to view mental life as intimately connected with physiological processes, as capable of investigation along experimental and physiological lines, and finally as susceptible of explanation in an evolutionary manner. Moreover, by the time the *Descent of Man* was published the weight of scientific authority, so heavily against Darwin at the time of the publication of the *Origin of Species* in 1859, had swung unmistakably to his support.

Another circumstance of probably more than negligible moment is found in the fact that the major interest of many psychologists has always been in the more narrowly analytical problems of mind. On these problems Darwinism has had little immediate bearing and has exercised only the smallest fructifying influence. Its contentions have seemed, therefore, to demand no very vigorous partisanship either one way or the other.

The effect of certain philosophic tendencies ought, no doubt, to be added to this brief survey of contributory influences, but the considerations already offered are probably sufficient to indicate in part, at least, why the publication of the doctrines of mental evolution expounded in the *Descent of Man* occasioned so little psychological flutter and in many quarters awakened so warm and enthusiastic a welcome. They also serve to explain why it is so difficult to assign with confidence the precise contribution of Darwin's thought to current conditions in psychology. Many convergent forces have been at work and the independent effects of each are hardly to be discriminated. Nevertheless, it is clear that Darwinism exercises a very potent influence in psychology, not alone as regards general standpoint and method, but also as regards certain specific doctrines.

In the matter of general method we may certainly attribute to Darwinism the larger part of the responsibility for the change which has brought into prominence functional and genetic psychology (including animal psychology), in distinction from the older and more conventional analytic psychology. Here again many influences have contributed to the final outcome, but it is fatuous to suppose that the genetic movement in psychology could have attained its present imposing dimensions had it not been for the inspiration of Darwin's achievements. The analytical methods will no doubt always retain a certain field of usefulness, and an indispensable one at that, but our larger and more significant generalizations, our more practically important forms of control over mental life are going to issue from the

**313**

pursuit of methods in which growth, development and the influence of environment, both social and physical, will be the cardinal factors, methods which will in other words apply Darwinian principles with, let us hope, Darwin's tireless patience.

Darwin's more specific contributions to psychology may be grouped under three main headings: (1) his doctrine of the evolution of instinct and the part played by intelligence in the process; (2) the evolution of mind from the lowest animal to the highest man; and (3) the expressions of emotion. This is the chronological order in which these topics were given publicity by Darwin and we may properly adopt it in discussing the problems involved.

## II.

The solution of the first issue, *i. e.*, the genesis of instinct and the part played by intelligence in such genesis, bears primarily perhaps on the field of animal psychology, but it certainly has a very definite interest for human psychology as well. At first blush it might seem that instinct is altogether a matter of muscular activities and neural mechanisms and that mentality has little or nothing to do with it. But a closer inspection of the actual manifestations of instinct serves to disabuse one's mind of that impression. Not only are human instincts honeycombed with psychic influences, but even animal instincts show themselves variable and adaptive to specific situations in ways which hardly permit any other interpretation than that of conscious adjustment. Take the imperious mating instinct as an instance. Among birds of many species there is every evidence that despite the impelling force of impulse, the female exercises a very definite choice in which to all appearances psychical impressions are potent. But the question still remains whether intelligence is a true cause in the *production* of instinctive acts, or whether it merely comes in occasionally to modify them. Herbert Spencer is cited with questionable justice as representing one extreme opinion in this matter.[1] It is alleged that he holds that instinct is simply compound reflex action and that

[1] Cf. Romanes, *Mental Evolution in Animals*, p. 256. I find it difficult to be certain from a reading of Spencer's own statement just what position he really holds on this matter.

it is always the precursor of intelligence. This is clearly the view of many modern physiologists and naturalists, of whom Bethe and Loeb are illustrations. From this standpoint consciousness is not essential to the formation of instinct. Among English and American writers G. H. Lewes and Cope represent the other extreme, maintaining that all instincts are originally intelligent conscious acts, from which conscious control has largely or wholly disappeared. Some authorities like Romanes have held that consciousness is at all times operative in instinct and that it is precisely the presence of consciousness which distinguishes instincts from mere reflexes. This general view held with sundry modifications by numerous writers, among others Wundt, is known as the 'lapsed intelligence' theory.

Darwin[1] himself seems to have been less interested in the question as to whether mind is always present in instinctive reactions than in the question of its relation to the origin of instinct. His view seems to have been that instincts are in part due to the inheritance of useful habits consciously acquired, and in part due to the effects of natural selection operating on chance variations in conduct. Of the two he regards natural selection as the more important, because many instincts cannot have been inherited habits (e. g., those of neuter insects), and because the selection of slight variations in action through many generations seems to him plausible by reason of the conclusive evidence of a similar process in the evolution of structures.

Against the natural selection argument, as it pertains to the supposed preservation of incremental variations of a useful sort, it has been urged that in not a few instincts this is an impossible assumption, because the whole value of the instinct depends on the appropriate execution of each step in a long series of acts, each one of which alone, and any group of which apart from the others, is useless. Natural selection could only furnish an adequate explanation provided the whole series of complex acts sprang into existence simultaneously. To suppose that this occurs is to assume the miraculous. Stated abstractedly this

[1] Cf. Darwin, *Origin of Species*, Ch. VIII.; Romanes, *Mental Evolution in Animals*, Appendix.

criticism appears forceful, but in view of our profound ignorance of the stages through which complex instincts have actually
passed, it seem wise to be conservative in estimating the significance of the criticism.

It will be noted also that Darwin speaks quite explicitly of
his belief that acquired habits are transmitted. The doubt which
attaches to this doctrine in the minds of competent contemporary
zoölogists is well known. Darwin quotes as illustrating his
point the alleged acquirement of fear of man by birds in certain
of the oceanic islands remote from the mainland subsequent to
the coming of men and the pursuit of hunting. Certain cases
of alleged transmission of characteristics as a result of mental
training among dogs appear also to have weighed heavily in
his mind.

If such acquirements *are* transmitted by heredity, then it
must be admitted that this factor, together with the natural
selection of such instinctive variations as arise naturally and
after the manner of structural variations, would no doubt largely
account for the phenomena with which we are familiar. But
as we have just pointed out, difficulties beset both parts of this
program.

A compromise view which is put forward with the joint
authority of Morgan, Osborn and Baldwin,[1] under the title
'organic selection,' maintains that consciously acquired habits
are probably not directly transmitted, but that consciousness
plays an indispensable part in the drama by enabling successive
generations of creatures to accommodate themselves to the vicis-
situdes of life while the slow changes are taking place which
finally issue in the completed instinct. Not only is consciousness operative in this way, but in all the higher forms of animal
life it is held that conscious imitative activities also play a part,
and with man a dominant part, in setting the racial pattern.
Natural selection serves to lop off the feeble and incompetent,
both among individuals and groups, while all this process is
going forward, but the successful issue is fundamentally dependent on conscious reactions during the critical formative stages.

In the midst of uncertainty and speculative ingenuity such

[1] Cf. Baldwin, *Development and Evolution*, especially Appendices A and B.

as this, many minds will look with hope and a certain relief on the efforts of a group of zoölogists and physiologists — illustrated by Jennings and Loeb — who have made persistent and in no small measure successful attempts to modify instinctive behavior by experimental methods, thus securing at once some rudimentary insight into the mechanics of the instincts, instead of waiting for nature to reveal her secrets at her pleasure. In the lower organisms where such experimental control is most feasible, already the dependence of certain forms of instinctive behavior on conditions of temperature, light and oxygenation has been demonstrated and it hardly seems unduly optimistic to hope that through such means we shall ere long be able to substitute for speculative theories on the *modus operandi* of instinctive behavior something more nearly resembling knowledge. At present we can only say that we know with reasonable certainty that many instinctive acts are accompanied by consciousness, that practically all of them are variable within limits, that some of them appear to be modified by conscious forces, that possibly consciousness has played a part in the formation of some of them as it seemingly plays a part in their actual workings, that natural selection would certainly account for many instincts and perhaps for all.

We come now to consider Darwin's view of mental evolution.

### III.

Darwin[1] held that the mind of civilized man is a direct outgrowth of the animal mind. He maintained that from the lowest animal upward we find evidence of mental processes which increase in range and power, but do not change in kind, until we meet their most complete expressions in man. In man himself he finds again no evidence of aught but continuity of development from the lowest savage to the highest genius.

Darwin not only teaches the continuity of mental evolution from the lowest to the highest forms of animal life, he also urges the value of mental factors in the operation of both natural and sexual selection. Men and animals alike that were alert and intelligent in their adaptive acts would enjoy a larger chance of

[1] Cf. Darwin, *The Descent of Man*, Chapters III. to V.

life and leave behind them a more numerous posterity. In those orders of animals where the female exercises selective control in the choice of a mate, he urges, as has already been indicated, that psychical factors enter in an important degree to determine the feminine preference.

His survey of mental characteristics on which these doctrines are based is somewhat naïve. The psychic qualities which he cites as a foundation for his statements are as follows : sensations, pleasure, pain, passions, emotions (terror, suspicion, fear, anger, courage, timidity, love, jealousy, emulation, sense of humor, wonder, curiosity), imitation, attention, memory, imagination (whose presence in animals he regards as proved by behavior indicating dreams), and reason, which in animals, he says, is closely allied with instinct. These categories are all taken quite simply and with no special effort to indicate precisely what may be meant by them. He contents himself by citing illustrations of animal behavior, which seem to him to indicate the presence of these several mental attributes.

He undertakes to fortify his general position by a refutation of the several stock arguments commonly advanced to support belief in the radical distinction between animals and man. Of these we may pause to mention only a few.

He meets the assertion that animals make no use of tools by citing the case of the chimpanzee who is said to use stones to open nuts, and by the case of the elephant who uses branches to protect himself from the assaults of flies. He might have cited many other similar cases, but it is to be observed that he makes no very satisfactory attempt to meet the further points that animals do not fashion utensils and that they do not use fire. For the present generation, however, this type of consideration has somewhat lost interest. He believes the opinion that animals do not form concepts and that they are incapable of making abstractions is not well founded. He cites as an instance of the appreciation by animals of something akin to an abstract idea, the attitude which a dog will assume in response to the exciting question, " Where is it?" The simple-mindedness of this conclusion must inevitably furnish amusement to the sophisticated animal psych logists of the present day. On the matter of language he occupies a position distinctly favorable to the possession of rudimentary language forms by animals. He cites the fact that many animals have calls expressive of emotion, and these calls he regards as essentially linguistic. He also mentions he use by parrots of significant words as a case demonstrating his contentions. Again, the sense of beauty has been held to be a purely human attribute. But this view Darwin feels is definitely controverted by the fondness which certain animals display, especially birds, for colors and plumage. The possession of conscience and the belief in God have frequently been urged as the sole possessions of humanity. To this assertion Darwin replies that the belief in God is not universal among human beings and hence not generically human, and the actions of many animals, notably dogs, indicate something closely akin to the feelings of conscience. To the contemporary psychologist all this sounds highly archaic and scientifically anachronistic and so no doubt it is. But in view of Darwin's extensive innocence of psychology, it represents, as he marshals his facts, an amazing range of original observation and a most intrepid mind.

In the last analysis, despite the statements of the preceding paragraph, Darwin regards the development of conscience, or the moral sense, as by far the most important practical distinction of man from the animals. He says, however, that any animal endowed with well marked social instincts, such as the parental or filial affections, would develop man's conscience as soon as he developed man's intellectual capacity, or even approximated it. The social and gregarious habits of many animals obviously furnish an excellent point of departure for such a development. Moreover, sympathy, which plays an important part in all moral evolution, seems to be manifested by certain animals. There is therefore no evidence anywhere for radical differences between man and the animals.

It may be of interest to remark certain typical divergences from this general position in which, however, Darwin has found not a few loyal followers. Indeed, at the present time it is undoubtedly the case that most psychologists share Darwin's main convictions as to the continuity of mental evolution from animal to man, less perhaps as a result of careful scrutiny of the facts than as a consequence of a powerful drift from every direction toward the belief in a common origin for human and animal characteristics. We feel more comfortable nowadays in a world where simple and uniform rules obtain.

Probably the most persistent and most substantial point of dissent from Darwin is represented by writers who like Mivart [1] hold that although men and animals have certain forms of conscious life in common, for instance, sentience and memory, man alone can frame true concepts, and man alone can use true signs, can create and use language. Only man has ideas. Whereas we find essential continuity from the lowest to the highest of *bodily* forms, in *mental* processes we meet a real break, separating the human and spiritual, from the merely sentient and brute.

This type of view has always commended itself to a certain stripe of religious belief, because of its seeming provision for a somewhat super-naturalistic element in man, and its protest against regarding him, or at least his ancestry, as substantially on a level with the beasts of the field.

Moreover, it can summon to its support not a little apparently valid evidence wherein alleged instances of the animal use of language and signs are shown capable of another and more rudimentary interpretation. We are, of course, unable to intrude upon the inner workings of the animal consciousness, and it must be confessed that in so far as we judge by external conduct, few, if any, of the instances adduced to prove the formation by animals of concepts or of language really furnish unequivocal evidence of the thing to be proved. Meantime, it should be clearly recognized that this position, as advanced by Mivart at least, does not rest for its severance of man from the animals simply on the classical contention that he has a soul while they possess only minds. It is a distinction in the field of mind itself, which is here emphasized, an ascription to man, as his unique possession, of capacities which constitute the higher stages of cognitive activities.

Another divergent line is represented by the celebrated

[1] Cf. Mivart, *The Origin of Human Reason.*

naturalist Wallace,[1] who shares with Darwin a part of the credit for that revolution of opinion in the scientific world which generally is characterized with Darwin's name. Wallace is apparently willing to grant as a mere hypothesis that man's mind has developed *pari passu* with man's body, but he absolutely refuses to admit that natural selection could have brought this result to pass. He calls attention to three great familiar instances of alleged discontinuity in nature as suggesting that we should be scientifically hospitable to the idea of discontinuity. First, there is the breach between the organic and the inorganic, a breach which seems daily to shrink, but which has not yet been over-spanned. Then there is the equally marvellous break between the organic and the sentient, the conscious. And finally there is the break between mere sentience and rational intelligence — the distinction upon which Mivart dwelt so insistently.

Wallace cannot seriously call in question the possibility that natural selection should affect such mental qualities as quickness of eye and ear, accuracy of memory of former dangers and the like. It is the higher more definitely human qualities which apparently afford him foundation for his position. For example, what he calls the 'mathematical faculty' and the 'faculty for music' seem to him too remote from the life-subserving functions to have had any survival value, and unless they have such value, his position must be granted as having force against natural selection. On such grounds, in any case, he rests his contention that there is in man a spiritual essence not inherited from his animal forbears to whom he owes his bodily structure. By virtue of this essence human progress is possible and a spiritual life beyond the grave assured, for spirit cannot perish.

In reading Wallace one feels the presence of a vein of mysticism and the impelling influence of religious pre-possessions . . . influences which may properly be given a hearing, but which must not be treated as standing on the same logical level with ordinary empirical evidence. Whether natural selection can reasonably explain mental development in its higher ranges, is however, a perfectly fair question and one which deserves, and from ethical writers at least has often received, serious consideration.

[1] Cf. Wallace, *Darwinism,* Ch. XV.

It seems perfectly clear that certain familiar intellectual and emotional endowments would have had a very positive survival value both among animals and men. Those individuals who were mentally quick and inventive, who were courageous, cunning and pushing, would certainly be at an advantage over those who failed in these characteristics. Other things equal, the latter would live shorter lives and leave fewer progeny. When one takes into account the conditions of life under gregarious or social circumstances, one sees clearly how in a group the social virtues of sympathy, bravery, self-sacrifice, etc., may condition the dominance of the group over competing groups and consequently how a survival value may attach to these mental and moral characteristics. All this is familiar and trite and probably true. But what is to be said of Wallace's case as it concerns mathematical, philosophical and musical capacities, to the possessors of which men have customarily paid large respect? Wherein do such characteristics display a survival value, and if they have none such, how can natural selection account for their preservation and cultivation?

The reply, I believe, is quite in keeping with the reply as to the survival value of sympathy and pity and self-sacrificing bravery. In course of mental evolution, no doubt many characteristics are developed which are either harmful or useless. The congenitally insane illustrate the appearance of harmful forms. Other forms appear which may be useless or even harmful to the occasional individual, but to the group as a whole they are highly valuable and by virtue of this fact they secure perpetuity, either by social imitation, or by direct heredity. Now we have only to assume the appearance of a mental strain which has such social value, to expect with certainty that it will be encouraged in most of those who possess it markedly. Music and mathematics and philosophy do not represent such highly occasional mental sports as Mr. Wallace implies. A respectable amount of each of these capacities is latent in all normal individuals. Propitious surroundings are not always at hand and other more seductive interests often secure the field in advance, so that these capacities remain latent and undeveloped. But nothing is more certain than this, that if society did not at least *consider* itself benefited by the cultivation of these tastes, they would speedily disappear along with the taste for collecting scalps and wampum.

In other words, Mr. Wallace and others of his way of thinking take their natural selection too narrrowly when they come to the higher ranges of mental life. They forget the social pressure which is there exercised, not to create but to develop certain capacities.

Still another view which not only accepts but magnifies discontinuity in natural phenomena is conceived not in the interests of any idealistic metaphysical or religious tenets, but rather in frank hostility to such. This is the view typified by Loeb,[1] who believes that many of the lower organisms have no consciousness at all. This is a view which in more sweeping form Descartes long ago made famous, though on grounds quite different from those of Loeb. For Loeb, man's mind is a natural product of the evolution of animal mind, but animal mind itself begins not necessarily in the protozoa, but presumably at a relatively advanced point among the metazoa, at a point, namely, where we find creatures able to profit by experience, able to learn.

Accepting the analogy of many chemical phenomena in which a critical stage is represented, before and after which the resulting phenomena are apparently entirely discontinuous (*e. g.*, the formation of liquid from gas under given conditions of temperature and pressure) he urges that until precisely the correct molecular conditions are represented in the protoplasm of the nervous system, no consciousness will appear. But the moment these conditions are given, mind will also be present. It is not necessary to assume mind, or associative memory, as he prefers to call it, wherever we find a nervous system, much less wherever we find protoplasm in a living state. We have a right to allege the presence of mind only when the actions of an organism indicate its presence, and our only criterion for this presence is, as was above stated, the capacity to learn by experience, to improve the reactions made to stimuli.

The difficulty with this criterion is practical, not theoretical.

[1] Cf. Loeb, *Physiology of the Brain*, particularly pages 213 ff.

If one could always say with assurance that animals can or can not learn, the task would be easy. Unhappily such is not the case. Some animals learn to better a reaction after a few attempts, others require dozens of trials. Even the frog, whose intellectual capacities were once regarded as nil, has now been proved capable, under the advantages of higher education, of making some progress, but it is a progress which taxes both pupil and teacher, for it may require hundreds of experiences to improve even a very simple reaction. The criterion proposed, while theoretically admirable, leaves us as a matter of fact in much the position we occupied before, *i. e.*, inability confidently to allege that any living creature is wholly lacking in mind. Even the lowly amœba manifests certain peculiarities of action which may betoken consciousness of a low order.

An examination of these variants on the Darwinian view of continuity in mental development leads one to feel that the balance of probability distinctly favors the original formulation. Not only does modern psychology disclaim in man at least any such sharp lines between conceptual thought and the lower levels of sentient mental life, as Mivart and Wallace postulate, it has on the contrary expended no little effort in analyzing and defending the presence of just these conceptual processes in the sensory and perceptual activities of mind. Binet's[1] essay on the psychology of reasoning is a typical example of this tendency, exhibiting as it does the implicit reasoning process involved in every definite perception. To perceive that this object before me is a desk, involves identifying this present visual experience with antecedent visual experiences in a way which closely resembles certain phases of the process in syllogistic inference. Nor has this tendency in psychology been in any way influenced by partisan Darwinian prepossessions, so far as I know. It has been the inevitable outcome of penetrating analysis. The use of conscious meanings does not suddenly burst forth full-blown in a mind which before had given no indication of such an achievement. The simplest mental acts which as human beings we can detect in ourselves have some increment, however small, of this consciousness of meaning, this embryonic form of con-

[1] Binet, *La Psychologie du Raisonnement.*

ceptual thought. Nevertheless, it must not be forgotten that animals have certainly not been as yet proved to reason in human ways. On this score Mivart and his cohorts must be given their dues.

Nor is the dividing line which Loeb has proposed likely to result in any radical alterations in the general Darwinian position. For not only do we find it difficult to use the criterion Loeb offers, *i. e.*, educability, but in point of fact we have considerable evidence at hand to show that even the lowest animal forms modify their behavior somewhat to meet changed conditions, and that these modifications are of a kind which in higher animals would be regarded as indicative of the presence of consciousness.

IV.

This brings us to the work on emotion. In his treatise on *The Expression of the Emotions* Darwin has brought together with characteristic patience and industry the most extended array of observations bearing on the subject, an array which has been of notable value to the defenders of the James-Lange theory of emotion. As finally put forth the work is a defense of three familiar theses concerning emotional expressions. The first holds that serviceable bodily reactions become habitual and become associated with the state of mind in connection with which they arose. When the mental state recurs, the bodily reactions recur also, although they may long since have lost any immediate and obvious utility. The clenching of the fist and the showing of the teeth in anger illustrate this conception. The second thesis, that of antithetic action, maintains that a state of mind opposed to one calling out a definite bodily attitude may evoke an opposite bodily attitude. As an illustration may be cited the fact that an angry cat naturally lashes its tail from side to side. On the other hand a cat which is pleased carries its tail erect and stiff. The third thesis, that of nervous overflow, holds that apart from the two previous principles of explanation, conditions of emotional excitement are prone to release more cortical energy than can be effectively disposed of in the usual ways, and the superfluity pours out in muscular contractions of the most various kinds.

So far as concerns the adequacy of these explanatory hypotheses, it may be said that in the light of our present knowledge the first affords a highly probable account of certain emotional reactions, while it is quite inadequate satisfactorily to explain others. The second hypothesis has always been viewed askance, as something of a scientific *tour de force*, while the third, which Darwin himself treats rather as a catch-all to take care of cases found bothersome to handle by his first two hypotheses, is probably of much more fundamental import than he imagined. In any event later writers have been unable to improve materially upon Darwin"s catalogue of the causative influences provocative of our emotional attitudes.

### V.

In conclusion we may venture a brief comment upon the methods now current in the study of evolving mind and more particularly upon the methods and points of view now dominant in animal psychology. A few words may also be added upon a group of problems suggested by Darwin's work.

The most marked and unmistakable change which we notice in method is the somewhat aggressive skepticism now everywhere entertained for the anecdotal foundation on which many of the early zoölogical doctrines about animals were based. Darwin himself quotes numerous tales to substantiate his positions and his disciples have far outdone the master. This condition of things has led not unnaturally to a reaction in favor of laboratory experiments and observations under conditions of control. To this procedure there is never lacking acrimonious protest on the part of those who hold that only under the conditions of nature can the intimate facts of animal life be seen and understood. No doubt there is a large measure of justice in this protest. But fortunately it is now possible in many of our laboratories and zoölogical stations to simulate with large success the conditions of life which are natural to many animal forms. The result has been a wealth of new material which promises quite to revolutionize many phases of animal lore. It seems not unreasonable to anticipate that the effect of such work will not only be felt in the direct increase of our reliable information gained through these channels, but also that the observation of animals in a state of nature will be rendered far more intelligent and precise by virtue of the suggestions which will be gained from work of this type. Certainly such work has already brought us new and more exacting standards of accuracy and taught us an invaluable caution and conservatism both in inference and in generalization.

Conspicuous among the many interesting psychological problems suggested by Darwin's work is that of the determination of mental types, species and genera, following rudely the analogy of species and genera in zoölogy. The practical difficulty in defining a species need occasion us no concern, because the *idea* of species has had great value, despite the perplexities attached to the satisfactory differentiations of particular classes. If the type of intelligence manifested by an animal be contingent upon the structure of its nervous system, as is apparently the case, it would seem to follow as a reasonable inference, that we might expect to find groups of animals evincing in their behavior psychic characteristics of a similar pattern, just as we find forms of nervous system highly similar to one another. It is of course conceivable that in different animals different nervous structures should function to produce similar psychic behavior. But even recognizing this possibility, it still ought to be feasible to group creatures together as belonging to various great psychical type-forms.

At present the common divisions follow other lines. Animals which belong to the same family, *e. g.*, the dogs, are thought of as resembling one another in general mental pattern and as differing from other animals partly in their instincts, but partly also in their capacity to learn non-instinctive reactions. This practical view of the matter leaves us with as many main patterns as there are genera and with no explicit and tangible description of any one. The other line of demarcation consists in cross-sectioning such a division as the preceding by distinguishing between such psychical characters as sentience, memory and reason, ascribing all these attributes to the higher creatures and denying one or another to the lower creatures. Amœba may be thought to have sentience, but not reason and only dubiously memory. The pigeon has sentience and memory, but probably not reason, whereas men and possibly some of the higher animals have all three capacities.

Obviously neither of these modes of classification affords us any real insight into psychic types. If Darwin's fertile investigations are to bear fruit in this direction in psychology, we must be able to portray the entire range of mental processes belonging to the great divisions of animal life, to show where and how these dividing lines part company with those which now bind animal forms together on structural lines. For ordinary zoölogical purposes the dog and the elephant have little in common except their mammalian hall-mark. But in their psychic types they may be very similar.

Such types may clearly be grouped around various central factors. Animals in which the so-called 'distance receptors' (auditory, visual, olfactory) are well-developed, may present a pattern with the psychic life all grouped about these processes. In other animals the 'contact and proprio-ceptive' organs may be the centers of psychic life and in consequence give rise to quite another mental pattern. In one or in both, the psychic operations may be of the most rudimentary and immediate sort, or they may, on the other hand, involve processes comparable with the simpler forms of human inference. The patterns may vary again in dependence upon the relatively large or relatively small amount of purely instinctive and reflex activity. They may vary with the phylogenetic antiquity of the form, newer types being more plastic than older ones. Many other principles of grouping will readily suggest themselves.

At the present moment we have the beginnings, but only the beginnings, of the necessary data for the solution of this general problem. We have learned, for example, that the mere presence of a sense organ does not argue such a use of it as casual inspection would suggest, much less such as is suggested by the analogy of human sense perception. We have accordingly learned caution in assuming that the sensory activities of animals involve the sort of consciousness which we know in ourselves. Indeed our whole tendency now-a-days is to recognize and frankly admit, that inasmuch as we must infer the psychic operations of animals wholly in terms of their behavior, we are under peculiar obligation to interpret their activities in the most conservative possible way. We know that the 'try-try-again, method' is the one commonly used by animals in solving laboratory problems. But we are for the most part profoundly ignorant as to just what occurs when progress is actually made, what sensory avenues are most important for giving information and how far the counterparts of human inference may at times be present. To secure these and dozens of other items of information needful for the execution of the program proposed will require long years of patient labor. Nevertheless, until this work is done, we shall remain powerless to describe the great stages of developing mind. The task is eminently worth while and is certain to be accomplished. Only when it is accomplished will it really be possible to entertain an intelligent judgment concerning the fundamental contentions of Darwinism concerning the evolution of mind.

# 26

Reprinted from *Psychol. Bull.* **40**(1):1-24 (1943)

## MULTIPLY, VARY, LET THE STRONGEST LIVE AND THE WEAKEST DIE—CHARLES DARWIN[1]

### BY CALVIN P. STONE

*Stanford University*

Even in remote times naturalists attempted to explain the origin and significance of diversity of instinctive behavior in animals. It was obvious to them that inherited patterns of behavior in bees and moths, songbirds and vultures, bears and hunting dogs were discontinuous phenomena. But how to account for discontinuity was indeed a baffling problem for the ancients; and so it is for scientists of the present day.

In 1842, the birth year of William James, whose life and work we are commemorating in the annual meeting of our Association, there were two widely held conceptions of the origin of diversity of instinctive behavior: *special creation* and *gradual evolution by the inheritance of adaptive habits.*

Special creationists generally regarded ·the species as immutable or permanent types. Major lines of diversity were assumed to have been created at the beginning of life on earth, or in successive eras thereafter, and minor diversities were ascribed to special circumstances of life which allowed individuals only in limited degrees to realize the fundamental characters of the species to which they belonged. Although the first half of the 19th century was not wholly free from dissenters from the foregoing conception of origin, it was lacking in variety of competing hypotheses which gave promise of unifying the legitimate speculation, hypotheses,

[1] Presidential Address for the Fiftieth Annual Meeting of the American Psychological Association. Because of the cancellation of the program of scientific papers scheduled for Boston and the substitution of a "skeletonized" business meeting in New York City in response to the request of the Office of Emergency Management that meetings be postponed for the duration of the war, this address, originally scheduled for Friday, September 4, 1942, was not delivered orally.

and facts of observation of that time. Quite appropriately the special creation theory was characterized as one that was "easy to scotch but hard to kill."

About 1801 Lamarck (17) made the inheritance of learned responses a basic postulate in his theory of gradual evolution of diversity in instincts. And so skillfully did he employ this postulate later on (1809) in the biological classic "Philosophie zoologique" to organize the available facts bearing on gradual evolution that his account temporarily overshadowed the earlier evolutionary theories of Buffon, St. Hilare, and Erasmus Darwin. It commanded the respectful attention of leading scientists on the continent, in Great Britain, and in the United States during three quarters of the 19th century. Spencer used it, Carpenter accepted it, Wundt endorsed it. Even Weismann who later sounded the death knell of this Lamarckian postulate actually countenanced it as late as 1880.

Lamarck assumed that all of the organisms of his time had descended from minute germs, the smallest and simplest of living matter, and that these germs were the product of spontaneous generation. As a general rule, behavioral patterns developed from the simple to the complex but under certain conditions progress was arrested and regressions set in. Basic was the assumption that circumstances of the *milieu externa* create in animals possessing a nervous system all of the fundamental "needs" (*besoins*) or "wants" relating to food, fecundation, avoidance of pain, and attainment of pleasure or happiness; and these, in turn, arouse adaptive movements which alleviate the needs. Changes of the living conditions regularly create new needs, or cause the alteration and disappearance of former needs thereby invoking disuse, waning and ultimate disappearance of adaptive movements, habits, or instinctive acts which had been functionally associated with them.

It naturally followed that whenever, for a considerable period of time, a group of closely related animals was isolated and subjected to circumstances of life (climate, geographical barriers, enemies, competition for space or food, etc.) which differed considerably from those to which the parent stock had been standardized in behavioral adaptations, a succession of variations eventuating in noticeable diversity would appear. Acting over only a short period of time, the altered circumstances would produce such minimal changes as one now observes between varieties within a species and, over geological eras, such gross differences as are observable in our time between contemporary orders, genera, and classes.   When external circumstances are relatively stable for a long period of time the individuals of a species living in close proximity eventually acquire approximately the same repertoire of adaptive habits.  By virtue of this, when viewed in man's life-span, they may appear to be invariable from generation to generation and thus provide the illusion of immutability of species.

Lamarck assumed that slowly developed adaptive habits are changed into hereditary behavioral characters, which thereafter are transmitted from parent to offspring without the necessity of tuition or individual learning.  The newly "acquired" instincts are subsequently modified by further additions and subtractions, each of which serves the biological end of adapting individuals or species to contemporary conditions of life.  Thus one may regard each complex instinct of bees and moths, songbirds and vultures, bears and hunting dogs as the end-product of a finite number of successful adaptations made in the history of the species.  Granting to Lamarck unlimited time and unlimited capacity in animals for the organization of adaptive movements which later become hereditary characters, we can hardly imagine a degree of instinctive specialization too complex to be accounted for by his theory of evolution.

But just how adaptive responses, individually learned, became transmissible by "generation"[2] was only superficially explained by Lamarck, this enigma of our day being passed over then as if only a commonplace fact of observation not worthy of prolonged discussion.  Without questioning, he assumed that habits which have become stereotyped and well nigh invariable with practice in their use, which run their course without apparent conscious direction as human automatisms are perceived to do, and which tend similarly to appear in individuals of a group living together, are the *veritable* essences of hereditary characters.

Lamarck did not deal systematically with the interrelationships of homeostatic mechanisms as did Claud Bernard in the sixties or Walter B. Cannon in the past two decades.  He did not clearly distinguish between agencies which initiate changes in the instincts of a species and those which bring to fruition in the in-

[2] The term "generation" is roughly equivalent to our concept of sexual reproduction.  In Darwin's time "congenital" was an alternative for hereditary.

dividual, in sequential order, the distinctive innate characters which differentiate between young and adults, adults and old, males and females, or the like-sex workers and queens among the bees and the ants. He said little to stimulate detailed study of the interplay of instinctive activities in animal populations, a topic more thoroughly understood by later workers, particularly the founders of the science of animal ecology. Nevertheless, Lamarck did psychobiology a service by according to behavioral evolution a place no less prominent than form and structure, an evaluation no one has rejected. He asserted with emphasis that behavioral adaptations are necessary forerunners or accompaniments of structural changes, the latter resulting from use and disuse of existing parts of the body. By attending to co-variations of adaptive movements and structural adaptations he was able to envisage a closely interwoven causal nexus in which the evolution of well-nigh countless correlated structures, forms, and instinctive acts has occurred in bygone eras (and may be occurring today), these having interrelations which hitherto had baffled the understanding of every naturalist who had witnessed and described them. Lamarck perceived and convincingly argued that no theory of descent could win adherents unless it gave a plausible account of the evolution of animal instincts. Probably more than any other scientist before his time he set the stage for fundamental speculation, observation, theorizing, and research on the origin of diversity in instinctive behavior. This has been a major interest of leading evolutionists during the past one hundred years.

## THE EVOLUTION OF INSTINCTS BY NATURAL SELECTION

A relatively independent point of view concerning the evolution of instincts began to take shape in the mind of Charles Darwin in 1842, the year of William James' birth. Referring to the earliest formulation of his views he says, in his autobiography (6), "In June 1842 I first allowed myself the satisfaction of writing a very brief abstract of my theory in pencil in 35 pages; and this was enlarged during the summer of 1844 into one of 230 pages, which I had fairly copied out and still possess." His son, Francis, who published these manuscripts in 1909 says that the 1842 paper "only came to light after my mother's death in 1896 when the house at Down was vacated. The Mss. was hidden in a cupboard under the stairs which was not used for papers of any value but rather as an overflow for matter which he did not wish to destroy" (7).

Doubt as to the immutability of species had not seriously occupied Darwin's mind prior to his voyage on the Beagle and the years immediately afterward (1837–39) when he was arranging and interpreting the observations made by himself and other scientists who reported on this voyage. So omnipresent had been behavioral variations in whatever instincts he chose to observe that it seemed he had only to discover rigorous selecting and isolating agents, capable of summating similarly oriented variations for a long period of time, to account for a degree of diversity equalling that found in local races of well-known species or in related species inhabiting islands which once were connected with the mainland.

By 1842 he had no doubt as to the demonstrability of ever-continuing variations in the instinctive behavior of all extant species living under conditions of domestication or in the feral state. And so far as he then could determine, *a priori*, there was no law of nature which limited the kind, the direction, the amount, or the perpetuity of variation in instinctive behavior. Already he had arrived at the conclusion which prompted him to say, in the first edition of the "Origin,"

> . . . it may not be a logical deduction, but to my imagination it is far more satisfactory to look at such instincts as the young cuckoo ejecting its foster-brothers,—ants making slaves,—the larvae of *Ichneumonidae* feeding within the live bodies of caterpillars,—not as specially endowed or created instincts, but as small consequences of one general law, leading to the advancement of all organic beings, namely, multiply, vary, let the strongest live and the weakest die (4, p. 244).

1. *Scope and limitation:* Darwin did not attempt in the first enunciation of his views to account for the "first origins of instincts and other mental attributes." He desired only to show how diversity could possibly have occurred in the great groups of animals of his day. He spoke, for example, of such instinctive acts as we commonly designate by the terms *fear, timidity*, and *wildness;* of those conditioned by diurnal or seasonal states of the body such as sleeping, hibernation, migration, and fecundation; of consensual movements such as pacing or trotting, erratic flying of "tumbler" pigeons, and pointing and shepherding in certain breeds of dogs; and of the so-called "industries" of animals, such as spinning of cocoons by insect larvae, fabrication of nests by weaver birds, erection of dams by beavers, construction of diverse kinds of cells by bees and wasps, and complicated family routines of the social insects pertaining to nursing, feeding, and the defense of young. These and others not enumerated could vary in respect to detail

of pattern, strength and perseverance, age at first appearance, latency or patency in successive generations, dependence on experience for normal development, or susceptibility to modification by tuition and the particular life situations for which the true instincts were not suited.

2. *Definition.* He perceived the difficulty of formulating a precise definition of instinct. While reminding himself in the 1842 essays[3] to define instinct, he merely discusses some of the important items the concept should entail. The context, however, indicates that he intended it to embrace (1) the more corporeal unlearned activities of animals which obey the same laws of transmission as structural traits when fertile races or interfertile species or genera are hybridized, and (2) complex acts in which the motivating impulse arises from conditions having an hereditary base, but in which quite variable details of behavior might appear as, for example, the migratory journeys of birds or reindeer.[4]

In the "Origin of Species" (1859), Darwin again avoided defining instinct on the ground that everyone understood what the term meant when it was used in a specific instance. Continuing, he says:

An action, which we ourselves should require experience to enable us to perform, when performed by an animal, more especially by a very young one, without any experience, and when performed by many individuals in the same way, without their knowing for what purpose it is performed, is usually said to be instinctive. But I could show that none of these characters of instinct are universal. A little dose, as Pierre Huber expresses it, of judgment or reason, often comes into play, even in animals very low in the scale of nature (4, p. 207).

With this conception, which was not entirely original with him, he was never satisfied, nevertheless he retained it unaltered in each

[3] In the 1842 essay he jotted down the words "Lord Broughham's definition" at a point where his own conception must have been in mind. But it is doubtful whether he expected to quote this definition, for in expanding this section later he merely says that "Lord Broughham insists strongly on ignorance of the end proposed being eminently characteristic of true instincts" (7, p. 117). It would seem that the jotting was to remind him to say that, in respect to ignorance of end, acquired instincts (habits which have become hereditary) differ in no essential way from the true instincts which are summations of variations naturally occurring in animals living in the feral state.

[4] I shall not deal with this aspect of the problem today. The subject received considerable attention at the hands of Romanes, Lloyd Morgan, and animal biologists during the last quarter of the nineteenth century. In the period beyond 1920 interest has been revived in the topic by students of animal migrations and also by those working in the field of animal drives.

revision of the "Origin," the last being completed in 1872. Although later authors have emended and possibly improved upon this basic idea, no one so far has been able to define the term in a manner satisfactory to all who have occasion to use it. The multiplication of diverse phenomena embraced by the word *instinct* has made it one of the most uncertain and abused words in the lexicon of psychological terms during the past 100 years. And recent attempts to banish it from general usage have accomplished little by way of freeing our science from the dilemma of multiple meanings. Unfortunately, these attempts are working to our disadvantage by diverting the attention of young researchers from a wealth of behavioral phenomena which are known to have great, although as yet not fully evaluated, theoretical and practical implications.

## VARIATION

Darwin foresaw the necessity of accounting as fully as possible for all behavioral variations that could possibly have contributed significantly to divergence from one or a few parent stocks. Variations were the building stones of evolution theory then, as they are today.

Believing that most variations in habits due to short-term influences, such as food deprivation, illness, injury, or exposure to heat or cold, were rarely if ever transmitted by "generation" and therefore could have had but little weight, he dismissed them as a class from consideration. A high degree of conjecture and arbitrariness on his part gave rise to inconsistencies and no small degree of confusion among those who regarded him an authority.

Although then unable to decipher the basic distinctions between the acquisitions belonging to the somatoplasm and those belonging to the germ plasm, as did Weismann and others in the eighties, he had no doubt as to the gonads playing an important if not essential role in the transmission of hereditary characters. While psychobiologists have been in essential agreement with this early conclusion, they dared not accept his judgment as to what individually developed responses originally had or later attained hereditary status. Darwin always was a very unreliable prophet on this point, as also were some of his followers during the latter third of the nineteenth century.

In these early essays he discussed chiefly two kinds of variation which could possibly have been the sources from which diversity in instinctive behavior arose: namely, (1) Differential habit formation, to which adhered the belief that some habit variants which fortuitously have adaptive value in the struggle for survival and are slowly acquired may attain hereditary status, and thereafter be passed from parents to offspring as "acquired" instincts without the necessity of practice; and (2) Gross hereditary variations of the saltatory type, known in his time as "sports," and small hereditary variations some of which are so minute as to require summation in successive generations before becoming noticeable to naturalists or animal fanciers. He desired to explain the diversification of instincts so reasonably that no thoughtful sceptic would reject the "theory of common descent of allied organisms from the difficulty of imagining the transitional stages in the various now most complicated and wonderful instincts." In so doing he gave about equal weight to the inheritance of learned responses and to hereditary variations. The following quotations reflect his views:

... almost infinitely numerous shades of disposition, of tastes, of peculiar movements, and even of individual actions, can be modified or acquired by one individual and transmitted to its offspring. . . . The inherited paces in the horse have no doubt been acquired by compulsion during the lives of the parents: and temper and tameness may be modified in a breed by the treatment which the individuals receive (7, p. 115).

The "transandantes" sheep in Spain, which for some centuries have been yearly taken a journey of several hundred miles from one province to another, know when the time comes, and show the greatest restlessness (like migratory birds in confinement), and are prevented with difficulty from starting by themselves, which they sometimes do, and find their own way. There is a case on good evidence of a sheep which, when she lambed, would return across a mountainous country to her own birth-place, although at other times of year not of a rambling disposition. Her lambs inherited this same disposition, and would go to produce their young on the farm whence their parent came; and so troublesome was this habit that the whole family was destroyed (7, p. 114).

I will briefly consider . . . one other class of instincts, which have often been advanced as truly wonderful, namely parents bringing food to their young which they themselves neither like nor partake of;—for instance, the common sparrow, a granivorous bird, feeding its young with caterpillars. . . . We may suppose either that the remote stock, whence the sparrow and other congenerous birds have descended, was insectivorous, and that its own habits and structures have been changed, whilst its ancient instincts with respect to its young have remained unchanged; or we may suppose that the parents have been induced to vary slightly the food of their young, by a slight scarcity of the proper kind (or by the instincts of some individuals not being so truly developed), and in this case those young which were most capable of surviving were necessarily most often preserved, and would themselves in time become parents, and would be similarly compelled to alter their food for their young (7, p. 126).

Once grant that dispositions, tastes, actions or habits can be slightly modified, either by slight congenital differences (we must suppose in the brain) or by the force of external circumstances, and that such slight modifications can be rendered inheritable,—a proposition which no one can reject,—and it will be difficult to put any limit to the complexity and wonder of the tastes and habits which may *possibly* be thus acquired (7, p. 126).

*1. The "acquired" instincts.* Whether Darwin had any misgivings in asserting that certain habits attain hereditary status cannot be determined from his earliest writings, but I am inclined to believe that he did not. The idea was not new. For almost a quarter of a century scientists had freely utilized it. Hence, he had no reason to fear that criticism of this assumption would "backfire" on the theory of descent, which it was intended to support. A few years later, quite independently, Spencer employed the idea without apology in his account of the compounding of reflexes to form new instincts or to alter the old ones. The method of compounding described was simple associative learning, in which contiguous factors of the external environment cause simple reflexes to be repeated again and again in particular orders and temporal spacings. Somehow, with many repetitions, these associated reflexes become fixed as hereditary compounds and are thereafter transmitted from one generation to another without the necessity of practice or repetition.

After some experimentation on pigeons and further consideration of facts collected from other sources, Darwin was disposed to de-emphasize the importance of "acquired" instincts as compared with hereditary variations. This was apparent in 1859, in the first edition of the "Origin of Species" and albeit with some wavering it continued for several years thereafter. Nonetheless he attempted to develop a provisional hypothesis that would serve several purposes, one of which was to explain the mechanism whereby habits can attain hereditary status. This he published (5) in 1865 under the name *pangenesis*. Today pangenesis has only historical significance; but in the sixties and for about three decades thereafter it served as a unifying principle for the coordination of a multiplicity of discordant beliefs and facts of observation.

This theory, so far as it applies to behavior, stipulates that every cell of the body, in every stage of life, discharges into the circulation minute particles or gemmules. The latter multiply by fission, at the same time preserving their essential characteristics and congregating in the gonads, particularly in the sperm and the ova. They mingle but preserve their identities at the time of fertilization and thus provide a liaison mechanism between parents and offspring. The gemmules have an affinity for nacent cells of the type which originally produced them and exert a controlling influence upon their proliferation and activities so as to cause them to recapitulate forms and functions which were characteristic of, or even peculiar to, the parents at specific ages. Assuming that cells of the nervous system mediate all adaptive movements, it naturally followed that the nerve cells responsible for specific habits in the parents would pass on to the offspring a heritage of gemmules capable of instating in these young a specific response or a repertoire of parent-like responses. No practice was required in typical instances and, since the gemmules were presumed to act at precisely the same age in the offspring as that in which the habits were developed in the parents, he could thus explain the origin of temporal and serial schedules which the instincts follow in their initial manifestation. Obviously the annexation of "acquired" instincts at any point on the life line, from the embryo to the aged, provided one of the most fertile sources of variation with which selective and isolating agencies could operate to produce some of the kinds of diversity present in our day.

To give full details of the workings of gemmules is not our intention. Suffice it to say, however, that this ingenious theory of the mechanism of transmission of learned responses was applicable also to the modification and transmission of true instincts. Furthermore it offered an explanation of latent instincts, reversion, blending, saltation, and dominance. The list is not exhaustive. Even the difficult case of graniferous sparrows which fed their young on larvae which they neither ate nor liked for themselves yielded to pangenesis. It was truly an all-purpose theory, directed to the inscrutable as well as the orderly processes of "generation."

In the mind of Darwin, pangenesis was only a provisional theory. It should stand or fall by the force of evidence submitted for and against it. He had not long to wait because in 1871 his cousin Francis Galton (11) devised an experimental method by which to put it on trial. He transfused the blood of one race of rabbits with distinctive morphological and behavioral characters into another that had noteworthy differences in homologous characters. Then, as soon as possible, he bred the recipients of the foreign blood to animals of their own race and awaited the appearance of characteristics of the blood donors in offspring from these matings. He assumed that gemmules from the blood of the donors would find their way into the sperm and/or ova of the hosts and thence into the offspring where they would exercise their usual functions in the manner hypothecated by Darwin. Not a single offspring in a rather elaborate series of tests showed behavior or morphological characters which deviated in the direction of the donors of blood. While not a perfect test of the theory, as Galton admitted, these experiments nevertheless had some weight on the negative side of the ledger. In 1875, Galton (12) published an alternative theory of heredity in which he assigned to the germ cells full responsibility, without aid of gemmules from the somatoplasm, of transmitting hereditary characters from parents to offspring. This paper denied the possibility of learned responses attaining hereditary status and thus altogether eliminated the "acquired" instincts from consideration. Eight years after this paper appeared Weismann gave substantial support to Galton's point of view in his epoch making treatise on the continuity of the germ plasm. This placed a stricture upon the Lamarckian hypothesis that on *a priori* grounds made it unacceptable to many scientists immediately thereafter.

Among certain men, however, the theory of pangenesis or derivatives therefrom continued to flourish, and further experiments were designed to put it under stress, among them being experiments relating to telegony. The upholders of telegony believed that the blood of a female which bore a hybrid offspring became contaminated ("infected") during the gestation period with the result that this condition would give to subsequent pureline offspring some of the characters of the hybrid. Thus an equine colt borne by a mother which the previous year had borne a mule-colt would have mulish characteristics; a pedigreed bitch if allowed to produce a litter by a mongrel sire would, when next mated to a pedigreed male of her own breed, bear one or more pups resembling the mongrel. Against this popular conception the celebrated Penycuik (9) experiment provided telling evidence. Equine mares were mated with a zebra stallion and allowed to rear hybrid offspring; then followed matings of the same mares with equine stallions. The behavioral traits of wildness, viciousness, and excitability of the zebra should have appeared in the equine foals, but none of them did. Bearing indirectly on telegony is the classical experiment of Heap (1890) in which two fertilized ova of the Angora breed of rabbits were introduced into the Fallopian tube

of a Belgian hare (**13**).  These fertilized eggs developed into normal
Angora rabbits which in no way appeared to deviate from the
characteristic features of their true parents.   Finally, in 1902
telegony was conclusively disproven by Darbishire (**3**) in a systematic study of the whirling tendency in "dancing" mice.  Non-
whirling mothers which had borne offspring begotten by dancer
males were subsequently mated to non-dancer males.  In no instance did whirlers appear from these matings.

Darwin personally supplied only inferential evidence in support of the inheritance of learned responses and for many years
only anecdotal evidence was supplied by others.  In the seventies,
however, Brown-Séquard reported behavior data which were interpreted as giving it support.  He described a small number of epileptic convulsions in guinea pigs which were the offspring of
parents in which epileptic convulsions had been produced experimentally by lesions in the spinal cord or in the sciatic nerve.  A few
years later Romanes repeated these experiments with only here and
there a result that supported the claims of his predecessor.  Neither
of these studies was convincing to careful experimenters of that
time because of inadequate controls of the genetic stock, the operations, and the symptoms displayed.  William James (**15**) did psychology an invaluable service in subjecting this experiment to
thoughtful scrutiny in his "Principles of Psychology" (1890), and
in that connection reviewing a great deal of morphological and
behavioral data previously offered in support of the inheritance of
acquired characters.  To his credit, be it said, he found it totally
unconvincing.

Within recent years the most sincere and persistent attempt to
cause a learned response to attain hereditary status was that of
McDougall (**19**).  Unfortunately, the results have been most difficult to interpret, both for him and for others, due, in part, to the
fact that complete records regarding the animals discarded as well
as those experimented upon were not preserved for retrospective
consideration.  With some reservations, however, McDougall interpreted his results as favoring the Lamarckian hypothesis;
others, competent to review them, have preferred to suspend judgment or to presume that reductions in learning rate such as he
has obtained would most likely arise from unintentional selective
breeding.  Whatever the final interpretation of these studies may
be, we may say now that in the final stages of the experiments it
was apparent to McDougall and to others that nothing even closely

resembling an "acquired" instinct was being set up. McDougall was unable to contrive a method of forcing the acquired responses into the germ plasm.

In view of the foregoing and still other lines of negative evidence, should we say, or hope, that the inheritance of learned responses as a source of hereditary variations is a dead issue? Neither would be justified. To a degree unequaled by any other postulate so far advanced, this conception superficially accounts for the small and the great steps in the evolution of diversity in a manner that is satisfying both to personal experience and to imagination. While this condition obtains, there will be able experimenters seeking new ways of making tenable what hitherto has been an unverified postulate.

*2. Hereditary variations.* Hereditary variations of the true and the "acquired" instincts, occurring in every direction, were considered the fundamental sources from which selecting and isolating agencies might create noteworthy diversity. Neither in 1842 nor in later years did Darwin assign much weight to gross variations as exemplified by "sports," except possibly when these were cultivated by man under artificial conditions. Telling against their importance was their rarity, and for that reason the small chance they would have in making their influence felt in competition with other animals already standardized for conditions then existing; also, among animals, as opposed to plants, the vast majority of "sports" described in the literature were monstrosities which because of organic weakness only rarely survived and begot offspring. Of course there were exceptions. The erratic flight of the tumbler pigeon might be considered an example of a "sport" that has been able to perpetuate its kind under conditions of domestication and selective breeding by pigeon fanciers, but which under natural conditions probably would never have become established as a variety or race. So also the pointing by bird dogs might be looked upon as a "sport" since this tendency was known to crop out now and then among various breeds without tuition; quite probably it had been preserved by dog fanciers through isolation and selective mating of individuals in which this novel response had appeared.

Since unequivocal examples of "sports" perpetuating themselves in the feral state were rare, there seemed to be no logical ground for questioning the wisdom of placing the chief burden on small variations. Moreover, this step was consistent with a basic tenet of Darwin's theory of descent which envisaged the abruptness

of transitions between behavioral series relating to any fundamental instinct, such as nesting in reptiles, birds, and rodents, as
the result of sporadic extinction of intermediates from a long line
of ancestral stocks,—these exhibiting continuous variations and
extending from remote antiquity to the present day.

A growing interest in discontinuous variation was apparent toward the end of the nineteenth century, owing largely to de Vries'
extensive work on mutant plants that were normal in development,
fertile *inter se*, and infertile or less fertile when crossed with ancestral or unrelated stock. Here in one generation was notable
diversity and with it an isolating mechanism by which the swamp-
ing effects of hybridization might be minimized or obviated while
the new type was becoming established. This work led de Vries
to discard Darwin's theory of pangenesis and to question his belief
that continuous variations provided the major sources for diversification. In this he was materially supported by Bateson and other
geneticists of that period. Their work, together with numerous
advances in knowledge of cell structure, particularly the chromosomal constituents of the nuclei, and the significance of meiosis,
knowledge which for the most part had gradually accumulated for
approximately 25 years, laid a foundation for immediate appreciation of Mendel's paper of 1866, the main tenets of which were independently confirmed by de Vries, Correns, and Tschermak in 1900.

In 1902 Darbishire (3) demonstrated that the Mendelian principles could be applied to behavioral characters of the Japanese
waltzing mouse. Experimental studies by a number of competent
observers had indicated that this type of locomotion is not acquired
by imitation or learned through tuition or practice. It appears
late in the nursing period and, although subject to minor variations
due to environmental influences, is not unlike other stable patterns
of instinctive behavior. Darbishire crossed pure-line waltzers with
pure-line European albinos that were free from the whirling tendency. All of the $F_1$ generation, the number running into the
hundreds, were free from the waltzing behavior. The $F_1$ hybrids
when crossed *inter se* gave ratios of 4 normal to 1 waltzer, instead
of the expected number if one assumes that waltzing is a recessive
unit character. Subsequent experiments by other workers make
the latter assumption tenable and yield the expected ratios. Need-
less to say, Darbishire's demonstration that an unlearned behavioral pattern is transmitted in breeding tests, somewhat as morphological characters are, tended to stimulate new lines of research

on the heredity of instinctive dispositions. Among the most striking of these were studies on laying hens.

The first egg-laying contest of national scope was held in England in 1897. Prior to that time practical poultry breeders had selected birds which matured early, laid eggs in the "off season," and did not interrupt the laying sequence with periods of broodiness. Although pure lines had not been developed in all of these traits, considerable progress in that direction had been made with respect to broodiness and early maturity,—sufficient at least to suggest the following tests. Hurst, in 1903, crossed pure-line Cochins with pure-line Black Hamburghs (14). All of the hens of the $F_1$ generation were good "sitters," broodiness usually appearing after the hens had laid about a dozen eggs. In this respect they resembled the Cochin but not the Hamburgh strain. The $F_2$ generation segregated so as to give a ratio of 3 broody hens to 1 non-broody hen. Further tests support the assumption that broodiness is transmitted as a dominant unit character and non-broodiness as a recessive unit character. Table I gives additional data showing the outcome of crossing several genetic types of males and females derived from White Leghorn and White Wyandotte races. Incomplete dominance, or possibly impurity of the original strains, may account for the ratios deviating somewhat more from the calculated ratios than would be expected. Excesses of non-broody hens sometimes result from the fact than an occasional broody-type does not display the broody behavior until the second year; correction for these cases harmonizes the empirical and the calculated ratios.

Before discussing the onset of laying in domestic hens, geneticists must make certain arbitrary distinctions as to what constitutes early and late layers. Provisionally, those beginning to lay between the ages of 4 and 8 months are designated as early, and those beginning between the ages of 9 and 13 months as late layers (14). Now if homozygous "earlies" are crossed with homozygous "lates" the $F_1$ generation tends to fall, with but few exceptions, into the category of "earlies." When the $F_1$ males and females are interbred their $F_2$ females approximate the ratio of 3 "earlies" to 1 "late." The results from back crosses and other experimental matings support the hypothesis that early maturity behaves as a dominant, and late maturity as a recessive unit character. Table II gives results from crossing animals whose gamete formulae are conjectured by controlled matings of the an-

TABLE I

BROODINESS (H FACTOR)

Daughters sired by White Leghorns and White Wyandottes From Hurst (14, p. 492)

H = broody; h = non-broody

| Matings | | | | Offspring | B. Grades (times Broody first season) | | | | | | | Observed | | Calculated | | |
| Sires | | Dams | | Daughters | Broody | | | | | | Non-Broody | Broody | Non-Broody | Broody | Non-Broody | |
| Nos. | Factors | Nos. | Factors | Nos. | 6 | 5 | 4 | 3 | 2 | 1 | 0 | | | | | |
|---|---|---|---|---|---|---|---|---|---|---|---|---|---|---|---|---|
| 1 | hh | 2 | HH | 6 | — | — | 1 | 1 | 1 | 3 | — | 6 | 0 | 6.00 | 0.00 | A |
| 1 | Hh | 2 | Hh | 10 | — | — | 1 | 1 | 4 | — | 4 | 6 | 4 | 7.50 | 2.50 | B |
| 2 | Hh | 3 | hh | 40 | 2 | 1 | — | 3 | 6 | 4 | 24 | 16 | 24 | 20.00 | 20.00 | C |
| 6 | hh | 18 | Hh | 50 | — | — | 1 | 6 | 5 | 5 | 33 | 17 | 33 | 25.00 | 25.00 | |
| 13 | hh | 41 | hh | 95 | — | — | — | 2 | 2 | 1 | 90 | 5 | 90 | 0.00 | 95.00 | D |
| 23 | — | 66 | — | 201 | 2 | 1 | 3 | 13 | 18 | 13 | 151 | 50 | 151 | 58.50 | 142.50 | |

*Mendelian expectation*: A—all Broody; B—3 Broody, 1 Non-broody; C—1 Broody, 1 Non-broody; D—all Non-Broody.

**345**

## TABLE II

### Sexual Maturity (Age at First Egg; E Factor)
Daughters sired by White Leghorns and White Wyandottes
E=early; e=late   From Hurst (14, p. 477)

| Sires Nos. | Sires Factors | Dams Nos. | Dams Factors | Offspring Daughters Nos. | 4 | 5 | 6 | 7 | 8 | 9 | 10 | 11 | 12 | 13 | Observed Early | Observed Late | Calculated Early | Calculated Late | |
|---|---|---|---|---|---|---|---|---|---|---|---|---|---|---|---|---|---|---|---|
| 9 | EE | 11 | EE | 61 | 1 | 12 | 23 | 20 | 5 | — | — | — | — | — | 61 | 0 | 61.00 | 0.00 | A |
| 9 | EE | 35 | Ee | 104 | — | 3 | 39 | 35 | 21 | 3 | — | — | — | — | 101 | 3 | 104.00 | 0.00 | A |
| 2 | Ee | 3 | EE | 18 | — | 3 | 7 | 8 | — | — | — | — | — | — | 18 | 0 | 18.00 | 0.00 | A |
| 3 | EE | 3 | ee | 23 | — | — | 4 | 11 | 8 | — | — | — | — | — | 23 | 0 | 23.00 | 0.00 | A |
| 6 | Ee | 21 | Ee | 82 | — | — | 16 | 19 | 25 | 13 | 5 | 3 | 1 | — | 60 | 22 | 61.50 | 20.50 | B |
| 1 | Ee | 7 | ee | 28 | — | — | 1 | 7 | 5 | 6 | 9 | — | — | — | 13 | 15 | 14.00 | 14.00 | C |
| 2 | ee | 4 | Ee | 15 | — | — | — | 2 | 7 | 3 | 3 | — | — | — | 9 | 6 | 7.50 | 7.50 | C |
| 1 | ee | 1 | ee | 4 | — | — | — | — | 1 | 1 | 1 | — | — | 1 | 1 | 3 | 0.00 | 4.00 | D |
| 33 | — | 85 | — | 335 | 1 | 18 | 90 | 102 | 75 | 26 | 18 | 3 | 1 | 1 | 286 | 49 | 289.00 | 46.00 | |

*Mendelian expectations:* A—all Early; B—3 Early, 1 Late; C—1 Early, 1 Late; D—all Late.

cestral stock. The empirical data conform rather closely to the calculated data. Onset of egg-laying, a sex-limited activity, is closely related to age of first estrus in domestic fowls. Although one cannot definitely say that early and late behavioral sexual maturity will behave as onset of egg-laying in genetic tests, there is analagous evidence that I shall not discuss which clearly indicates that this would be the result.

Still other applications of the Mendelian method of studying variation and inheritance of instinctive reactions might be given. The number of cases, however, is extremely small as compared with that in which somatic characters have been studied. This is due in part to rarity of inter-specific fertility between species that have distinctive homologous instincts. It is due also to the decided preference geneticists have shown for structural, as contrasted with functional, characters. Animal psycholgists, for some unknown reason, have not had even sufficient interest in the topic to keep the growing literature assembled, to say nothing of preparing themselves for creditable research in the field. Fortunately, a few biologists are again developing interests in this subject and are taking the necessary steps to determine within what limits the laws of variation derived from studies of the transmission of structures may be applied to representative instinctive and other behavioral characters.

*3. Instigation and Realization:* In 1842 Darwin had only tentative suggestions relating to the initiation of hereditary variations. Without thoroughly weighing the matter he stated that significant diversity could arise from the interbreeding of races in which behavioral homologues were noticeably different, e.g., wildness, timidity, or ferocity. In developing this point he said, in 1844,

When once two or more races are formed, or if more than one race, or species fertile *inter se*, originally existed in a wild state, their crossing becomes a most copious source of new races. When two well-marked races are crossed the offspring in the first generation take more or less after either parent or are quite intermediate between them, or rarely assume characters in some degree new. In the second and several succeeding generations, the offspring are generally found to vary exceedingly, one compared with another, and many revert to their ancestral forms. This greater variability in succeeding generations seems analogous to the breaking or variability of organic beings after having been bred for some generations under domestication (7, p. 68).

In the "Origin" he de-emphasized the importance of crossing of races or species as a means of initiating variations which, having adaptive value, might be the initial step in diversification. The change in viewpoint expressed in 1859 probably resulted from his experiences in pigeon breeding wherein he observed the rapidity with which a mongrel race develops when indiscriminate matings are permitted between two initially different races, as most probably would obtain in nature. In the main his final viewpoint was not unlike that expressed by scientists of our day. Hybridization ordinarily adds nothing, except possibly in rare instances in which it accelerates the rate of mutation (8). It chiefly reveals.

In keeping with beliefs commonly held in 1842 Darwin stated that various agents might act directly upon the germ cells so as to instigate hereditary variations. The most important of these were diet, climate, toxic and infectious agents, and sudden changes in living conditions. For many years he spoke of the profuseness of variation occurring in domesticated animals and especially the sudden changes produced by bringing them from the wild state to an artificial habitat. He believed that these agencies somehow caused the reproductive organs to fail "in their ordinary functions of producing new organic beings closely like their parents." Today we speak of two, and only two, processes initiating hereditary variation: namely, gene mutation and chromosomal changes. To these are accredited all initial variation, whether small or large, continuous or discrete. The agencies mentioned by Darwin have significance only if they effect mutations of genes or produce chromosomal changes. So far the vast majority of these initial changes have occurred spontaneously, i.e., from causes largely unknown. Recently a few noteworthy somatic mutations have been caused by irradiation of the germinal cells.

In making the foregoing summary statements I have omitted essential landmarks in the unfolding of discoveries relating to initiation of variations; to some of these we now return.

*a. Sex determination:* Between 1875 and 1900 the main points relating to *maturation* of the germ cells and the union of nuclei from ovum and sperm had been revealed; yet no one as yet had a clue to the solution of the age-old problem of sex determination. MacClung in 1902 found an accessory chromosome in insects which he related to sex determination (18). In 1907 Correns postulated two kinds of male gametes, one determining the male and the other determining the female (2). In one well-known type of sex determination (XY), found in *Drosophila* and most of the mammals so far studied, the males have a pair of unlike sex chromo-

somes (XY) and the females a pair of like-sex chromosomes (XX .
In another type (WZ), common in birds, the female has the pair
of unlike sex chromosomes and the male the like pair. Among the
*Hymenoptera* (bees, wasps, ants), a few of the *Homoptera* (white
flies, scale insects), and a few other species of insects a still different
type of sex determination is found. The males have only half as
many chromosomes (haploid) as the females (diploid). For example, the drone of the honey bee has 16 whereas the workers and
the queens have 32 chromosomes. This results from the fact that
the queen does not release sperm upon all of the eggs as they are
laid. Those not fertilized develop parthenogenetically into males
and have only the chromosomes of the unfertilized egg; the fertilized eggs develop into females in which the chromosomes of both
sperm and egg are summated.

To say that different genes residing only in the sex chromosomes have full responsibility for the initiation of development
which eventuates in diverse primary and secondary sexual behavior between the sexes within a species and between them in
closely and distantly related species would be incorrect. Yet it is
quite in keeping with the available evidence to credit them with
primary leadership in the instigation of this process. This is a
first step in accounting for ontogenesis of one large group of instinctive responses. How far it may be extended in explaining
phylogenesis of the same remains to be determined.

*b. Sex differentiation:* What control genes may exercise beyond
the initial differentiation is largely conjectural at the present time.
It is known, however, that the differentiation of primary and secondary sexual instincts in vertebrates is always preceded by the
appearance of chemical substances from the endocrine glands.
These are operative in developmental processes that produce the
adult sexual activities, such as unlearned vocalizations and pos-
tural lures that attract males and females to each other during the
"mating" season; fighting by males for exclusive control of females
during certain phases of the reproductive cycle; copulation; serial
acts having to do with laying and incubating eggs or with parturition; nidification; hiding, feeding, and defending of offspring, and
age of onset, periodicity, and time of waning of many of these instinctive activities. From the fact that quite diverse behavior patterns are produced by the same substances in different races or
species it is inferred that there is some degree of genic regulation
of both production and utilization of the endocrine substances.

In the honey bee still different extrinsic factors contribute to differentiation during the developmental period. The workers and queens are alike as to their chromosomal make-up. A female embryo may become a worker or a queen. Which way it develops depends on how it is reared. Those becoming workers are kept in small cells and fed upon pollen from the third day of embryonal life; those becoming queens are reared in large cells and fed on royal jelly throughout the embryonal period. While we await the time when experimental embryologists can delineate the precise manner in which the extrinsic factors affect differentiation, we have the satisfaction of knowing that diversification is limited to a short period of embryonal and early adult life. Moreover, the problem to be solved falls in with those of morphogenesis for which a few promising methods of attack are now available. Again we must remind ourselves, however, that we are concerned here with ontogenesis rather than phylogenesis and that there is no guarantee that elucidation of the first will clarify the second.

*c. Autosomal instincts:* Although our data on autosomal inheritance of unlearned behavior are less abundant and exact than those relating to sex, they indicate that gene complexes serve as instigators and regulators of variation. The whirling tendency in mice is a recessive Mendelian character based on developmental defects of the inner ear. It is not associated with any lethal factor and is neither sex-linked nor linked with the factors for agouti, albinism, pink-eye, dilution, brown, Dutch spotting, short-ear, or kinky-tail (10). Pacing as a mode of locomotion arises spontaneously as a mutation in dogs, horses, and other quadrupeds. When pure-line trotting and pacing horses are hybridized, it behaves as a recessive unit character. It is now apparent that the basis of wildness and savageness in rats is inherited in gene-controlled patterns. According to Keeler (16) most of the tame strains of albinos employed in American laboratories bear the black gene or the black and piebald genes combined, the coat-color effects of which are masked by the albino gene. These tame strains appeared in our time as mutants from the wild Norway stock. Some of the hunting responses of dogs are transmitted as hereditary characters although the relationships are still somewhat obscure. Fighting and non-fighting mice have been subjected to extensive genetic analyses with results that leave no doubt as to their being transmitted as hereditary characters, despite the fact that they are easily masked by experience.

When appropriate methods of selection and isolation are applied to the foregoing hereditary variations, and still others not mentioned, many kinds and degrees of diversity may be produced.

### SELECTION: NATURAL AND SEXUAL

Without selection, variation would count for nothing in the production of notable diversity in instinctive activities. Conversely, selection is impotent without hereditary variations on which to work. These ideas had become apparent to Darwin following his voyage on the Beagle. Upon his return he began to assemble evidence, from all available sources, to support a plausible account of the selective mechanisms in nature whereby notable diversity could have developed as a necessary consequence of the struggle for survival through successive additions of behavioral adaptations.

He assumed that *Nature* selects animals in the feral state as practical breeders or fanciers choose those under domestication, but always without transcendental guidance or orthodirectional plan. From variations continually occurring in every direction (as a result of mutations and chromosomal changes, one now adds) nature selects those which *fortuitously* have adaptive value to their possessors which gives them an advantage over those not possessing equivalent variations. Sexual selection is only a special type of natural selection. Insofar as it pertains to instinctive behavior, it purports to account for only one or two classes of aggressive instincts and a few classes of preferential responses pertaining to mateships.

To what extent natural selection can account for the original hereditary adaptive behavior is still controversial. The question cannot be settled one way or the other by weight of the evidence now available. We know that in the case of dichotomies like pacing and trotting or whirling and non-whirling little more is accomplished after pure lines have been established, beyond strengthening the vigor or frequency of manifestation. In onset of puberty in hens, mice, rats, swine, and many other animals notable reductions have been made, although practical limits are finally reached because somatic maturity can no longer be coordinated with behavioral maturity. Also, selection has eradicated broodiness in certain races of domestic hens, a gain which, when coupled with early maturity and winter laying, has enormous economic worth to the poultry industry. Furthermore, relatively tame races of rats have been developed side by side with parent stock which is no tamer than that living in the wild state. Mutations among rats at the Wistar Institute clearly suggest a plausible explanation of the "wild dogs" of Cuba which, as an obsession, overrun the books of Darwin. Even relevant statements can be made on the transmission of hereditary characters among the "neuter" insects, troublesome cases for Darwin and his followers. Yet despite considerable thought and planning to this end no evolutionist or practical breeder has ever contrived a simple scheme for intruding upon the "mating" flight of the honey bee, *Apis mellifica*, with a view to eliminating it entirely. The bee industry could well afford to offer a million dollars to the man who first produces a colony of honey bees that will mate in the laboratory as do the geneticists' special, *Drosophila melanogaster*.

### ISOLATING MECHANISMS

The necessity of isolation in early stages of diversification was perceived by all of the early evolutionists, but it was not well developed as a topic in evolutionary theory before the time of Lamarck and Charles Darwin. Isolation became a controversial topic during the second half of the nineteenth century but finally the consensus of opinion as to its importance stabilized at a point not essentially different from that expressed by Darwin in 1859. It is now apparent that isolating devices were no less instrumental in affording conditions for diversification of instincts than of somatic characters.

Among fundamental researches devoted to isolation are those dealing with psychological incompatibilities which prevent or minimize the crossing of races or interfertile species, thereby masking or eradicating small gains in diversification. Instincts which are presumed to be the product of isolation in turn become most effective isolating mechanisms themselves. Instances are numerous and, time permitting, would be most interesting to consider.

As a final word, and without pausing to summarize the points I have elected to stress in this brief survey of a century of progress, may I express extreme gratitude to the well-nigh innumerable biologists who, unmindful of "academic" criticisms of instinct, have continued to undertake fundamental research on the topic. Questions of origin and evolution have given them a common theme, a harmonizing principle for diverse undertakings. Biologists are now laying foundations for unparalleled expansion in a hitherto unemphasized phase of animal psychology, one that is not revolutionary but highly useful: namely, the field of

## Behavioral Ecology

Animal psychologists have neglected the study and appraisal of this important topic. Therefore, I can think of no better attitude with which to indoctrinate our colleagues of tomorrow who would make animal psychology their specialty than one of constant vigilance for opportunities to study the instincts as they are related to the subject of behavioral ecology.

### BIBLIOGRAPHY

1. ALLEN, E., DANFORTH, C. A., & DOISEY, E. A.  Sex and internal secretions. Baltimore: Williams & Wilkins, 1939.
2. CORRENS, C.  Die Bestimmung und Vererbung des Geschlechts. Berlin: 1907.
3. DARBISHIRE, A. D.  Note on the results of crossing Japanese waltzing mice with European albino races. *Biometrika*, 1902–1903, **2**, 1st·rept., 101–104; 2nd rept., 165–174; 3rd rept., 282–285.
4. DARWIN, CHARLES.  On the origin of species. London: John Murray, 1859.
5. DARWIN, CHARLES.  Animals and plants under domestication. II. (2nd ed., rev.) New York: D. Appleton & Co., 1890.
6. DARWIN, FRANCIS.  Life and letters of Charles Darwin. I. New York: D. Appleton & Co., 1891.
7. DARWIN, FRANCIS.  The foundations of the Origin of Species. Cambridge: University Press, 1909.
8. DOBZHANSKY, T.  Genetics and the Origin of Species (2nd ed.) New York: Columbia University Press, 1941.
9. EWART, J. C.  The Penycuik experiments. London: Adam & Charles Black, 1899.
10. GATES, W. H.  The Japanese waltzing mouse: its origin, heredity, and relation to the genetic characters of other varieties of mice. Part III. Carnegie Instn. Washington Publ. No. 337, 1926, 83–138.
11. GALTON, FRANCIS.  Experiments in pangenesis, etc. *Proc. Roy. Soc.* (London) 1871, **19**, 393–410.
12. GALTON, FRANCIS.  A theory of heredity. *The Contemporary Rev.*, 1875, **27**, 80–95.
13. HEAP, WALTER.  Preliminary note on the transplantation and growth of mammalian ova within a uterine foster-mother. *Proc. Royal Soc.* (London), 1890, **48**, 457–458.
14. HURST, C. C.  Experiments in genetics. Cambridge: University Press, 1925.
15. JAMES, WM.  Principles of psychology. II. New York: Henry Holt & Co., 1890.
16. KEELER, C. E.  Personal communication.
17. LAMARCK, J. B.  Philosophie zoologique. I. (Rev. Ed.) Paris: C. Martins, 1873.
18. MacCLUNG, C. E.  The accessory chromosome—sex determinant? *Biol. Bull.*, 1902, **3**, 43–84.
19. McDOUGALL, WM.  Second report on a Lamarckian experiment. *Brit. J. Psychol.*, 1930, **20**, 201–218.

# AUTHOR CITATION INDEX

# SUBJECT INDEX

# About the Editor

DONALD ALLEN DEWSBURY is a professor of psychology at the University of Florida. His research interests relate to comparative animal behavior with emphasis on the study of adaptive significance, reproductive behavior, the use of the comparative method, and the behavior of rodents.

Dr. Dewsbury received his A. B. degree from Bucknell University in 1961 and his Ph.D. from the University of Michigan in 1965. He was an N.S.F. post-doctoral fellow in the laboratory of Dr. Frank A. Beach at the University of California, Berkeley in 1965–1966. His published scientific papers number over 150. Dr. Dewsbury's books include *Comparative Psychology: A Modern Survey* (co-edited with D. A. Rethlingshafer, McGraw-Hill, 1973), *Comparative Animal Behavior* (McGraw-Hill, 1978), and *Sex and Behavior: Status and Prospectus* (co-edited with T. E. McGill and B. D. Sachs, Plenum, 1978), *Mammalian Sexual Behavior* (Hutchinson Ross, 1981), and *Comparative Psychology in the Twentieth Century* (Hutchinson Ross, 1983). He is a member of a dozen scientific organizations and has served as Treasurer and President of the Animal Behavior Society.